The Rulers of British Africa
1870-1914

The Rulers of British Africa
1870-1914

L. H. GANN & PETER DUIGNAN

HOOVER INSTITUTION
PUBLICATIONS

Stanford University Press, Stanford, California

1978

Stanford University Press
Stanford, California
© 1978 by the Board of Trustees of the
Leland Stanford Junior University
Printed in the United States of America
ISBN 0-8047-0981-5
LC 77-92945

Sources of photographs on pp. 187–96: 1, 3, 4, 9–12, 14–17, 19,
Royal Commonwealth Society. 2, Longmans, Green and Company.
5, B.B.C. Radio Times. 6, 7, 13, 18, 20, Colonial Office Library.
8, George Allen and Unwin.

Contents

Ten pages of photographs follow p. 186

Tables

Preface

The decline and fall of the British empire in Africa has occasioned an outpouring of printed books, monographs and travelers' reports, learned compendia, and popular novels. The imperial record has been defended in terms of a civilizing mission—and more often condemned as the source of all the evils besetting present-day Africa. Modern historians, however, have not taken much interest in the nuts and bolts of the imperial edifice. Relatively few academic works deal with the men who actually built and administered the empire, their failures and their achievements. "Eurocentric" studies have indeed become somewhat unfashionable and even suspect to a generation of scholars determined to rewrite African history in African terms.

We ourselves have a different interpretation. We place these pioneers among the creators of modern Africa. They were the new Romans who built the foundations of the states that now cover the map of Africa; they traced the boundaries, shaped modern armies and bureaucracies; they helped to create Western-style economies. This work, like our recently published parallel study, *The German Rulers of Africa, 1884–1914*, is designed to elucidate the sociological and functional characteristics, the achievements as well as the shortcomings of the white empire builders, civilian and military, during the age of the "New Imperialism" in Africa.

The older kind of imperial history that professed to enlighten British readers on how "black savages" succumbed to "white heroes" has rightly seen its days. But there is still a need for an impartial assessment of the erstwhile rulers' role in Africa. The most important of the post-imperial studies that touch on this particular subject in British Africa is Robert Heussler's *Yesterday's Rulers: The Making of the British Colonial Service*. It is a model of its kind. It deals with the district officer in Africa—his social background and the manner in which he was selected. Our own study is concerned with the military, technical, and administrative elite for the whole of sub-Saharan Africa. We treat the central organization and the machinery of government on the spot; but we also cover the technicians and such ancillary services as the Crown agents for the Colonies, things that are usually omitted from accounts of colonial governance. We have tried to place the military and civilian bureaucracies into the wider social and economic framework in which they operated.

Our present work, then, is designed to show how the British ran their African empire during the formative 40 years or more preceding World War I. It is meant as a contribution to Euro-African history, to the record of Western expansion and Western cultural transfusion in Africa. We trust that it will be of interest to Africanists and to students of British history and of comparative colonialism; to specialists in the history of administration; and to sociologists interested in the formation of military and civilian elites.

During the age of the "New Imperialism," the British acquired a huge, though short-lived, empire in Africa, an empire that for the most part did not last the life span of a single grandmother. It comprised many peoples, Stone Age hunters and advanced farming communities, stateless societies depending on small neighborhood units and powerful feudal lordships. Had we attempted to provide an exhaustive account of the British impact on each people or on each colony, we would have had to fill many volumes. As in our study of the German empire builders, we have based our work on case histories and selected samples, on published sources along with some use of archival material. We have tried to blend the thematic with the chronological approach; hence our readers must forgive a certain amount of repetition.

We gratefully acknowledge permission from A. P. Watt and Son, and from Doubleday and Company to reprint selections from Kipling's poetry. We would also like to thank the following for permission to reproduce pictures: the B.B.C. Radio Times, the Royal Commonwealth Society, the Colonial Office Library, George Allen and Unwin, and Longmans, Green and Company.

Our work has been helped by generous assistance from the staffs of the Hoover Institution, Stanford University, Rhodes House at Oxford, the British Museum and Public Record Office, the Royal Commonwealth Society, and the Commonwealth Office Library. Professors D. Brokensha, D. K. Fieldhouse, A. H. M. Kirk-Greene, C. W. Newbury, I. F. Nicolson, R. E. Robinson, and P. D. L. Stansky have read the manuscript in part or in its entirety. Their help and advice have been of great benefit in the completion of this work. The National Endowment for the Humanities has provided financial support, as have the John Simon Guggenheim Memorial Foundation and the Committee for African Studies, Stanford University.

We thank them all for their assistance, and we absolve one and all from responsibility for any defects remaining in this work.

L.H.G.

P.D.

Stanford, California

June 1977

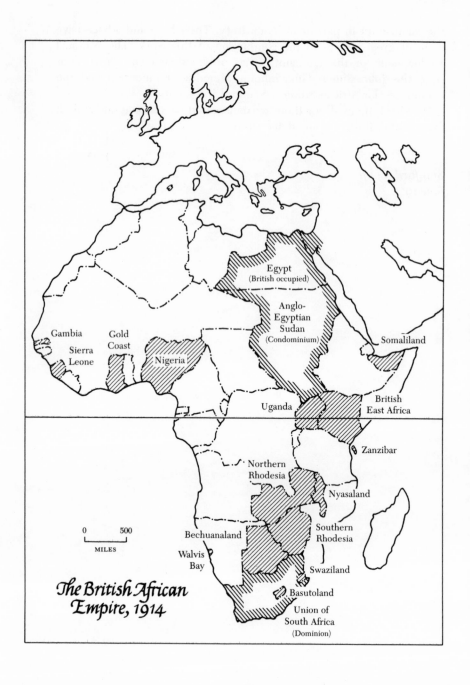

Gambia

Gold
Coast

Sierra
Leone

Nigeria

Egypt
(British occupied)

Anglo-
Egyptian
Sudan
(Condominium)

Somaliland

Uganda

British
East Africa

Zanzibar

Northern
Rhodesia

Nyasaland

Bechuanaland

Southern
Rhodesia

Walvis
Bay

Swaziland

Basutoland

Union of
South Africa
(Dominion)

0   500

MILES

*The British African
Empire, 1914*

The Rulers of British Africa
1870-1914

ONE

Introduction

On a momentous June day in 1897 a resplendent procession passed through London the likes of which the townspeople had never seen before. Fifty thousand troops had assembled from every part of the British Empire to celebrate Queen Victoria's Diamond Jubilee. There were fighting men in bearskin caps, turbans, fezzes, and digger hats. Kings, dukes, and rajahs rode in a procession that glittered with jewels and decorations. Between them they represented the greatest empire in history, an empire that covered one-fourth of the world's surface and was the mightiest maritime power in existence.

The intensity of social concern in the Victorian age exceeded all preceding periods of history. There were brilliant achievements in literature, history, medicine, and science. The era was equally creative in the fields of social and political organization. Institutions now mistakenly regarded as traditionally British—Parliament, civil service, clubs, colleges, trade unions, the Public Record Office, local governments—owed their existence or their modern form to Victorian innovators.

British investors placed their funds in the remotest corners of the globe.* They helped to build railways and factories in the United States; they invested in South African gold mines and stockyards in Argentina. On the eve of World War I, British capital abroad had grown to something like a quarter of or a third of the total holdings owned by British capitalists; current foreign investments may have slightly exceeded home investments.[1] The greater part of British funds went to the United States and the "white dominions," followed

---

* Selected data on the British economy in this period are presented in Appendix A, pp. 371–73.

by India and Argentina, with the tropical colonies acquired as the result of the "new imperialism" playing but an insignificant part.

British bankers were among the world's most powerful. In 1914 the total assets held by the Big Five (the leading joint-stock banks) amounted to £731.8 million, more than 40 times the annual revenue of the Union of South Africa (£17.3 million) and six times that of Italy (£114.6 million). British currency, firmly founded on gold, seemed the world's safest.

The commerce of the British Isles was tremendous in its variety and magnitude. The United Kingdom on paper showed an unfavorable balance of trade, but the gap was easily closed by invisible exports, the proceeds of shipping, banking, and insurance services, and remittances earned from foreign investments. Great Britain remained the world's most important free-trading power. The reputation of free trade had grown somewhat tarnished during the long depression years from the 1870's to the 1890's, but economic recovery brought new confidence. The majority of British voters would have no truck with advocates of protection, whose proposed tariffs threatened to put up food prices. The system of governance found challengers among certain militants: Irish nationalists, women, trade unionists, and socialist intellectuals. Yet the belief in capitalism as a working system in Great Britain was not seriously shaken in the decade preceding World War I.

The island metropole of this great empire was relatively prosperous. The so-called Great Depression—starting in 1873 and broken by bursts of recoveries during the 1880's—had receded. Real wages had risen during that period, though they were to drop slightly after the turn of the century. Except for Ireland, the population of the United Kingdom vastly expanded. Yet from the mid-nineteenth century the crime rate had lessened in a truly astonishing fashion, making pre–World War I Britain one of the most secure and perhaps one of the most crime-free societies in the industrialized world. In 1910 the number of convictions for all offenses in the United Kingdom was considerably less than the number of serious assaults in the city of San Francisco in 1973.[2]

The British people of 1897 could look back on half a century of unbroken and spectacular advances in every department of life. The Victorian age saw more advances in the lives of the common people than all the preceding ages. Despite the aesthetes' censure of "dark Satanic mills," the factory lords had done more to improve the condition of England than had any of its kings. However unsightly in appearance, factories turned out cheap goods in profusion: soap, underwear, shoes, margarine, iron bedsteads, and towels. Industrial forms of production provided inexpensive transport, brick houses, municipal sewers, proper sanitation, and piped water—reducing sickness, lowering the death rates, and adding to the decencies of life. The misery of the traditional rural cottage—insanitary, overcrowded, ridden with insects and rats, picturesque only to itinerant philosophers—was happily diminishing. An ever-increasing percentage of the population was able to enjoy a healthier and more dignified form of existence and the British death rate became the lowest among all the great European powers.

Industrial progress, however, had neither eliminated poverty nor leveled the social disparities of British society. In London the distinction of St. James Square, the solidity of Kensington, and the respectability of Hampstead Heath were offset by the drab wretchedness of Stepney and Whitechapel. The inhabitants of the East End and other members of the outcast world who lived *In Darkest England*—the title of a popular book written by the founder of the Salvation Army— were as mysterious, as alien, and as frightening to the respectable classes as were the denizens of "darkest Africa." An amateur sociologist like the well-to-do shipowner Charles Booth investigated metropolitan misery with the same mixture of methodological discipline and social concern that anthropologists soon would show in their study of South Sea islanders and Africans. Booth's great work, *Life and Labour of the People in London* (1891–1903), was designed to reveal "the numerical relation which poverty, misery and depravity bear to regular earnings and comparative comfort." Booth's work and a host of similar studies revealed a netherworld of ill-paid proletarians, of abandoned children, of whores, pimps, and thieves. This "darkest England" became the scene of a new missionary endeavor, secular as well as religious in inspiration, intended to change British society. To many Englishmen, misery now appeared not as a divinely appointed affliction but as a social ill to be cured by social action, a challenge that was being met and would continue to be met in the future.

Such optimism, like the British belief in capitalism, was not untinged with apprehension. Of social critics there were many; and whatever their political views, they all pointed to the "condition of England" as the overriding issue: the stark contrasts between the rich and the poor. Champions of the new imperialism like Joseph Chamberlain and Cecil Rhodes became convinced that only by developing the imperial estate, only by finding new overseas markets and new overseas sources of raw materials, could England feed its growing population and supply its industries, thereby avoiding civil strife. British economists were seriously concerned with foreign competition. The empire's economy continued to expand but at a slower rate than the economies of Germany and the United States. Progress in technical education, in modern managerial techniques, and in the application of science to industry was not equal to German advancement. Even the Grand Fleet, Britain's pride, the greatest navy on earth, was inferior in training and technology to the High Seas Fleet that the Germans began to build after the turn of the century.

Agriculture also had its troubles, for unlike France and Germany, Britain lacked tariffs that might have protected farmers from the competition of food producers in the United States, the dominions, and Argentina. Between 1892 and 1912 British landowners decreased the area under cultivation in the kingdom while the Germans were expanding theirs. The Germans produced more wheat, potatoes, and other foodstuffs per acre than the British. Great titled landowners and minor landed gentlemen remained a powerful component of British life, but noble wealth increasingly came to depend on City investments and on judicious marriage alliances with banking houses rather than on income from the land. As Oscar Wilde's formidable dowager and brilliant amateur sociologist Lady Bracknell put it in "The Importance of Being Earnest": "What between the duties expected of one during one's lifetime, and the duties exacted from one after one's death, land has ceased to be either a profit or a pleasure. It gives one position and prevents one from keeping it up. That's all that can be said about land."[3]

Nevertheless, the island kingdom still had awesome resources. Great Britain may no longer have been the world's only great industrial power as it had been in 1870, but the United Kingdom was still—at the turn of the century—the greatest European producer of coal and pig iron. The British turned out more steel than Russia, France, and the Austro-Hungarian monarchy together. Unlike German industries, those in Britain owed little or nothing to tariffs or government subsidies. The firms stood on their own feet. British people of all classes generally were better off than Germans of a corresponding social level. London was the center of world finance; Berlin came a long way behind. As a result, the leaders of German public opinion and commercial life often had that peculiar kind of inferiority complex regarding the British—that unpleasant mixture of envy, admiration, and sense of grievance characteristic of the *parvenu*.

Great Britain enjoyed other, less tangible advantages. Of all the industrialized states of Europe, it had the most cohesive and most unified ruling class. British society remained immensely and intricately stratified, but the aristocracy did not form an impenetrable caste. Only the first-born sons of lords inherited their fathers' title; their younger brothers had to make do with courtesy titles and imperceptible merging into the highest ranks of the bourgeoisie. There were also opportunities for commoners to rise into the aristocracy. Merchant princes, railway builders, and bankers could aspire to the highest social ranks of the realm in a manner unthinkable in Germany. So could a gifted physician like Joseph Lister, an adaptable politician like Benjamin Disraeli, or a popular poet like Alfred Tennyson, who rose from a parsonage to a peerage.

The governing class thus varied in social composition, But overall, it derived its ethos from the country gentlemen of England. Well-to-do businessmen or successful professional people could become part of the gentry by purchasing landed estates, looking after their tenants with the paternal concern expected of their rank, and sending their sons to Public Schools. Victorians looked askance at the narrowly trained specialist—whether "rootless" French career officers of the Bonapartist kind, Prussian civil servants trained in a restrictive code of legal and administrative efficiency, or Scottish engineers, good at their job, but without "the makings of a gentleman." The worship of the well-born amateur pervaded every aspect of Victorian life—army, church, academia, civil service. The cult even percolated into industry, often with fateful results in all fields of endeavors that required technical expertise of a supposedly "narrow" kind. The Victorians' love for unqualified gentlemen proved a burdensome legacy to subsequent generations forced to cope with problems different from those that had troubled their forebears. But given the right environment, the gentlemen did remarkably well. They lacked the narrow caste spirit of the Prussian nobility; they were more open to newcomers. They had a more genuine sense of public spirit than even that represented by the Prussian Haltung.

The advantages and disadvantages of their ethos were apparent in every part of life. Military officers, outside technical branches like the Royal Engineers, were not expected to spend much time at studying the principles of warfare. They prized "on-the-job" training. They valued social skills and the art of fox-hunting. Many of them were extremely well read, as evidenced by magnificent regimental libraries. Many more were deeply religious in the style of an Anglican manse. During the second part of the nineteenth century the officers acquired a growing sense of social consciousness of a kind that had been almost absent in the army that had fought in the Crimean War when the Redcoats still included many foreign mercenaries. The late-Victorian infantry officer might be deficient in technical training. But he was expected to display a paternalistic concern for the welfare of his soldiers, a concern that extended to the soldiers' families and dependents. He took this sense of social obligation back into civilian life. The best Victorian officers took these attitudes with them when they left the army to stand for local elections in Great Britain, or enter Parliament, or take up colonial appointments.

The civilian administrators shared this same ethos. The best of them combined the gentry virtues with a policy of domestic reform that likewise seeped into the colonies, combining a sense of family responsibility with social concern. For an example we might take the Gorst family, not at all a famous lineage but an interesting one. Sir John Gorst the Elder (1835–1916) was a gentleman's son who did brilliantly at Cambridge. He was awarded a fellowship, but preferred to explore New Zealand, where he became embroiled in Anglo-Maori diplomacy at a troubled time during the country's history. He lived through a "native outbreak" as civil commissioner and went in fear of his life. On his return to England, he successively became a Tory MP in the reformist tradition of Lord Beaconsfield, a member of Lord Randolph Churchill's "Fourth Party," and a minor Conservative officeholder. Later he was an unsuccessful Liberal candidate for a parliamentary seat at Preston, his home town. He was one of those many Victorian gentlemen who tried both to maintain the social order and to ameliorate the condition of the poor—their housing, education, and personal well-being.

His eldest, Sir Eldon Gorst (1861–1911), carried on the paternal tradition. His life work represented the "overspill" of domestic reformism into the empire. He went to Cambridge, his father's university, and subsequently entered the Foreign Service. He was posted to Cairo, where in 1892 he succeeded Milner as under secretary for finance; later he became adviser to the Egyptian government and then, in 1907, succeeded Lord Cromer in the position of His Majesty's agent and consul general, a viceregal position. Gorst Senior had been a Tory democrat, determined to link the mass of British workingmen to the governing classes. His son tried to reconcile Great Britain's Egyptian subjects to imperial rule. The task was to be accomplished by a judicious mixture of administrative reforms, low taxation, balanced budgets, and limited self-government. Had his career not been cut short by cancer, Sir Eldon Gorst might have made his name as a great viceroy, as well known to imperial historiography as Cromer, Kitchener, and Lugard. Today, the Gorsts are known only to specialists. But it was they, and people like them, who built the Victorian empire.

British society was divided into innumerable religious and irreligious sects. Of unbelievers there were many—especially among the slum dwellers. But organized religion nevertheless remained a powerful force. The Bible and the Book of Common Prayer profoundly influenced the style of public discourse. Theological tracts and sermons between them accounted for a larger percentage of publications than any other branch of literature. Victorian and Edwardian religiosity easily blended into secular reform. Poverty, most Victorians believed, was neither a holy nor an inevitable state. The best way to improve society was not by taking up the sword, but by encouraging men to better their condition, and by giving help to children, sick people, prisoners—indeed to all who could not look after their own in the hurly-burly of free enterprise. This spirit of reform helped to inspire the Victorian missionary movements, designed to lift up the heathen in the bush like the heathen in the slums. Victorian religiosity also played its part in developing colonial trusteeship doctrines of a more secular kind.

Despite the influence of organized religion in Victorian life, there was nothing like the bitter division into clericals and anticlericals that separated French society. Soldiers were apt to look down on civilians, and civilians in turn were apt to criticize the military. But the armed forces—like the world of banking, the Established Church, and the secular administration—were headed by gentlemen. The soldiers and sailors who held a commission from the queen did not regard themselves as a separate estate, with their own jurisdiction over cases of honor, as German officers did. Political parties might clash bitterly over a great variety of issues, but the parliamentary system was in good working order. The parliamentarians in turn were linked by ties of personal interest and family connections to the world of commerce, banking, and industry, and also to the world of the clubs and the world of the universities, in a manner that softened social clashes within the ruling strata.

Expressed in terms of numbers—the number of soldiers on parade and of policemen on the beat—the British state machinery was agreeably restricted and agreeably civilian in outlook. The British subject's person and property were secure. Constitutional liberties were real rather than sham. The British judicature and the British civil service were adjudged among the world's most incorruptible; the British police were accounted the world's most humane constabulary. Great Britain, as the centuries shifted, had reached its apogee, a point never again to be attained in the island's history. And one of the most visible marks of that ascendancy was the vast African empire it had acquired during the last quarter of the nineteenth century.

Great Britain and the Scramble for Africa

During the 1870's and the early 1880's, Africa—from the British imperial strategist's standpoint—was a continent of outposts. Within the framework of British capitalism, Africa played a negligible part. Britain's most important stake was in South Africa, where in 1806 the British had permanently annexed the Cape Colony. Located along the vital route to India, the Cape became the principal base for British naval operations in the South Atlantic. The British later secured control of Natal, fronting on the Indian Ocean, and claimed a vague suzerainty over the interior, where emigrant Boer trekkers, anxious to escape British overlordship, had set up two autonomous republics— the Orange Free State and the Transvaal.

British power centered on the Cape Colony, the country with the largest white population in Africa (236,785 out of a total of 720,984 in 1875). The colony was distinguished by a complex ethnic caste pattern. English-speaking whites dominated urban enterprise, business, the army, and administration; Afrikaans-speaking—and a lesser number of English-speaking—farmers were supreme in the countryside; Eurafricans and Africans stood at the bottom of the ladder as artisans and laborers. The Europeans were divided along lines of language and culture, but they were sufficiently strong to obtain a form of self-government. In 1852 the Cape legislature became purely elective, with a "color-blind" franchise based on property qualifications that gave the vote to the bulk of the European residents and a handful of Eurafricans and Bantu-speaking voters. In Natal the British settlers were supreme; European planters succeeded in hiring indentured laborers from India, whose presence further complicated southern Africa's intricate ethnic mosaic.

In the eyes of most British statesmen South Africa was a permanent headache. It was a land of conflict: conflict between white frontiersmen and the African communities beyond the pale of settlement; conflict between the Europeans and an "internal proletariat" of Africans and Eurafricans (Coloreds); conflict between the European "colonials" on the one hand, and "imperially" oriented administrators and missionaries on the other; conflict between differing social strata within the white community; conflict between Britons and Boers—both of them minorities within the predominantly African and mixed population. British governors were expected to keep the peace with a small administrative establishment, a modest revenue, and a tiny military force. In 1880 only five battalions were available for the whole of southern Africa. High regimental morale did not prevent widespread desertion; indeed, the Transvaal, temporarily and unsuccessfully annexed in 1877, was regarded by British enlisted men as one of the worst stations in the empire.

The British also had to deal with a number of independent African states whose power, as yet, was very far from negligible. Lesotho (Basutoland), a collection of peoples welded into a state by the genius of King Mosheshwe, derived some protection from its mountainous terrain; the Sotho (Basuto) forces, mounted on hardy ponies and armed with firearms, possessed considerable mobility. Sotho diplomacy excelled at playing off Briton against Boer, and generally looked for British assistance against the trekkers. Zululand, on the frontier of Natal, formed a highly centralized monarchy of a different kind, a "Black Sparta" that relied on raiding, war, and cattle farming—the greatest of several "spear kingdoms" scattered over southern Africa. The Zulu struggled against the Transvaalers, as well as against their African neighbors; they relied on strong forces of well-drilled infantry, armed with spears and oxhide shields. The Zulu state continued to be a formidable factor in local politics until its armies were crushed by the British at Ulundi in 1879.

From the economic standpoint, South Africa's importance at first was small. In 1880 the Cape Colony exported goods worth £7,710,000 —a puny sum by the standards of contemporary British mercantile statistics, but still more than four times the value of the traffic between all British West African colonies and the United Kingdom. The prosperity of the South African colonies, such as it was, depended on the sale of primary products—cane sugar, hides, skins, ostrich feathers, mohair, and particularly merino wool.

The discovery of the Kimberley "dry diggings" in 1870 brought the colonists a new and sudden source of prosperity. The Kimberley diamond mines became a magnet that attracted African workers from as far afield as the Upper Zambezi Valley. In addition, scores of Europeans—most of them English-speaking—made their way into the interior, and the British urban element within the Cape was greatly strengthened. The South African colonies came to occupy a peculiarly important place within the British imperial dispensation in Africa. Alone in sub-Saharan Africa, South Africa—by the 1880's—had a fairly large white population, including miners and artisans with specialized skills. Alone in Africa, South Africa had the makings of a coal-mining industry. It obtained credit through a relatively intricate banking system linked to the London money market. The Cape Colony was the first sub-Saharan territory to acquire the rudiments of a modern economic infrastructure. These advantages enabled the colony for a time to play the primary role in the life of southern Africa. In the person of Cecil Rhodes, who was to become both a major mining magnate and prime minister of the Cape, the colony developed an imperialist drive of its own.

Next to South Africa from the British merchants' standpoint, the most important part of the continent was the West Coast, especially the tropical forest area. West Africa produced peanuts and, above all, palm oil, a valuable commodity that had a variety of uses and was produced by Africans using little capital and rudimentary methods. Among other things, it was required for the preparation of margarine and soap, for oil cakes used as cattle feed, and for industrial lubricants. In the Gold Coast cocoa became a peasants' crop after the turn of the century, when it became a popular drink in Europe; it was also an essential raw material for the manufacture of chocolate, introduced in Switzerland in 1876. In countries lying outside the tropical forest zone, like Gambia, the place of palm oil was taken by groundnuts, a crop valuable as a food and in the fabrication of soap. Like palm oil, groundnuts were produced by indigenous cultivators and required little capital. All three—palm oil, cocoa, and groundnuts—were produced by smallholders, who in their turn provided importers with a market for a variety of merchandise: liquor above all, but also textiles, trinkets, and tools.

British merchants traded over vast areas in West Africa. But Britain's territorial stake in the region counted for little during the 1870's. South of Senegal, a French colony, the British held a narrow strip of territory along the Gambia River. The Gambia was a magnificent waterway, but the British could make little use of its opportunities. Bathurst, the capital of Gambia, stood in the midst of pestilential marshes; and though Europeans could happily settle in the Mediterranean climate of the Cape or the healthy plateau country of the South African interior, they suffered heavily from the many tropical diseases endemic to West Africa. Malaria infected the river valley, and mosquito-borne sicknesses for long loomed as a deadly barrier to white commercial penetration. African dealers did some business in peanuts, kola nuts, and other agricultural produce. But the volume of trade was small, and the British at one time seriously considered abandoning the country to the French.

Farther south, the British were established in Sierra Leone, where liberated slaves, black veterans who had fought under the Union Jack in the American War of Independence, and civilian settlers from other parts of the New World and Africa had coalesced into an Afro-British population, English by language, African by origin and sympathy. Freetown, the capital, possessed one of the finest harbors in West Africa and became an important base for British naval operations against the slave trade. The town also was a center of commerce in palm oil and peanuts, and—with its shops, shipping agencies, and newspaper office—became one of the few places where a modified form of the British Victorian tradition struck root in black Africa. Sierra Leone creoles, English-speaking people of mixed descent, benefited to some extent from the British connection. They pushed outward along the coast and inward into the hinterland, where they made their name as traders, clerks, factors, interpreters, government employees, and missionaries—voluntary or involuntary agents of Afro-British expansion.

The bulk of British West African commerce centered on what was then known to geographers as Lower Guinea. At the Gold Coast the British occupied a number of forts on the littoral. Their influence depended on trade and on alliances with the coastal peoples against the warlike Ashanti kingdom of the interior; but the administrators were unable to confine their countrymen's economic activities to the shore. In 1865 a Parliamentary Select Committee, disturbed by the expenditure entailed by Britain's West African obligations, advocated a partial and gradual withdrawal. But traders throughout British West Africa wanted more, not less, protection, and the committee's resolutions had but limited impact on British policy. The British could not pull out. Neither could they escape the complications of a turbulent frontier. Friction with the Ashanti continued, and the British were drawn deeper into warlike enterprise.

Farther east, white traders initially worked in partnership with the small city-states along the Niger delta, which profited from an increasing trade in palm oil. The development of steam-propelled riverboats and the prophylactic use of quinine, however, gradually enabled British traders to penetrate inland; the old system of collaboration with the river states by diplomatic means supported by seapower broke down. By the 1870's four British companies were operating in the Niger Valley, and navigation extended some 600 miles into the interior. British commercial penetration occasioned widespread conflict. African palm-oil brokers in control of the strategic river courses and creeks tried to keep out the interlopers. British merchants then called on their government for protection, and the 1870's saw a good deal of stiff fighting. As long as British vessels remained in the vicinity of inland trading posts, the merchants did good business. When the dry season set in and warships could no longer move upriver, Africans resumed their attack. Barter and battle alternated with the regularity of the seasons.

In East Africa Britain's trade was considerably less than on the west coast, and its East African commerce gave much less scope to small peasant cultivators. Principal British imports centered on luxury goods, including ivory, a commodity obtained through the skills of professional hunters; sugar, grown mainly on Mauritian plantations; and cloves, derived from Arab-owned estates on the island of Zanzibar. Britain's political influence in the Sultanate of Zanzibar depended on a partnership with a local Islamic oligarchy of great estate owners and merchants. But in Zanzibar, as at Constantinople, British policy rested on unresolved contradictions. On the one hand, Britain wanted to enforce reforms acceptable to the British humanitarian conscience; these reforms hinged on free trade, free wage labor, and the benevolent treatment of the weak. On the other hand, the home government wanted to avoid expensive commitments, and therefore looked to traditional rulers to carry out reforms that were incompatible with traditional institutions.

In East Africa the British were determined to wipe out the Muslim slave trade, one of the props sustaining the social system of Zanzibar. This obliged them to play an ever-increasing role in the affairs of the sultanate. At the same time British Indian financiers and businessmen acquired growing influence within the island's economy. In 1869 the Suez Canal was opened, and Western European ships bound for India could avoid the long haul around the Cape. Four years later the British—relying on their overwhelming seapower—succeeded in closing the Zanzibari slave markets, with the result that the sultan became ever more dependent on Royal Navy support.

During the 1870's, therefore, British power in many parts of Africa still depended on a system of indirect influence exercised through consuls, missionaries, and traders, and sometimes through captains of cruisers and gunboats. In another 20 years the British had acquired what appeared to be the greatest empire in African history. Admittedly, the enormous areas painted Royal Red on the map were as yet a disparate medley, underadministered and underfinanced. Their trade, for the most part, was minimal. They lacked political cohesion. They were devoid of governmental uniformity—an ill-assorted amalgam of Crown colonies and protectorates, territories under settler self-government, and vast areas under the rule of chartered companies. Their military establishment was small, their revenue mostly insignificant. (See Table 1.) Many African communities nominally under the Union Jack were unaware that they were supposedly the subjects of a White Queen who dwelt thousands of miles away in an unknown island. Effective occupation was not completed until about 1914; everywhere, claims had preceded conquest. Even so, British territorial expansion was on a stupendous scale, part of a wider design by which the European colonial powers had partitioned the bulk of Africa.

The literature on the Scramble for Africa and the British share in the partition fills many library shelves.[4] But a few salient points emerge. The Scramble was not a unified venture. By the late nineteenth century there were many points of Euro-African contacts, all with a logic of their own, and all capable of generating expansive policies of their own. The partition of Africa was not determined from one or two geographical centers, any more than it arose from any single set of causes. Each major European acquisition, however, might upset the local balance of power; each new imperial acquisition was apt to provoke new efforts on the part of imperial competitors.

In North Africa the fight for the expansion of Europe was linked to the fortunes of the declining Ottoman Empire, faced from without by the Russian threat, and from within by financial ruin, by the agitation of subject nationalities, and by the inability of its ruling class to reform its military, economic, and administrative institutions at a pace sufficiently swift to meet the new challenges to Ottoman power. Frightened by the Russian threat to their dominions, the Turks in 1878 agreed to hand over the administration of Cyprus to Great Britain in return for British support. Britain in turn allowed France a "free hand" in Tunisia.

Great Britain and France, moreover, were both deeply involved in Egypt, an autonomous country still nominally under Ottoman suzerainty. Benefitting from a rapidly rising world demand for cotton, Egypt had attempted to effect a far-reaching program of modernization; but

TABLE 1
The Formal British Empire in Africa, 1893

Territory	Area (Square miles)	Estimated population	Number of Europeans	Value of exports (£1,000)	Form of government
Southern Africa					
Basutoland	10,293	220,000	—	—	Protectorate (under high commissioner for South Africa)
Bechuanaland	270,000	100,000	5,000	—	Crown colony, protectorate
Cape Colony (including African areas annexed to colony)	221,310	1,530,000	377,000	13,157	"Self-governing colony"
Natal	20,460	544,000	48,000	1,615	"Self-governing colony"
St. Helena	47	4,116	—	1,338	Crown colony
Rhodesia (Northern and Southern)	439,575	1,000,000	c. 3,000	—	Chartered company
East and Central Africa					
Mauritius	705	371,000	—	1,478	Crown colony
British East Africa Protectorate (including Uganda)	c. 340,000	c. 4,000,000?	c. 200	86	Chartered company
Zanzibar	1,000	100,000?	c. 200	1,002	Protectorate
British Central Africa Protectorate	37,000	800,000	c. 345	—	Protectorate
West Africa					
Gold Coast	46,000	1,500,000	—	722	Crown colony, protectorate
Lagos	20,000	3,000,000	—	836	Crown colony
Sierra Leone	15,000	—	—	398	Crown colony
Gambia	15,000	—	—	204	Crown colony
Niger Protectorate	—		—	988	Protectorate
Niger Territories	374,000	30,000,000	—	406	Chartered company

SOURCE: The Statesman's Yearbook, 1894.

the khedive's plans were far too ambitious for his limited resources and inefficient administration. In 1876 he went bankrupt. Great Britain and France assumed financial control over his country. Foreign intervention led to an ineffective uprising led by Egyptian army officers— the country's partly Westernized military intelligentsia. The French would not intervene, so the British acted by themselves and in 1882 crushed the Egyptian forces at Tel-el-Kebir.

The British did not originally intend to stay. But once having entered the country, they found withdrawal problematical. Imperial strategists no longer regarded Constantinople as the key to the Near East. They now looked on Alexandria as the pivot of their position in the eastern Mediterranean. Egypt seemed essential for the control of the naval route to India, and British influence in the country was consolidated. Intervention in Egypt in turn helped to involve the British in the troubles of the Sudan, which was reconquered by an Anglo-Egyptian force in 1898 and safeguarded against French claims by a British threat of war.

South Africa was another point of departure for imperial expansion. The discovery of diamonds in the Cape had far-reaching consequences for the country's economic future. More British immigrants came into the country to benefit from the newfound mining wealth. So great were the profits from diamonds that producers could largely pay for the initial development of the industry from their own earnings and still accumulate sufficient funds for investment in other enterprises. Additional opportunities arose in 1886, when gold was discovered at the Witwatersrand in the Transvaal. A new mining frontier came into being, giving rise to a new Anglo-Cape imperialist impulse that looked for further territorial acquisitions beyond the Limpopo River, where Rhodes and his associates mistakenly expected to find a "Second Rand." In the 1890's the Union Jack was implanted in what later became Southern and Northern Rhodesia and also in Nyasaland, a missionary stronghold dear to the Scottish humanitarian conscience.

In West Africa, France and Great Britain had been competitors of long standing. During the 1880's the French embarked on a vigorous expansion policy. The position was further complicated by the irruption of two "new" powers: Belgium, and the recently unified German Reich. Lack of space prevents us from recapitulating the complex story of their diplomatic dealings. Suffice it to say that Belgium obtained a lien on the Congo (later known as Zaïre), and the Germans rapidly acquired an African empire comprising Togo, Cameroun, and South-West Africa. Not to be left behind, the British vastly extended their possessions. Faced with competition from the French, in 1885 the British united the territories between Lagos and Cameroun into the Niger Protectorate. A year later they issued a charter to the Royal Niger Company. Anglo-French rivalry continued, but after numerous disputes, Great Britain and France agreed to a settlement (1898) that largely completed the diplomatic partition of West Africa. Meantime, the British had consolidated a substantial territorial bloc in East Africa; they acquired Uganda, British Somaliland, and Kenya (known as the British East Africa Protectorate), while the Germans acquired the bulk of what is now Tanzania.

At the time of the partition these newly acquired territories were a puny part of the British economy. Except for the Cape, their exports were negligible. But even the Cape accounted for only a minor proportion of Britain's imperial trade; Cape exports in 1893 amounted to just £13,156,589, compared with £65,952,699 for Australia and £218,094,865 for the United Kingdom itself. In terms of foreign trade and investment, the African continent played a marginal role within the framework of British capitalism during the Scramble for Africa.

TABLE 2

Principal Items of Trade Between the United Kingdom and
the Union of South Africa, 1910

(In £)

Item	Value
Principal UK exports to South Africa	
Apparel	2,834,929
Iron and steel manufactures	2,309,636
Machinery	2,018,059
Cotton manufactures	1,980,533
Leather manufactures	1,246,699
Woolen manufactures	1,007,600
Chemicals	433,742
All UK exports to South Africa	19,451,561
Principal UK imports from South Africa	
Diamonds	8,480,875
Sheep's wool	3,930,746
Ornamental feathers	2,002,907
Metals and ores	929,202
Mohair wool	801,444
Sheepskins	568,279
Corn	514,742
All UK imports from South Africa	18,754,275

SOURCE: *Whitaker's Almanac* (London, 1912), p. 583.

TABLE 3

Trade of the United Kingdom with Selected Countries and Possessions, 1910

(In £)

Territory	UK's imports	UK's exports
Union of South Africa	18,754,275	19,451,561
Nigeria	3,242,941	6,375,500
Gold Coast	1,065,314	1,792,183
East Africa	268,001	369,921
Denmark	19,464,059	5,970,910
Argentina	29,009,738	19,710,537
Total trade with all countries and possessions	678,257,024	534,145,817

SOURCE: Same as Table 2, pp. 490, 491, 583.
NOTE: For figures on British overseas investments, see Table A.1, p. 371, below.

The importance of Great Britain's economic stake in Africa increased somewhat after partition had been completed. The development of African-centered lobbies was the result more than the cause of the Scramble. As the years went by, British commerce in Africa grew in both volume and diversity. Liquor lost its pride of place.* Tea, coffee, salt, tinned food, and other luxuries figured more prominently than before among African imports. Western-made clothes, plows, hatchets, sewing machines, bicycles, and pocket watches became common items of trade. European mining and railway companies required a broad range of new equipment—pumps, cranes, steam locomotives, iron rails, and such.

Nevertheless, sub-Saharan Africa did not hold a major place in the British economy before World War I. By 1910 a quarter of a century after partition had begun, Britain's only important trading partner on the continent was South Africa; but even Anglo–South African commerce was considerably less important than the traffic between, say, Great Britain and Argentina. (See Tables 2 and 3.) Nigeria came second on the list of African trading partners, yet its value in British traffic was far less than that between Britain and Denmark, a minor European country. From the standpoint of the British businessman, a relatively recent acquisition like the British East Africa Protectorate was almost valueless; yet lobbies continued for imperial acquisitions and for increased African trade.

* In fact, liquor dominated the West Coast trade during much of the nineteenth century. The bulk, however, consisted of spirits distilled in Germany and other continental countries. In 1897 foreign firms exported 2,984,327 gallons of liquor to West Africa; this compares with a mere 179,176 gallons of British exports to all parts of the empire.

How far, then, did economic motives determine the partition of Africa? According to past critics of empire like J. A. Hobson and Leonard Woolf, the "New Imperialism" was the brainchild of commerce and investment. When all is said and done, the British soldier in the 1870's went to battle against the Ashanti to promote the sale of British cotton. He marched on Pretoria a generation later to safeguard the wealth of British mineowners in the Transvaal. Marxists later elaborated these interpretations by stressing the growth of metropolitan monopolies, the domination of industry by finance, the need to compensate for falling profits at home by conquests abroad, and the change in the character of trade from consumption goods, such as textiles, to investment goods, such as mining equipment. Bankers wanted to protect their investments and to gain super profits; hence the politicians turned to empire.[5]

These interpretations have many weaknesses. The structure of British finance in the Victorian and Edwardian eras was by no means monopolistic. British banks did not dominate the manufacturing industries. British investors seldom earned super profits in the colonies. Indeed, many investors lost their capital, and others were content with low-yield investments like railways. The export of merchandise other than investment goods continued, even though commodities shipped abroad became technically more complex, with bicycles and sewing machines gaining on hatchets and beads. During the age of the "New Imperialism," moreover, the bulk of British monied men continued to place their faith in free trade, a sensible policy at a time when developed sovereign countries like the United States absorbed infinitely more British investments than the British African colonies.

Our own interpretation lacks the simplicity of the Hobson-Woolf school. As we see it, the economic motive was only one among many. A desire for security, a search for glory, nationalism, the Europeans' belief in their civilizing mission, were equal in importance to purely economic factors in impelling the whites on the course of empire. The economic factors themselves were more diverse and more complex than Woolf and Hobson assumed. Scientific and industrial development had further widened the already enormous gap between the states of northwestern Europe and the indigenous societies of sub-Saharan Africa. During the second part of the nineteenth century, for instance, the prophylactic use of quinine helped to raise the mosquito barrier that had shut off much of the African interior. The steam engine was successfully applied to land and water transport, bringing about a complete transformation in production, logistics, and war.

Rifles and Maxim guns revolutionized the techniques of conquest. The whites, moreover, held the ideological initiative and convinced themselves that African conquest would benefit both the metropolitan powers and their newly gained subjects. Colonialism, in fact, became a form of social gospel that appealed both to the missionaries of secular progress and to the missionaries of the Holy Word.

During the 1880's British policy makers also became increasingly concerned with protecting British trade against foreign pressure at a time when the economy was suffering from a serious and extended depression. Before this period London's approach to the future of British trade had been optimistic; British commerce should receive fair and equal—not favored—treatment overseas, and all would be well. Britain prided itself on its position as the "workshop of the world"; "universal free trade" seemed destined to bring peace to a strife-torn world.

The situation changed after 1880. Growing competition from factories in France—and above all, in Germany and the United States— began to trouble British exporters; so did the long-sustained depression that had begun in the 1870's, and the trend to protectionism abroad. In the harsher economic climate of the 1880's territorial expansion on the part of foreign powers seemed to require a more positive British response: intervention to secure freedom of trade or, failing all else, "prophylactic annexations" designed to safeguard markets of the future. Trade overseas came to be linked with full employment and social peace at home. British policy makers grew increasingly determined that other nations should not preempt potentially valuable regions and exclude British commerce. At the same time their conviction strengthened that the traditional African states could not modernize the continent, and that the advance of military and scientific technology rendered European rule inevitable.

Local lobbies played their part. In West Africa, for example, local trading firms suffered severely from the fall in prices for palm oil and other tropical products during the worldwide depression. The slump also struck the African middlemen at the Atlantic shore, and Africans attempted to increase their prices, raise their tolls, and keep out interlopers. European merchants, for their part, became increasingly anxious to push into the interior, cut out the coastal middlemen, eliminate local African trade monopolies, and increase the turnover of trade by building railways. Many white merchants thus began to press for a more active policy of territorial expansion.

The advance of the mining frontier from southern to south-central

Africa had similar consequences. European ivory hunters had found no difficulty in adjusting to the ways of a military monarchy such as that of the Ndebele (Matabele), based on herding and raiding for captives and cattle. But once European miners settled in Mashonaland, along the outer periphery of the Ndebele kingdom (1890), they decided that there could be no peaceful coexistence between an economy based on wage labor and one based on war. The Ndebele had no wish to give up raiding. But Ndebele raids on the local African population left white miners without labor, and white shopkeepers without customers. In the settlers' eyes the exigencies of profit and humanity alike called for conquest.

Economic pressure groups, however, did not operate in a vacuum; they were effective only when their demands coincided with those of other pressure groups. As John Flint puts it for West Africa:

In the broad perspective, the British government and its officials were not manipulated . . . by traders' lobbies or chambers of commerce. The traders were themselves too divided to mount monolithic pressures by the regional differences of their trade . . . and by the personal antagonisms between strong-minded characters such as Goldie [Sir George Goldie, founder of Nigeria], A. L. Jones the shipping magnate, John Holt of Liverpool, and numerous lesser figures. Even had this disunity been overcome, British politicians and government officials . . . were not of a background or temperament to accept dictation from traders. Their frame of reference was still essentially aristocratic; they regarded themselves as responsible administrators who based their decisions on higher concepts of British interests than those which could be advocated by any lobby. [Thus] the "official mind" made its decisions in light of what *it* assessed were the needs of British commerce.[6]

Political and Intellectual Lobbies

Now away sail our ships far away o'er the sea,
    Far away with our gallant and brave;
The loud war-cry is sounding like the wild revelrie,
    And our heroes dash on to their grave;
For the fierce Zulu tribes have risen in their might,
    And in thousands swept down on our few;
But these braves only yielded when crushed in the fight,
    Man to man their colors were true.

Popular Victorian broadsheets rarely liked halftones in their value judgments, and in the Zulu war of 1879 the issues were apparently clear cut.[7] Not even the most tender-minded humanitarians had much good to say about the warlike Zulu people, whose armies terrorized their African neighbors and even seemed to threaten British settlers in Natal. Rapid victory seemed assured, for the Martini-Henry rifle was expected to do wonders against oxhide shields and assegais. Hence the news of the battle of Isandhlwana, in which an entire British battalion was wiped out, came as a stunning blow. A fashionable bootmaker remarked to an officer ordered out to Zululand, "Very sad business, sir, nothing like it in England since I can remember. We lost three customers by it."[8]

The British Army quickly redeemed its reputation. A small but well-led and well-disciplined detachment, 80 men in all, repulsed a Zulu force numbering some 4,000 warriors. Disraeli, with his political instinct, seized his chance; his showmanship turned a minor engagement into a magnificent victory. Eleven members of the unit were awarded the Victoria Cross, making this the most highly decorated battle in British history. Rorke's Drift—more important in the public eye than the overthrow of Zulu might in the subsequent battle of Ulundi—made up for political incompetence in dealing with South African affairs and for incapability in the proper administration of the army.

Disraeli's government had no economic stake in Zululand; the settlers' lobby in Natal was of minor importance. This conquest seemed to the British essentially a defensive operation to calm a turbulent frontier. It signified an imperialism of conspicuous display. For Disraeli's government never pursued a consistent policy of territorial expansion, despite his avowed imperial sentiments and his emphasis on splendid titles and speeches. During his most important ministry, between 1874 and 1880, he established a central government for New Zealand, constituted the colony of Fiji, annexed the Transvaal—a backward colony whose mineral resources were as yet unknown—attempted to federate the various South African colonies, and waged frontier campaigns in Afghanistan and Zululand; in 1877 his government proclaimed the queen to be Empress of India.

Disraeli's imperialism was of a kind that appealed to conservative clubs and officers' messes. In addition, imperialism began to have a growing attraction for many newspaper readers. The majority of London's daily newspapers were Conservative, addressing them selves to the middle and upper-middle classes.[9] Their techniques for presenting news was simple. A correspondent making his way through the African bush—often an army officer or a geographer—wrote lengthy dispatches in stately and somewhat turgid English; these appeared in print with little or no alteration. A lead writer devoid of a

more interesting subject would then comment on the news in magisterial fashion. The comments varied widely in tone; even the Conservative press was by no means a consistent advocate of imperial
expansion. As Lord Salisbury said in 1884, "The misfortune—the root
difficulty—we have in dealing with imperial questions . . . is that public opinion in a large sense takes no note of them. Unless some star-
tling question appealing to their humanity arises, the constituencies
are quite indifferent."*

The poorly educated—the mass of the population—rarely read the
daily papers, with their complex syntax and elaborate vocabulary. In
an age innocent of radio and television, the British populace mainly
drew its news and much of its entertainment from a variety of Sunday
papers that had served the public for several decades with a diet of
sport, sex, and crime. Included were *Titbits*, pioneer in this particular
form of journalism, *Answers*, *Comic Cuts*, and *Home Chats*. Even the
Daily Mail, one of the first "popular dailies," considered itself at first
to be an imitation of *The Times*. Not perhaps until 1903, when the
Daily Mirror first appeared on the newsstands, did the flavor of
Titbits seep into the daily press. In so far as they dealt with overseas
questions, these organs liked their imperialism well-spiced—with red-
coated fusiliers chasing naked savages through the bush and saving
beauteous maidens from a fate worse than death.

The extent of newspaper influence is hard to assess. There is not
the slightest evidence that a statesman like Disraeli allowed his policy
to be determined by editors. Yet as an institution, the press became
increasingly powerful toward the end of the century. Joseph Chamberlain was initiated at an early stage of his career into the art of harness-
ing newspapers to his support. According to his own reminiscences,
several Conservative ministers were in constant touch with editors of
The Times, the *Standard*, the *Daily News*, and the *Pall Mall Gazette*.
W. T. Stead, editor of the *Pall Mall Gazette* and one of the proponents
of the new journalism, had grown aware of the potential represented
by the press during the British campaign against the "Bulgarian atroci-
ties" committed by the Turks in the Balkans. Stead was inspired by a
queer blend of national assertiveness, religious hysteria, and social
uplift, which led him to formulate a new doctrine of what the press
ought to represent—"the worthy leader of a regimented people"—and
as such he avowed himself an imperialist "within the limits of sanity

---

The Times at first had little respect for Rhodes's dealings with Lobengula, king of
the Ndebele; its attitude changed only toward the end of 1889, when Rhodes's conquest
of Mashonaland seemed assured.

and the Ten Commandments."[10] The new journalism had arrived, based on mass readership—but only after the empire had been acquired.

In addition to the imperialism of mess, club, editor's office, and public bar, there was the imperialism of church and chapel. This was a pervasive force, with numerous ramifications and a powerful moral impact. The missionary lobbies were organized into countless societies, Nonconformist and Anglican, which wielded considerable influence. Mission journals had a wide readership. Once a year there was a great gathering in London of missionary and humanitarian societies for the May Meetings. These were commonly held in Exeter Hall in the Strand, which has given its name to the colonial policy advocated within its walls. At these meetings, missionaries from the "foreign field" were themselves a great attraction; their letters were sometimes read aloud if they could not come in person.

Missionaries became skilled in the art of parliamentary lobbying, in buttonholing politicians and journalists, and in making the right ministerial contacts. They drew financial support from many social strata—from skilled workers to great landowners. Missionary pressure groups played a direct and important part in the British acquisition of Yorubaland, Nyasaland, and Uganda, where Britain's economic stake was negligible. And by indirection they were at least in part responsible for British expansion into other areas of Africa, constantly importuning government officials to occupy new territory to save the Africans from German, French, or Portuguese rule. A missionary career appealed to committed men anxious to serve the downtrodden in faraway lands and willing to risk their health—or even their lives— in doing so. It also provided a means of social promotion to many a man whose father had earned his living as a gardener, a farm laborer, or a shopkeeper.

The inspirational imperialism represented by Livingstone and his imitators had many facets. It appealed to evangelical members of the Established Church and to Nonconformists alike. It often went with a doctrine of sudden conversion, the believer's intense conviction that he had been "saved" at an identifiable time on an identifiable date. Inspirational imperialism commonly entailed a missionary belief in intervention on behalf of the persecuted—be they Armenians and Bulgarians subject to Ottoman domination, Africans harried by Sudanese or by Swahili slave traders, or Boer farmers. As prime minister, William Gladstone made use of the militant conscience vote to support a Liberal policy in Ireland and the Near East. But the militant conscience was hard to control, and in 1884, when General C. G. Gordon found himself besieged by Muslims in Khartoum, the humanitarians joined with the militarists to vilify the minister who had abandoned a Christian to his fate.

The Livingstonian tradition also appealed to secular reformers, who were grouped into associations such as the Anti-Slavery and Aborigines Protection Society, founded in 1838 at the insistence of Sir Thomas Fowell Buxton, a British prison reformer and a militant opponent of slavery. Supporters of the society rejected the abuses that went with imperialism. They believed in a policy of free labor and free trade. They repudiated economic coercion in all its forms. They stood for due process in law, and they had no truck with monopolies—chartered or otherwise. But they accepted empire in principle as a right of dominion to be held in trust for the backward and the weak.

The society's journal, the *Anti-Slavery Reporter*, claimed that the rulers' first responsibility was to wipe out slavery and the slave trade. But this was just one of several pressing responsibilities. First of all, the society insisted, the "natives should be protected against the evils of liquor. For this purpose, it set up a Native Races and Liquor Traffic United Committee in 1887, a body that appealed to the temperance lobbies throughout Britain. Second, the "natives" must be secure in their persons and property. And, finally, "punitive expeditions" against ill-armed Africans should be opposed. The doctrine of "native rights" was worked out more fully by Henry Fox Bourne, the society's secretary. The African, he argued, had three fundamental rights: a right to his land, a right to the free practice of his own customs and institutions, and a right to an equal share in "all the beneficial arrangements" introduced into his country by the white man. The conquerors might not forcibly appropriate his land or produce, or impose labor contracts. Barbaric institutions should be suppressed, but only by means of "reasonable persuasion." The colonizing powers should aim, not at the material advantage of the white man, but at the "moral advantage of his subjects."[11]

The Aborigines Protection Society wielded a good deal of influence among educated men and especially among such important groups as journalists, merchants, clergymen, university teachers, and officials. The officeholders of the society held a variety of positions in national and local politics; they were also active in missionary and secular movements directed toward domestic reform. (For instance, Sir Thomas Buxton took a prominent position in the affairs of Essex; he was also treasurer of the Church Mission Society. His son, Noel Edward Noel-

Buxton, a co-president of the Aborigines Protection Society, was a Liberal and later a Labour MP. He was connected with a host of good causes in Britain, including the Save the Children Fund, the Miners' Welfare Committee, and the National Laymen's Missionary Movement.) The society was skilled at lobbying; its deputations were received by ministers and members of Parliament. Above all, it stood for a positive creed of imperialism, for power sanctified by trust. In economic terms, it appealed to all those who wished to develop Africa by means of an economic partnership between traders and African cultivators. In political terms, it placed stress on the services of enlightened administrators capable of defending backward peoples against the exactions of concessionaires and settlers. Not surprisingly, the society's creed made a profound impact on the best practitioners of empire themselves and later found official expression in British trusteeship doctrines.

The society's tradition appealed to a variety of reformers at home and abroad. (The Gesellschaft für Eingeborenenschutz, for instance, was founded in Germany specifically on the model of the Aborigines Protection Society.) A number of British associations were formed to deal with specific issues, including the organization in 1904 of the Congo Reform Association under the auspices of E. D. Morel to combat Belgian abuses in the Congo. The list of Morel's supporters is impressive for both their social distinction and their political range. Morel attracted missionaries like Grattan Guiness and atheists like Fox Bourne; he derived support from members of Parliament in all parties. The names and titles of his officeholders would have delighted the most snobbish London hostesses—Lords Beauchamp, Aberdeen, Listowel, and Mayo; the bishops of Southwark and Liverpool; prominent Nonconformists like John Clifford and R. J. Campbell; the fashionable journalists, including Harold Spender and St. Loe Strachey. There was support also from men traditionally powerful in humanitarian circles: from businessmen like John Holt, Alfred Emmott, and William Cadbury; from colonial administrators like Sir Harry Johnston, Sir George Denton, Sir William MacGregor, and Sir Percy Girouard.

These societies were elite bodies. Their influence derived from political and social contacts within the ruling stratum; they worked in collaboration with other political groups and with one another. They stood for reform. But they also stood for the expansion of empire in a good cause. In 1873 the Aborigines Protection Society joined with another imperial-minded association, the Royal Colonial Institute, for the purpose of urging the annexation of Fiji.

The Royal Colonial Institute (now the Royal Commonwealth Society) had started its career in 1868 as the Colonial Society, its founders at first eschewing the use of the title "Royal" because the Royal College of Surgeons would not share the same initials with an upstart body. The society encouraged imperialism when most people in Great Britain were not interested in expansion. Its original object was to oppose critics who believed that Britain's white-settlement colonies would inevitably cut adrift from the motherland; it was determined to promote the unity of the empire and to spread knowledge concerning its different parts. It built up an important library, published its annual *Proceedings* and from 1910 onward a monthly journal entitled *United Empire*; it conducted discussions and held lunches and an annual dinner in the City to which important businessmen and visiting colonial officials were invited. On 11 June 1874 the institute held its first annual *conversazione* and began monthly dinners at the South Kensington Museum (now known as the Victoria and Albert Museum). Its membership at that time was only 500, and visitors from overseas were few, but the affair was a great success and more than 500 people attended. From 1897 to 1909 the membership expanded by only a few hundred a year; the greatest growth came between 1909 and 1915, when 6,377 members were added, bringing the total to 11,000. The society thus grew most rapidly after the empire had been acquired.[12]

The Royal Colonial Institute was strictly an Establishment body centered mainly in London and the home counties. There were branches in various parts of Great Britain and the empire, but Birmingham was the only great commercial provincial city with African interests where the society was represented; no branch was formed in Liverpool, Manchester, or Sheffield. Its members were overwhelmingly Anglo-Saxon, though a few Indians, West Indians, and creoles were admitted to its ranks. Membership itself was evidence of the highest respectability. In 1892 some 10 percent of the resident fellows were members of such distinguished London clubs as the Carlton, Oriental, Athenaeum, United Service, and Conservative. Nearly a third of the governing board belonged to the peerage or to royalty, and another third were knights. It attracted colonial civil servants, professional soldiers, scientists, and literary men—including Tennyson, the poet laureate, and imperialist-minded historians like J. A. Froude and J. R. Seeley. Its leadership comprised men of all parties, even though Conservatives came to dominate its ranks. Its council took good care to expel the few deviants who disgraced the institute's name. One of its fellows was called on to resign after "unseemly behavior" at a banquet; another—

from the Cape Colony—was struck off the roll on being sentenced to hard labor for embezzlement. The ordinary member, however, was unlikely to appear in a police court.

In typically British fashion, the society maintained a residential club to provide a convenient meeting ground for members on leave or on a visit to Great Britain. It supported the creation of bodies like the Imperial Institute, set up in 1887 to promote research and disseminate information concerning the empire. During the Boer War it raised a small force, a group of Scouts known as Loch's Horse. And just before the outbreak of World War I it set up a masonic lodge for "the purpose of enhancing ties of empire." [13]

The imperial cause also was supported by a variety of learned societies, one of the most influential being the Geographical Society, which originated in 1827—characteristically, as a London club, the Travellers'. Subsequently it absorbed the African Association, an organization dating from the end of the eighteenth century and formed to promote the exploration of Africa. In 1859 the society was incorporated under the sought-after title "Royal," and the letters FRGS (Fellow of the Royal Geographical Society) became for a time a mark of social and professional distinction among geographers. It published the *Geographical Journal*. It promoted expeditions on the part of great explorers like Livingstone, Sir Richard Burton, J. H. Speke, J. A. Grant, and Joseph Thomson, whose rivalries—academic and personal—enlivened the society's proceedings. Like the Royal Colonial Institute, it attracted a great number of distinguished men; its officeholders were drawn from leading men interested in the empire, and Goldie was elected president in 1893. It also served as a forum for political struggles; Frederick (later Lord) Lugard, for example, used the society as a battleground to attack Goldie and the entire principle of chartered government.

Colonial issues were aired in a variety of other learned bodies, all of which were essentially in tune with an age that believed without question in the superiority of Western civilization over primitive cultures. The Royal Anthropological Institute of Great Britain and Ireland, founded in 1843, published a number of journals, particularly its own annual *Proceedings* and a quarterly entitled *Man*; these remain important source books, not merely for the development of African studies, but also for the scholarly concerns and prejudices of British academics. Another such association was the Royal African Society, founded in 1901, which published *African Affairs*, a journal widely found on the tea tables of intellectually active colonial officials.

Late-Victorian imperialism also was supported by intellectuals like J. R. Seeley, professor of modern history at Cambridge from 1869 to his death in 1895. Seeley and his successors stood for a more pessimistic interpretation of world history than Livingstone, who represented the religious faith and secular confidence of the mid-Victorian era, when Great Britain had stood supreme as the greatest industrial and free-trading power in the world.

The new imperial historiographers looked beyond Great Britain—and indeed beyond Europe—to Russia and the United States. They believed that the United States, the product of steam and technological innovation, would turn into the giant power of the future, and that America's power would be matched by Russia's. Once Russia had improved its communications, perfected its technology, and consolidated its regime, its power would loom like a specter over Europe. France and Germany, the two powers of the old Europe, would sink to second-rate status. The two super powers would come to overshadow the other great powers as completely as Macedonia had overshadowed the Athenian *polis* of antiquity, or as Spain and France had towered over Florence during the Renaissance. Great Britain would have to decide whether it would drop to the level of a European state or would weld its empire into a third global power linked by kinship, culture, and self-interest to the United States in a great Anglo-Saxon partnership. Only a great consolidated and developed empire, it was felt, would ensure Great Britain's survival as a world power, a doctrine born of apprehension for the future, and one that continued to animate imperial statesmen like Sir Godfrey Huggins in the twentieth century.

The imperial mystique was widely linked with a fervent faith in the notion that the white-settlement colonies were destined to join in a transmaritime fraternity of equals. These notions helped to inspire a group of young Oxford men, mostly drawn from New College, who gathered round Lord Milner in order to rebuild South Africa after the Boer War. Milner's "Kindergarten" later solidified into the Round Table movement, formed in London in 1909 for the purpose of reconciling self-government in these dominions-to-be with closer imperial union. The Round Table was supported by an impressive group of intellectuals, including Ramsay Muir, Reginald Coupland, and above all, Lionel Curtis. Their views were disseminated in a journal known as *Round Table*; they were discussed by groups set up in Great Britain and the dominions. Financial support came from South African magnates such as Sir Abe Bailey, and from Lord Salisbury, Lord Selborne, and the Rhodes Trust. The Round Table group failed to understand either the force or the divisiveness of dominion nationalism; within the context of Africa, they never understood the Afrikaners, much less the Africans. They did try to come to terms, however, with the growing desire for self-government in India and reached a considerable degree of unanimity regarding imperial autonomy long before anything of the kind was accepted by most of their contemporaries.

Opponents of imperialism during the late-Victorian and Edwardian eras were incomparably weaker than the champions. Yet the influence of critics was far from negligible. Opposition to imperial expansion was perhaps most widespread in what ethnocentric Englishmen were pleased to describe as the "Celtic Fringe"—Ireland, Scotland, and Wales. Militant socialists and militant pacifists would have nothing to do with overseas conquest, though many Fabian reformers approved of colonial rule as a means of bringing efficiency to primitive cultures. The Treasury, with its rigid financial integrity and its ingrained belief in economy, commonly attempted to block new commitments. So did radical-minded MPs like Henry Labouchere.

This was an unusual man. His grandfather had married into the Baring banking family, hence "Labby" was never short of cash to indulge his love of the turf. After Eton and Cambridge, he served in various legations from Washington to Constantinople, and in 1880 won Northampton for the Radicals. He became a successful journalist, edited a paper of his own entitled *Truth*, and was known in the House of Commons as "the Truthful Member for Northampton." Labouchere's version of the truth often diverged from facts, but was always presented with intense passion. He believed that "Africa belonged to the Africans"; he considered the directors of the great chartered companies "moneyed adventurers" who filled their own pockets under the guise of the common weal. According to Labouchere, the British South Africa Company had as little right to establish its rule in Mashonaland "as an African chief would have to turn the Mayor and aldermen or Town Council out of the Townhall of Birmingham and shoot down any alderman or Town Councillors who resented these high-handed proceedings."[14] His ally in the fight against the chartered companies was the *Star*, a Radical evening paper founded in 1888, which rejected the Social Darwinism that some thinkers were fond of applying to imperial problems, and the belief that might made right in the development of new countries.

In the higher reaches of British politics, the humanitarian and noninterventionist standpoint was represented most effectively by Gladstone, who was both a classical scholar and a deeply religious man with a profound interest in the Greek Orthodox Church and the cultures of southeastern Europe. Gladstone—with his Liberal supporters—increasingly came to identify himself with peoples whom he regarded as downtrodden Christian peasantries. He supported the Irish rural masses against their Protestant landlords; he backed the Bulgarians against their Ottoman suzerains. He looked to home rule for Ireland and to independence for the Balkan nations. He withdrew from the Transvaal, and condemned what he regarded as unnecessary displays of military prowess in the borderlands of India. But even Gladstone never dreamt of dismantling the empire. He was capable of taking a strong line against Russia over a border issue in Afghanistan; he refused to hand Cyprus to Greece; he authorized the occupation of Egypt.

Indeed, the success of imperial policy itself created new imperial lobbies and popularized a variety of imperial creeds. By the late 1890's the Liberal Party, once the stronghold of those who believed in keeping down taxes and avoiding imperial entanglements, had become almost as imperialistic as the Conservatives. An imperial faith had become supreme at the court, at the great universities, in the Public Schools, in the armed services, in the Established Church, in the City of London and the chambers of commerce of the major provincial towns. Imperialism joined with Social Darwinism, with the creed of those who believed in the rights of "superior" over "inferior" peoples, in the victory of "healthy" over "dying" nations, black or white. Imperialism also appealed to a great number of idealists, mainly middle-class people, who considered colonialism as a means of doing good, as an engine for improving the natives of the African bush as well as the denizens of the British slums. Imperialism was, among other things, then, a form of social reformism. As such, it made an especially potent appeal to the British administrative establishment. The creed of a minority gradually gained popularity, and by the 1890's colonialism acquired a wider—though by no means a universal—appeal in Great Britain.

Critics of imperialism, however, received impetus from the Boer War. In its aftermath colonialism and finance capital came under bitter attack from both traditionally pacific Radicals and Catholic critics of society like Hilaire Belloc. These sentiments sometimes blended with anti-Jewish outbursts against the "hooknosed financiers" who supposedly had pushed Great Britain into an inglorious war. The financial interpretation of imperialism was elaborated by the journalist J. A. Hobson, who was convinced that European capitalism suffered from a permanent crisis of domestic underconsumption. In his view capitalists merely created empires to earn higher profits on their overseas investments—a view later taken over by Lenin, who admired Hobson as a great bourgeois historian.

But neither Hobson nor Labouchere, neither the bulk of Fabian intellectuals nor the mass of Labour Party voters, condemned empire out of hand. They criticized the way in which Great Britain ruled its colonies, but not the fact that it ruled them. India and Egypt, the critics had it, should be slowly guided toward self-government. But the peoples of sub-Saharan Africa were still in their minority and had a long way yet to go under the tutelage of their British guardians. That tutelage must be benevolent—but it must continue. Even the Radicals were pragmatic. As Bernard Porter puts it, men like Hobson and Morel indeed managed to imperialize the Radical critique of empire.[15]

British Territorial and Economic Lobbies

Economic interests concerned with Africa clustered in certain areas of the United Kingdom, each with its own peculiar characteristics. The older form of imperialism that hinged on mercantile and missionary expansion derived particularly strong support from the north and northwest of England, and from Scotland, where shipping and shipbuilding firms—especially those connected with Glasgow—had a material interest in expanding African commerce. Scottish missionaries played a major part in shaping a new imperial philosophy. Moreover, Scotland was a major source of educated workers willing to migrate to Africa. Unlike the British system, the nineteenth-century state school system in Scotland involved the mass of the people. Young Scots not only learned how to read and to reckon, but acquired a widespread respect for intellectual ability. Every institution of society, churches and universities alike, emphasized the virtues of hard work, a creed exceedingly useful to a nation many of whose sons had to emigrate in order to make a living.

The greatest representative of Scottish missionary imperialism was David Livingstone, whose life might be called one of the great success stories of Victorian England. Born into a working-class family in 1813, he started life as a laborer in a cotton factory, won promotions by dogged hard work, and then became a medical missionary to South Africa. The dramatic character of his career was heightened in public appeal by his heroic death in the wilds of Central Africa and a ceremonial interment in Westminster Abbey. Livingstone was a great traveler, a man of science, a pioneer in tropical medicine, and a Protestant hero. To working-class people he was one of themselves, a factory worker who had made good; to wealthy industrialists he was a man who preached social peace at home and commercial expansion abroad; to believers of all classes he spoke for the spread of the Gospel; to men of science he was remarkable as an accurate observer, a man of the cloth who looked at African societies more with the detachment of a clinical diagnostician than with the zeal of a bigoted Hot Gospeller.

Livingstone, moreover, was remarkable as a theorist of African development. In his eyes the African was not a depraved savage but a rational man, capable of responding to the demands of the market. He felt that the slave trade, the curse of Africa, could never be stopped by sermons or even by gunboats. In order to break the stranglehold of slave traders over wide regions of Central Africa, the Christian powers must develop the legitimate commerce and indigenous resources of the continent, applying steam power to African land and river transport and helping the Africans to develop new trade goods. By doing so they would help not only the Africans but themselves, supplying European industries with both new sources of raw materials like cotton and new markets. The growth of wealth would make for progress, and social amelioration would allow the Gospel to spread. Africans, however, required outside assistance to create the new world of Livingstone's imagination. He therefore called God's blessing on any European power that would shoulder the task of extirpating the traffic in slaves and create a new economy. Christianity and commerce, he wrote, based on free trade and an Afro-European partnership, would uplift Africa.

No pioneer of Africa ever struck the public imagination more than David Livingstone. His books ran into countless editions and were translated into every European tongue. In an age in which publishers put out more works on theology and related subjects than on any other theme, his writings formed part of a great body of literature that was acceptable Sabbath reading in Evangelical and Nonconformist families who would never have defiled the day of rest with secular reading. New missionary societies were formed to commemorate his death in 1873, and scores of young men from Cambridge and Oxford joined to carry out Livingstone's dream.

Some of Livingstone's disciples became missionaries, but others turned to trade, and there was always a close connection between the two. In 1878, for example, Glasgow shipbuilders and merchants established the African Lakes Company, a commercial body designed to supply the Scottish missions in what is now Malawi and to introduce "legitimate trade" into the African interior. Perhaps the most prominent promoter of what might be called the Presbyterian school of imperialism was William (later Sir William) Mackinnon, who was born in the village of Campbeltown on the Kintyre peninsula in Argyllshire in 1823. His formal education was limited to elementary school, which he left to become a grocery clerk. No shadow of impropriety or scandal ever touched him. He acted in accordance with God's injunctions as revealed by the Bible, and believed that he had earned the Almighty's favor. God's special regard seemed to advance Mackinnon's earthly fortune; he became a great shipping magnate with extensive East African interests and in the late 1880's founded a chartered company—the Imperial British East African Company—which governed that area until 1895.

In England itself the most important pillar of empire was Lancashire. It was the country's greatest producer of cotton goods, just as the West Riding of Yorkshire was its main manufacturer of woolens, and both regions shipped the bulk of their exports through Liverpool. That port had been a slave-trading center in the 1700's, but in the nineteenth century the city switched wholly to "legitimate trade." It also built ships and processed tropical crops like tobacco and vegetable oil. Liverpool's university was one of the new centers of civic learning, with departments distinguished in subjects connected with tropical research such as parasitology and entomology, as well as a world-famous school of tropical medicine, founded in 1898.

Liverpool was likewise closely linked to Manchester, the world's most important center of the cotton industry. In the 1800's most of the spinning, weaving, dyeing, and bleaching moved increasingly to the city's economic hinterland, and Manchester devoted itself to warehousing, buying, selling, and banking. By tradition it was famed for a sturdy civic culture maintained by cotton lords whose stately villas in Chorlton-upon-Medlock have now lost their former splendor and house a more transient population. The city was wedded to free trade, Protestant Nonconformity, and a strong commitment to social improvement and missionary work.

The most notable champion of the free-trading merchants was Mary Kingsley—the unhappy daughter of distinguished parents.[16] Her father George was a physician, who loved to travel; at home he browbeat his daughter and taught her no subject but German so that she might help him in his research. As a chronic invalid, her mother could

only add to the girl's wretchedness. Mary's appearance was grim—
thin, flat-chested, sour-faced. The death of both parents left her free,
and in 1895 she sailed to Africa to study fish. As she was to write later,
"Dead tired and feeling no one had need of me any more I went to
West Africa to die."[17]

Mary Kingsley wrote two books on the experiences of her 18 months
on the continent, *Travels in West Africa* (1897) and *West African
Studies* (1899). She braved lions and elephants, snakes and leopards,
hostile tribesmen and dangerous waters. She drove a lion from her tent
and a crocodile from her canoe. And she became an admirer of the
European traders, who were scorned in England as drunken, evil
"palm oil ruffians." She understood their loneliness and drunkenness,
and respected their knowledge of African customs and ways of life.

No one knows, who has not been to visit Africa, how terrible is the life of a
white man in one of these out-of-the-way factories, with no white society, and
with nothing to look at, day out and day in, but the one set of objects—the
forest, the river, and the beach, which in a place like Osoamokita you cannot
leave for months at a time, and of which you soon know every plank and
stone.[18]

In England she became a fierce polemicist, known as "Liverpool's
hired assassin" to some of her critics. She censured all that was dear to
conventional Victorian family men—missionaries, temperance leagues,
and the Aborigines Protection Society. She defended the Liverpool,
London, and Manchester merchants and the liquor trade on the
reasonable grounds that Africans were not easily debauched by liquor
like American Indians or Maoris. She denied that there was much
drunkenness in Africa—indeed one saw much less indulgence among
Africans than could be seen "any Saturday you choose in a couple of
hours on the Vauxhall Road."[19] Africans preferred to drink their own
brew, not the imported product. She pointed out that liquor was used
mostly as currency and for ritual occasions.

Liquor in fact was an essential article of trade, at least in the early
days of empire, when its duties had provided the bulk of the revenue
raised by the West African colonies.* Yet even though British expansion in West Africa had owed much to pressure from mercantile inter-

---

*In 1894 the Gold Coast and Lagos derived 60 percent of their revenue from the
liquor traffic, and the Niger Protectorate about 80 percent; in French West Africa the
average was about 70 percent. The amount imported was not that great; it was estimated
to be under a gallon annually per person—less than the amount consumed in the United
Kingdom. See Great Britain, *Papers Relative to the Liquor Trade in West Africa*, Parliamentary Command Papers, C. 8480 (1897), p. 16.

ests anxious to safeguard their commerce against French penetration and French protectionism, the Colonial Office attempted to restrict or prevent the import of spirits from the 1890's onward, drawing criticism from the traders, as well as from Mary Kingsley. Neither she nor the old-time traders liked the "new colonialism" advocated by Joseph Chamberlain, the colonial secretary who was determined to develop the imperial estates. The new approach seemed to imply higher taxes, more government regulations, and a free hand for military men eager to win battles and medals at the traders' expense. As John Flint points out, Chamberlain's policy spelled the end of the traders' dream of a great West African chartered company.

Mary Kingsley looked back to the days when colonial government was small, with little control, few regulations, and low taxes—when the traders did what they wanted. She opposed social change, railroads, and harbors; she hated the new dynamism of Chamberlain and his officials. Of Lord Lugard she said that she hoped he would "drown . . . in his own ink-pot." Colonial rule was supposed to be expensive and wasteful, so her solution was simply: remove all colonial officials and missionaries, and leave everything to the traders. They would rule through a grand council of representatives nominated by the chambers of commerce of Liverpool, Manchester, London, Bristol, and Glasgow. Africans would be governed indirectly through their chiefs. There would be few officers and no taxes.[20] But by the turn of the century her ideas were becoming out of date. She went to South Africa to nurse during the Boer War and died there in 1900 of an infection.

Commercial interests were turning to Africa for reasons that did not concern just selling gin to blacks. Lancashire had become economically vulnerable to interrupted supplies of cotton. Civil war in the United States had brought about the so-called cotton famine by shutting off access to American-grown supplies, and the ravages of the boll weevil in American cotton fields during the 1890's threatened still another economic disaster. Lancashire businessmen thus were increasingly attracted by a more active policy of imperial development, and more among them were converted to Chamberlain's cause. For the express purpose of stimulating the improvement, cultivation, and export of African cotton, the British Cotton Growing Association was founded in 1902. Its president was Sir Alfred Jones, a great West African shipping magnate. He was born a Welshman, but in his multifarious positions as senior partner in the Elder, Dempster shipping line, chairman of the Bank of British West Africa, president of the Liverpool Chamber of Commerce, member of the 1904 Tariff Commission, and founder of the Liverpool School of Tropical Medicine, he personified what might be called a Lancashire school of empire.

The steel magnates of Birmingham were no less devoted than the textile manufacturers to the cause of empire. Birmingham was an unusual city. It had played a vigorous part in the battle for parliamentary reform and for technological advancement. In some ways it had an almost American character, with its insistence on civic improvements —parks, libraries, hospitals—its spirit of self help, its machine politics, and its supposedly plebeian vigor. Birmingham worked metal in all its forms—screws, machine tools, rifles, railway carriages, fencing, cages, and bathtubs.

The greatest representative of the city's industries and politics was Joseph Chamberlain, manufacturer, mayor, and later the most influential of British colonial secretaries, whose political career will be detailed in a later section. Suffice it to say at this point that Chamberlain was an outsider in some ways: a Unitarian and not a member of the Established Church, a manufacturer unconnected with landed wealth, a product of London University rather than Oxford. Unlike the majority of leading British politicians, Chamberlain became a convinced proponent of protection in the form of preferential tariffs for empire-made goods, a policy that split his party. He also vigorously supported a forward policy against the Boers in South Africa and helped to steer Britain into the second Anglo–South African war, thereby incurring bitter hostility from "Little Englanders" like Lloyd George, who opposed the war and who believed that the stake of the Chamberlain clan in the armaments industry influenced their political stance. Or, as *Punch* put it, "The more the Empire expands, the more the Chamberlains contract."

Lloyd George, who apparently had employed two full-time investigators to ferret out details concerning the Chamberlain fortunes, never proved the point he wished to insinuate. Joseph Chamberlain did not benefit from illegitimate government contracts. Much less was his warlike policy inspired by a desire to profit from arms deals. But Lloyd George's attack on Chamberlain in the House of Commons did show the manner in which the family's fortunes were linked to weaponry. The Chamberlains, for instance, had holdings in Hoskins and Sons, a Birmingham firm that acted as contractors for the Admiralty. The family also held an interest in the Birmingham Trust, which in turn had holdings in other manufacturing companies under contract to the Admiralty, including Eliot's Metal Company, which produced boilers for the navy and furnished supplies for naval dockyards. On top of this, the Chamberlains were connected with Kynoch and Company, a manufacturer of cordite and explosives, and with the Birmingham Small Arms Company.[21] Birmingham had become an arsenal of empire.

Gentlemen and Chartered Companies

Chamberlain's involvement in industry caused little popular and less parliamentary indignation. He belonged to a political world in which the center of political gravity was shifting from landed to manufacturing interests. According to Elie Halévy's analysis, 250 of the some 670 members of Parliament in 1895 were businessmen—manufacturers, merchants, mine owners, brewers, and bankers. Many of the remaining MP's—barristers, military officers, or country gentlemen of leisure —were tied to business by similar bonds. The gentry had been widely forced to make up for the fall in food prices by acquiring shares in limited liability companies, and MPs frequently found places on the boards of such firms.[22] By itself, the landed gentry was no longer a great political force outside of the local affairs in more remote rural counties.

The colonial "outcrop" of the landed gentry played but a limited part in colonial politics. Once the African empire had come into existence, some noblemen—including the Duke of Westminster, Lord Winterton, and Lord Wolverton—invested in Northern Rhodesian or Kenyan estates, gambling on a future rise in land values. Kenya actually attracted a few aristocratic immigrants, men such as Hugh Cholmondeley (later Lord Delamere), heir to a minor estate in England and one of Kenya's greatest pioneers. These gentlemen, entitled to a seat in the House of Lords and connected to the best families in Great Britain, achieved importance in limited areas like the White Highlands of Kenya. The Association of Northern Rhodesian Farmers Resident in England was formed by estate owners, turning a handful of Northern Rhodesian whites into one of the best-represented communities in the empire. But aristocrats were a minor element of the population in the largest British settler communities, those centering on Southern Rhodesia and South Africa. The African empire remained essentially a middle-class affair.

Aristocrats did not initiate the great chartered companies that acted as pacemakers of British rule, though they joined the boards of these enterprises, lending their social connections and an air of respectability, if not distinction. The actual empire builders, like Rhodes, a parson's son, and Goldie, a member of the Manx squirearchy who had chosen a middle-class corps—the Royal Engineers—over a more socially distinguished regiment, had no great social pretensions.

Chartered companies varied considerably in political power and financial backing. But they did have certain features in common. They had links to London, the world's greatest financial center. They represented imperialism on the limited liability principle. Private shareholders would take the risks of empire building without involving the British taxpayer; private shareholders would garner the profits, if any. The pioneers of chartered enterprise did not think primarily of making money. They aimed at enlarging the empire; they dreamed of painting the map red. Chartered enterprise, of course, brought economic and social advantages for insiders—directors' fees, invitations to great country houses, membership in select clubs, consultations with the colonial secretary and even the prime minister, confidential information of a kind that might prove useful on the stock exchange. But men like Rhodes and Goldie were not in the chartered business only for the cash it might bring, and most of their shareholders failed to make money. In the promoters' eyes chartered enterprise was, above all, a form of public service. These companies could take risks that government was unwilling to shoulder. Without costing the taxpayer anything and before imperialism had become a popular cause, the chartered company could reserve large areas of Africa for British influence and trade.

A broad division shows two categories of chartered companies: those linked to shipping and commerce, and those connected with mining and railway investment. The most important of the companies in the first category was the Royal Niger Company, an export-import firm that capitalized on the introduction of steamships in the West African trade. The use of steam had been pioneered by the African Steamship Company, a shipping firm founded by a group of British shipowners in 1852. Competition between the company and its rivals lowered freight rates considerably, until the lines were virtually amalgamated in 1890 under control of Elder, Dempster and Company. Transport between England and West Africa was cheapened and regularized, so that merchants now could deal profitably in bulky goods like palm oil, cocoa, and copra. Meanwhile, British shipbuilders had learned how to construct small stern-wheeled steamboats suitable for going up the Niger, largely creating the Niger trade and helping to open the Nigerian hinterland to white businessmen.

The steamship also changed the machinery and organization of trade. On the one hand, steam navigation gave rise to great shipping companies that confined themselves to carrying other people's cargoes. On the other, numerous small traders availed themselves of this opening; as competition increased, the profits of many individual dealers sharply declined. Their predicament worsened as a result of a general trade depression, and the British merchants became increasingly disposed to look to their home government for protection against both the encroachment of European foreigners and the exactions of African middlemen, whose tolls and internecine conflict combined to raise the prices of export crops.

The story has been expertly told of the commercial amalgamation that united Liverpool, Glasgow, and Bristol firms in a larger body. There is also excellent literature on the origins and development of the Royal Niger Company.[23] Suffice it to say that the company was formed in 1879 (taking the name the United African Company, which was changed in 1882 to the National African Company) after the price of palm oil, palm kernels, and shea butter had dropped to almost one-half in Europe. Under the stress of its losses, the company insisted on obtaining a royal charter (1886).

The company's founder, Sir George Taubman Goldie, was not a trader of the conventional kind. A son of the gentry, an ex-officer of the Royal Engineers, a member of the Naval and Military Club and of the Royal Yacht Squadron, and a religious skeptic to boot, his tastes and social connections were very different from those of the ordinary West African merchant. He looked on the company as an instrument for countering French encroachment and extending the bounds of Britain's empire. Government, however, proved to be an expensive business.* The company then tried to meet the costs of imperial rule by imposing a de facto trade monopoly of the kind repugnant to the Lancashire tradition and specifically forbidden by its charter. These practices aroused bitter opposition among British traders who had not been admitted to the inner circle; the company failed to garner the golden riches anticipated by its shareholders, and in 1900 its charter was withdrawn and a British protectorate established.

---

*The company's administrative organization was, in fact, slender. It was run by a council in London and directed operations in Nigeria through an agent general, three provincial and 12 district superintendents. The company maintained a small military police force, consisting of 424 Hausa and Yoruba; it owned a small and lightly armed river fleet and a battery. Real power rested with Goldie.

In East Africa, as we have seen, the leading exponent of chartered enterprise and railway investment was William Mackinnon, who combined his evangelical fervor and British patriotism with a bitter hatred of Germany. His chosen instrument was the Imperial British East African Company, like the Royal Niger Company, a trading firm. It received its royal charter in 1889. As John S. Galbraith, Mackinnon's biographer, has noted, the subscribers represented the upper reaches of Anglo-Scottish society. Business interests, philanthropy, independent wealth, and distinguished public service were blended into a governing board with East African and Indian interests; it could command respect from any government, Liberal or Tory. Four board members were themselves MPs. The former grocer's clerk had risen in society and become a power in the land.[24]

The Imperial British East African Company, however, proved an economic failure and surrendered its charter in 1895. East Africa lacked an easily accessible source of wealth, and the enterprise had begun with an inadequate economic base. The company could not compete in trade with Indian merchants from the coast; the income from custom revenue was inadequate to support even a rudimentary form of Western government; agricultural development was impossible without railway construction that the company, with its limited resources, could not afford.

An economic constellation of a very different kind was represented by the British South Africa Company. It was the most powerful and the longest-lived of modern British chartered enterprises and deserves more attention than the others. Cecil Rhodes, its founder, was a remarkable man.[25] A vicar's son turned company promoter, a dreamer, schemer, and pioneer, he mingled the values of the parsonage, the City, and the frontier. According to his own entry for *Who's Who*,

he kept the drag at Oxford; rode daily for two hours at 6 A.M.; read chiefly the classics, of which he had a fine collection, with a separate library of typewritten translations executed specially for him; Froude and Carlyle he admired universally; favourite reading, biography and history; knew Gibbon almost by heart; favourite work of fiction, *Vanity Fair*, which he admired more than any single work in literature; collected old furniture, china and curios generally, with a preference for anything Dutch; had a Sir Joshua Reynolds; fond of nearly all old fashions; fond of old things, particularly old oak chests; went in greatly for gardening, especially rose culture; good pyramid player; a fair shot; had a menagerie on Table Mountain; visited his lions there every day when he could; his zebras, ostriches, and buck of all kind were not caged, but ran wild in enclosed tracts of the mountain side.[26]

Rhodes's economic power was extensive. He arrived in South Africa in search of his fortune, first trying cotton farming, then going to the diamond digs at Kimberley. He gradually established control over the South African diamond industry, and later acquired an important stake in the gold mines of the Witwatersrand, which were themselves financed to a considerable extent from diamond profits. Rhodes represented the expansionist-minded segment of the South African mining industry. He looked to the "Far North," that is to say, the lands beyond the Limpopo River, for additional mineral wealth and for as yet untapped labor resources. In his eyes territorial expansion was needed also to preempt the claims of European competitors in the interior. Colonization in the Far North would unite Boer and Briton in a joint task. It would afford new opportunities of settlement for white farmers from South Africa. The Cape Colony, of which Rhodes became prime minister in 1890, would become the main gateway into the interior and establish its supremacy over the Transvaal. British immigration inland would make the British element supreme in South Africa. Expansion north of the Limpopo would finally form the stepping-stone of a new empire that would stretch from the Cape to Cairo, rivaling the British Raj in India.

Rhodes meant to link the new African empire by means of a transcontinental railway on the American model. The new railway imperialism, paralleled in France by projects even more visionary, owed little to considerations of immediate gain. Manufacturers of locomotives and steel rails might make money on the spot. But shareholders in the lines themselves could not look forward to substantial dividends for many years to come. The traffic on the new lines at first was small, the distances great, and the financial outlay enormous. The lines were built not so much to serve existing demands as to develop wealth in the more distant future and, above all, to serve as the framework of empire. Such speculations frightened Lord Salisbury, who thought that Rhodes was quite mad.

Salisbury was only one of Rhodes's many opponents before the company got its charter.[27] Imperialists like Chamberlain remembered Rhodes's opposition to the "imperial factor" and felt he was an Afrikaner. Exeter Hall and the Aborigines Protection Society mistrusted his motives and felt that African interests could only be protected by London. An old enemy from Bechuanaland, the Reverend John Mackenzie, whipped up missionary and humanitarian opposition. The government itself had to be won over. The Treasury and the Foreign Office feared Rhodes's adventures would cost Britain money or would alienate foreign nations. His application for a charter in 1889 provoked a barrage of questions in Parliament, and the sale of arms to the Ndebele was attacked.

To follow Rhodes through the negotiations surrounding the charter is to realize his mastery of intrigue and his skill at compromise, and to perceive how opinion had divided on the question of overseas expansion. Rhodes seemed to wear a thousand masks. With businessmen he became practical: he won the support of Lord Gifford by buying out his Exploring Company. To the missionaries he stressed the advantages of white rule and opening the country to Christianity—he promised that no liquor would be sold to Africans. To the editor W. T. Stead he appeared as a great imperialist, aflame with desire to spread the benefits of Anglo-Saxon civilization to the backward Africans. Stead's *Pall Mall Gazette* helped convince the British public that Rhodes "was the savior of the British Empire."[28] Through Stead, Rhodes made friends with Moberly Bell, the managing editor of *The Times*, and the Reverend John Verschoyle, an editor of the *Fortnightly Review*; thereafter he received favorable publicity from these men. An article in the *Fortnightly Review* (1889) by his friend Sir Charles Metcalfe, of the Bechuanaland Railway Syndicate, stressed the danger of the German advance in Africa while holding out the dream of British expansion from the Cape to Cairo. For his help Metcalfe received Rhodes's promise to build a railway through Bechuanaland.

Opposition in Parliament was largely stilled or neutralized. Sir John Swinburne, who first attacked Rhodes's company, was pacified when Rhodes bought out his business associate Lord Gifford. The gift of £10,000 to the Irish nationalist Charles Stewart Parnell won over the Irish vote and counterbalanced the missionary-humanitarian strength in Parliament.

Initially Rhodes worked through the warlike Ndebele people; in return for cash, guns, and the promise of a gunboat he secured an extensive mining concession in what later became Southern Rhodesia. His proceedings at first roused bitter criticism at home. The colonial secretary, Sir Henry Holland (later Lord Knutsford), suggested that the gunboat was "for protection against foreign aggression." Under pressure, the government expressed disapproval of the gift of guns and ammunition to King Lobengula, but the secretary later accepted the view that the rifle was more humane than an assegai.*

Rhodes's group, joined by Lord Gifford's Exploring Company, ap-

---

*The opposition was silenced also by being told that the rifles the Ndebele were getting were no good.

plied for a charter on 30 April 1889. It was understood that important Britons serving on the board of directors would speed up its grant. Rhodes thus requested the Duke of Abercorn—son-in-law of the Prince of Wales—the Duke of Fife, and Earl Grey, a landed magnate, to become directors. Lord Knutsford now could assure the queen of the company's integrity. The government was won over by pressure from Rhodes's new friends, and by the force of the argument by Hercules Robinson, the high commissioner of South Africa, and Lord Knutsford that granting the charter would "relieve Her Majesty's government from diplomatic difficulties and heavy expenditures."[29] The charter was granted 29 October 1889. Rhodes's South African Company became the British South African Company and was linked with British capitalist interests.

Known simply as the Charter, the British South Africa Company was by far the most successful of all chartered companies. Unlike the Royal Niger Company or the African Lakes Company, it did not look to trade for its income, but to investments in mining, farming, and railway enterprises. It had a much broader financial base than the other chartered companies; its economic management was vastly superior to that of the imperial government. Yet during the whole of the period in which it was in charge of governing the two Rhodesias, the company failed to pay any dividends to its stockholders. Its days of prosperity began only after it had rid itself of its administrative duties (1923–24).*

The "New Imperialism," to sum up, drew its main support from the upper-middle classes and the middle classes, and only slightly from the aristocracy and the petty bourgeoisie. It derived added backing from local colonial societies, such as the settler communities at the Cape and in Australia. It represented a great variety of strands—commercial, financial, missionary, military, and humanitarian. It was by no means uniform in nature, but contained disparate and conflicting elements. The imperial movement was facilitated by the growing gap between the resources—technological, scientific, and military—of the industrialized Western states and the indigenous societies of tropical Africa.

---

*The British South Africa Company garnered a handsome compensation from the Southern Rhodesian taxpayers for its land and mineral rights, and it profited from a variety of mining and railway ventures. Even so, the Charter was only a minor power within the framework of British capitalism. By 1928 its authorized share capital stood at £6,500,000, against an issued share capital of £42,800,000 for the Imperial Tobacco Company and an authorized share capital of £65,000,000 for Imperial Chemical Industries.

The "New Imperialism" contained a strong sense of social idealism. The "savage" in the bush was to be uplifted and improved in the same manner as the lower classes in the slum. Missionary and imperial endeavor represented in many ways an "overspill" from domestic reformism. The "New Imperialism" was also born of fear, fear of an uncertain future when great continental powers might reduce Great Britain to insignificance, unless the island kingdom extended its power while there was still time.

TWO

The Colonial Office

Of all the world's modern empires, the British was the most diverse and the most decentralized. It comprised a great variety of polities; it lacked a single administrative center. Protectorates like British East Africa (later Kenya) and British Central Africa (later Nyasaland) at first fell under the jurisdiction of the Foreign Office before being transferred to Colonial Office control. The War Office appointed military governors for possessions like Malta, Bermuda, and Gibraltar. Sarawak, though a British protectorate, was governed by a white rajah. Egypt, a key dependency, was legally not part of the British Empire at all; British power was exercised through the British consul-general, backed by a handful of officials and an army of occupation. The Indian subcontinent, subject to the British queen-empress, was administered through the Indian civil service, a brilliant group of officials selected through one of the most demanding examination systems in the world; the Indian empire was supervised by the India Office, its representative in London. The Sudan, nominally co-administered with Egypt but de facto a British dependency, was governed by a separate service under the Foreign Office.

The "self-governing colonies," later known as dominions, enjoyed full autonomy and were represented in London by their own agents-general, who to all intents and purposes had ambassadorial standing. Northern and Southern Rhodesia were administered by a commercial concern, the British South Africa Company, loosely supervised by the Colonial Office. Finally, there was the colonial empire properly speaking, a diverse group of colonies run by the Colonial Office, scattered geographically, varied in economic potential and social structure. There was then no system. As a minister of the Crown reminded a colonial conference in 1927:

Strictly speaking, there is, of course, no Colonial Empire, and no such thing
as a Colonial Service. . . . I deal in this office with some thirty-six different
Governments, each entirely separate from the rest, each administratively,
financially, legislatively self-contained. Each, whether it deals with nearly
20 million people over an area as large as Central Europe, or with 20,000
people on a scattered handful of islands, has its own Administrative Service,
its own Medical Service, its own Agricultural, Public Works, and other technical Services, its own scale of pay, its own pensions.[1]

Each one of these colonies, the speaker might have added, had its
own sense of territorial identity; the British rulers who communicated
with one another sometimes addressed their opposite numbers in
other dependencies in the style of contending powers. For instance,
the dispatches exchanged between the government of India and the
authorities in charge of Southern Rhodesia with regard to the Indian
labor questions on occasion were marked by an almost contemporary
kind of hostility.

There was no single colonial service. The Indian civil service was an
independent body recruited by competitive examinations. The Foreign Office recruited its own officers for the areas under its sway; it
also oversaw the Sudan political service. Within sub-Saharan Africa
there were separate services for the chartered companies; even within
the British South Africa Company's territories there were at first three
separate administrative units, one each for Southern Rhodesia, Northeastern Rhodesia, and Northwestern Rhodesia. The territories run by
the Colonial Office through all our period had their own separate
services (only in 1932 did a unified colonial administrative service
come into existence). The administration of the Colonial Office was
likewise organized on separate lines. Members belonged to the home
civil service, and their conditions of employment, as well as their general outlook on government, often differed widely from those of the
men on the spot.

This dispersal of administrative power was reflected even in the
physical construction of the offices. In the 1850's Sir Gilbert Scott
designed a great building complex to house these centers of government. He would have preferred monumental Gothic, but Gothic had
come to be identified with Toryism, and when the Whigs returned to
power, Lord Palmerston insisted on an Italianate Renaissance style.
Sir Gilbert shuddered with horror, but complied. In 1875 a new structure went up on the south side of Downing Street within walking
distance of the great clubs and the Houses of Parliament and near the
prime minister's residence. Sir Gilbert's edifice, a hollow block, lacked

originality in design but possessed great dignity. The Colonial Office, adorned with symbolic figures of empire and portrait medallions of former colonial secretaries, was in the northwest corner of the block, the India Office was placed in the southwest, and the Foreign Office— the most exclusive of them all—was located in the northeast.

In those days the Colonial Office was a pleasant place in which to work. It had the air of a stately West End club with great influence and a small membership—solid, high-minded, and devoted. The corridors and rooms were high and narrow, the furniture of dark mahogany upholstered in leather. The building was lit by gas. No clattering of typewriters as yet disturbed the calm; dispatches were copied by clerks in beautiful copperplate handwriting and bound in great volumes. Office administration was a simple matter. The colonial secretary's room had a long, heavy, mahogany sideboard with a brass rack above it that held a number of leather-covered boxes containing secret papers: cabinet papers were in red containers, the others mostly in black; copies of recent communications to and from colonial governments went into green boxes. On top of the boxes lay files tied with red tape (hence the phrase). Some were waiting for consideration by the secretary; others had just come back from his office with his minutes noted in red ink. Only the colonial secretary might use this color. Life was unhurried; manners were dignified. During the 1850's juniors were kept in their place and huddled together in offices that were little better than boxes.

Neither was there any undue familiarity between the various offices charged with Great Britain's imperial destinies. Indeed, physical contact between them was restricted. Between the Foreign Office and the India Office there was a communicating door at the end of a long passage on the first floor. But no one below the rank of under-secretary was allowed to use the key. Each office, moreover, had perfected the art of snubbing an unwelcome visitor in a gentlemanly fashion. Brigadier-General Trevor Ternan, a soldier not unduly troubled by timidity, recalled the reception he got when he had to call on the Indian Office at Lord Salisbury's behest in order to ask for some military reinforcements.

Lord Salisbury's suggestion that a battalion should be sent from India to Uganda was received coldly, and I gathered that we were looked upon as little better than outsiders, almost as conspirators with fell designs upon the safety of the great Indian Empire. His Lordship [Lord Hamilton], when he spoke, conveyed the impression that he considered the officials of the Foreign Office side of the building as hardly more than imbeciles.[2]

During much of the nineteenth century working habits do not appear to have been excessively strict. Sir William Baillie-Hamilton, who entered the Colonial Office in 1864, recalled that in the olden days his supervisor was satisfied if the juniors appeared punctually at twelve noon and did not leave before five-thirty at night. The old gentleman himself was careful not to impair his own constitution by overwork.

It was his daily habit, after luncheon, to ensconce himself in a cunningly designed rocking-chair, and for exactly one hour, to devote himself, ostensibly, to the perusal of old *Quarterly Reviews*, to which it was understood that bygone members of his family had been extensive contributors, and from which he doubtlessly acquired much edification and support.[3]

But working habits improved and, according to Sir Robert Herbert (permanent under-secretary between 1871 and 1892), it had "a high character as being an office in which the work is well done, and the men work well together with a gentlemanly good feeling."[4]

The Men

The ethos of the modern Colonial Office, high-minded and "improving," owed a great deal to Sir James Stephen (under-secretary from 1836 to 1847). Stephen had been a leading member of the Aborigines Protective Society—the only time he ever worked on the Sabbath Day was spent on drawing up the bill for the emancipation of the slaves in 1833. To many white colonists, in places as far apart as Jamaica and New Zealand, Stephen—lampooned variously as "Mr. Mother-Country" or "Mr. Over-Secretary"—represented all that was worst in imperial control, with its peculiar blend of negrophilism and officious interference, snobbery, and mealy-mouthed economy. To his admirers, Stephen was an early representative of imperial trusteeship. But whether the Colonial Office was loved or hated, its real powers were at first rigidly circumscribed. The office increasingly gained in importance after 1854, when the outbreak of the Crimean War led to the appointment of a separate secretary of state for the colonies to relieve the secretary of state for war of colonial business. No further changes were made at the ministerial level until 1925, when the Dominion Office was established. But the growth in importance was not paralleled by a growth in staff. As late as 1872 the Colonial Office still had just 26 first-division clerks; and only a few of these men were senior officials.*

*An 1870 Order in Council established two types of examination: "Regulation I" examinations, which were designed to recruit university graduates for the higher posi-

Sir Robert Herbert himself represented an age of high-minded aristocratic patronage. His father was the younger son of the Earl of Carnarvon, and young Robert spent his childhood at his father's estate at Ickleton, Cambridgeshire, where he was educated by private tutors. The senior Herbert remained rooted in his village. He spent much time at his country home, and filled the usual positions of magistrate and deputy-lieutenant of the County of Cambridgeshire. In 1844 Robert was sent to Eton, where he met Lord Carnarvon, his first cousin and future chief of the Colonial Office, and also got to know many other boys who later rose to head various government departments. From Eton he went to Balliol College, Oxford. Balliol at the time trained numerous future civil servants for service at home; later the college became one of the principal recruiting grounds for the colonial service overseas. In common with many higher civil servants of the late nineteenth century, Herbert began his official career as a private secretary. He first served under Gladstone, and later went to Queensland, where he acquired a thorough understanding of "responsible government" in a settler colony. He was popular in Australia, especially among the powerful landowners of the outback, who appreciated Herbert's interest in agriculture, and his "sound" ideas regarding finance. Later he served under John Bright, the militant free trader, at the Board of Trade, and subsequently transferred to the Colonial Office as assistant under-secretary.

Herbert played an important part in implementing a variety of reforms at the Colonial Office. There was a sharper division of labor. Clerks were assigned more demanding work. In 1872 the Colonial Office, following Foreign Office precedents, authorized under-secretaries to sign dispatches on behalf of the secretary, an innovation that in practice increased the power of senior permanent officials. In addition, like other government departments, the Colonial Office had begun in 1856 to fill clerkships by open competition. "Upper-division" clerks were drawn from the great universities and received substantial salaries, and promotion was entirely on merit. The lowlier class of clerk was expected to carry out routine and simple supervisory tasks, and could not expect promotion to the "first division."

In theory the examination system was a break with the age of patronage; critics complained that examinations would induce "cramming," that the system was nothing but a "schoolmaster's ramp," designed to

---

tions, and "Regulation II" examinations, which were aimed at filling the lowlier posts. Vacancies in the Colonial Office, as in other departments, later came to be filled by a civil service commission.

give more power to the universities, and that it would give an unto-
ward advantage to "swots" over gentlemen. In practice, the examination system did not justify these fears. Examinations continued to
stress Latin and Greek, thereby ensuring that most of the new clerks
continued to come from homes with a solid middle-class or upper-
middle-class background, with fathers who could afford to educate
their sons in a Public School and in one of the great universities.

In general the Colonial Office wanted moral qualities—integrity,
esprit de corps—rather more than intelligence; "the habits and manners of a gentleman" were looked for, not trained men. And it recruited some very capable men. Henry Edward (Cardinal) Manning
served for two years as a clerk; Geoffrey Dawson (editor of *The Times*),
Professors A. B. Keith, H. F. Egerton, and Sir C. P. Lucas (editor
of the *Historical Geography Series on the Empire*), and two secretaries of state (Sir Henry Holland and Sidney Webb) all started their
careers as clerks in the Colonial Office. But the office also had that special British distrust of modern languages; one Colonial Office official
noted "that a good linguist is never a man of high principle."[5]

In social terms the Colonial Office did not occupy as high a position
as the Foreign Office, whose members held about the same status
within the British administration as Guards officers within the army.
Intellectually, the Colonial Office may not have been quite on a par
with the Treasury, the main stronghold of free trade orthodoxy, the
department that supposedly attracted the best brains in the civil service. The Colonial Office did not have quite as many classicists as the
Treasury; a considerable number of its officials had made their way
through grammar schools rather than Public Schools; a substantial
proportion had studied subjects like mathematics, law, or even engineering, subjects not normally familiar in the upper echelons of the
Foreign Office.

Even so, the Colonial Office enjoyed a solid social status, one much
superior to that of, say, the Reichskolonialamt in Germany or the
Ministère des Colonies in Belgium. As Brian Blakeley points out, of
the 11 second-class clerks who entered the office between 1877 and
1889 only one was not a university man; seven came from Oxford, two
from Cambridge, one from Aberdeen University. Most candidates
came from solid families; they were the kind of men who would have
secured commissions in the Royal Artillery or in a first-class infantry
regiment like the Royal Fusiliers had they chosen to serve the queen
in uniform. The industrial and mercantile bourgeoisie, in whose interest the empire was supposedly being expanded, was little repre-

sented. The service instead had a church and professional flavor, with a heavy scent of the parsonage. It consisted of men with a mission in life, men who regarded colonialism as a venture in applied philanthropy—not as an enterprise designed to maximize metropolitan profits. Five of the group analyzed by Blakeley were sons of clergymen; the others came from families headed respectively by a physician, a well-to-do draper, a university-trained designer, and a chartered accountant.

Academically, they were a distinguished crew. The Colonial Office had no time for third-raters; it was full of Exhibitioners and Scholars (men who had won highly competitive scholarships to colleges at Oxford and Cambridge). Its senior officers commonly had a First (a first class in the final examinations for a Bachelor of Arts degree, a distinction confined to a small percentage of all candidates and an honor that opened the way to academic employment in Great Britain). Indeed, the seven principal clerks who worked at the Colonial Office in 1914 could all have been transferred as a body to the senior common room of any Oxbridge college.[6] Their society was marked by that same touch of masculine fellowship that characterized a West End club, a Guards officers' mess, and an Oxford common room. They were bound together by common ties of church, school, and university. Many of them had shared memories of having served as prefects in a House, of having studied with the same tutor, or rowed in the same boat. They understood the same literary allusions; they smiled at the same limericks. They read the same books. They took much pride in being men of culture rather than specialists. They were schooled in the works of Plato, Caesar, and Thucydides, not those of Hegel and Marx. They argued well and they wrote well. They cultivated similar styles of polite understatement.

Yet these men were at the same time adaptable, and on the whole managed to acquire considerable proficiency in an extraordinary variety of subjects. They read copiously; indeed, the *Blue Books* they periodically produced at the request of the secretary or the colonial governments had that magisterial catholicity normally associated only with the *Encyclopaedia Britannica*, with headings like "agriculture," "bankruptcy," "botanical gardens," "catalogues," "councils," and "criminals." They were chosen also for a capacity to think and act like gentlemen, for their "tact, good manners, and savoir faire," and for a precise knowledge of the things that were done and not done in English society. They were constitutionally incapable of accepting graft; even Satan himself would have hesitated to offer a financial bribe to a first-class clerk in Downing Street. They lacked the bent for legal and administrative studies that distinguished their German and French colleagues, and they tended to be a higher caliber than their French equivalents. (The French found it difficult to recruit first-class men into the colonial ministry and overseas service because of the preliminary training required, and because most Frenchmen preferred the home service.) They belonged to clubs. Sir Robert Herbert's clubs were the Savile, the Cosmopolitan, the Athenaeum, and Grillion's—where he had an opportunity to meet leading statesmen of both major parties, an opportunity that would have been denied to a senior civil servant in Belgium and France, where anticlericals were not on terms of social ease with Catholics, or in Germany, where merchants and Freisinnige did not mingle with Pomeranian landowners.

The interests and talents of the men in the Colonial Office were remarkably varied. Edward (later Sir Edward) Marsh, for instance, was a brilliant classical scholar at Cambridge, where he had won every conceivable distinction. He was a patron of the arts and poetry, an inveterate first-nighter at West End theaters, and a translator of Horace and of La Fontaine. Much of his career was spent as private secretary to various colonial secretaries—most notably, Winston Churchill, who appreciated his stylistic elegance. Herbert (later Sir Herbert) Read, an Oxford "First," was the originator of a great drive against tropical disease that marked the first quarter of the twentieth century. E. R. Darnley, for many years head of the West Indian Department, took a single-minded interest in the problems of whaling, and set in motion a great oceanic research organization. John Green, who had done brilliantly in the Natural Science Tripos at Cambridge, was a geologist of renown. Others took up entomology, currency, surveying, and other specialized subjects, and acquired "if not a professional, at any rate a respectable, amateur status."[7] Their work was their hobby. Their office and a nearby West End club were home—all the more so since many of them chose to remain bachelors.

With a strong esprit de corps and a well-developed collegiate sense, the men in the Colonial Office trusted one another implicitly. Whatever their background—Anglican or Presbyterian, Tory or Liberal—they were apt to be "improvers" with a strong sense of social responsibility. Some of them indeed left the service in order to devote themselves to social reform. Others interrupted their careers for many years to that end. For instance G. W. Johnson, who entered the office in 1881, subsequently served as editor of the *Christian Socialist*; he was also chairman of Morley College, a center for adult education in

London; a director of the London Missionary Society; a leader in the Women's Suffrage Movement; and a "tower of strength" to the Association for Moral and Social Hygiene. Sidney Webb (Lord Passfield) and Sydney Olivier went on to acquire fame in the Fabian Society. Even the most conservative were inclined to champion good causes, and some of them—becoming disillusioned with the restrictions and routines of the Colonial Office—joined the overseas service.

Others had less admirable qualities, and few were well versed in economics. Had the British desired to emphasize the development of the colonies in the interest of British capital, they would have done better to take the emergent British local government services for their model. During the later colonial period, local government came to take up a greater variety of tasks than those handled by any other such systems in the world. British boroughs were responsible for services as varied as the provision of police protection, sewerage, water and gas, electricity, housing, transport, public libraries, parks, and clinics, among many others. The administrative elite of the boroughs consisted of a consolidated Administrative, Professional, and Technical Division.[8] When it came to economic or commercial affairs, Colonial Office officials were apt to be censorious—with that peculiar whiff of snobbery derived from the parsonage and the homes of the minor gentry. They were inclined to look down their noses at businessmen. They had a faintly offensive contempt for "moneybags," including, for example, the directors of the British South Africa Company or indeed of any chartered company. They tended to snub merchants, traders, and farmers on social and aesthetic as well as political grounds. In many cases they did not even think very highly of their own civil servants overseas. Sir George Bowen, who served as governor of Queensland, New Zealand, Victoria, and Mauritius, figured in departmental communications as "a pompous donkey"; Sir John Pope Hennessey, who served as governor in West Africa and other outposts of empire, was said to be "vain, unscrupulous, wanting in sound judgment and common sense, and prone to quarrel with his subordinates."[9]

There were other criticisms. The empire they tried to rule was too big and diverse for the available staff. In 1862 it numbered 48, in 1871, 50; and in 1934, 404. Before the 1890's the staff had few modern aids such as typewriters, telephones, or the telegraph. Permanent officials in London rarely visited the colonies, and so knew little of the difficulties faced by the men on the spot. Some even had trouble with exotic geography. According to an apocryphal story, a certain colonial secretary, on being asked by a society hostess at a dinner party to give the precise location of the Virgin Islands, replied simply, "As far as possible from the Isle of Man!" The lack of personal administrative experience overseas meant that Colonial Office officials were not always sympathetic to or even had any grasp of local problems. Lord Lugard complained of two other critical faults: the overruling of governors' recommendations by the Colonial Office staff, and the interference in the details of administration by men who had never worked in Africa. The Colonial Office, he wrote, should not decide such questions as how many pieces of an official's baggage were to be carried free by rail, or what pay increase a work foreman was entitled to.[10]

Perhaps the major weakness of rule by the Colonial Office was its reluctance to consult with other departments, a reluctance that represented the diversity of interests and the lack of coordination between the Treasury, the War Office, the Admiralty, and the India Office, all of them concerned in some measure with imperial problems, all of them with departmental traditions and preconceptions of their own. The War Office was inclined to take a narrowly military view; the Admiralty thought, above all, in terms of imperial communications, of naval bases, coaling stations, and cables. The India Office behaved almost like a foreign government, magisterial and aloof, apt to lecture other official bodies in terms of evangelical morality.

But from the Colonial Office's point of view, the Treasury was the main hindrance, with its small staff and its determination to scrutinize all expenditures as burdens on the British taxpayer. Treasury officials, containing within their ranks some of the ablest men in the British bureaucracy, did not hesitate to lecture their colleagues in other departments on every subject under the sun—from economic planning and naval strategy to the proper layout of botanical gardens. The upshot of their reasoning was usually simple: Spend less! To give but one example: the Treasury refused to provide the funds for Consul E. H. Hewett's journey to West Africa. The delay cost Britain a colony —the Camerouns. Only Lord Granville's private inquiry to the chancellor of the exchequer, pointedly asking whether the country was being governed by the cabinet or by the Treasury's clerks, got Hewett the funds. By the time he arrived the Germans had already negotiated treaties with the local chiefs. Henceforth in his career, Hewett was known as "Too-Late" Hewett.[11] Much time was lost in consulting other departments, and many programs and policies were spoiled by Treasury vetoes at the end of deliberations. Still, the historian Henry Hall concluded, after studying the minutes and activities of the permanent officials of the Colonial Office, that they "were men of great talents and industry, with abundant good sense, possessed of a saving gift of humor, and actuated by a desire to do all they could for the benefit of the colonies."[12]

The rulers of empire were preoccupied to an extraordinary degree with the minutiae of honors, precedence, and decorations. To most of them there was a world of difference between a simple Kt. (Knight Bachelor) and a KT (Knight of the Thistle). They knew exactly that according to the official Table of Precedency, a member 4th Class of the Royal Victorian Order ranked just behind a Companion of the Order of the Bath, and a Companion of the Order of the Bath behind a Master in Lunacy. One of Herbert's more important duties was to advise the colonial secretary on who deserved official honors and decorations. Colonial justices usually received knighthoods because of their position; eminent colonists obtained distinctions in order to quiet their clamor, reward a favor, or redress a geographical imbalance. Soldiers were honored for victories, albeit sparingly, lest too many military appointments lower the prestige of the Order of St. Michael and St. George. But above all, honors were given for governmental service; hence most colonial governors got a knighthood. Financial, academic, or scientific distinction carried no comparable weight, though achievement in these areas was not wholly ignored.

The Machinery of Colonial Government

A domain as decentralized and as diverse in its political structure as the British Empire was administered naturally on the geographical principle. In 1872, at a time when investment in the colonies was increasing and colonial markets were acquiring added importance, the office was reorganized into two geographical departments, one concerned with territories like the West Indies, the other with North America, Australia, Africa, and the Mediterranean. In addition, there was a smaller General Department. The work of administration increased slowly. Between 1853 and 1873 the total number of letters and dispatches received by the office rose from 11,519 to 14,001. For the most part, the scope of these messages was limited to general problems of government, finance, justice, and defense. The local administrator's principal task was to protect his subjects' personal rights and property, leaving economic development to the beneficent operation of private enterprise and taking care not to raise the ire of the Treasury by asking for funds to run his colony.

The structure of the central administration reflected the British class system as a whole. Broadly speaking, the first-division clerks represented the upper-middle and middle classes with their gentry linkages and aspirations. The lower-level personnel derived mainly from the petty bourgeoisie and the upper working class. Taken as a whole, the higher metropolitan bureaucracy was a small and able elite, cohesive, gentlemanly, infused with that spirit of improvement that characterized the Victorian middle classes as a whole. The scope of bureaucratic interference was as yet limited, and conformed to the notions of a society that spent little more than 10 percent of its gross national product on public expenditure. Hence the greatest empire in the history of the world, covering about one-fourth of the world's surface, was supervised at "home" by a few hundred civil servants, relying on a military force much smaller than that available to any great European power. It was a remarkable achievement.

Limited government accorded with accepted British notions of free trade. But irrespective of theory, limited government was also inevitable as long as communications remained slow and deficient. Mail service throughout the greater part of the nineteenth century was infrequent, and a dispatch that missed the mail packet might be delayed for months. Under these conditions, Colonial Office clerks geared their work to the departure of the mails and took life easy during the intervals between sailings.

Gradually, however, shipping lines improved their performance. In 1857, for example, the *Dane*, a small boat displacing 530 tons, inaugurated a regular mail service to Table Bay (South Africa) and completed its first journey in 44 days. The *Tintagel Castle*, built about four decades later—a more comfortable and larger vessel with 5,531 tons displacement—did the trip in three weeks. As mail schedules improved, messages began to stream into the Colonial Office in ever-greater quantities (see Table 4), so that the clerks now worked under continual rather than intermittent pressure. Senior officials in London no longer had to wait many months for a reply and could therefore take a greater interest in the minutiae of government overseas.

The telegraph had an even more immediate impact on the routine of the office. In 1879 the first cable was laid to Cape Town and, for a time, Britannia ruled over the world's cable lines. By 1892, when Herbert retired, the Colonial Office received over 3,500 cables a year; eight years later the number had grown to 10,000. Telgrams helped to speed up the work of government. The colonial secretary or his deputy was forced to make an increasing number of decisions quickly —sometimes based on the barest information. However, the telegraph

TABLE 4

Growth of the Colonial Office's Letter and Cable Traffic, 1870–1900

| Year | Letters and dispatches | | | Total telegrams received |
	Received	Sent	Total	
1870	13,541	12,136	25,677	800
1880	20,367	18,084	38,451	2,800
1890	25,313	21,457	46,770	3,500
1900	42,700	41,700	84,400	10,000

SOURCE: Henry L. Hall, *The Colonial Office* (London, 1937), p. 24.

did not necessarily improve the Colonial Office's control over strong and self-willed subordinates. It could be used also as a quick means of announcing a fait accompli, such as Queensland's annexation of New Guinea in 1883, and thus introduced a new note of uncertainty into government.

Governors were obviously important in the development or the lack of development of a colony. For example, Governor Alfred Moloney in the Gold Coast had prepared himself for his governorship with a course of instruction at the Royal Botanical Gardens at Kew. He encouraged rubber production and the search for export crops, and in 1882 sent a circular to all his officers instructing them to investigate gums, resins, waxes, fruits, seeds, dyestuffs, and the like. But all the colonial secretaries, whether the governors helped or not, sought to improve the economic life of the colonies by developing new crops and industries, and the Colonial Office encouraged colonial products exhibitions and stock breeding. Its officials met with the four governors of West Africa to plan how the Kew Gardens could be more helpful. A stock farm was established in Trinidad in 1879. A program to instruct cultivators in improved methods of animal husbandry was launched in West Africa in about the same period. Concern with the death rate in Africa led the office to fund medical research and a sanitation program.

The new era, with its steamships, telegraph, cables, and typewriters, its cult of scientific endeavor and efficiency, found its most dynamic representative in Joseph Chamberlain, colonial secretary from 1895 to 1903. But Chamberlain was not the inventor of colonial development; it had been the policy of the Colonial Office to improve the colonial estates for some time. Chamberlain merely pushed this program more intensively and successfully. When he assumed charge at the Colonial Office Chamberlain, like his German counterpart

Bernhard Dernburg, was *homo novus*, a new man. In spite of his courage, strong will, and diligence, he was disliked by many of the establishment for his poor taste and rough, crude manners. He did not come from a great Public School; he had not been to Oxford or Cambridge; he was a Unitarian by faith and a radical in domestic politics. His father had made a good deal of money by manufacturing boots. Joseph Chamberlain made even more in the screw business, so much so that he was able to retire at an early age with independent means, determined to make a name for himself in public life.

Chamberlain was the kind of man who would have done as well in America as he did in England. He entered municipal politics in Birmingham and rose from the school board to the mayor's office. His administration cleared slums, provided an efficient supply of gas and water, opened a great park, an art gallery, and a public library. He also built up a powerful party machine and became one of the most influential members of the Liberal Party. Despite his radicalism, however, in 1886 he broke away from the Liberals on Gladstone's projected Irish Home Rule Bill. The faction that he led, the Liberal Unionists, were determined to maintain the unity of the empire and eventually gave their support to the Tories. In 1895 Chamberlain became colonial secretary in Lord Salisbury's government.

He was quite unlike any colonial secretary who had ever held the office before. He did not regard it as a lowly post to be used as a stepping-stone to higher things, but as a key position in its own right, and remained in office until 1903, longer than most of his predecessors. With his belief in close collaboration with the white territories, in 1900 he successfully passed the Commonwealth of Australia Act, which established the modern dominion. He was eager to cooperate with both Germany and the United States, but was inclined to take a strong line against the French—even risking war—and against the Boers, whom he helped drive into armed resistance.

To Chamberlain in Great Britain, as with Dernburg in Germany, the colonies proper were an undeveloped estate whose potential should be unlocked by a proper combination of scientific endeavor and managerial skill. But Chamberlain, unlike the serene free traders of an earlier generation, also had a streak of pessimism. Chamberlain was deeply troubled about the manner in which Great Britain seemed to be losing its industrial primacy. The exports of British manufactures to Europe and the United States were on the decline. British wealth continued to expand, but not at the same rate as that of Germany or the United States. An increasing proportion of British wealth, moreover, derived from "invisible" exports, from such things as the proceeds of British banking enterprise and the services rendered in the insurance business. Chamberlain felt convinced that invisible exports were less likely to benefit the working classes than exports of manufactured goods that gave employment to large numbers of Englishmen. He believed, moreover, that the empire would provide protected markets to British manufacturers. Great Britain was threatened by long-term industrial obsolescence; protection would provide a much needed economic defense. As far as Chamberlain was concerned, only a strong imperial policy would protect British entrepreneurs against future exclusion from colonial markets at the hands of foreign competitors. He had no doubt that scientific colonialism would benefit both the employers and the workers, both the rulers and the ruled, and he was willing to accept the challenge.[13]

Chamberlain placed increased reliance on the Crown agents for the colonies, the men who looked after the financial affairs and public works programs of the dependent empire. (Their work will be discussed in greater detail in a subsequent section.) Whereas the Treasury stood for accustomed notions of laissez-faire, the Crown agents helped to pioneer many forms of state enterprise in the colonies. Chamberlain's ideas found a warm welcome in the Crown agents' office. In turn, he appreciated their work, and in 1900 Sir Montague Ommanney, the chief Crown agent, an ex–Royal Engineers officer and a man of outstanding ability, was promoted to be permanent under-secretary at the Colonial Office. His appointment marked a further shift within the bureaucratic balance of power.[14] Under the new dispensation, the rule of cheeseparing at Downing Street gave way to a design of developing the colonies by the judicious investment of public money in communications and other public works. Funds became available, for instance, for building state railways in Sierra Leone, the Gold Coast, and Nigeria. Chamberlain likewise gave permission to Rhodes to run a railway through Bechuanaland. He used his influence so that the Foreign Office agreed to the reoccupation of the Sudan and began work on the Uganda railway. In 1900 he steered through Parliament the Colonial Stocks Act, which enabled the colonies to borrow at favorable terms on the London market by classifying their bonds as trustee securities. All this was accomplished in the teeth of Treasury opposition.

Above all, Chamberlain took a vigorous part in the systematic offensive against tropical disease that was to change the fortunes of tropical Africa. In 1897 Sir Patrick Manson (1844–1922), a Scottish

surgeon who had made his name by studying parasitical diseases in
Hong Kong, became medical adviser to the Colonial Office. In the
same year Ronald Ross completed his study on the life cycle of the
malaria parasite, a spectacular triumph. In 1899 Chamberlain helped
to found the London School of Tropical Medicine.

Chamberlain was also interested in technical reforms. He was concerned with office management, the internal delegation of responsibility, and systematic collaboration with scientific bodies outside the office proper. His permanent staff, however, did not share his interest
in such matters. The modern Colonial Office, with its proclivity for
advisory boards and its emphasis on economic and social development,
took form after Chamberlain left office. Between 1904 and 1907, for
instance, the Colonial Office set up a variety of new advisory committees on technical questions, the Tropical Diseases Research Fund, the
Entomological Research Committee, the Colonial Veterinary Committee, and the Colonial Survey Committee. World War I brought further
administrative changes, prompting old-timers to rail at "the virus of
departmentalism which infected the office so swiftly and pervasively
after 1919."[15]

In terms of administrative organization, Chamberlain improved office management within his ministry. He tried to introduce a greater
degree of uniformity by transferring the various protectorates from the
Foreign Office to the Colonial Office (incidentally increasing the power
of his office). The process began with Nigeria in 1900; it was completed thanks to his successors—except for the Sudan condominium—
by 1913. He also made some attempts to unify the colonial service—
a task that proved to be beyond his grasp, but he at least managed
in 1896 to consolidate the entrance examination for administrators and
other officers with the regular civil service examination.*

Above all, Chamberlain introduced a new spirit, a new sense of
urgency into the office of colonial secretary. He gave a lead to his
successors by actually visiting the empire he was meant to rule, and
he gave greater say to the men on the spot. For instance, he gave
small dinner parties to which he invited both members of his own
staff and colonial service officers on leave, some of them quite junior.

---

*In 1932 Lord Passfield (Sidney Webb), a Labour colonial secretary, finally unified
the colonial service with the express intention of helping the more backward, insalubrious, and penurious colonies. A colonial legal service was formed in 1933; a colonial
medical service in 1934; forestry, agricultural, and veterinary services in 1935; and
survey, mining, geological, postal, and custom services in 1938.

When the port had gone round . . . Joe would take his glass and sit down by the youngest member of the Colonial Service in the room. "Got an axe to grind?" he would say, and the man, if he were wise, would bring out some darling scheme for the welfare of the tribe he governed, but which an unsympathetic Secretariat had shelved. Joe would listen carefully and, if he thought there was something in it, would do something about it. O yes, Joe was a great man.[16]

These notions of Chamberlain's were not, of course, new. Herbert, for instance, had taken a considerable interest in railway development and spent a great deal of time on problems of logistics. But Chamberlain's approach was much more systematic than Herbert's or anyone else's. The Colonial Office now had a planner and a plan. Pressure from shipping and merchant interests, cotton manufacturers, and others pushed government into providing some infrastructure to develop West Africa. Railways and roads and ports were built. Humanitarian interests dictated health measures. The official plans called for the development of trade, and governors were appointed who were qualified to push this through. For example, Sir William MacGregor, governor of Lagos, and Sir Ralph Moor, governor of the Niger Coast Protectorate, both stressed agricultural development by experimentation, supplying farmers with test seed, seedlings, and saplings from the government botanical gardens. Seedlings for coffee, kola, cocoa, maize, oil-palm, and citrus and other fruits produced at the Royal Botanical Gardens at Kew helped to improve the people's diet and led to the development of economic crops. Farmers were instructed in cultivation, and gardeners and demonstrators were provided. New steel machetes made it easier to clear the bush, and new crops were planted for food and export. Commercially valuable plants were brought from the West Indies, and American experts in cotton-growing and stock-raising came to Lagos. These people not only tried to develop new export crops, but planted new trees to conserve and develop forest resources as well.

These policies continued under the Southern Protectorate of Nigeria, which united these two formerly separate colonies. Like its predecessors, the protectorate encouraged agriculture and market gardening. It introduced new crops and experimented in agriculture. It established a botanical garden and an experimental cotton plantation, and brought in cattle from Barbados. Though many projects failed, some succeeded, notably those involving mangoes, tobacco, firewood plantations, cocoa, kapok, cinnamon, raffia, and kola. The protectorate administration also experimented with jute, castor oil, bananas, maize, and groundnuts.[17]

Still, for all Chamberlain's achievements, he did not change the Colonial Office in any fundamental way; it remained static. "His efforts to make imperialism more efficient, responsive, and adventuresome were contrary to the attitude and function of administration. Its institutions resisted many of his reforms and frustrated his policies and programs. Inadvertently he weakened its structure when he imposed burdens upon it which it was not designed to take."[18]

The Colonial Office expanded more significantly under Chamberlain's immediate successors as the empire grew and as the Foreign Office transferred various territories to its control. In 1904 the Central Africa Protectorate passed under the surveillance of the Colonial Office; a year later the British East Africa Protectorate followed suit. They were put in charge of a new East African Department, along with Uganda and Somaliland. In 1907 the Colonial Office was thoroughly reorganized, with the geographic and other departments consolidated into three large departments, each headed by an assistant under-secretary. The white self-governing colonies (later known as dominions) had called for the creation of a separate ministry to handle relations between themselves and the United Kingdom. The Colonial Office would not go all the way. But it did agree to form a separate Dominions Department. Within this department, one section was responsible for Canada, Australia, and New Zealand; a second looked after the four self-governing states in South Africa (Cape, Natal, Transvaal, and Orange Free State), plus Northern and Southern Rhodesia, Basutoland, Swaziland, and Bechuanaland.

The second department, called the Crown Colonies Department, comprised several divisions: the West Indian Division, the Eastern Division (responsible for a great variety of Asian possessions outside India), the West African and Mediterranean Division (which incongruously grouped Gambia, Sierra Leone, and the Gold Coast with Gibraltar, Malta, and Cyprus), the Niger Division (for Nigeria), and the East African Division (concerned with Uganda, Somaliland, British East Africa, Nyasaland, and Zanzibar). Separate offices were responsible for medical work in tropical Africa, for the West African Frontier Force, and the King's African Rifles.

The third department was aptly called the General Department, with tasks as varied as personnel management, audit, pensions, indentured labor, postal communications, and copyright, as well as precedence, ceremonies, honors, and quarantine. In addition, the Colonial

Office could draw on the services of a legal adviser and of a Colonial Audit Department, a separate administrative entity connected with the office but not part of it. On paper, this structure might sound complex; in practice it was still quite small. As late as 1914 the Colonial Office employed fewer than 140 persons, from the secretary of state down to the office porters. Fewer than 50 of these men were included in the first division.*

The geographic sections commonly had four men of the first rank. Each section was headed by a principal clerk (later known as assistant secretary), who was generally assisted by one first-class clerk (later known as the principal clerk) and two second-class clerks (later assistant principals, the second lieutenants of administration). By this date, as noted, all first-division men had been brought under the civil service. The top-most civil service officeholder, the true senior to all these men, was the permanent under-secretary. He was a man of distinction, was always knighted, and exercised great influence on the conduct of the office. He represented the administrative gentry within the British class structure, and was the principal adviser to the secretary of state for the colonies. The secretary, often a baronet or a Peer of the Realm, had a seat in the British legislature; as a political appointee, his tenure of office was necessarily much briefer than that of his senior civil servant.† In addition there was a parliamentary under-secretary, a politician whose main task was to represent the office in Parliament.

Parliament's control over the Colonial Office was limited. In general, the legislature took little or no notice of colonial affairs; from 1810 to 1890 only 4 percent to 10 percent of the debates were on colonial matters, including Australia, New Zealand, and Canada, which took up most of the time. "The house gets livelier and better filled when a dog-tax bill comes up," complained a Nova Scotian delegate.[19] Parliament could pass a motion for a select committee to study a colonial question; it could debate or ask questions. There also was an annual discussion of Colonial Office budget estimates. But the

---

*The establishment then consisted of the permanent under-secretary, two assistant under-secretaries (each in charge of a division), one chief clerk, a legal adviser, a legal assistant, four private and assistant private secretaries (these served the colonial secretary or his deputy and were normally destined for positions of influence), seven principal clerks, fifteen first-class clerks, and eighteen second-class clerks (*The Colonial Office List*, London, 1946, pp. xv–xviii).

† Between 1874 and 1914 there were 13 secretaries of state for the colonies; most of them regarded the Colonial Office merely as a stepping-stone in their political careers. During the same period there were only six permanent under-secretaries. For a list of both groups of titleholders in our period, see Appendix B, p. 374.

number of questions asked in Parliament were few—seven in 1849, 21 in 1893, still only 32 in 1913.

In its actual functions, the Colonial Office, even in 1913, still reflected the collegiate system of the "upper division," with its cohesion and social homogeneity, in which both senior and junior members had their recognized places. Each incoming communication was sent to the registry of the appropriate department, where it was docketed. A second-class clerk (assistant principal) began a process of minuting; the document then went up the Colonial Office bureaucracy, being minuted in turn by the more senior members. (Some of these minutes were remarkably learned, and still make interesting reading.) When the file reached an official who felt that he had sufficient authority to dispose of the matter, he added the words "at once" to his minute and initials. If he did not want to take any action at all—a not uncommon occurrence in an age of limited government—he wrote "put by." The file would then be returned, generally to the second-class clerk, for the drafting of a reply based on the minute of the authorizing official. Important communications might be drafted in the first instance by a higher official, but followed essentially the same procedure. In order to reduce the need to search through a mass of files for the background regarding any particular matter, second-class clerks periodically compiled the most important communications on the subject; these were specially printed as "Confidential Prints" for internal use.

This system gave considerable responsibilities to junior members of the Colonial Office—far greater than those entrusted to their peers in France or Germany. Indeed, at times the British system permitted important policy decisions to be made by relatively junior men simply because senior civil servants and politicians had failed to make an adequate study of the documents. Thus the land policy adopted in Kenya, which was the subject of nearly ten years' controversy between the Colonial Office and the settlers, originated in a memorandum drafted in 1905 by W. D. Ellis, at the time a first-class clerk. Like many of his colleagues, Ellis was contemptuous of the small white entrepreneur and regretted that the Colonial Office was not strong enough to adopt a policy of "the EAP [East African Protectorate] for the Indian and the native. No whites except capitalists need apply."[20]

Whatever the private opinion of the Colonial Office by those who manned it, their workmanship was high. The office had its own library; books and files were reasonably accessible, and information was drawn from a wide variety of sources. Reports from the governors and their subordinates or from field commanders provided many data. Local newspapers were scanned; letters from missionary societies, traders, and people with friends or relatives in the colonies all were used as sources. British papers were read carefully, and officials on home leave were encouraged to drop by the office to discuss affairs in the colony. There was no complex superstructure of research departments, intelligence sections, and advisory committees. Memorandums were always read instead of leading a twilight existence in a bureaucratic limbo. The number of decision-makers concerned with a specific issue was small. By 1921, when the office had grown somewhat, the total number of persons involved in the question of self-government for Southern Rhodesia did not exceed ten.[21] This group included everyone who ever perused a file on the subject, from Winston Churchill, the secretary of state, down to G. H. Creasey (later Sir Gerald Creasey), then an unknown assistant principal who had joined the Colonial Office a year before. Morale was high, cohesion was great, and within the limits set by convention, government was effective.

The Crown Agents for the Colonies

The Colonial Office was administered by gentlemen ill-qualified to run business ventures. The bulk of the housekeeping chores of government fell to the three Crown agents for the colonies and their staff. This office had originated in 1833, when the Treasury set up a body designed to take care of all Crown business in Great Britain. As the empire expanded, the agents' tasks became ever more numerous and varied, and their staff grew accordingly. The Crown agents acted as the commercial and financial agents of the Crown colonies (agents-general dealt with those who had "responsible government"), and had all sorts of responsibilities. They managed the bulk of Crown colony borrowing and investment in Great Britain. They took charge of all purchases and technical assistance not obtainable in a colony or an adjacent British possession. They dealt with surveys, shipping contracts, commissary supply, and insurance; they selected officials for multiple technical posts; they oversaw the building of bridges, lighthouses, and railways; they supplied bank notes and postage stamps; they invested surplus funds on behalf of British colonial territories; they undertook to disburse half pay and pensions to colonial officers. They bought livestock for colonial agricultural departments. They acted for the various public utility boards of the colonies, electricity commissions, railway and coal corporations, city councils, and harbor boards. The professional staff advised and were consulted on most building activities—they designed

TABLE 5

Commissions and Other Business Charges of the Crown Agents for the Colonies, 1899–1906

(In £)

Year	Commercial, railway, and general business			Financial, loan, and related business		Total debited	Total net income from commissions and other collections
	Stores and equipment purchased and shipped	Commissions collected thereon	Inspection fees	Transactions	Charges collected thereon		
1899	2,019,415.0.0	16,217.18.2		5,595,118.0.0	8,391.19.5	7,614,533.0.0	24,609.17.7
1900	2,211,711.0.0	17,328.2.11		7,584,026.0.0	8,202.2.7	9,795,737.0.0	25,530.5.6
1901	2,064,528.0.0	17,998.3.8		11,786,502.0.0	12,859.8.3	13,851,030.0.0	30,857.11.11
1902	2,124,557.0.0	19,291.4.11		20,678,836.0.0	25,260.6.10	22,803,393.0.0	44,551.11.9
1903	3,596,638.0.0	33,617.10.4		90,192,269.0.0	13,030.10.5	93,789,607.0.0	46,648.0.9
1904	2,541,935.16.4	22,638.3.8	3,059.5.11	22,903,900.18.7	16,461.13.11	25,445,836.14.11	42,159.3.6
1905	2,080,481.16.11	17,428.12.10	7,690.3.0	24,219,301.8.11	19,276.5.8	26,299,783.5.10	44,395.1.6
1906	2,133,659.8.2	21,670.6.11	14,401.12.10	22,537,962.8.9	34,183.0.9[a]	24,671,621.16.11	70,255.0.6

SOURCE: Victor Ponko, Jr., "Economic Management in a Free-Trade Empire," *Journal of Economic History*, 26, no. 3 (Sept. 1966): 377.

[a] Of this amount, £16,123.10 was commission for the investigation and redemption during the period 1902–6 of the outstanding liabilities of the government of the late South African Republic.

bridges and furniture and advised on railway equipment. All material was inspected by the Crown agents' department before being shipped overseas. The organization had its own testing laboratory; arranged packing and shipping; handled the issue of colonial loans and investment funds; and acted as publishers for official publications and as booksellers for a variety of items printed overseas.[22] The Crown agents, unlike the run-of-the-mill department, were able to pay for the cost of their own staff and operations with the revenue derived from their activities. From the design of a postage stamp to the purchase and feeding of a giraffe, there was no task the department was not prepared to handle for a fee. The organization therefore had a bureaucratic ideology of its own. Whereas the Treasury stood for accustomed notions of laissez-faire, the Crown agents and the men who carried out their orders were willing to promote public enterprise.

The Crown agents were subject to the general supervision of the colonial secretary. But their department was more like a commercial firm than a government agency. Far from relying on tax-supported subsidies, the agents made a profit by charging commissions on loans, commissions on the purchase of stores, inspection fees, and the like (See Table 5.) They were loyal to the local colonial governments they served. In the words of an official dispatch, "They act in discharge of their business not in any sense as agents of Her Majesty's government but as the agents of each colony that employs."[23]

The internal management of the Crown agents' office was notably unsystematic, in a curiously British fashion. No clear line of demarcation was drawn in relation to the authority and responsibility of the agents themselves. As things operated in 1908, the senior agent concerned himself with organization, discipline, and finance, and with the building of railways in China and Africa; the second-ranking man handled a variety of public works projects such as harbors, and all railways not within his senior colleague's realm of responsibility; and the third agent dealt with the agents' numerous other tasks, from the recruitment of personnel to the printing of colonial postage stamps. The need for unanimous consent in major decisions was never laid down in law. In theory, this system should have made for economic disaster. In practice, the office worked well. Its financial troubles in the 1970's derived from the profligacy and incompetence of a later generation that prided itself on its abilities in the field of "scientific" management.

The staff of the organization increased steadily with the march of empire, albeit at a modest rate in the early days. In 1881 its personnel still numbered only 33; in 1908 the figure had grown to 200; and by

1914 the staff had swelled to more than 350 persons—over twice the total employed in the Colonial Office. The Crown agents had their own departments for engineering and engineering inspection, insurance, shipping, and the like. They had their own draftsmen and engineering assistants; they had their own experts on virtually everything within their purview, from railways, harbor works, and water and sanitary services to shipbuilding, architecture, and furniture design. Their department pioneered in modern office methods and was among the first to employ "lady typewriters." Generally speaking, the agents were honest and efficient; they formed an essential—though little recognized—link in the day-by-day operations of empire.

Within the British colonial establishment, the Crown agents occupied a curious intermediate position. They were linked to the Colonial Office, but not part of it. The agents were first lodged in the basement of the old Colonial Office building, side by side with the messengers, porters, and the housekeeper and his wife, but eventually they moved into their own offices at Whitehall Gardens, with a separate shipping room, warehouse, and packing stores. The most senior officials of the organization belonged to the social universe of the universities, the great government departments and clubs. Sir Ernest Blake, who served as a senior Crown agent from 1881 to 1909, was a clergyman's son who had risen high in the Colonial Office, where he first made his name as private secretary to the Earl of Kimberley and later as head of a department. Of the six Crown agents who served between 1880 and 1914, all but one had come from the Colonial Office; all had practical experience as administrators or engineers.

The medium-level and junior employees of the Crown agents, on the other hand, did not form part of the Colonial Office world and did not share its social prestige. They enjoyed the same pay rates and pensions as members of the civil service, but they were not civil servants. They were a hard working and competent lot, socially connected to the City rather than to the higher layers of the bureaucracy. The Crown agents and their staff more or less viewed their office as an old-established mercantile house, a Victorian family firm, proud of its probity, its versatility and far-flung operations, and the internal harmony and esprit de corps that prevailed within its walls. By 1908 the Crown agents were acting for at least 24 dependent colonies and 11 protectorates. They also transacted a good deal of financial business for a number of self-governing colonies, including the Cape Colony, Natal, and Orange River Colony (the old Orange Free State), and West Australia.

Their work freed the colonial secretary from the troublesome—and the almost socially demeaning—task of running a financial and commercial establishment. From this arrangement the Colonial Office derived considerable advantages. As Vincent Ponko, a historian of the office, points out, in a 12-month period before World War I the Crown agents might have received as many as 9,000 orders necessitating some 24,000 contracts of varying kinds. Since a period of time often elapsed before a contract for a financial project was let, the agents commonly invested their clients' funds for them, more or less at their own discretion and on their own responsibility. The system operated on the basis of trust of a kind that could exist only in a society where private business and public administration were linked by informal ties of school, class, and clubland.

No critic ever questioned the integrity of the Crown agents. When, after 1878, they increasingly came under attack, it was not because of any whiff of corruption but because of their penchant to conduct their affairs in a spirit of social selectivity. And indeed, they do seem to have handled the business of placing colonial loans in the City almost as a "family affair." Instead of raising capital by public subscription, the agents preferred to seek the advice of favored financial houses on the rate they were likely to get for any particular issue, then used the services of these houses to sell the loan to other favored financial firms that in turn dealt with the public. The same exclusive spirit was displayed in the purchase and shipment of stores and in the overseeing of engineering contracts, activities in which the agents and staff exercised a strict and sometimes over-zealous quality control. In reply to charges of social favoritism, the Crown agents argued that they dealt only with selected firms whose honesty and efficiency were assured. Any firm in Great Britain that could satisfy them of its competence, or any colonial firm recommended by the appropriate governor, could go on the list, they said; moreover, any firm they rejected was entitled to appeal to the colonial secretary. But for all this, colonial governors often complained that local firms had difficulty in being admitted into the inner circle of approved establishments. The Crown agents' refusal to listen to colonial advice supposedly resulted from an ignorance of local requirements. Their reliance on tendering firms located in Britain was said to work hardships on local businesses.

In retrospect, the pros and cons of this debate are not easy to decide. There is no evidence that the Crown agents deliberately discriminated against colonial enterprise. The colonies probably raised their loans on terms as favorable as they would have been able to secure under any other system. They were furnished with merchandise of acceptable quality. But there seems little doubt that the Crown agents operated in the same spirit of economic paternalism that dominated the Colonial Office. Their practices were defended on the grounds that open bidding for contracts would raise prices, hinder the application of existing quality-control arrangements, increase the risks and costs of transportation, and generally work to the disadvantage of the colonies. Their clients were regarded as immature wards to be defended against the wiles of unscrupulous entrepreneurs by a select class of economic guardians. The Crown agents considered themselves watchdogs, appointed for the purpose of preventing the Crown colonies from making mistakes in the fields of purchases, construction, and finance. The Colonial Office and the Crown agents alike were convinced that British businessmen would seek selfishly to exploit the economic opportunities of a colony unless held in check by a benevolent, and often overbearing, bureaucracy.[24]

Within these limits, the Crown agents did their task well and efficiently. Their ideology, however, was far removed from free trade pure and simple, for it presumed that business and the state should cooperate for a common prosperity. While the Treasury continued to uphold the cause of economy, low taxation, free trade, and budgetary restraint, the Crown agents stood for state intervention in the economy. Not surprisingly, reformers like E. D. Morel, a spokesman for the Liverpool West African merchants as well as a militant humanitarian, called for the abolition of the Crown agents' department. Morel objected to rising public expenditure in the West African colonies. He criticized extensive public works constructed, as he thought, on the most impractical lines, without adequate safeguards, without proper tenders. He equally censured grants-in-aid and public loans. In his view, government should aim at the expansion of the West African export trade. Let the government abstain from fighting expensive wars. Let the government keep down taxes. Let the government abandon the mischievous notion that increased public revenue signified prosperity. Then all would be well. Morel, however, was fighting a losing cause. The Crown agents went from strength to strength; and so did the interventionist tradition that they represented within the British official establishment.

THREE

The Army

Queen Victoria's army seemed to foreigners a magnificent military anachronism. In an age when Great Britain led the world in manufacturing skills, its army was accounted among the most backward of European military establishments. "Of late, the British Army has much improved," a German professional soldier wrote with an air of unconscious patronage just before the outbreak of World War I. "The Territorial Army (the reserve forces) are of inadequate quality; but the regular forces, once mobilized, should not be far behind other European armies in general efficiency."[1]

In fact the army was well adjusted to the tasks that it was supposed to carry out. It was designed, in the first place, for "imperial policing," for fighting "small wars" and minor campaigns on the frontiers of empire. In the event of a European war, it was to provide an expeditionary force, an army not numerically on a par with the great conscript armies, but sufficiently large to support an ally and to demonstrate a sense of national commitment. Finally, when the need arose, it proved capable of acting as a cadre on which a citizens' army could be built during World War I, while the nation prepared for battle behind the shield of the Royal Navy.

The British Army: An Overview

After the downfall of Napoleon in 1815, the British Army was not called on to fight in any great conflict other than the Crimean War through the rest of the century; hence there was little incentive for improvement. Indeed, it had no General Staff until 1907, when an Imperial Conference drew up plans for the creation of a body that ensured, for the first time in history, that the troops of all units in the empire were organized, trained, and equipped on identical lines. Great Britain, moreover, was the only great European power that did not rely on conscription. And the British fighting man was expensive to maintain—as Rudyard Kipling remarked, in his "Arithmetic of the Frontier":[2]

> One sword-knot stolen from the camp
>   Will pay for all the school expenses
> Of any Kurrum Valley scamp
>   Who knows no word of moods and tenses,
> But, being blessed with perfect sight,
> Picks off our messmates left and right.
>
> With home-bred hordes the hillsides teem.
>   The troopships bring us one by one,
> At vast expense of time and steam,
>   To slay Afridis where they run.
> The "captives of our bow and spear"
> Are cheap, alas! as we are dear.

Yet in comparison with his peers in civil life, Tommy Atkins was poorly paid. So poorly, in fact, that even the "respectable poor" were apt to look with pity or contempt on a brother, cousin, or friend who "went for a soldier."

The officer corps varied tremendously in quality. The summary judgment of a modern British historian, that it was "an expression of late Victorian upper-class society, rich, snobbish, and corsetted by etiquette," is much exaggerated.[3] Certainly the army contained many a competent and well-trained company and battalion commander. There were scientific and efficient generals like Sir Garnet Wolseley, celebrated by Gilbert and Sullivan as "the very model of a modern Major-General," a man who boasted not of his gallantry and dash, but of his other qualifications:

> I am very good at integral and differential calculus,
> I know all the scientific names of beings animalculous.

Nevertheless, the officer's commission was more a status symbol than a certificate of professional competence. The serious study of military problems received but lukewarm encouragement. "Talking shop" at table was considered "bad form"; in many regiments, officers were discouraged from sitting for staff college entrance examinations. Formal schooling, moreover, did not necessarily profit a man. Even Douglas Haig, an educated soldier (later supreme British commander in World War I), remained constrained by the prejudices of the mess. After the disasters sustained by the British Army at the hands of well-trained marksmen in the First Boer War (1881), his military judgment was in some matters hardly better than that of a boulevard journalist or a duchess. "Personally I think," he wrote in a private letter, "our regiments of Cavalry should be armed in equal proportions, viz. half the Cavalry should have swords; the other lances—but I believe that a good hog spear would be better than the existing long lance."[4]

Yet when all is said and done, the army generally did its primary job well—that is, imperial policing and fighting "small wars" on the far-flung frontiers of empire. And it did so at an amazingly small cost. By the standards of European conscript armies, its size remained minuscule. Exclusive of the "Native Army" in India, there were about 212,000 men in the British regular forces in 1897. Of these, 72,000 were stationed in India, 32,000 on various colonial posts throughout the world, and the rest at "home"—a home that included Ireland, one of the most disaffected provinces in the empire. Even the General Staff, when one was finally organized, began as a modest undertaking. Charged with directing an army spread thin all over the globe, the "Imperial" General Staff did not in fact take any part in the formulation of imperial strategy until 1915, when Sir William Robertson became its chief. In sum, throughout the Victorian era, especially, the British Army suffered from many deficiencies in its central direction, central intelligence, and training; large-scale maneuvers, for instance, essential to the fashioning of an effective army, only began during the 1890's. Yet this army sufficed to hold the greatest empire the world had ever known, covering one-quarter of the earth's surface. In doing so, to be sure, it could rely on the support of the largest fleet in existence. But the army also had positive qualities of its own that were used by the British to shore up their huge imperial structure.

The army was both flexible and diverse—more of an armed federation than a unified force. There was the "Native Army" in India, numbering some 147,000 men in 1897 and linked to the British units there on the basis of one British to two Indian regiments per brigade. Its rank and file consisted of mercenaries drawn from a great variety of ethnic groups—Rajputs, Jats, Sikhs, Gurkhas, and other "martial races." Its officers were mostly British—generally upper-middle class in origin, devoid of the aristocratic prestige that characterized the Guards regiments and the smart cavalry formations at home. This army had its own esprit de corps and its own hierarchy of prestige. It counted among its number men like Sir Bindon Blood, whose name reads like a pseudonym but whose deeds were genuine enough. An Irish-born engineer officer, Blood received his majority in the Zulu war of 1879, served with distinction on the Northwest Frontier, made a considerable impression on Winston Churchill, rose to the rank of general, and became a Knight Commander of the Order of the British Empire.

The Indian Army was a formidable force. The British Army proper may have been small by the standards of Europe, but the British Army in India, numbering well over 200,000 men on a permanent war footing, was the most powerful armed force in Southeast Asia. Its territory was also a much better base than Great Britain for the minor wars and punitive expeditions involved in expanding and consolidating the British Empire in East Africa and Asia. There were plenty of recruits to fill its ranks. There was plenty of space to exercise its regiments. The major expense of its maintenance did not fall on the British taxpayer, but on the Indian government. The Indian Army had its own mystique, derived both from past conquests and from the ongoing feats of the tribesmen in its ranks—Afridis, Wazirs, Mohmads, riflemen inured to guerrilla tactics in the hills—whose forays received inordinate publicity from their opponents. In addition, the army held fast to the memory of the Indian mutiny, a large-scale rising of indigenous *sepoys* whose incidents were made known to Victorian schoolboys in Tennyson's famous "In Defence of Lucknow":

> Banner of England, not for a season, O banner of Britain, hast thou
> Floated in conquering battle or flapt to the battle-cry!
> Never with mightier glory than when we had rear'd thee on high
> Flying at top of the roofs in the ghastly siege of Lucknow.

Like the old Austro-Hungarian Army, the Indian Army was cemented by an officer class mostly foreign in speech, habits, and origin to the other ranks. Its reliability was sometimes questioned, and it was weak on the technical side. But it could and did act as an imperial reservoir of individual officers and of entire units willing to serve in Africa. Indian Army officers assisted Sir Harry Johnston, the first British commissioner of the newly established Central Africa Protectorate (later Nyasaland). Indian troops, Bengal cavalry, Madras sappers, Bombay infantry, and others took a leading part in the expedition against Ethiopia (1867–68), a campaign unsurpassed in the history of war as a model of logistic performance in roadless, uncharted mountain country.

The West India Regiment was like the Indian Army in miniature.

It consisted of professional fighting men drawn from the West Indies and, up to the early 1880's, from Sierra Leone and Gambia. Its commissioned officers—and most of the noncommissioned—came from Great Britain, and the regiment saw service in countries as far afield as Central America and the Gold Coast.

In addition, the frontier of white settlement created its own style of military organization. The self-governing colonies of Natal and Cape Colony maintained their own forces, militia-like, comparable in training and outlook to volunteer units raised in Australia and North America—local-born men officered by "colonials," whom British officers were apt to patronize or disregard. The value of these troops varied greatly. In Natal the Royal Natal Carabineers (formed in 1855) at first elected their own officers and provided their own horses and uniforms, drawing only their weapons from the government. These and other mounted units consisted mostly of established settlers, men who were both good horsemen and excellent shots with years of experience in the bush. Infantrymen, such as the Maritzburg Rifles, were recruited from local merchants, clerks, and civil servants who enlisted for local defense. At their best, these units were comparable to mounted Boer riflemen; at their worst, they were worthless braggarts, hard to mobilize and harder still to keep under arms.

The defense of the South African frontier hinged mostly on British regulars. One of the best units was the 8th Light Dragoons, which played a decisive part on the eastern frontier of the Cape, scene of innumerable "Kaffir wars" that ended only in 1877. By reason of long service in southern Africa, the Dragoons became completely identified with the Boers in their knowledge of the terrain, in their political sympathies, in their social attitudes, and even in their grasp of Afrikaans. Crack foot regiments like the Black Watch gave up their resplendent uniforms in favor of locally made canvas blouses, broadbrimmed hats, and whatever footwear could be secured on the spot. Beards were in fashion, and the men were taught to forget the upright military carriage to which they had been accustomed and to stroll along bush paths at a comfortable slouch, never raising their voices above a whisper. The soldiers learned to fight like Africans. They usually moved in single file, with flankers deployed on either side of the path, on the lookout for an attack from the trees or the thicket. In case of ambush, the men were instructed to charge straight at the enemy, for the bush, they learned, was never as impenetrable as it looked. The British, like their opponents, became past masters in the art of raiding the enemy's cattle and seizing his crop, fully aware that economic warfare was the best way to bring a pastoral enemy to his knees.

The frontier was fertile also in technological and organizational innovation. The British first used the machine gun in the Zulu war of 1879. Every other kind of experimental arm was tried out on the eastern Cape. The Minié rifle was first fired there in battle, and so was a large-bore weapon made in Edinburgh that fired a small conical shell. British soldiers perfected the art of musketry, and by the middle of the nineteenth century the best marksmen at the Cape came to consider the effective range of infantry as something better than 800 yards. In order to pacify the frontier, the British created in 1855 a paramilitary unit, the Frontier Armed and Mounted Police. The men of the FAMP were mounted constabulary, equipped with double-barreled percussion guns, bowie knives, and revolvers, and dressed in a comfortable uniform of brown cord and slouch hats that made them look more like gamekeepers than troopers. This was the ancestor of many other mounted forces, half military and half police, bodies like the British South Africa Police in early Rhodesia and the Landespolizei in German South-West Africa, which proved to be both the most effective and the most economical military means of armed domination at the time.

Frontier experiences encouraged British military intellectuals to think about "small wars," a subject neglected in other European military schools. According to Colonel C. E. Callwell, one of the ablest military theoreticians of the Edwardian era, "small wars" consisted of campaigns undertaken for prestige, pacification, or conquest. Annexation campaigns, he suggested, commonly passed through two distinct stages: the overthrow of the enemy—usually effected by a few decisive engagements—and a period of guerrilla warfare. In such conflicts, marked by ambushes, by surprise assaults and quick retreats, the enemy enjoyed a strategic superiority. On the other hand, "superior armaments, the force of discipline, a definite and acknowledged chain of responsibility, *esprit de corps*, the moral force of civilization [worked] together to give a trained and organized army an incontestable advantage from the point of view of tactics." In these circumstances, said Callwell, "the object to be sought for clearly is to fight, not to manoeuvre, to meet the hostile forces in open battle, not to compel them to give way by having recourse to strategy. . . . To beat irregular opponents and savages, the most efficacious plan is to engage them on every possible occasion."[5]

For better or for worse, the colonial experience profoundly affected

British military thought. True, it induced many ordinary Englishmen and perhaps many of their leaders, too, to believe that great campaigns might be won at small loss in lives and money, and that the blood toll would necessarily be paid by a few well-delineated segments of British society—the poor from the cities and the countryside and the gentlemen from town and country houses. But it also habituated officers to action in many parts of the world under many different conditions. Moreover, the frontier taught the British some valuable lessons in the art of warfare. They learned how to put their faith in aggressive tactics and offensive strategies. The annals of British colonial warfare are full of engagements initiated by small forces against opponents greatly superior in number, though inferior in firepower. More valuable in the long run, since these methods proved of little account against such later foes as the Boers, was the expertise the British overseas army gained in logistic matters. Probably no other power would have managed, as Britain did at the turn of the century, to send several hundred thousand men to South Africa and keep them supplied there.

Out of necessity, the army learned how to move supplies over mountain country, across deserts, through jungles and bush, a difficult problem at a time when an economy-minded government and a stingy Treasury might overlook a lost battle but never a big expense account. At the beginning of the 1870's the railway age had scarcely begun in Africa. There were only two short rail lines in Egypt; and with the exception of 152 miles in the Cape and Natal, there were no tracks in all of Africa south of the Sahara. Warfare moved at the speed of an ox wagon, and few wagons ever covered more than ten miles a day. A sandy drift or a flooded river could bring a column to a halt; a smashed wheel or a broken axle could take a week to repair. Expeditions such as the invasion of Zululand in 1879 required an extraordinary degree of organization, forethought, and managerial skill. The British managed to beat their opponents, despite a brilliant Zulu victory at Isandhlwana the same year. In the end, the Zulu kingdom was smashed.

They were equally successful in drawn-out guerrilla struggles such as the conflict with the "Kaffirs" on the eastern frontier of the Cape that lasted until the end of the 1870's. The British had better weapons than their opponents, but technology on its own was not the decisive factor. The technological gap that existed in the 1950's between lightly armed Algerian partisans and French regulars equipped with helicopters, walkie-talkies, armored cars, and a host of other devices was much greater than that existing between a British infantry battalion and a Xhosa force a century before. British strength lay in unity of command, a high degree of discipline, and supply facilities far superior to those of the enemy. African guerrillas did not enjoy any privileged sanctuaries, places inaccessible to British troops for political reasons. Nor were African warriors able to command much sympathy within the British metropole at a time when even Karl Marx praised the progressive role of the British in India and Friedrich Engels welcomed the French conquest of Algeria.

Organizationally, the victorious British Army was not much more than a loose collection of regiments that reacted in a dissimilar fashion to the uneven impact of military change. Some corps were highly professional in their outlook, such as the Royal Engineers, whose colonels, according to Kipling, were "married, mad, or Methodist." The infantry and cavalry regiments, however, were far different from such units, both in organization and in their approach to warfare. After the Cardwell reforms, the recruitment of regiments was linked to specific geographical areas, an arrangement that helped to make the army more popular at home and created strong territorial affiliation.* The British soldier was moved to fight not so much from a sense of patriotism as from an intense loyalty to his particular "mob," the Seaforth Highlanders or the South Wales Borderers, or whatever. In the British Army, unlike continental armies, the fighting unit was not the regiment but the battalion, a unit that consisted, on home station, of eight companies—each with about three officers, ten noncommissioned officers, and from 85 to 110 private soldiers—and was commanded by a lieutenant-colonel. The system allowed commanding officers enormous scope in stamping their own personality on the battalion. There was a much higher proportion of officers to men than was customary in most continental armies (about one officer to 36 men, against one to about 60). It proved particularly suitable for small wars

---

*The so-called Cardwell system, introduced in 1873 by Edward Cardwell, a Gladstonian Liberal, was designed to provide regiments with permanent homes. Overseas service was reduced in length. Battalions were paired for alternate tours at home and abroad, their personnel becoming interchangeable. The "linked battalion" system was not universally applied. It had to be modified, for example, in relation to the South African service. But the reforms did succeed in their object of allocating strategic depots and recruiting areas in Great Britain to particular units that in turn were linked to militia battalions. In 1881 Hugh Childers, a Gladstonian like Cardwell, further modified the system. County titles were allotted to regiments previously known only by numbers. Like so many other great creations—the club, the Public School, the cult of games-playing—the county-associated regiment in time came to be looked upon as part of an immemorial tradition. From this reorganization 69 regiments of the line emerged. By 1914, 157 regular battalions were available, the largest volunteer force in the world.

and police actions, since it enabled commanders to detach small units for independent action. This organizational structure was not superseded until 1913, when battalions were reorganized into four rifle companies.

The Martini-Henry rifle, introduced in 1871, was the infantryman's main weapon. It was capable of killing an opponent at up to 1,000 yards if handled by an expert, but prone to jam and apt to bruise a marksman's shoulder or even cause his nose to bleed because of the rifle's terrific kickback. The Martini-Henry, the last of the blackpowder rifles, was replaced in 1889 by the Lee-Metford, which was in turn superseded in 1899 by the Lee-Enfield, a sturdy, reliable, bolt-action magazine rifle that any reasonably well-coordinated recruit could learn to fire with considerable accuracy. The development of the machine gun was relatively neglected in the British Army, and at the beginning of World War I the German infantry formations, both in Europe and in East Africa, enjoyed a considerable superiority in automatic weapons.

The army formed a society peculiarly its own, distinct in religious and class background from British society at large. It contained but a small proportion of Nonconformists, a group composed in good part of respectable tradesmen and skilled craftsmen who tended to look on the queen's forces with suspicion or disapproval. Private soldiers were drawn largely from the working class, both rural and urban. Many were Catholics, most of these Irishmen. Nevertheless, "the army was in fact one of the few institutions in which the notion had ever taken root of the United Kingdom as an entity which constituted something more than an uneasy conjunction of England, Scotland, and Ireland."[6]

In 1830 more than half of the ordinaries had derived from the "Celtic Fringe" (42.2 percent Irish and 13.5 percent Scottish). But by the end of the century this demographic imbalance—a potential danger to the stability of British rule in Ireland—had been eliminated. In 1890 only 14.2 percent of the men in the army were Irish, just slightly above their 12.5 percent representation in the United Kingdom as a whole; before ten years had passed, Scotsmen made up 8 percent of the army compared with 10.5 percent of the entire population. Ireland's share of officers was likewise roughly balanced, though far more of the Irish-born men were Protestants than the size of Ireland's Protestant community would indicate. On a purely per capita basis, the Church of Ireland was apparently the most army-oriented denomination in the British Isles.

The army derived tremendous benefit from the reforms instituted

by Lord Cardwell, one of the greatest "Victorian improvers." Cardwell, a product of Winchester and Balliol, served as secretary for war
in the Gladstone government of 1868–74. He exemplified in his
person that spirit of methodical efficiency associated with the Public
School at its best. He abolished the savage punishments that had been
inflicted on delinquent soldiers in the past. He ended the purchase
of commissions. He withdrew troops from the self-governing colonies.
He reformed the volunteer system; he equipped the infantry with
breech-loading rifles. He established the "linked battalion" system
mentioned earlier, a pattern that endured in its essentials until the
eve of World War I. He rearranged regiments according to geographical districts, so that volunteers would serve in units in which the same
dialect was spoken and the same local prejudices shared. Reorganization did not always work smoothly. The fusion of certain regiments
involved all kinds of anomalies. But by the 1900's the process was
complete. British regiments developed a peculiar family atmosphere,
so that a man posted from one battalion to another found himself in
an equally familiar background. Above all, Cardwell introduced a system of short-term enlistments, designed to provide Great Britain with
an army of young professional soldiers who would serve for a limited
number of years, then return to civilian life, settle down to a trade
(possibly one learned in the army), and spend additional time in the
reserves.

The system was extraordinarily successful. The onetime army of
aging professionals disappeared. The average British soldier came to
be a tough volunteer serving on a short-term contract, supported by a
regular army reserve, youthful, well trained, capable of being instantly
called to the colors. As a result of these reforms, the army lost some
of its former unpopularity. It ceased to be regarded by the nation
either as a threat to English liberties or as an academy of drinking,
idleness, and whoring. Philanthropists built schools for soldiers and
soldiers' homes. Reformers organized the Boys Brigade (begun in Glasgow in 1883) and kindred organizations designed to inculcate into the
young "habits of Obedience, Reverence, Discipline, Self-Respect,
and all that tends towards a true Christian manliness"—qualities that
early Victorians had looked for in the chapel rather than on the barrack
square.

The Victorian army's esprit de corps was high. It centered on individual regiments whose cohesion any football team might have envied.
Many soldiers—but particularly the officers—identified themselves
with particular regiments, sons following fathers into the same unit

for generations. Regiments had their distinctive personalities, which were apt to reflect the social characteristics of the area from which they had been recruited. The Royal Fusiliers was a London regiment; a corporal in its ranks who did not know Cockney rhyming slang would have had a hard time. After many Polish, Lithuanian, and Russian Jews had settled in the London East End at the end of the century, the regiment also attracted Jewish recruits—so much so that during World War I there were jokes about the "Royal Jewsiliers." There were Scottish Highland regiments, famed for their fighting ability and for their cult of real and—more often—supposed Highland traditions. The Cameronian Scottish Rifles, on the other hand, were vociferously "Lowland" in orientation.[7] They did not have pipers—only drummers. They did not wear kilts. Their trews were of a dark green-and-black tartan, their bonnets had black pompons, and their buttons were black —all indicative of their Puritan Covenanter origin and their not wholly deserved reputation for earnestness, sobriety, and frugality. Their regimental march was "The Nut Brown Maid," to which the regiment naturally had its own words. One verse, the lament of a Scotsman faced with qualifying for the extra allowance that went with a classification as a "first-calls shot," went as follows:

> Och bring the Target nearer!
> Och bring the Target nearer, ha!
> I cannot see the Target,
> It's oo'er far awa!
> My eyes they cano' see it!
> I'm shootin' for me pay.
> Och bring the Target nearer,
> It's oo'er far awa!

The regiment drew its officers from the gentry and the upper-middle and upper classes. The officers' mess was their home; the battalion was their life. Their training emphasized courage, honor, and physical fitness. Games were important; field craft and the art of organizing night marches much less so. About half the noncommissioned officers were of lower-middle-class or respectable working-class background. They came from homes where it was usually accounted a disgrace to put on the queen's uniform. Accordingly they had a strong desire to make good, and displayed tremendous attachment to the military world. About 70 percent of the other ranks came from the slums of Glasgow. Filthy, ragged, and underfed, they had good reason to join an army that built up their physique and gave them pride. The battalion became their home. In battle they displayed incredible courage and stamina, even though they had little ability to think for themselves and little chance to acquire any new skills beyond those of a purely military kind.[8]

The ordinary soldier was tough and resilient, though physically not very impressive. Infantrymen needed to be only five feet four inches tall, with a chest measurement of 33 inches on enlistment; but they soon broadened out. Their enlistment was normally for a period of 12 years, of which seven were spent with the colors. During the years he spent under arms, the British soldier's training emphasized discipline, spit and polish, instant, automatic obedience. Two and one-half months were devoted to "square bashing"—to enable recruits to conduct themselves in public like soldiers. Bayonet drill was excellent. Musketry standards were far below those obtaining in Boer and many British "colonial" formations. Two hundred rounds of ammunition per man were nonetheless allowed for the so-called recruit courses, and the same number for trained soldiers. After the Second Boer War, however, marksmanship vastly improved, and the professional British infantryman was a better shot than any of his European rivals.

Combat training likewise left much to be desired. During the 1890's only 18 days a year were spent in company field exercises. Noncommissioned officers received instruction in map-reading, map-making, and direction-finding, but these skills were not taught to ordinary soldiers, who were told by their corporals that privates were paid to obey and not to think. Mounted infantry training was considerably better in the sense that more emphasis was laid on individual initiative; but mounted infantry courses, like the regular infantry courses, only lasted for two and a half months. Cavalrymen, in contrast, spent six to eight months learning how to use the carbine, the sword, and the lance. They were famed for their horsemanship. But again, field training and drill in firearms were neglected in favor of equitation and regimental glitter. Only three months a year were devoted to field training in squadrons. Soldiers of all ranks, from private to field marshal, were ill-prepared to cope with the task of fighting in large formations or commanding them. Well into the Edwardian age, the British Army continued to see its task as fighting "small wars."

British soldiers, whatever their rank, valued their regimental traditions, more so perhaps than any other soldiers in history. Troopers and officers alike placed an extraordinary stress on regimental memories, regimental achievements, and regimental quirks. Individual regiments vied with each other and often developed long-standing friendships or enmities. The pride of the regiment grew out of its history, its badges and buttons, its silver, its battle honors and colors. The regimental system had an elaborate ceremonial, an intricate order of precedence, and a jealously guarded set of privileges, such as the prerogative of the Royal Fusiliers to march through the City of London with fixed bayonets, colors flying, and drums beating.

There were isolated islands of professionalism within these regiments, but by and large the officers regarded their units as social clubs, or perhaps rather as a sort of itinerant country house in which the officers corresponded to the gentry, and the sergeants to the "upper servants," with their own complex order of precedence. The enlisted men, though derived largely from the rural and urban working class, also included some numbers of the déclassés, the gentleman-rankers immortalized by Kipling as the legion of the lost ones and the cohort of the damned. In the more fashionable regiments (though not in the Frontier Armed and Mounted Police) an extraordinary degree of attention was devoted to the ceremonial side of warfare, to the cut of uniforms and other aspects of military haberdashery, to the minutiae of drill, and to the finer points of etiquette. Messes abounded with strange customs, more reminiscent of Public Schools than of military establishments. There were marvelous true-life stories—of the officer who carried a pony upstairs for a bet or of the horse that by reason of its distinguished service had its hooves encased in silver. At Laing's Nek, in the First Boer War (1881), a British bayonet attack against Boer trenches withered away under an appalling fusillade. Nearly all the British officers died at once. Among them was the commander's ADC, who fell shouting "floreat Etona"—a scene immortalized in countless Victorian illustrations celebrating deeds that won the empire.

Yet one of this army's many virtues was precisely its lack of professionalism. Of all the great European powers, Great Britain had the most civilian-minded military establishment. The all-male camaraderie that existed in a British officers' mess was no different in kind from the spirit prevailing in a club or even in the senior common room of an Oxford college. Officers prided themselves on being gentlemen rather than military specialists. Their outlook differed little from that of civilian dignitaries. The British officer, unlike the Prussian, saw nothing wrong in wearing civilian clothes off duty. The British Army had nothing comparable to the military class privileges of the German officer corps, with its courts of honors and dueling ceremonial. The homogeneity of the British ruling stratum was reflected in its administrative structure. The War Office was essentially a civilian body, headed by a civilian minister of the Crown. The Colonial Office was equally civilian in composition. There were no military strongholds within its organization comparable to the administrative enclaves controlled by soldiers within the French colonial administration.

The Army in Africa

The British colonial forces in Africa were small. As late as 1902 the military strength of the British units in all of West Africa, East Africa, Uganda, Nyasaland, and Northern Rhodesia was something under 11,500 men. This was strikingly small both in relation to the forces available to the French or the Belgians and in relation to the vast size of Great Britain's tropical African empire. The white manpower requirements of these forces were even more limited. In fact, the British required fewer than 300 European commissioned and noncommissioned officers to run them.

The control of these forces was highly decentralized. Governmental policy during the 1890's assumed that the army's regular forces (defined by statute and raised by parliamentary consent) were to be employed mainly in the defense of coaling stations, maritime fortresses, and occasional expeditions. The internal defense of colonies and protectorates accordingly rested with locally raised corps, usually called police, constabularies, or "Rifles," regulated by local ordinances and controlled by the local civil authorities. These forces included units like the Royal Niger Constabulary, whose organization and equipment had a profound effect on many future colonial forces. Under the stewardship of Joseph Chamberlain, the defense of the West African colonies was entrusted to a new formation, the West African (later the Royal West African) Frontier Force, an imperial unit—unlike the constabularies—though locally raised. In 1901 the War Office successfully recommended a similar system for the East African colonies, leading to the unit that later came to be known as the King's African Rifles. Both of these units were controlled through inspectors-general appointed with the consent of the War Office, but they continued to be at the service of the local governor, who acted also as commander-in-chief.

The governor's military powers were thus far from nominal. In some British colonies, moreover, civilians actually supervised the day-to-day conduct of military operations, something unheard of in the Kaiser's service. Harry Johnston, the first British commissioner of the Central Africa protectorate, was as untypical an empire-builder as the imagination might conceive. In 1891 he was appointed to take charge of a forlorn outpost where British influence was limited to a few mission stations and trading posts. Within a few years, the ex-art student—plump, squeaky-voiced, and undersized—had wrought a complete transformation. With the help of a handful of British officers seconded from the Indian Army, he organized a small but efficient force of Sikhs and some African levies. Aided by a few gunboats supplied by the Admiralty, Johnston smashed the local supremacy of Yao chieftains and Swahilispeaking slave traders. There was plenty of friction between Johnston and his subordinates, but none suggested that a professional military man would be disgraced by serving under a self-taught soldier who had never worn a uniform.

In purely technical terms, the army was quite prepared for the task of imperial policing. The army's code of conduct emphasized the virtues of civilian control. The British police force, built up in the nineteenth century as a civilian body, owed a great debt to light infantry officers of the Peninsular campaigns of the Napoleonic wars. In its approach to military supervision, the British army overseas in turn emphasized civilian preeminence over the military, minimum use of force for the purpose of repressing public commotions, and the need for collaboration with the civilian power for the purpose of restoring public order.[9]

The army, as we have seen, also proved capable of organizational pioneering to fit the needs of the frontier. Alone among the European powers, Great Britain developed the use of mounted infantry for colonial warfare. Taken as a whole, the army was well up to the demands put to it by the enemy, be they Indian mountaineers, Zulu spearmen, or Sudanese dervishes. The British could successfully tackle even relatively well-organized indigenous armies in West Africa, schooled in the art of jungle fighting and supplied with a fair number of firearms.

The gentlemen-amateur, educated in a Public School, may not have been well read in the professional literature dealing with great European conflicts. But whatever his educational deficiencies, he did no worse in colonial campaigns than his confrères in the Belgian Army, where an ability to pass examinations, especially examinations in "practical" and scientific subjects was highly prized. A knowledge of military theoreticians like Hamley and Jomini did not, in fact, appear particularly useful in training a diverse lot of mercenaries—Yao, Sikh, or Ngoni—or in fighting small campaigns in places as different as Ashanti, Zululand, and Afghanistan—in mountains, desert, or jungle country, where climate, disease, and inadequate supplies were greater perils than enemy bullets. For the purpose of fighting "small wars," the British system, with its emphasis on drill, ceremonial, athletic prowess, personal risk taking, and "good form," was supremely functional. The very disparity in social status and education between officers and other ranks emphasized the leaders' prestige; British discipline was superb. (Even among African troops there were few mutinies.) By and large, British company and platoon commanders kept the confidence of their men by giving a good account of themselves in small-scale actions that put a premium on the physical stamina, courage, initiative, and personal leadership qualities of youthful subalterns, rather than on the technical abilities of their elders in the more senior ranks. At the same time, the army had sufficient specialists for the more technical jobs. The logistic and medical scandals of the Crimean War were not repeated. The Royal Engineers turned out to be good railway builders; and British army doctors learned how to cope with all manner of unfamiliar health problems.

The failings of the late-Victorian army only became obvious when it had to deal with European irregulars, supported by highly trained professional cadres. In the Second Boer War (1899–1902) the British faced a formidable force, mounted Boer sharpshooters armed with modern rifles, habituated to fighting on the veld, and supported by artillery detachments equipped with Krupp guns. The initial British performance was deplorable. (In fairness to the British, it is worth remembering that the highly trained German Army experienced very similar difficulties during the South-West African rising of 1904–7. The Germans had to mobilize something like 17,000 men to put down Herero and Nama fighters. The task of eliminating mounted Nama guerrillas skilled in partisan warfare proved extremely hard.) But the British, unlike the Germans, had no proper General Staff. The British Army, in other words, had no corporate memory, no planning, and no analytical faculty of a corporate kind. Above all, British officers, habituated to almost inevitable victories in scores of minor engagements, commonly despised the Afrikaners. "They are given to more boasting . . . than the Americans, but at heart they are cowards, and cowards that would be relentless to a fallen foe," wrote General Sir Garnet Wolseley. "They have all the cunning and cruelty of the Kaffir without his courage or his honesty. They knew that they could not stand up against our troops for an hour."[10] Boer victories won by marksmanship were explained away as unsporting acts or even massacres worthy of savages. Moreover, there was a widespread belief that the cowardly Boers must have been aroused to resistance by Fenians or other agitators.[11] (A number of Irish nationalists, as well as volunteers drawn from the European continent, did in fact fight on the Boer side.)

The British regarded themselves as agents of economic rationality and progress in South Africa. The Afrikaners were supposedly backward farmers, wedded to an archaic form of social organization, idle and unproductive—just like Africans. In the same way, the British underestimated the Boers in the military sphere. Many an officer was convinced, for instance, that the Afrikaners would run like rabbits if forced to fight against regulars. But in the matter of military tactics the rationality was all on the Boers' side: at a time when the British infantrymen relied on volleys, mounted Afrikaner riflemen were able to select their targets and pick them off as they chose. To smartly dressed Dragoons, the Boers looked little better than ragamuffins in arms: ill-kempt, bearded men with dirty long hair, wearing sweaty flannel shirts, baggy corduroy trousers, and coats that barely held together. Yet these men—lacking conventional discipline and little addicted to glamorizing war, but well armed, well mounted, and accustomed to the veld—were able to wipe out a British force in open country by murderous rifle fire, shedding so much blood that even the most hardened Afrikaner frontiersmen were sickened by the sight of what they had accomplished.

British commanders lost the First Boer War because they remained wedded to outdated weapons and outdated tactics, much like their opposite numbers in Zulu and Ndebele *impis*, who likewise failed to adjust their military institutions to the changing realities of the battlefield. The British Redcoats, like the gorgeously plumed Ndebele warriors of Rhodesia, had been spoiled by a succession of relatively easy victories over weaker opponents. The ceremonial of the British regimental review, like that of the Ndebele Great Dance, was therefore apt to obtain priority over up-to-date battle drill. Even the Gordon Highlanders, one of the best regiments of the British Army, battle-hardened on the Afghanistan frontier, failed at the battle of Majuba (1881). The British military establishment proved slow to profit from its mistakes. Troops who marched into battle in the Second Boer War were led at first with the same fatuous incompetence as those of 1881, only on a larger and more disastrous scale.

Just over a decade later, the British Army once more went to war—this time against the Kaiser's Germany. The British Expeditionary Force that landed in France in 1914 was considerably more professional in spirit than the army of Disraeli's age. Socially, it had changed surprisingly little. (As indicated in the tabulation on p. 91, the share of middle-class officers had risen slightly; the proportion of "aristocratic" officers had declined. But the percentage of "gentry" officers had stayed the same, at just under one-third. Many of the so-called middle-class officers were identified in life-style, social aspirations, origin, or education with the landed interests.) This army had benefited considerably from the lessons of the Boer War. Its mobilization procedure was efficient, its discipline admirable, its musketry deadly, its morale superb. British equipment was better than French equipment; British tactics were well-suited to mobile warfare. This army could take incredible casualties without flinching. Its cohesion and the officers' spirit of self-sacrifice astonished even the most hostile critics. Civilian supremacy, or better perhaps—the supremacy of the gentleman—was taken for granted. Internal quarrels between "frocks" (civilians) and "brasshats" (senior military officers) had none of the ferocity that marked civilian-military infighting in Germany. No British "brasshat" ever dreamed of dominating the state in the way General Ludendorff did in Germany.

For all its manifold virtues, the army had paid a heavy price for its colonial commitments, its cult of the gentleman, its remoteness from industrial society, and its isolation from the people at large. The bulk of the British nation assumed that future wars would be like colonial wars. There might be initial disasters, but armed conflict would be restrained and not excessively bloody. There was little sense that modern land war would require total mobilization and entail enormous casualties. The generals thought in similar terms, in terms of mobile warfare of the southern African pattern, with rapid sweeps in which horsemen would play a leading part. They could not, however, envisage a modern Materialschlacht dependent on industrial mass production. The great majority of gentleman-officers had little interest in the technology of war. The bulk of the private soldiers, mainly drawn from the proletariat, were poorly trained in manual skills. In terms of physical equipment, the army was desperately short of those weapons that a great manufacturing power should best have been able to provide—machine guns, mortars, hand-grenades, barbed wire, and, above all, shells of every size and description. Despite progress made with the internal combustion engine, the army had made no experiments for transporting troops in trucks, for pulling guns by tracked vehicles, or for building armored cars.

The generals thought in terms of mobile warfare, conducted by relatively lightly armed troops, especially cavalry. Their army was superbly trained for "small wars" along the periphery of empire. It had made no serious provision for trench fighting, the coming form of warfare, one widely practiced already in the Russo-Japanese War and even the American Civil War. Tactical innovations such as elastic defense, infiltration, the employment of machine guns as the pivot of battle owed more to German than to British ingenuity. The colonial achievement, though great, had exacted a heavy price from the army in terms of technological efficiency; the full cost in socio-military terms can never be fully assessed.

Gentlemen in Arms

> The sand of the desert is sodden red,
> Red with the wreck of a square that broke;
> The Gatling's jammed and the Colonel dead,
> And the regiment blind with dust and smoke.
> The river of death has brimmed his banks,
> And England's far, and Honour's a name,
> But the voice of a schoolboy rallies the ranks:
> Play up! Play up! and play the game!

Sir Henry Newbolt's poetry does not find many admirers today—least of all in a British Army that has since overcome disasters infinitely greater than any experienced in a Victorian frontier foray.[12] But in his time Newbolt's observations were accurate enough. British colonial units still formed squares in "cannibal-chasing" campaigns. These squares were sometimes broken, and there were bloody disasters in remote places. The vast majority of British officers were Public School men. In Victorian England the Public School played a major part in amalgamating the urban upper-middle classes—sprung from trade and industry—with the landed gentry, creating a common ethos for members of both the civil and the military establishment. With its cult of games-playing and the team spirit, its stress on good form, its cast-iron prohibition of those "things that are never done," the Public School helped to shape the British Army.

In theory, the British officer corps varied in birth and breeding. After 1871 gentlemen anxious to serve in the army could no longer purchase commissions. According to *The Army Book for the British Empire*, 50 percent of the officer candidates for the infantry and cavalry entered the army by open competition through the Royal

Military College at Sandhurst, 25 percent by competition from the militia, and the remaining 25 percent from various sources, most notably the universities and the colonial military forces.[13] Sandhurst therefore occupied a position of peculiar importance within the country's military establishment. The RMC—situated in a pleasant part of Berkshire a few miles from the railway station at Camberley, and one of the country's first professional training institutions—provided a military education of varying length for cadets seeking commissions in the infantry and the cavalry.* Academic standards were not high. Training took no account of technological advances, especially in the fields of weapons and logistics. The cadets, moreover, were never quite subjected to the Spartan regime that then prevailed at the Hauptkadettenanstalt at Lichterfelde in Germany. Nevertheless, Sandhurst was no picnic. The students were taught drill, musketry, equitation, gymnastics, tactics, military administration, and law. Entrants to Sandhurst, like those to all other English professional schools at the time, came largely from the propertied classes. Far from seeking exemption from military service for their sons, British middle-class and upper-middle-class fathers regarded commissioned service for the Crown as a privilege for their offspring—a form of social investment worth a good deal of money. They could generally afford, by one means or another, to give their sons a good general education, to pay the Sandhurst college fees (about £150 a year at the beginning of the twentieth century), and, since junior officers usually needed extra income, to supplement a subaltern's pay with an allowance, a subsidy that could range from £150 a year in one of the less distinguished infantry regiments to £600 or more in a smart cavalry regiment. In social terms, the British officer corps was thus fairly homogeneous, though by no means uniform—as was the British governing class as a whole.

Attendance at Sandhurst did perhaps make some difference in the selection of applicants for higher command, but was not essential for a successful military career. The British Army, moreover, was innocent

---

*"Gentleman cadets" destined for the Royal Artillery or the Royal Engineers took their instruction at the Royal Military Academy at Woolwich, not at Sandhurst. The course there was two years. Both institutions were small; hence students and instructors came to know one another reasonably well. (Woolwich had 200 cadets and Sandhurst 360 cadets in 1897.) The Staff College at Camberley, which was designed for the higher training of staff officers, accommodated 64 students. Courses took two years to complete. Graduates were entitled to place the letters "psc" after their names, but their prestige and standing in the army in no wise corresponded to that of German General Staff officers.

of the political and religious dissensions between Catholics and anti-clericals that played such an important part in the armed forces of the Third Republic. Some corps were clearly less prestigious than others; but there was no equivalent to the French Infanterie de Marine, whose officers were Republican in sympathy, anticlerical by conviction, lower class by origin, and self-consciously distinct from their colleagues in other branches. Most of the British officers simply looked on themselves as gentlemen. They belonged to a group neither commoner nor noble, but a social amalgam oriented toward the values of the squirearchy and drawn from a wide economic spectrum: the professions, business, the military, the civil service, and the land.

In terms of social origin a gentleman with a house in London and a small estate in Kent cannot easily be classed as rural or urban. Moreover, categories such as "aristocracy" and "middle class," employed in the tabulation below, are somewhat arbitrary, for the peerage tended to shade off into the gentry, and the gentry to merge into the higher strata of the upper middle class. Consequently, the following figures on the social status of British officers have more of an illustrative than a statistical value.[14]

Year	Aristocracy	Landed gentry	Middle class
1830	21%	32%	47%
1875	18	32	50
1912	9	32	59

In Great Britain, as in Germany, holders of aristocratic names preferred to join the Guards, the cavalry, or favored line regiments that often were the preserve of local aristocratic or gentry families; the social status of an English regiment was apt to rise with the proximity to London of its depot. Units like the Royal Engineers (highly qualified technicians), the Royal Marines, less favored line regiments—and above all, colonial constabularies—drew most of their officers from the middle class. They were usually sons of clergymen, civil servants, lawyers, merchants, or other army officers. Nevertheless, there was a certain amount of social mobility within the military, especially along the colonial frontiers.

The service conditions of a British regimental officer were superior to those of his colleagues in continental armies. Promotion came faster —a feature linked to the relatively small size of British formations, where companies were commanded by majors instead of captains as in Germany, and battalions by lieutenant-colonels instead of majors. By 1908 or so a British first lieutenant could expect to be promoted to the

TABLE 6

Average Annual Pay (Excluding Allowances) of British, French, and
German Infantry Officers, c. 1908

(In £)

Rank	British Army	French Army	German Army
Lieutenant-colonel	328	263	292
Major	248	224	292
Captain	210	139–200	150–195
First lieutenant	118	101–120	78
Second lieutenant	94	93	45–60

SOURCE: Encyclopaedia Britannica, 11th ed. (London, 1911), 20: 18.

rank of captain within seven to eight and a half years of his first commission, and to make major after fifteen to twenty years. In the Indian
Army, a subaltern was automatically promoted to captain after nine
years, and to major after fifteen to twenty. In the German Army at the
time, the senior Oberleutnant was normally thirty-seven to thirty-
eight years old, the senior captain forty-seven to forty-eight. A British
regimental officer also drew higher pay than his German and French
counterparts. (See Table 6.)

Still, as an instrument of social mobility, the British Army could in
no wise compare with the French Army, where something like one-
third of the commissioned officers had been promoted from the ranks.
The British ruling class did not look with a kindly eye on gentleman
rankers, sons of good families who had enlisted in order to escape from
the unwelcome attentions of creditors, police detectives, or ill-used
ladyloves. But for the high-spirited adventurer there was no disgrace
in enlisting as a trooper in, say, the Bechuanaland Border Police, a
crack unit where a young man could rapidly gain distinction. In fact,
some of the early muster rolls of the British South Africa Police—
formed in 1889 to safeguard the territories assigned to the British
South Africa Company north of the Limpopo—read like a membership
list of a good London club, with names like the Honorable Frederick
Rossmore Wauchope Eveleigh de Moleyns gracing their pages.

The frontier also provided opportunities for a few men of humble
degree to rise into society. One of these was William Bodle, a Sussex
man born in Alfriston, who began his military career by enlisting as a
lad in the Sherwood Foresters. Transferring to the 6th Inniskilling
Dragoons—a mounted regiment with a South African connection of
long standing—in order to fight the Zulu, Bodle saw a good deal of

action in various parts of Southern Africa and rose to the rank of regimental sergeant major (RSM) in the Bechuanaland Border Police. After the British occupation of Mashonaland (1890), he left the military for a time and became a storekeeper in the bush. Three years later the British South Africa Company decided to make war on the Ndebele, kinsmen of the Zulu, whose armies seemed to pose a constant threat to the northern outposts of the white settlement frontier in southern Africa. Bodle had made the right decision: the British South Africa Company needed experienced fighters, and his regimental connections with the 6th Inniskilling Dragoons proved invaluable.

Military transfers and promotions in the British colonial forces depended heavily on regimental and personal links, a sort of military "Old Boys" network. This was in considerable contrast to the German colonial forces, where careers hinged to some extent on links to the General Staff. Whereas regimental connections do not seem to have played much of a part in the staffing of the Schutztruppe in German East Africa, for example, they certainly accounted for the fact that three of the first five commandants of the British South Africa Police were drawn from the 6th Inniskilling Dragoons. Bodle was the third in the line. The Dragoons were not very intellectual chaps; they refused for many years to let their officers sit for staff college examinations. But they had a splendid fighting record, and they knew how to look after their own. Bodle obtained a commission as an inspector, and served in the Matabeleland campaign and in the Jameson Raid. A few years later he was elevated to the rank of commandant, a bluff, forceful man with a barrack-room manner, who continued to be known respectfully as "the RSM" even when he was a colonel. He retired from the force in 1909, rejoined the military in World War I, and ended as brigadier general in command of a brigade.

Bodle's career would not have found a parallel in the German Army

TABLE 7

Annual Average of Rankers Appointed to Commissions (Combatants Only), 1885–1908

Period	Average	Period	Average
1885–88	34 [a]	1899–1902	35 [b]
1889–92	25	1903–8	14
1893–98	19		

SOURCE: *Encyclopaedia Britannica*, 11th ed. (London, 1911), 20: 21.
    [a] Sudan War and other campaigns.   [b] South African War.

of the Wilhelmian era. Neither would there have been an equivalent for the checkered career of Valentine Baker (1827–89), brother of Sir Samuel Baker, the great African explorer. Valentine was born in Ensfield, England, the son of a wealthy merchant with great estates in Mauritius and Jamaica. After working for a time as a pioneer farmer in Ceylon, he joined the Ceylon Rifles as an ensign. From there he transferred to the 13th Lancers, and distinguished himself in both the Crimean War and the Kaffir War (1855–57). A man with a keen and incisive mind, Baker received rapid promotion and at forty-seven had become assistant quartermaster-general. Married to a squire's daughter, he appeared to be a happy man, destined for the highest military honors that his country could bestow. Then his life turned into a melodrama. In 1875 he was convicted of "indecently assaulting a young lady in a railway carriage."[15] He was sentenced to a year in jail and dismissed in disgrace from the army. A German officer would have been compelled by public opinion to blow his brains out. Baker instead joined the Turkish Army, where brilliant officers guilty of assaulting young ladies in railway carriages were not barred from promotion. He was made a pasha and a major general, and served with distinction in the Russo-Turkish War (1876–78); however, he never succeeded either in reestablishing his place in British society or in getting his name into *Who's Who*.

The ordinary colonial officer's career was less controversial. Given the great variety of British military, police, and constabulary units in the colonies, we have not attempted to trace the career of every commanding officer in these formations. But a study of the life stories of the various commandants and inspectors-general who were in charge of the King's African Rifles, the British South Africa Police, and the West African Frontier Force before World War I shows a fairly consistent pattern.[16] Except for Bodle, they were middle or upper-middle class in origin. Their fathers had been soldiers, or had made their way in the church or in the professions, including the civil service. They had joined the army by way of the Public School and Sandhurst (the path taken by Major-General Sir Reginald Hoskins, inspector-general of the King's African Rifles, 1913–15), or through the militia, or through Cambridge and Sandhurst (Brigadier-General Sir William Manning), or straight from a Public School (Brigadier-General George Hancock Thesiger—like Manning, a predecessor of Hoskins). Of the 14 officers whose biographical data—some of them incomplete—we have examined, at least three had gone to Harrow, one each to Eton, Charterhouse, and Westminster, and several more to minor Public

Schools. At least two had attended Oxford and Cambridge. (These figures represent the general situation in the British Army, whose officers, by the end of the nineteenth century, had come to be increasingly educated in the Public Schools.)

Before coming to Africa, most of these men had seen service in other parts of the empire, and some had undertaken administrative tasks besides soldiering. Major-General Sir Alfred Edwards, commandant-general of the Rhodesian forces 1912–23, had previously served as chief constable of the metropolitan police in London. A considerable number, especially of the inspectors-general of the West African Frontier Force, had seen service in India and were apt to feel especially at home in Northern Nigeria, where native princes ruled in splendor and where polo was a popular regimental game. As regards regimental antecedents, eight had been infantry officers (including four riflemen), five had been commissioned in mounted units (three Inniskilling Dragoons, one Dragoon Guardsman, and one Hussar), and one was an artilleryman. Ten of these men later attained the rank of general officer, and eight of these were knighted.

Hunting and shooting were among their recreations, and United Services among their clubs. Some wrote books with titles like *Some Experiences of an Old Bromsgrovian: Soldiering in Afghanistan, Egypt, and Uganda*, by Brigadier-General Trevor Ternan, a former commandant of the Uganda Rifles. Their politics were apt to be of the Tory-no-nonsense kind. For instance, Brigadier-General John Sanctuary Nicholson, an Old Harrovian and an ex-Hussar, returned to England after World War I and secured election to Parliament as a "Constitutional Independent Conservative—Anti-Waste."

By and large, they enjoyed war. As Winston Churchill put it, while still a subaltern serving on the Northwest Frontier of India:

I would that it were in my power to convey to the reader who has not had the fortune to live with troops on service some just appreciation of the compensations of war. The healthy open-air life, the vivid incidents, the excitement, the generous and cheery friendships, the chances of distinction which are open to all, invest life with keener interest, and rarer pleasures. The uncertainty and importance of the present reduce the past and future to comparative insignificance, and clear the mind of minor worries. And when all is over, memories remain which few men do not hold precious. As to the hardships, these though severe, may be endured. Besides all this, the chances of learning about the next world are infinitely greater.[17]

Without exception, they were a resilient lot. After patiently enduring the hardships of a Public School education at Bromsgrove, Ternan

was commissioned in the West Suffolks, and almost immediately sailed
to India in a small, 4,000-ton troopship into which more than 2,000
officers and men were squeezed. The subalterns were given berths in
what was known as the Pandemonium, a dark hole below the water-
line. On shipboard, the young officers were expected to maintain
discipline not only among the soldiers, but also among the soldiers'
wives. This was not an easy task, for the sights and language that
greeted the orderly officer on his rounds were of a kind that "do not
allow of adequate description in cold print. It is sufficient to say that
the heat, especially in the Red Sea, is undoubtedly very great, but
even that hardly seemed to warrant the habit some of the ladies acquired of entirely discarding any clothing whatever, and receiving the
blushing orderly officer and his embarrassed orderly sergeant in that
insufficient costume with hilarious mirth."[18]

Subsequent military service, for Ternan as well as for many others,
included tours of duty in Afghanistan and Egypt. Here he widened his
military experience by learning how to deal with mutinous soldiers,
dishonest payclerks, and hostile warriors of every description.

Whereas officers who joined the British South Africa Police tended
to stay in Rhodesia, the majority of those who signed up for units like
the Uganda Rifles and the West African Frontier Force probably
looked on their assignment as a step to promotion in other units.
Within the military hierarchy, the new African regiments were far less
prestigious than the Indian Army, a force that attracted many able
officers anxious to make their career overseas. The British South Africa
Police ranked the highest of all the African units. Service in the force
continued to appeal to well-born young men from "home," men who
by some mischance had failed to get into Sandhurst. These men often
looked on service in the ranks of a mounted body as a means of gaining
a commission in a highly trained, smart, well-mounted troop, and
of subsequently settling in a land of opportunity. In terms of prestige,
The King's African Rifles supposedly stood slightly higher than the
West African Frontier Force; East Africa was famed for its hunting and
West Africa for its fevers. Even so, Northern Nigeria attracted a substantial number of officers with Indian experience. Service with the
West African Frontier Force was regarded as a likely step to promotion
in the army as a whole, and also as a way for impecunious officers to
earn enough to pay off their debts.

The direct influence on the British Army of colonial regiments like
the West African Frontier Force was negligible. But the indirect impact of the colonies on the military establishment was considerable.

Only the Guards regiments were never posted abroad, other than to "home stations" like Gibraltar, Malta, and Egypt. A large number of officers belonging to other formations were wont to make a name for themselves along the outposts of empire in India, Afghanistan, the Gold Coast, or South Africa, and many of them later attained civil office, a metropolitan appointment, or a minor governorship. They included men like Lord Lugard, who began his African career in Nyasaland, and General Sir James Willcocks, a commandant of the West Africa Frontier Force, whose career culminated with a governorship in the Bermudas, a distinguished record in polo, and an honorary doctorate from Amherst College. Some acquired an academic reputation, as did Sir Charles Warren, the soldier who secured Bechuanaland for the British Crown. Warren, like so many other distinguished colonial soldiers, was a Royal Engineer. He was also a fine archaeologist, whose accomplishments included the first archaeological survey of the Holy Land. A few men attained national and even international fame.

One of the most influential of these campaigners was Sir Garnet Wolseley (1833–1913). Wolseley's personality does not appear to have been overattractive. Disraeli described him as an egotist and a braggart; others used even more scathing terms. But he was a true professional soldier, a man who contributed to military literature, who insisted on efficiency, accuracy, and organization.[19] "All Sir Garnet" deservedly became military slang for "all okay." Worst of all from the traditionalists' point of view, Wolseley believed in promotion by merit rather than by seniority. He cultivated the acquaintance of war correspondents, a tribe still considered socially unacceptable by the more old-fashioned, and he was an expert in logistics. Whereas his rival, Sir Frederick (later Lord) Roberts, appealed to Tories, Wolseley was the rising hope of the Liberals, who described him as "Our Only General." Still more shocking, he insisted that officers should appeal to the enlisted man's intelligence and sense of honor, that the army should emphasize welfare as well as discipline, and that its leaders should regard themselves as soldiers rather than as "officers and gentlemen."

Wolseley campaigned widely—in India, in the Crimea, in Egypt, in West Africa, and in South Africa, attaining every possible distinction until his mind became clouded by mental illness. His entourage included a devoted group of officers, many of whom subsequently attained prominent though not necessarily distinguished positions in the history of the British Army. The Wolseley ring included many trained staff officers, but its very existence reflected the difficulties engendered by the absence of a General Staff, and occasioned many charges of favoritism. Among his protégés were a number of able men who played a considerable part in developing irregular tactics on the frontier, though their record was often marred by later misfortunes of war. Sir George Colley, for example, a leader of great personal bravery, was defeated and killed by the Afrikaners in the battle of Majuba Hill (1881). Sir Redvers Buller made a name for himself in South Africa, where he commanded a mounted frontier unit composed of "British, Boers, and aliens," and taught his troopers to rely on the carbine rather than the saber. But Buller proved no match for the Boers. After a number of serious reverses, he was relieved of his command, and his career fizzled out. Colonel J. F. (later Major General Sir) Frederick Maurice was another member of the Wolseley ring whose military career ended badly. He was a prolific and able writer on military subjects, and one of the leading British military intellectuals of the period. But he came under a cloud in 1918, when he publicly denied the accuracy of certain ministerial statements regarding army matters. For this breach of discipline, he was retired from the army and spent out his days as a university professor and principal of a workingmen's college.

Lord Roberts, Wolseley's great rival and the center of another ring, was a man of considerable abilities. An excellent cavalry commander, he was popular among his men, and was selected as Buller's replacement in South Africa at a time when snobbish prejudice against officers of the Indian Army was still widespread within the metropolitan military establishment. In a private letter, Wolseley described him as a "cute, little jobbing showman" and "a snob as regards Dukes and Earls." But in South Africa Roberts proved he was no showman. He captured Pretoria, and in 1900 returned to England in triumph, long before the Boers had been overcome. He was apostrophized by Kipling, awarded a grant of £100,000 by Parliament, and given a peerage by the queen. As Earl Roberts of Kandahar, Pretoria, and Waterford, he briefly succeeded Wolseley as commander-in-chief until the abolition of the office in 1904. At the outbreak of World War I, Roberts was seventy-two years old. Eager to serve as ever, he again put on uniform, went to France, and died of a chill.

Commoners in Arms

British noncommissioned officers occupied both a more fortunate and a less desirable position than their German counterparts. Unlike

TABLE 8

Rates of Pay, Daily and Deferred, of Other Ranks, 1881–1884

Rank	Rate	Rank	Rate
Sergeant major	5s.	Corporal	1s. 10d.
Color sergeant	3s. 2d.	Drummer	1s. 3d.
Sergeant	2s. 6d.	Private	1s. 2d.

SOURCE: W. H. Goodenough and J. C. Dalton, comps., *The Army Book for the British Empire* (London, 1893), p. 149.

NOTE: Deferred pay was a proportion of the salary that was set aside as compulsory savings.

the German Army, the British Army made provision for a small quota of ranker officers, allowing a few sergeants and sergeants major to rise from the ranks each year. According to one source, between 1898 and 1902, 136 men (not counting quartermasters and riding masters) were appointed to commissions, an average of about 27 a year.[20] The *Encyclopaedia Britannica*, the source used for the figures shown in Table 7, gives a substantially higher average, but in any event both figures reflect a higher-than-normal promotion rate. As the table makes clear, the number of such promotions jumped substantially in a war situation.

A handful of these men achieved high rank; one of them, Sir William Robertson, even became a field marshal. But in general the path of a ranker officer was hard. Social prejudice apart, life in an officers' mess was apt to be expensive. Uniforms, entertaining, sporting, and social obligations involved a considerable outlay in fashionable regiments, though not in minor colonial constabularies. Officers were therefore well-advised to have private means. Shortly after the end of the Second Boer War, a witness told a commission that the army only wanted officers who could command from £150 to £1,500 a year.

From the financial standpoint, a senior noncommissioned officer was considerably better off than a young lieutenant without a private income and with a good deal of social and sartorial expense. In accepting a commission a sergeant major stood to take a sizable loss. First of all, he had to give up free food, clothing, and accommodation. On top of this, he earned a relatively decent salary—as much as 35s. a week in the 1880's (when a private made only a little over 8s; see Table 8). During the same period an agricultural worker in Durham earned about 18s. at the height of the summer season, a fitter in Tyneside about 31s., a mason in Liverpool about 36s. 8d., a printer in Glasgow about 32s. 6d., and a coal hewer in Lanark about 32s.[21]

Still, there was the future to think about. British NCOs suffered

certain retirement disabilities compared with their German counterparts. A retired sergeant in Germany was more likely to get a minor
civil service job than his British confrère. From 1893 onward, both the
British War Office and the Post Office began to give preference to
retired NCOs. Even so, many a former sergeant had to eke out his
pension by working as a commissionaire outside a London club or
hotel, a feature of military life not lost on Kipling. The situation described by Kipling and other reformers led to the creation of the Corps
of Commissionaires, which did much to raise the employment prospects of former warrant officers, who acquired a reputation as a lower-
middle-class "elite group" by reason of their employment with distinguished City banks.

In their educational attainments, most British NCO's likewise seem
to have suffered in comparison to their opposite numbers in the German Army, though not in the French. The British Army did not require any educational qualifications from recruits on enlistment. Only
the Royal Engineers and a few other specialist corps expected newcomers to know how to read and write. In 1870 an Act of Parliament
at last laid the groundwork for universal education in Great Britain.
The army introduced corresponding reforms, the military taking steps
to spread literacy within its ranks to equal the proficiency shown by
Prussian conscripts. Sergeants were expected to acquire a Second
Class certificate, and senior noncommissioned and warrant officers a
First Class certificate. But at the end of the nineteenth century most
British soldiers except for Scotsmen were still poorly schooled. "It cannot be doubted," two British experts concluded, "that the high reputation as soldiers, so deservedly enjoyed by Scotsmen, is largely due to
the fact that in Scotland education has been enforced on all classes for
more than two centuries, and that a wholly illiterate Scotsman is almost
unknown.[22] Scottish- and Ulster-born sergeants, like Scottish-born
missionaries and "artisan missionaries," thus seem to have played a
particularly important part in the training of Africans.

Both Marx and Kipling had praise for the British NCO. "The native
army, organized and trained by the British drill-sergeant, was the *sine
qua non* of Indian self-emancipation," wrote the German philoso-
pher.[23] A British noncommissioned officer could turn the Indians into
fighting men, said Kipling. The British sergeant's not-unsubstantial
part in colonial development and military history in fact remains to be
written. In the so-called native African units, there were almost as
many senior British NCOs as British officers. The Uganda Rifles at
the turn of the century, for instance, had 36 British officers and 21

British sergeants, against 1,952 African NCOs and men.* The European sergeants handled a great deal of regimental administration. They played an important part in training, and they were sometimes seconded to local constabularies. But British NCOs, unlike those in the German and Belgian armies, were but rarely called on to assume any responsibility in civil governance, a field normally reserved for ex officio gentlemen.

Seen as a whole, the British military cadres in Africa represented a peculiar combination, drawn from specialized segments of the gentry and the middle classes, as well as the petty bourgeoisie and upper-working-class of Great Britain. In terms of physical conquest, their achievement was astounding. The British occupied and held a vast empire with an outlay of European manpower hardly adequate to police a minor British city. To a considerable extent, their achievement depended on a superior military and civilian technology. But they primarily succeeded because of their organization, discipline, and cohesion, and because of that intangible factor of morale, the cement of armies and of states.

* In peacetime a British battalion on foreign duty had 1,011 men: 29 officers, a regimental sergeant major, 44 sergeants, 16 drummers, and 921 rank and filers.

FOUR

Military Organization and Campaigns

When the Germans and Belgians embarked on wars of conquest in Africa, they relied almost entirely on locally raised African troops commanded by European officers—the sole major exception being the great German campaign in South-West Africa, 1904–7. This reflected to a considerable degree the marginal nature of their colonial commitments in Africa. The British deployed their military forces in Africa in a far more extensive fashion. They used troops drawn from the mother country and from imperial dependencies in other parts of the world. They created local militias, both white and black. They raised regular forces in colonial territories, sometimes by private entrepreneurs but more often by colonial administrators. Viewed in sociological terms, the difference in strategy might be likened to a shift from migrant to local military labor, both white and black.

The Ashanti Campaign, 1873–1874

The use of European troops in the tropics was far from popular. Late-Victorian strategists generally condemned the use of white soldiers in rain forests and bush on the grounds that white men could neither brave a hostile climate nor withstand exotic diseases. But there were exceptions, such as the British campaign commanded by Sir Garnet Wolseley against the kingdom of Ashanti (Asante) in what is now the hinterland of Ghana (Gold Coast). Winwood Reade, author, traveler, and *Times* correspondent, covered the expedition, attached to the 42nd Foot Regiment (Black Watch), where he faced enemy fire and contracted dysentery. He returned home broken in health, though still well enough to tell *The Story of the Ashanti Campaign*, a book he published almost immediately, in 1874, that spared neither the policy of the cabinet nor the strategy of the army. But his views were unusual.

Wolseley was an immensely popular commander, even though his personal philosophy did not accord with the Nonconformist conscience. He had two great bugbears: one was inefficiency, the other monogamy in the tropics.

> I have always had the firmest conviction that as long as monogamy is insisted upon as a sine qua non, Christianity can never spread in any tropical countries. The best and some of the finest characters of whom we read in the Old Testament had many wives or concubines, and any attempt to put such a practice down in eastern countries will I am sure stop the spread of Christ's religion, for to be faithful to one woman all your life is against every instinct of human nature.[1]

He kept these views for his journal rather than for church parade. As regards his public image, the commander-in-chief ensured the historiographic aspect of his campaign with the same thoroughness that he devoted to logistics, health services, and press relations. Henry (later General Sir Henry) Brackenbury wrote *The Ashanti War*, the standard work on the subject; he was Wolseley's military secretary. Wolseley's private secretary, J. F. (later Major General Sir Frederick) Maurice, acted as special correspondent for the *London Daily News*, compiled a volume devoted to *The Ashanti War*, and co-authored a *Life of Lord Wolseley*.

Works written in such proximity with the commander-in-chief were not likely to diminish his reputation. But for all their sympathy with the British cause, these correspondents had a stirring tale to tell. By the standards of the West Coast, Ashanti was an important military power. Its armies were disciplined, its chiefs renowned in war, its arsenals well stocked with muskets, and its support services far better than in most African armies; the Ashanti even had their own corps of medical orderlies. Ashanti, however, had numerous weaknesses, too. It possessed neither artillery nor Gatling guns, modern weapons that the Ashanti musketeers could not have maintained even had they acquired them.

In a more general sense, Ashanti was apparently in a state of economic and political disorder—no doubt because much of its power had been built on the slave trade. The British had probably played the greatest role in Ashanti's decline by abolishing the slave traffic in the early nineteenth century. Following on this, the price of slaves had dropped sharply, and Ashanti purchasing power had diminished. An

increasing number of slaves were then used for human sacrifice—a
feature in Ashanti religion that outraged the British humanitarian conscience. But a more important issue between the British and the
Ashanti was the kingdom's claim to authority over the Fante states
along the coast, communities that in turn relied on the wavering and
uncertain protection of Great Britain. For the Ashanti, an occupation
of the Atlantic littoral seemed to promise many advantages. They
could trade directly with Europeans along the coast and lower their
costs by cutting out the Fante middlemen. The importation of firearms, restricted by the Fante for strategic reasons, would become
easier. The monarchy would be able to collect both tribute from the
Fante and ground rents from the British for the forts and castles they
occupied on the coast. Above all, the Ashanti were unwilling to accept
the Dutch sale of the important coastal city of Elmina to Great Britain
(1872). This transfer, as they saw it, would further weaken their already
shaky authority over the coastal regions. The British would have to
yield or depart.[2]

The British, however, were ready to take up the challenge and in-
vade the hinterland, a risky decision in the light of the problems posed
by tropical disease, a harsh climate, and a difficult terrain. Their assembled forces consisted of some African levies; the 2d battalion of
the Rifle Brigade, the 23d Royal Welsh Fusiliers, and the 42d Highlanders—about 2,500 whites in all; also units from the West India Regiment, as well as detachments of engineers, artillery, and auxiliary
services. Thousands of carriers supported the British effort. The British commissary estimated that they would need at least 8,500; 400 tons
of food were required to make up 30 days' ration for 6,500 men.

The campaign was launched in the fall of 1873. The British plan
of attack resembled the favorite Ashanti strategy of sending several
separate but coordinated columns against the enemy. The main body
under Wolseley comprised 1,509 whites and 708 blacks, a force that
advanced in a hollow square with the service personnel and two seven-
pounders in the center and two rocket projectors at each wing. This,
the famous British square—the best-known formation in British military history—was not square at all. It was an offensive and defensive
formation showing extra fronts to flanks and rear, and oddly resembled
the battle order of African warriors like the Meru of Mount Kenya,
whose cattle-raiding forces were formed in rough rectangles protected
by scouts.[3] It arose from the need to protect supplies and sometimes
wounded men, artillery, and carriers. When moving through the bush,
commanders often adopted the "elastic square"; this involved march-

ing with a strong, compact rear guard capable of closing up quickly, and with units in parallel columns on either flank, detailed to close into position and deploy at a given signal. The square was particularly useful for maintaining control over the troops and giving them the confidence and cohesion possessed by a compact group.

In theory, the Ashanti should have abandoned their capital, just as the Russians had relinquished Moscow to Napoleon. They might have relied on protracted guerrilla warfare, waiting until losses from disease and minor skirmishes had weakened the British Army, angered an economy-minded Treasury, and upset an equally parsimonious Parliament. But the Ashanti were convinced that they could not give up Kumasi, the political, administrative, and ritual center of their kingdom, without fighting—a decision that was to be paralleled in numerous other campaigns waged by West Africans against the whites. Instead, the Ashanti settled on a "spider-and-fly" strategy. Wolseley was to be lured into the interior, then held at a strong defensive position at Amoafo, a site designed to cover the capital, and cut off from the coast by convergent columns. Given the Ashanti's numerical superiority and their proficiency in fighting in the bush, where dense undergrowth diminished the British superiority in firepower, the Ashanti plan was not unreasonable. But it failed to work. With guns whose effective range was only some 50 yards, the Ashanti could make no reply to British rockets and the two seven-pounders. In the end, the battle of Amoafo cost the British relatively little in the way of casualties: four dead, 194 wounded. The number of Ashanti casualties, though never clearly established, was certainly many times higher. After hard marching and harder fighting, the British reached Kumasi— abandoned by its people and showing copious evidence of human sacrifice.

Wolseley was now anxious to return to the coast. Kumasi was largely destroyed. The rains had begun. The British wounded had to be carried back, and supplies were running out. The Ashanti were also in a parlous state. The fall of the capital had shaken the monarchy to its foundations, and the Ashanti finally signed a peace treaty at Fomena on 13 February 1874. They agreed to pay an indemnity (assessed at a figure so high that it could not be paid), vowed to stop human sacrifice (an essential feature of their religion), and promised to make far-reaching territorial concessions and to keep open the trade routes. For the time being, the Ashanti state fell into pieces, and Kofi Karikari, its king, was deposed. However, his successor, Mensa Bonu, was able to reassert Ashanti authority over some of the breakaway territories.

Even śo, Wolseley's achievement had been remarkable. His arrangements for health and supply services had been exceptionally efficient. Campaigning in one of the world's most insalubrious areas, the British lost no more than 55 soldiers from disease. There were no administrative breakdowns; there were none of the scandals that had marred the Crimean War. Honors were showered on him. He was made a Knight Grand Cross of the Order of St. Michael and St. George, and received the Knight Commandership of the Bath, a parliamentary vote of thanks, several honorary degrees, and a purse of £25,000. The bulk of the British forces engaged in the war returned to their respective home stations. Wolseley had proven that a British army—harried by heat and torrents of rain, insect bites and disease and enemy musketry, but properly supplied and well dosed with quinine—could march, fight, and win in the bush.

But Wolseley had not solved the Ashanti problem. A "force of intervention" drawn from afar failed to bring Ashanti permanently into the British orbit of empire, free trade, and humanitarian reform. The revival of Ashanti power, the expansion of French and German influence in the immediate vicinity of the Gold Coast, widespread dissidence among Ashanti's unwilling allies, and the inability of the British to force their social policies on the kingdom all helped to bring about a major shift in British policy. In 1896 another expedition occupied Kumasi.* The reigning Ashanti king was deposed. A serious rebellion was put down in 1900, and the next year Ashanti formally became a British protectorate.

Organization of the Black Colonial Forces

West Africa

Throughout most of the nineteenth century, the defense of local British interests on the West Coast depended on the Royal Navy, the West India Regiment—whose personnel were assumed to be more resistant to disease and cheaper to maintain than whites—and several small local forces. These included the Lagos Constabulary, composed originally of freed "Hausa" slaves (the term Hausa relating to a language group); the Sierra Leone Frontier Police, popularly known as the Frontiers, made up of Creoles, Mende, and Temne; and a constabulary raised by the Royal Niger Company. Other forces included

---

*This force, led by Sir Francis Scott, consisted of the 2d West India Regiment, the 2d West Yorkshire Regiment, 1,000 men of the Gold Coast Constabulary, and some irregular levies.

the Niger Coast Constabulary, composed primarily of Yoruba and Ibo and formed in 1893 for the defense of the Oil Rivers Protectorate, and the Gold Coast Constabulary, set up in 1879 with an initial complement of 16 whites and 1,203 Africans. In terms of size, none of these forces amounted to much: the Frontiers had only 17 officers, 23 NCOs, and 300 men. Their military prestige was small, and their reputation among Africans as employers apparently left much to be desired.

In 1897 Joseph Chamberlain, then two years into his tenure as colonial secretary, decided to put an end to this untidy arrangement. He took steps to raise a regular military force—the West African Frontier Force (familiarly known as the WAFF, pronounced "Woff").[4] The WAFF's immediate object was to cope with disturbances like the hut tax revolt of 1898 in Sierra Leone, a rising that caused special disquiet at a time when the Anglo-French dispute over the Niger was at its height, but the force had a wider imperial significance. It was intended also for general service in West Africa against an assumed French threat. Imperial strategists viewed Sierra Leone both as the key to the defense of British territory in West Africa and as a "strategic colony" in the imperial chain by reason of its importance as a coaling station. In the event of war, British seapower was expected to prevent a European opponent from supplying and reinforcing local African forces or using West Africa as a base for an attack against India. British maritime superiority would thus multiply the effectiveness of the WAFF many times over. But Chamberlain, for all his concern with the broader picture, clearly regarded West Africa as important in its own right, not merely as a bastion for the defense of the Indian empire; between 1897 and 1898 he was determined to fight the French over West African issues, if need be. The WAFF, though small, provided him with an indispensable military instrument.

Still, the WAFF had many weaknesses. It was in no sense of the word an army. Its highest officer was an inspector-general with limited powers, assisted by a small section in the Colonial Office. There was no colonial military department in London, and in 1910 a mere five officers were responsible for all the activities of the WAFF (and also of the King's African Rifles in East Africa). Given the WAFF's area of responsibility, which covered the most populous parts of West Africa, its size was unimpressive; all the more so since the French had a much larger force in West Africa, and France—rather than Germany—seemed to be the real enemy. But British seapower was supreme, and France could not have withstood a maritime challenge.

In 1901 the WAFF consisted of six battalions, divided into 45 com-

TABLE 9

Composition of the West African Frontier Force, 1901

Battalion number	Unit	Companies	Gun batteries (75 mm.)	Officers	Other ranks
1st and 2d	Northern Nigeria Regiment	16	2	54	2,400
3d	Southern Nigeria Regiment	8	2	38	1,250
4th	Gold Coast Regiment	12	2	35	1,657
5th	Sierra Leone Regiment	6	—	17	498
6th	Lagos Battalion	3	—	15	503

SOURCE: A. Haywood and F. A. S. Clarke, *The History of the Royal West African Frontier Force* (Aldershot, Eng., 1964).

panies and distributed as shown in Table 9. Like other British units, it had a high proportion of officers to enlisted men—159 to 6,308, roughly one officer for 39 men. As in other colonial units, the officers were British. So were most of the senior British NCOs, though there were a few "native officers" risen from the ranks and equivalent, to all intents and purposes, to senior warrant officers. The British, who did not enforce conscription at home, likewise relied on volunteers in their colonies—unlike the Belgians and the French—though they had no compunction about drafting carriers. Black soldiers in British uniform were not expected to perform as much construction work or fatigue duty as their colleagues in the service of the continental powers. But they probably spent more time on drill parade than the others put in at hard labor.

In recruiting their forces, the British were guided by their traditional respect for "martial races"; they relied mainly on backwoodsmen, most of them Muslims. The bulk of the Nigerian soldiers were either Hausa-speakers, some of them born in the French-controlled hinterland, or Yoruba. Initially the Nupe were also recruited in Nigeria, but they were later eliminated. The Kanuri were welcome recruits. So were the Ibo, who supplied most of the technicians and signallers and were the educational elite of the force. For many years, the WAFF maintained its predominantly Muslim character, especially after the Islamic emirates had become reconciled to British rule by Lord Lugard—who served also as the WAFF's first commandant. However, the religious composition of the force changed with the spread of education and the money economy after World War I; a large proportion of the Northern Nigeria Regiment then consisted of volunteers from the more backward, pagan communities of the Niger and Benue valleys and the hill country beyond. Muslim lords came to regard the regiment as an instrument of British domination, fit only for heathen and city laborers, and as an academy of drinking, whoring, and other practices repugnant to Islam.[5] The ethnic composition of the WAFF also changed over time, with the result that by 1914 the force was an ethnic mosaic. Hausa- and Yoruba-speakers, for instance, now accounted for only about one-half of the Northern Nigeria Regiment; the remainder were drawn from a great variety of ethnic groups. Each battalion was ethnically balanced in such a way that no single group would prevail in any one major unit. Yet the force attained a considerable degree of military cohesion.

Most African privates, like their opposite numbers in British regular regiments, came from the lowest strata of society. West African townsmen, a vociferous and politically conscious group, were only accepted into the WAFF during World War I, when the British had consolidated their authority to such an extent that they no longer considered urban Africans to be a threat to military discipline. Ashanti volunteers were likewise unwelcome to British recruiters, owing to the distrust prevalent among British administrators for the stubborn Ashanti resistance to conquest. Like their fellow colonialists, the British relied at first on ex-slaves, aliens in the land where they served, men who owed everything to the colonial forces that clothed them, fed them, paid them, protected them against their former masters, and often placed them in positions of power. African soldiers and policemen enjoyed considerable prestige among the uneducated. Literate Africans, however, were apt to despise the men in uniform. As the *West African Standard*, the mouthpiece of educated Africans, reported with some exaggeration:

From Ijebu to the further interior, there is one painful cry echoing from town to town, from city to city, of the evil deeds of the Lagos constabulary. Goods have been seized from traders; maidens have been assaulted, youths have been plundered; men have been browbeaten and women have been robbed. Neither the family altar nor the family hearth has escaped their daring. Travellers of all ages have suffered from their cupidity, avarice, rudeness and effrontery, and there has been none to deliver, none to redress.[6]

The supply of ex-slaves began to dry up by the end of the nineteenth century as slave-raiding and slave-trading were progressively eliminated. Ex-slaves, moreover, were prone to desert when they could. The British then tried to fill their local forces by inducing veterans to reenlist and by sending out recruiting teams into villages. The military authorities worked to improve the soldiers' diet; they paid better bonuses on enlistment; they arranged for wives to join their husbands on military posts. But they did not succeed in raising the social level of the colonial forces, which continued to be drawn primarily from the dregs of society. The colonial forces, on the other hand, began to instill a sense of professional pride and cohesion into these onetime outcasts. They also became an instrument of social advancement. On retirement, the more intelligent veterans were appointed government agents in the hinterland and thereby brought home to the villagers the shift from old to new values. Some recruits learned how to read and write in their own languages. Many had an elementary familiarity with the English language. Not surprisingly, the ex-soldier joined the graduate of the mission school in purveying the white man's ways.

In consolidating their colonial army and creating a new esprit de corps, the British—as was their wont—developed a most intricate and at times bizarre ceremonial designed to give color and dignity to an otherwise drab and often monotonous existence in the bush. It served also as a disciplinary device. The ordinary soldier may not have stood high in local prestige. But for the first time in his life he received regular pay and wore a uniform in which he learned to take pride. He acquired a spirit of regimental loyalty that successfully took the place of patriotism or political ideology.

The battalions adopted distinctive songs, crests, mess appointments, and unit flags. One marched to the tune of "The Lincolnshire Poacher," another to "The Orangeman," and still another to "La Paloma." The Sierra Leone Battalion favored "In South Carolina's Sunny Clime." For its unit emblem, the 5th Battalion took an antelope, the 6th a warthog. Some also kept living specimens of their crest; the 1st battalion, for instance, had a *burtu* bird as large as a turkey and reputedly able to eat knives, forks, and bicycle tires. To vary the routine of the officers' mess, various battalions developed formal "ordeals." In the 4th battalion newcomers dining for the first time at guest night had to climb to the top of the mess flagstaff and drink a bottle of beer hoisted up by the halyard.

Next to the colonel, the most important man in each battalion was the RSM, who much later came to be an African. He chided the subalterns, supervised the NCOs, and drilled the men. In the Sierra Leone Battalion he was responsible for teaching the men how to sing "God Save the Queen" and to recite the Lord's Prayer, a duty not thought to be in conflict with their profession of Islam. There were games aplenty. The British Army, no less than the Public Schools, promoted sports, and was instrumental in spreading British-style athletics to all corners of the Empire. And likewise the values that went with these sports. The British, for instance, considered the employment of magic in a sports competition unfair; as late as 1937 the programs for the annual regimental sports still confirmed in print that "any team of individuals displaying a juju, or anything purporting to be a juju, will be disqualified."

Ideally, the officers' existence correspond to the "club-polo-boy-fetch-whisky" image, nostalgically conjured up in Gilbert-and-Sullivan style by a British WAFF officer campaigning in East Africa in World War I:[7]

> Are you fond of your sport or a glass of old port,
> Or is it merely the spending of pennies
> Which will make you forget the bullets and wet,
> Would you sooner have cricket or tennis?
> You can get all these things, live richly like kings,
> Play your bridge, sing in quartet or solo,
> Kick a Rugby football, dance in the Club Hall,
> Or show off your prowess at polo.
> Disguised as a toff, you can sample the golf,
> To your hand you'll find ready each plaything;
> Quite peeled of your bark you may swim about stark,
> Or when draped, take a turn at mixed bathing;
> And when those are over, return to your clover,
> In which at the Club you're residing;
> Gossip on the verandah or go and philander,
> The war and its worries deriding.

But the realities of service in the bush differed greatly from the stereotype. Life was hard. Accommodation in bush houses, fashioned of mud with grass roofs and with matting "doors" and "windows," was crude and unhealthy. Despite the lessons taught by the Wolseley campaign, the West African Frontier Force continued to suffer from sickness, especially from malaria and blackwater fever. As an official report stated drily, "Timber for hutting had to be used to a great extent for making coffins."*

---

*A. Haywood and F. A. S. Clarke, *The History of the Royal West African Frontier Force* (Aldershot, Eng., 1964), p. 39. In Lagos in 1896, 28 of the 150 whites in service died within a few months. By 1926 the regular use of quinine and improved accommodation had vastly improved health conditions, with the result that only 42 of an estimated 5,000 whites in Nigeria died in one year.

The high initial rate of sickness was, to some extent, a symptom of over-lenient regimental management. Unpleasant though the side effects of quinine might be, patients on sick parade could have been put up on charges by their company commanders for failing to take their regular dose as a prophylactic. But there were other and more serious weaknesses. The WAFF early was subject to indiscipline. In 1900, for instance, a mutiny broke out among troops serving on the Gold Coast, and 150 armed men set out from Cape Coast to Sierra Leone, plundering where they went. The mutiny was finally put down by a detachment of the Central Africa Regiment, which trapped the mutineers against impenetrable marshes and cut off their retreat.

To some extent, lack of discipline was a reflection on the officers, who varied in quality. Most of the WAFF commanding officers were transfers from the regular army, and included men of the caliber of Hugh Montague (later Viscount) Trenchard—who was quite unlike the stereotype of the pukka sahib. The son of a bankrupt businessman, Trenchard's formal education left much to be desired, and he barely passed his army entrance examination. But "Boom," as he was called, was tough, powerful, and a natural leader of men. He served with distinction during the South African War, first with the Bushmen Corps of the Imperial Yeomanry and later with the Canadian Scouts. He recovered from serious wounds, and was subsequently posted to West Africa, where he became commandant of the Southern Nigeria Regiment of the WAFF. As was the case with many British officers, his colonial service proved a starting point for a distinguished career. During World War I he was an outstanding airman; he was the founder and later chief of staff of the Royal Air Force, and one of the most uncompromising advocates of independent air power. He was equally versatile in his civilian abilities. At the king's urging, he served for a time as commissioner of the metropolitan police. He was also appointed chairman of the United Africa Company and a director of Goodyear's British subsidiary. But for all these connections, he was nevertheless able to sympathize with the Labour Party and the trade unions, organizations that did not regard his Royal Air Force as a military upstart, redolent of grease and petrol, in the manner affected by some of the tradition-minded soldiers.

In the first years of the WAFF many of the junior officers were not up to their task. The force initially contained a high proportion of men who had been commissioned in the militia and had advanced through local West African constabularies, with the result that they were inadequately trained for the military profession. However, the officer corps was not short of volunteers. Service in the WAFF gave junior lieutenants a chance to take part in a "scrap" and to escape from the boredom of life in home garrisons, with its frequent tours of duty as orderly officers. In Africa officers had a "bush allowance," some chance of promotion to "local" rank, and many opportunities for polo, racing, shooting, and fishing. On paper, at any rate, the pay looked excellent. (See Table 10.) A lieutenant in the WAFF made between £300 and £350 a year, about three times as much as his brother officer at home or—to give a civilian equivalent—three times as much as the resident medical superintendent in a big London hospital.

Service abroad was equally popular among the more venturesome kind of British NCO. A regimental sergeant major in the WAFF earned nearly as much as a captain in a metropolitan unit, and his length of service in West Africa counted for double. Servants and food were cheap. The only officers weighed down by serious financial problems were married men—especially subalterns—with children to educate. "Lieutenants can't marry," said an army adage. "Captains may marry, majors should marry, colonels must marry," for a colonel's lady was a social asset, but a lieutenant's wife was a financial encumbrance as well as an occasional embarrassment. Nevertheless, a job in the colonies seemed attractive to many a poorer officer without an income of his own. The WAFF thus attracted applicants from many regiments of the line, who came to regard the force as a new home.

Ordinary African soldiers were firmly integrated into this stratified society. But they had much more personal freedom than the British privates of the Home Army. The troops fed themselves, receiving "chop money" each week in addition to their monthly pay. All African soldiers except recruits had wives in barracks, who cooked for their husbands and swept the huts and the company grounds. Each company had its headwoman, the *magajia*—responsible for the cleanliness of the barracks and for the dress, deportment, and morals of the wives. The headwoman attended on company "request day," when grievances and suggestions could be aired. Sporting a red sash, she accompanied officers on their inspection rounds, and when matters did not come up to her expectations, her wrath was more fearsome than the RSM's.

For its armament, the WAFF relied on light weapons. These included a small number of Maxims—at most one per company.* It

---

*Machine guns were first used by the British Army in the Zulu war of 1879. The British then employed the multi-barreled Gatling, heavy, cumbrous, and apt to jam. In 1889 Sir Hiram Maxim invented a new weapon in which the recoil caused by the explosion was used to load, fire, and eject the next shot. The Maxim began to be used

TABLE 10

Comparative Annual Salaries of European Military and Civil Officers (Including Duty Pay), 1909

(In £)

West African Frontier Force	
Lt. colonel (commandant, Southern Nigeria Regiment)	900 (+156)
Major	600 (+96)
Captain	400 (+46)
Lieutenant	300–350
Regimental sergeant major	156 (+36)
Sergeant (1st rating)	120 (+24)
King's African Rifles	
Lt. colonel (commandant, Uganda Battalion)	700 (+144)
Captain (company commander)	400 (+48)
Lieutenant	325–350
Regimental sergeant major	156 (+36)

WEST AFRICA	
Southern Nigeria civil administration	
Provincial commissioner	1,000–1,200 (+200/240)
Assistant provincial commissioner	600–900 (+140/240)
District commissioner (1st grade)	500–600 (+100)
Assistant district commissioner	300–400
European chief clerk	250–300
Wharf inspector (Traffic Dept.)	200–250
EAST AFRICA	
Uganda civil administration	
Provincial commissioner	600–700
District commissioner	400–500
Assistant district commissioner	250–350
Clerk-storeskeeper (Survey Dept.)	180
Overseer (Cotton Dept.)	150

SOURCE: *Colonial Office List, 1910.*
NOTE: Figures in parentheses denote duty pay.

also had a small artillery force (equipped at first with seven-pounders and later with 2.95 mountain guns). The men initially carried antique carbines (replaced in time with Lee-Enfield .303 magazine rifles). Withal, the WAFF was one of the most hard-worked forces in the empire. Up to nearly the outbreak of World War I, the force was consistently engaged in some action or another. It was burdened especially by the numerous small campaigns occasioned by Sir Frederick Lugard's military-minded and aggressive approach to British rule in Northern Nigeria. His policy reflected his military ambitions, and differed considerably from the more pacific traditions of the Lagos Protectorate administration.

At first, standards of bush fighting were low. Until the beginning of the twentiety century, the British normally advanced in single file along a path, headed by an advance guard but with no troops deployed in the bush. Whenever the column encountered opposition, sections turned right and left, firing blindly into the thicket, where their shots were not likely to hit a target. A determined enemy would rely on defensive positions made up of stockades built of logs six feet high, backed sometimes with rocks and boulders three to four feet thick. These entrenched positions were held by musketeers with "Dane" guns (cheap imported muskets). Dense smoke, caused by the damp atmosphere of the thick undergrowth and bush fires, prevented the combatants from seeing more than a few yards. The seven-pounders and Maxims would be fired at the point from which the greatest volume of noise proceeded. The enemy would advance again, firing volleys. This procedure continued until the enemy had enough, but generally occasioned few losses to the enemy and numerous casualties to the British, as well as prodigious expenditure on ammunition and heavy dependence on carriers.

During the Ashanti campaign of 1900 bush warfare tactics were considerably improved. A line of scouts from each company was deployed on each side of the path. Men worked in pairs, the leader of the file using his machete to cut a path forward while the rear man of the file kept his rifle ready for defense. The column kept in touch with the two files next to the path. The art of reconnoitering improved, so that

---

in the British Army about 1891, but became a standard weapon only in 1894. It was employed in Ashanti, in Matabeleland, in the Sudan, and on the Northwest Frontier of India. Conventional officers long regarded it as suited mainly for stopping sudden rushes of tribal warriors. A good deal of prejudice continued against its use in regular warfare, with the result that the British Expeditionary Force that took to the field in 1914 was quite inadequately equipped with automatic infantry weapons.

columns no longer stumbled unaware on enemy stockades. In addition, long vulnerable columns were broken into self-supporting sections, with carriers marching in closed ranks to prevent their deserting or falling into enemy hands. In Nigeria, as everywhere else in Africa, the porter became the linchpin of the army; in a rough average, about two to three porters were required to support one rifleman.*

Against Fulani horsemen in the north, on the other hand, the British continued to use the square formation. In actions such as the Kano-Sokoto expedition of 1903, the British once again learned that cavalry charges against steady infantry well-supplied with firearms were useless—as ineffective in the Nigerian savanna as on the South African veld. By 1914 the WAFF had been transformed from a colonial backwoods force to an efficient unit capable of participating in operations against a European enemy. Nevertheless, its fighting proficiency probably never quite matched the level of the French or German colonial forces. The WAFF made less use of automatic fire than the East African Schutztruppe. It did not carry out many successful night operations. This weakness reflected to some extent a lack of reliable intelligence and trustworthy local guides.

East and Central Africa

Military developments in East Africa in some ways resembled those of West Africa. In the early stages of empire building, British leaders drew heavily on indigenous methods of organization and warfare. There was the same initial reliance on scratch forces—undisciplined and sometimes mutinous—that were ultimately turned into highly structured constabularies. Specialized labor migrants, Indians and Sudanese, played the same essential role as the Hausa in West Africa, stiffening the pioneer units until they could be replaced by local men at a cheaper rate of pay. In East as well as West Africa some of the earliest wage laborers were soldiers. The military forces were among the first employers forced to cope with labor unrest, strikes, and armed violence—or mutinies as they were uniformly termed by the men in charge. Finally there was the same process of military rationalization and consolidation, leading to the creation of a unified multi-battalion regimental structure extending over several territories. There was a good deal of violence, which was linked to the far-flung struggle against the Swahili-speaking freebooters, slave traders, and ivory

---

*Thanks to the use of carriers, the British West African formations were the most mobile of all the units deployed in the hilly jungle country of Burma in World War II, and when they were supplied by air, among the most flexible.

hunters who were penetrating inland from the coast. Violence came to be associated also with European settlement, which set up its own tensions along a new settlers' frontier in the highlands of Kenya, where white colonists, Masai, and Nandi came to blows.

In British Central Africa the first British-controlled force was raised by the African Lakes Company, which soon after its formation in 1878 became involved in local politics, and clashed with the Swahili-speaking ("Arab") slave traders ensconced in fortified stockades along the north end of Lake Nyasa. The Lakes Company relied on two local African allies, the Nkonde and the Mambwe, which supplied levies in exchange for spoils of captured ivory and gunpowder. But despite assistance from Lugard, the company could not at first make any serious impression on the well-armed Arabs. In addition, the British had to contend with warlike Yao communities. To the Yao, the trade in captives and elephant tusks was the main means of securing guns, cloth, and beads from the Arabs, and raiding for slaves was closely linked to internecine warfare between the petty Yao chiefs. The commerce in men was associated also with the constant search for new land on the part of expanding Yao groups, and with their institution of domestic bondage. They were well armed with muskets and fought skillfully from behind cover. But they would not cooperate among themselves. Moreover, they were menaced by hostile local Nyanja communities, many of whom sided with the British.

Yet Yao fighting men, once defeated, were all too willing to enlist in the British service. The instrument of their defeat was Harry Johnston, the first British commissioner of the Central African Protectorate, who recruited Makua and Zanzibari mercenaries to that end. He also called in Sikh troops from India, cheaper to employ and better able to stand the climate than whites, but more disciplined than African levies. Gunboats supplied by the Admiralty enabled Johnston to interrupt the enemy's seaborne communications, to interefere with his trade, to being rapid concentrations of troops to press the attack on various points of the lake's shore, and to avoid marching through difficult country around much of the lake. By 1896 the area had been more or less subdued. The protectorate's forces then consisted of nine British officers and one British sergeant major, 180 Sikhs, and about 1,000 African *askaris* (professional fighting men), armed porters, and policemen. The following year saw a reorganization of the British forces—known as the Central Africa Rifles, later the Central Africa Regiment—into six locally recruited companies of 120 men each: three Tonga, two Yao, and one Marimba. The British subsequently phased out the Sikhs, fearing that the high rates of pay for African service would interfere with recruiting for the Indian Army, and especially after the Indian government began voicing its objections to the frequent requests for troops to serve in Africa.[8] Thereafter, the protectorate relied exclusively on locally enlisted men, who were paid at the rate of 5s. a month plus food and accommodation, the remuneration normally paid to an unskilled plantation worker. Nyasaland, by this time, was becoming a major exporter of labor to the Rhodesias and South Africa. Its own wage economy was restricted by a lack of natural resources, a lack of transport, and a small European economic base —limited mainly to coffee and later tea plantations in the southern highlands. The Central Africa Regiment therefore had little difficulty in recruiting soldiers for a second battalion, raised in 1899 specifically for service abroad.

The Uganda Rifles had as checkered an origin as the forces in Central Africa. In 1890 Lugard arrived in the kingdom of Buganda, having taken service with the Imperial British East Africa Company. The country was then on the verge of civil war between hostile factions, each using a religious designation—Muslim, Catholic, or Protestant—in the struggle for power within the kingdom. Lugard's force consisted of a handful of Sudanese, Swahili, and Somali mercenaries. Supported by a great mass of Baganda levies, he defeated the Muslim faction and his Baganda allies dispersed.

Lugard's force was more like a slave trader's levy than an army. Most of the original Sudanese in fact came from the north. But their ranks were constantly thinned by campaigning in the service of Emin Pasha, the governor of the Sudan, and they were replaced by recruits drawn from many communities. As a result the term Sudanese became as much a generic name in Central Africa as Hausa was in West Africa (or as the Swede was in the Thirty Years' War in Germany). In any event the employment of the true Sudanese entailed many risks. They were accompanied by their families and followers, whose rapacity became a byword.

Sudanese officers, self-appointed leaders risen from the ranks, had no personal loyalty to the British, and together with their men developed many grievances. Their pay ranged from 5s. 4d. a month for a private to £4 5s. for an officer—as compared with 20s. paid to a private by the Germans in East Africa. In most districts, moreover, wages were issued not in cash but in cloth, an expensive and uncertain form of payment, owing to wastage from theft, loss, and damage in transit and to the fluctuations in its value. Since transport was primitive and dependent on porters, trade goods and rations for the troops were often in short supply. Most of the British officers seconded to the Sudanese had no experience in handling African soldiers. Many of them remained for only one tour, and few made any attempt to learn their language. The troops were incensed at field service that called for long periods away from their wives and families. Being the only trained troops in the country, they felt that they had little to fear if they took the law into their own hands.

In 1897 the Sudanese mutinied. There was a drawn-out engagement between the rebels (some 600 Sudanese led by experienced Sudanese officers, plus 200 Baganda Muslims) and the government forces (10 Europeans, 17 Sikhs, and 340 half-trained Zanzibaris). The mutineers failed to overrun the government's defensive position and fell back. More sepoys arrived from India, and the Europeans now took the offensive against the insurgents, who had built up their own stations, were well organized in companies and under strict discipline, and had the cooperation of some of the surrounding communities—especially the Lango. The British created a field force of four companies, supported by Baganda, Acholi, Madi, and Bari levies. Flying columns combed the Lango country and seized the enemy's cattle, goats, and sheep. The troops lived precariously on captured beasts and sweet potatoes grubbed from African tillers, always moving by forced marches and continuously searching the dense bush, until the mutineers were destroyed.

Other campaigns of the Uganda Rifles entailed operations against more primitive peoples, such as the Nandi, expert bowmen who, though they could not easily hit an individual target straight on at much over 30 yards, were able to inflict heavy casualties from three times that distance by using a high trajectory. The Nandi operated out of fortifieds caves, which sheltered cattle as well as men. The British enlisted Masai auxiliaries to help root them out. From a central base camp, flying columns consisting of about 40 Uganda Rifles and 100 Masai spearmen traversed the wooded hills and valleys of Nandi country. The Masai acted as a screen and did particularly well in attacking cave strongholds, their bodies protected from arrows by their hide shields, and full of confidence as long as they were supported by rifle fire. Again economic pressure did its work. The Masai-British columns captured cattle, seized grain stores, and finally reduced the Nandi to obedience.

The Uganda Rifles were also called on to cope with mounted opponents—Somali warriors in the drought-ridden Jubaland province of

TABLE 11

Composition of the King's African Rifles, 1902

Battalion number	Area	Companies
1st	Central Africa	8
2d	Central Africa	6
3d	East Africa	8 [a]
4th	Uganda	9
5th	Uganda	4

SOURCE: Hubert Moyse-Bartlett, *The King's African Rifles: A Study in the Military History of East and Central Africa, 1890–1945* (Aldershot, Eng., 1956).
[a] Includes one camel company.

East Africa, where the British employed a specially raised camel company, as well as Indian units, in order to repress raids and intertribal disputes.

In 1902 the three existing units—the Central Africa Regiment, the East Africa Rifles, and the Uganda Rifles—were amalgamated into a single regiment known as the King's African Rifles (KAR, administered initially by the Foreign Office, then put under the authority of the Colonial Office and supervised by an inspector-general), which was responsible for the defense of British East Africa, Uganda, and the Central Africa Protectorate. Northern Rhodesia, administered by the British South Africa Company, was outside the KAR's purview, the British pax there being enforced first by the Northern Rhodesia police, and then, in 1912, by the Northern Rhodesia Regiment. The KAR was armed with .303 rifles and also had a few seven-pounders, plus some Hotchkiss and Maxim guns. Initially, the force consisted of five battalions, with 35 companies in all, manned by 104 officers and 4,597 African other ranks. (See Table 11.) The imperial government and the settlers alike, however, pressed for a reduction of this force on the grounds that "the tribes were peaceful" and taxes should be diminished. By 1911 the KAR thus amounted to no more than three battalions—17 companies—almost a negligible force, given the area of its responsibilities.

The KAR at first was not the kind of unit in which a conscientious officer liked to serve. Richard Meinertzhagen arrived in Kenya to join it in 1902. Meinertzhagen was an unusual man, an Old Harrovian, who later made a name for himself in guerrilla warfare, Zionist politics, and the study of birds—and he was far from squeamish. But he was shocked by what he saw. His men were infested with lice, their uniforms greasy with dirt, their rifles corroded by rust. They were sullen, their discipline brutal. An askari who had saluted so smartly that the officer to whom the courtesy had been addressed was flung off his horse received ten lashes with a rhino whip. A second, found in bed with the sergeant major's wife, got 20; and a third was sentenced to 25 for calling his sergeant's mother and father a crocodile and a hyena, respectively.[9] If Meinertzhagen is to be believed, the officers were a sorry bunch. One drank himself into a stupor every night. Another preferred boys to women for his pleasure. Some brought their African mistresses into the mess. Most were heavily in debt. Meinertzhagen, and others like him, determined to improve regimental management. To a considerable extent they succeeded, as shown by the fine performance of the KAR against the Germans in World War I.

Still, when it came to native warfare, Meinertzhagen's methods in these years of conquest differed little from those of his opponents. On one occasion a newly appointed and inexperienced district officer sent an African policeman into a village to arrest the headman over some theft. But the policeman unfortunately arrived at the village in the middle of a festive ceremony, and unable to speak a word of Kikuyu, threatened the headman with a loaded gun, whereupon the villagers killed him. Meinertzhagen determined on quick action lest delay be taken as a sign of weakness. At night a spy reported that the population of several villages had joined in an orgiastic celebration around the mutilated corpse, and intended later to attack Fort Hall, a British station. A half-hour before drawn Meinertzhagen surrounded the village with 20 soldiers and 20 policemen. Bonfires were blazing, and by their light he could distinguish warriors dancing themselves into a state of frenzy. His men charged, one volley alone killing 17 Kikuyu. The British party combed the whole area, burned all the huts, seized the sheep and the goats, and killed every villager who still showed any fight. By early afternoon about 30 warriors lay dead. "So," Meinertzhagen wrote in his diary that night, "order once more reigns in the Kenya District."[10]

Meinertzhagen took even more rigorous action when some Kikuyu caught a European settler on his way to buy sheep, pegged the unfortunate man to the ground, and drowned him by wedging open his mouth and urinating into it. In reprisal, Meinertzhagen cordoned off the offenders' village at night and ordered his men to kill all but the children. His troops bayoneted every living soul, including grandmothers. The colonel, it might be added, felt no special resentment against the Kikuyu as a people. A well-educated, highly literate man, and a nephew of Beatrice Webb to boot, he was acquainted with enlightened opinion in England. Personally, he considered that the Kikuyu, being first-comers, had a better right to the land than white immigrants. But Meinertzhagen was a soldier; he was convinced that peace could be enforced only by toughness. Given the tremendous numerical disparity between the British and Kikuyu forces in an area where three white men, with 70 black soldiers and policemen, were responsible for the security of a region as big as Yorkshire, armed force—he thought—would have to be employed to the hilt. And this he did.

Settlers in Arms

European settlers never came to West Africa. British East Africa (later known as Kenya) came to be regarded as a "white man's country"; but even there the settlers never attained political sovereignty. Rhodesia followed a different pattern. When Rhodes decided to occupy Mashonaland, he had three main considerations. He wished to build a new British community in the interior that would cut off the Transvaal from its hinterland and ensure a British balance of power against the Afrikaner republics in a future South African federation. He believed also that a second Rand lay buried beneath the northern veld, and hoped that its wealth would finance his colonizing ventures. Third, he was bent on spreading British middle-class civilization and doing away with the independent native polities of the interior, either by peaceful penetration or by force of arms.

Rhodes entrusted the venture to Frank Johnson, a twenty-four-year-old prospector with extensive experience of the north and a sound background of service in various colonial mounted units and in the Bechuanaland Border Police. The undertaking rested on a commercial contract whereby Johnson pledged to organize a Pioneer Corps on semi-military lines in return for a fee of £87,500 (later increased to £90,400) and a land grant beyond the Limpopo River. Johnson's men were highly paid, and included doctors, lawyers, and stockbrokers, as well as miners and farmers, butchers and builders—the idea being to create the nucleus of a self-sustaining civilian community. The corps contained a considerable percentage of young volunteers of good social standing. Sons of peers served next to cowpunchers; clerks mingled with prospectors; and one troop was known as the gentlemanly troop because the majority were brokers.

A large proportion of the men hailed from the South African Cape, from Cape Town, Kimberley, or the Eastern Province; and throughout its formative years, the new white community remained closely linked to the Cape. Rhodes, in fact, apparently discouraged Johnson from collecting any of the retired and highly trained veterans of the colonial military units; he insisted instead that the recruits should include sons of leading Cape families. Johnson at first could not understand Rhodes's reasons, but his inquiry elicited an answer wholly in keeping with Rhodes's strange mixture of realism, cynicism, and gambling instincts. The Ndebele might cut off or massacre the expedition. What could then save the pioneers? Only imperial intervention. How could this be ensured? Only by agitation on the part of worried and well-connected fathers in the Cape.[11]

Johnson originally intended to advance without a secure base or properly guarded lines of communication. Instead, the force would carry supplies and ammunition for a year, and would rely on careful training and discipline. The high commissioner for South Africa, however, would not hear of such a scheme. He insisted that the force must be accompanied by a strong body of mounted police in order to prevent a repetition of the 1879 disaster at Isandhlwana, so the British South Africa Company rather unwillingly organized a mounted force. Its nucleus, one-fifth of its strength, consisted of a few specially recruited transfers from the Bechuanaland Border Police. The remainder was a mixed body—young men in search of adventure, a few scalawags, but generally a good type of man, similar in social origin to the pioneers, though not so well paid.[12]

The expedition that set out in June 1890 was made up of some 180 members of Johnson's Pioneer Corps and 500 members of the British South Africa Police. The command of the combined force was entrusted to Lieutenant-Colonel Edward Graham Pennefather, an officer of the 6th Dragoons who had served against the Zulu and the Boers. His column was well equipped, the expedition curiously combining the military technology of the backveld with that of the Industrial Revolution. There were ox-wagons and Maxim guns. There was also a steam-driven generator to provide current for a searchlight that swept the veld at night to prevent surprise attacks. Johnson, a good organizer, carefully worked out an elaborate drill for his 84 wagons, which were grouped into three divisions; and the teams were taught to maneuver with military precision and to advance where possible in broad formations. Single file was used only where the terrain made it necessary. There were carefully worked-out rules for making camp at night. Depending on the nature of the ground, the wagons drew up in one, two, or three separate laagers, with the water carts and other light rolling stock inside and machine guns or seven-pounders at each corner, protected by proper breastworks of sandbags.

The Ndebele's only chance would have been to catch the column by surprise in broken country or in a night assault, but Lobengula—though he had over 17,000 warriors—realized the difficulty of such a task, and allowed the column to proceed without striking a blow. The pioneers safely reached their destination on 12 September 1890, where a small fort—Fort Salisbury—was built. They then dispersed to look for the promised Ophir.

The early settlers formed a kind of armed aristocracy among the indigenous people, making a scanty livelihood from prospecting, transport contracting, and share-pushing. They knew how to ride and shoot, and they knew the veld; and the British South Africa Company, always intent on economy, though that the colonists would be well able to look after themselves in local clashes with Africans. The directors resented expenditure on the British South Africa Police, an efficient military body well adapted to irregular mounted warfare. They wanted profits rather than war, and in 1892 the force was cut to the bone, defense of the country largely being left to the colonists, who were organized into a volunteer force and supported by a small troop of artillery stationed at Salisbury. In case of emergency these units could be supplemented by a burgher force of some 1,500 men, liable to serve under their field cornets in time of war, a system copied from the Boers and one well suited to frontier conditions. The citizen-soldiers proved their worth when fighting broke out against Lobengula in 1893.

The chartered administration did not originally want war, hoping slowly to erode the Ndebele's social system by getting them to serve for wages; but the Ndebele tried to maintain their warrior state and persisted in raiding parts of Mashonaland. Local settlers, especially in the Fort Victoria region, were set on ending the Ndebele forays, which were interfering with their African labor and bringing economic enterprise to a halt. The Ndebele state, for its part, was geared to war and could not readjust its social institutions, even though Lobengula was anxious to maintain peace.

In 1893 war broke out. The Ndebele could mobilize some 12,500 men to face the colonists. Their fighting men, divided into regiments and well disciplined, were armed with spears, ox-hide shields, and knobkerries. In addition, they had at least 1,000 Martini-Henry rifles. Ndebele riflemen, however, did not know how to maintain firearms and were poor shots. Ndebele spearmen proved no match for mounted burghers with superior firepower and mobility, for they were unable to tear themselves away from the time-honored shock tactics that had secured them so many victories in the past. They remained wedded to a military doctrine that attack must invariably prevail over defense.[13] The settlers, led by Leander Starr Jameson, fielded a force of about 1,100 men and successfully employed the Maxim gun, an automatic weapon that more conventional soldiers tended to underestimate. The tactical use of wagons as mobile pivots gave the settlers an additional advantage, and after a few fierce and bloody battles the Ndebele "spear kingdom" rapidly collapsed, much to the surprise of the more orthodox military men, who thought that far more white troops would be required.

The settlers could conquer a country, but they lacked the means to consolidate their gains. A weak and undifferentiated backveld economy failed to yield the expected profits. Administration remained a scratch affair, oppressive and inefficient. Intelligence was almost nonexistent. The rigid social separation between whites and blacks probably helped to prevent information from seeping through to the authorities. Moreover, the British South Africa Company's constant need to economize, coupled with the colonists' overconfidence, precluded the maintenance of an effective defense organization. Most of the mounted police, the country's only full-time military cadre, were withdrawn for service in the disastrous Jameson Raid of December 1895, and in March 1896 the Ndebele seized their chance and struck. Many—though by no means all—of the Shona communities subsequently joined the insurgents. Others decided to sit on the fence or support the whites, the military politics of the rebellion being determined, in some degree, by existing precolonial cleavages. The organization of the rising hinged partly on the remnants of the Ndebele state organization, partly on pre-existing chieftainships, and partly on the fraternity of spirit mediums who supposedly voiced the wishes of tribal deities and ancestors. The rebels murdered many isolated settlers, avoided pitched battles, and stuck to guerrilla tactics. This time, the colonists found themselves with their backs to the wall.

The rebels outnumbered their opponents by almost seven to one. Many possessed firearms, including some modern rifles; and their performance was vastly superior to that of the Ndebele armies in 1893, as the casualty figures in Table 12 show. The settlers lost more than one-tenth of their number, double the percentage of losses suffered in the 1893 conflict (and a notably large proportion compared with the losses suffered by Europeans in the Mau Mau and Algerian

TABLE 12

Estimated Number of Battle Casualties in Matabeleland, 1893 and 1896

Date	Casualties	Numbers engaged	Percentage of numbers engaged
1893			
Company forces	63	1,116	5.6%
Ndebele	3,500	12,500	28.0
1896			
Company forces	134	1,200	11.2
Ndebele	600	7,000	8.6

SOURCE: R. F. H. Summers and C. W. Pagden, *The Warriors* (Cape Town, 1970), p. 136.
NOTE: Contemporary sources differ somewhat on the casualty figures.

campaigns). For a time all European economic enterprise came to a stop. The chartered company's administration found itself in desperate financial straits. But the settlers enjoyed high morale. They believed that history was on their side, and that insurgents simply fought with the grim desperation born of despair. British power backed the colonists. A force of imperial mounted riflemen was hurried to Rhodesia, while the company equipped a relief force in South Africa.

Once again, the whites enjoyed superior mobility through the use of mounted troops. They were skilled in building laagers. At Bulawayo, for instance, experienced white builders and miners put up defenses strengthened by machine guns, barbed wire, and mines, and the rebels wisely never risked an assault on "hedgehog" positions that would have proved difficult even to seasoned white infantrymen. Soon the Europeans managed to seize the strategic initiative. The bands of warriors were broken up and kept on the move. The whites seized crops and cattle, thus imposing a kind of economic blockade on their opponents, who never managed to work out a concerted strategy. The Ndebele, still with the remnants of a centralized state organization, negotiated as a body and concluded peace with Rhodes. Lacking any kind of common political leadership, the insurgent Mashona communities were unable to hold out for much longer, and in 1897 resistance collapsed.

The British South Africa Company, determined that Rhodesia should never again go through the same bloody experience, now made its police force the first line of defense. The British South Africa Police (BSAP), formed in 1889, was an elite unit from the outset, relatively well paid, versatile, highly disciplined, and drilled with the precision of a Guards regiment.[14] The force attracted many young men from good British families, recruits who for one reason or another could not secure commissions at home. Many joined the police on short-term engagements simply for a chance to go abroad and see a new country. In some ways the force acted as an unofficial settlement scheme, since many of the men who were mustered out chose to make their homes in Rhodesia. Military and educational standards were high, and promotions frequent. The BSAP, like the colonial administration, lacked a separate officer class, and its social organization reflected the spirit of relative equality found within the settler population as a whole.

Southern Rhodesia, from the start, was regarded as a "white man's country," and the main emphasis always lay on the European component. As a result, the British took a very different view of its military needs there, as opposed to Northern Rhodesia, where the policing was left to Africans serving under European officers and NCOs.* The BSAP nevertheless remained small, numbering at the turn of the century only 750 Europeans and 400 African auxiliaries. The white troopers constituted a significant segment of Southern Rhodesia's European population, which then totaled about 11,000, but in an African population of more than 500,000, this worked out to only about 1.5 men per thousand. The BSAP, therefore, had to rely on a high standard of training and on the cooperation or at least quiescence of the indigenous population.

From the start, the BSAP's principal task was policing, aimed more at prevention than punishment. Constant patrolling on horse and mule enforced respect for the company's law, and provided the administration with a great deal of general information to supplement reports received from the native commissioners. But the corps was also prepared to fight as a military body, and in fact was organized into two small cavalry regiments, each with a full headquarters staff.

The administration, caught napping once, remained obsessed with the fear of another outbreak, even though Africans began to adjust themselves to changing conditions. Many of them began to make some money from selling crops and livestock. Many more went to work for wages. The spirit mediums and minor chiefs involved in the rebellion lost heavily in prestige. European military officers nevertheless devoted a good deal of thought to their capabilities in the event of a new emergency, and the authorities felt the need for a supplemental European force. In 1898 the administration set up the Southern

---

*The Northern Rhodesian Regiment, formed in 1912 by amalgamating two small regional constabularies, had 750 African troopers and 27 British officers and NCOs.

Rhodesia Volunteers, a mounted corps supported by cyclists, sig-
nalers, and engineers, with a tiny permanent nucleus. Training never
reached a high level of efficiency. Membership fluctuated as settlers
drifted in and out of the country, but morale was high, reflecting the
camaraderie of a country where almost everybody knew everybody
else. The corps would have proved a welcome reinforcement in case
of local skirmishes, but the test—when it came—proved to be of a
different nature.

When Southern Rhodesia was drawn into the Boer War—an inter-
white civil war as much as an imperial campaign—the Africans remained quiet, and the colonist-volunteers found themselves face to
face with a European enemy similar to themselves in outlook and
possessed of formidable fighting power. Under these circumstances
the authorities used the volunteers only in detachments, and drew on
them mainly as a general reserve. The administration raised a new
unit, the Rhodesia Regiment, a mounted infantry formation recruited
by voluntary enlistment that gave an excellent account of itself in
battle.

Southern Rhodesia possessed a high proportion of young men.
Many settlers had seen action before. Many were familiar with veld
craft and veld lore, for though the great majority of the population
lived in townships rather than on farms in the bush, the settlements
were so small that riding and shooting were virtually the only amusements. On the whole, the settlers lived tough lives, and the quality
of the regiment's recruits was good. Indeed, British patriotism and
imperial sentiment ran so strong that by 1901 some 1,700 men had put
on uniform, a full 15 percent of the country's total white population.

When the men came back from the war, the country picked up
where it had left off. The BSAP was reduced, and in 1903 the two
divisions in Mashonaland and Matabeleland were amalgamated. The
country was divided into nine districts, each under an inspector with
a troop of some 40 officers and men. This system gave way in 1913 to
a more "civilian" type of organization based on districts that coincided
with magisterial areas, and a number of specialist sections were developed, including a criminal investigation department. Volunteers continued to drill, but there was no regular military force. The police,
then numbering 550 whites and 600 Africans, were charged with the
dual duty of external defense and maintaining internal order.

By now the British South Africa Company had lived down its reputation as a band of filibustering capitalists, acquired as a result of the
Jameson Raid. An Order in Council accordingly transferred the overall

control of the military police forces from the high commissioner to a commandant general, who was paid by the company and appointed by it with the colonial secretary's approval. The headquarters' staff was strengthened, a mobilization scheme was completed, and a department of defense was created by the company to provide for the security of both Southern and Northern Rhodesia.

The Boer War, 1899–1902

The South African War—known to Afrikaners as the Second Freedom War—marked a watershed in British military history.[15] The conflict began as a small colonial affair, an imperial venture financed on a shoestring and fought against an opponent considered hardly on a par with warlike Indian mountaineers. British fire-eaters like Weston Alexander Jarvis, an officer in the Rhodesia Regiment, complained that the Londoners' war hysteria was really "quite *infra dig*," and calculated to give the Boers—"those rotten skunks who are no good except behind a stone"[16]—an undue sense of their own importance. The war ended, however only after the greatest military effort the British had ever made. Some 449,000 men were mobilized on the British side, the vast majority of whom had to be shipped in from Britain. For the first time in colonial warfare the regular army proved far too small for its task, even after the reserves had been called out. Militia and yeomanry alike volunteered for foreign service almost to a man; Canada and Australia also raised contingents for service in South Africa. Some 53,000 British soldiers were recruited in South Africa itself. It was the largest undertaking ever made by English-speaking South Africans—including a number of Anglophilic Afrikaners—and gave to the conflict something of the character of a South African civil war, comparable in certain respects to other nineteenth-century wars of unification. What started as an armed clash—fought in the traditional manner, designed to protect civilians and to confine hostilities to soldiers—ended in something approaching total war, an all-out conflict in which the British burned farms, interned civilians, and partially wrecked the farming economy on which Boer resistance depended.

Equally significant from the military standpoint was the Jameson Raid, which should rightly be regarded as part of the war itself. The raid was the work of Rhodes's principal lieutenant, Leander Starr Jameson. At the end of 1895 he crossed into the territory of the Transvaal with some 600 horsemen, mostly Rhodesian police, in a raid designed to coincide with a British rising on the Witwatersrand aimed at overthrowing the administration of President Paul Kruger, an inveterate foe of British supremacy, and installing a pro-British government. It was bungled in comic-opera fashion by a small band of well-connected young men who, in the historian Edgar Holt's felicitous phrase, supplied in class what they lacked in mass. Nevertheless, the raid contained in embryo the elements of the "indirect aggression" and "Fifth Column" activities of the twentieth century, complete with the organization of an armed uprising within the borders of a nominally friendly state, the dispatch of "volunteers" from outside, and the employment of worldwide propaganda.

The war was equally significant in its political aspects. Behind a vast array of quarrels over matters such as the British immigrants' franchise, there was the deeper question of whether Britons or Boers should be supreme in South Africa. The British would not give way because they considered South Africa an indispensable strategic link of empire. The Boers would not yield, for they saw themselves as the ultimate masters of a subcontinent. Britons and Boers alike were misled by demographic projections for the future at a time when there were no reliable population statistics. Both Kruger and Sir Alfred (later Lord) Milner, the British high commissioner, seem to have believed that the Uitlanders (European settlers, mainly though not entirely of British descent) would come to outnumber the Afrikaners in the Transvaal unless their immigration was checked. In fact, the Afrikaners outnumbered the Uitlanders; and the Boers' rate of natural increase—much higher than the newer arrivals—was bound to leave the demographic balance in their favor.

Compared with these political issues, the economic ones were of minor importance. The British did not fight to make their investment safe from the exactions of unenlightened pastoralists. The Boers were not nearly so hard on the mining concerns in South Africa as the British South Africa Company was on concessionaires in neighboring Rhodesia. The Boer government at the Witwatersrand might have been inefficient and sometimes corrupt; but it was not against economic progress as such. The Boers were not bewildered Biblical herdsmen at war with an economic system they did not understand. They did not want to crush the mining industry. They did not want to drive out the Uitlanders. They wanted political and military supremacy, an objective that they attained half a century later.

As regards the military management of the war, criticism of British military leadership can be overdone. At the beginning of the war the British were heavily outnumbered. In August 1899, when negotiations with President Kruger had almost broken down, the British forces in South Africa amounted to no more than 6,000 men. "Protest," Kruger snorted to a British emissary, "we have the guns; you have not." The British speedily took steps to repair this deficiency. But the dispatch of several hundred thousand men to fight on the other side of the world was something never before attempted in the history of warfare. British military tactics, based to a considerable extent on the methods used in "small wars" against colonial peoples, proved ineffective. (In the war against the Germans, 1870–71, the French had likewise found that experience gained in fighting North African Arabs and Berbers often constituted a disqualification rather than an asset in a general charged with fighting a European army.) Finally, but not least, the British were criticized for taking so long to put down an enemy that never mobilized more than 87,000 men, and never fielded more than half that number at any one time. But only a few years later the Germans likewise had to deploy a total of something like 17,000 white troops against a much smaller force made up of Herero irregulars and of Nama horsemen employing the selfsame mounted guerrilla tactics that made the Afrikaners so hard to beat.

British Liberal critics, especially, made great play of "the methods of barbarism" supposedly employed by the British. But compared with the accepted continental methods of dealing with ununiformed *francs-tireurs* or with the ruthless practices of General William Tecumseh Sherman in the American Civil War, the British fought humanely. The conflict was the last of the "gentleman's wars." It was one between two ruling races, neither of which wanted to call on African soldiers, and it marked an ideological watershed. Popular enthusiasm was mobilized in Great Britain; tens of thousands flocked to the colors. But the war, for the first time, led to widespread imperial self-questioning. The British Radical J. A. Hobson wrote his critique *Imperialism: A Study* as a result of having covered South Africa as a journalist. S. P. Bunting, descendant of a distinguished Wesleyan family and a founder of the Communist Party of South Africa, had been a onetime volunteer, anxious to fight for queen and country.

Above all, the war revealed an astonishing amount of incompetent leadership among the army's well-born generals. One of these was Lord Paul Sanford Methuen, KCVO, CB, CMG, a member of the Wolseley "ring" who had soldiered in Ashanti, the Sudan, and Bechuanaland, and had served as the British military attaché at Berlin. He was later made governor of Natal and then of Malta. He was all that a Victorian officer was expected to be. "Lord Methuen," wrote an admirer, "is a Peer and a Guardsman, and a distinguished officer to boot. But he is also a genuine flesh-and-blood Briton, in whom sporting and athletic tastes are strongly developed." He was mentioned in dispatches at the battle of Tel-el-Kebir. He even challenged a London cabby to a fight and beat him. And "if at times he has indulged in exaggerated language, Methuen's dispatches have had a decidedly English and soldierly ring about them, especially when the tide of success seemed for the moment to have turned."[17]

Methuen was brave enough; he personally led a charge; he was wounded in action, and was later captured by the Boers. But he lacked originality. He made successive frontal attacks on well-entrenched positions at Belmont, Graspaan, and the Modder River. Though recorded as victories, these actions cost him severe losses. He charged again at Magersfontein; the Highland Brigade was nearly halved. A private of the Black Watch wrote of his regiment's experience:[18]

> Tell you the tale of battle, well there's not much to tell;
> Nine hundred men went to the slaughter, and nigh four hundred fell.
> Wire and Mauser rifle, thirst and a burning sun
> Knocked down by hundreds ere the day was done.

When the reports of the battle reached Edinburgh there was general mourning. Shops closed, and women were crying in the streets. Magersfontein was a minor calamity by modern standards—Methuen lost 210 killed—but worse was to come. The days that elapsed between 10 and 17 December 1899 were known as "Black Week," the worst beating known to British arms for a century.

The British defeats revealed a great number of organizational and administrative weaknesses, quite apart from those derived from an unintelligent reliance on frontal assaults against a highly mobile and well-concealed mounted infantry. The initial British operations were marked by a general lack of coordinated planning and by inefficiency in the decentralization of command. These deficiencies did not matter in "small wars," where only a few thousand troops were in action, but were fatal in a war with great bodies of armed men operating in divisional rather than battalion or company strength.* There were never

---

*At this time a British cavalry division on war duty was composed of two brigades, two horse-drawn batteries, one mounted infantry battalion, and various specialist troops. All together it had six machine guns, 12 field guns, and nearly 450 vehicles of different kinds; its strength was 327 officers and 6,701 other ranks. An infantry division was composed of two infantry brigades, three batteries of field artillery, and specialist troops. It had four machine guns, 18 field guns, and just under 400 vehicles; its strength stood at 324 officers and 10,073 men.

enough maps. Intelligence and scouting before and during actions were often inadequate. Unlike the Boers, the troops were handicapped by an inordinately long transport "tail." British cavalrymen were weighed down by heavy equipment, slow to move, reluctant to dismount, and ill-trained to shoot from horseback. Their ability to turn and maneuver their horses was inferior to the Boers'. Though the British had some excellent mounted infantry, such as the Rhodesia Regiment, they attempted at first to fight a mobile war on the veld by relying mainly on slow-moving infantry. Their infantry weapons were inferior to the Boers', the Lee-Metford .303 rifle being a less-efficient weapon than the German clip-loading Mauser .275 employed by the Afrikaners. The Boers also had the edge in gunnery and artillery tactics. Their guns, manufactured by Krupp in Germany, outranged the British 15-pound howitzers, and were skillfully handled and concealed. The Boer "Pom-Pom," a one-pounder manufactured by Vickers-Armstrong, delivered rapid fire with deadly effect; this weapon had been rejected by the British ordnance department as "an unnecessary refinement." At times, moreover, the Boers made unexpectedly good use of railway transport for bringing up troops and supplies to the front.

Speaking in more general terms, the British, like their continental competitors, had failed to learn the main lessons of the American Civil War: infantrymen, however brave, were no longer in a position to storm properly entrenched positions, except at the cost of exorbitant casualties from rifle and machine-gun fire; and horsemen charging point-blank with sabers or lances were helpless against well-trained infantry armed with accurate breechloaders. It was fortunate for the British that the Boers also had great military weaknesses. The Afrikaners had magnificent tacticians, but they lacked strategists. Their council of war system, which was linked to the Boer socio-military structure with its insistence on decentralization and popular control, only made things worse. Instead of pursuing a war of movement that would carry hostilities into the Cape Colony, and at the same time organizing insurrections among the Afrikaners in the south, the Boers uselessly locked up large bodies of troops in sieges. These put a premium on the ingenuity of British miners and artisans in constructing defense works impregnable to the enemy's mounted forces.

The British were perfectly capable of learning. In addition, they could draw on a group of able younger officers skilled in adapting the lessons of irregular warfare to large-scale operations. These included H. C. O. (later Viscount) Plumer, who was an Eton and Sandhurst man. He rose to regimental major in the York and Lancaster Regiment, and then saw service in the Sudan and in the Ndebele rebellion, in which he commanded a mounted rifle corps. In the South African War he led the Rhodesia Regiment and made its name in the relief of Mafeking (1899), a feat that caused outbursts of hysterical rejoicing in London. During World War I he became one of the most successful British commanders on the Western front; he never favored costly do-or-die ventures such as the terrible offensive against Passchendaele Ridge.

One of his comrades-in-arms was R. S. S. Baden-Powell (later Baron Baden-Powell of Gilwell), who first won fame by his defense of Mafeking. The son of a "Reverend Professor" at Oxford, Baden-Powell began his career in a conventional way. He went to Charterhouse and later served with the 13th Hussars in India and Afghanistan. Like Plumer, he fought in the Ndebele rebellion, where he learned a great deal from African methods of warfare and distinguished himself as a scout. He also had a knack for publicity. He loved to draw cartoons, act in amateur theatricals, and play practical jokes. He wrote books on a great variety of subjects, from cavalry tactics to pig-sticking, and was a successful newspaper writer. His book *The Downfall of Prempeh*, based on contributions to the *Daily Chronicle*, still stands today as one of the best accounts of the Ashanti expedition of 1896, in which he served on special duty in charge of local levies. Newspaper correspondents were not a popular breed among servants of empire.

> He wrote for certain papers, which—as everybody knows
> Is worse than serving in a shop, or chasing off the crows.

Thus wrote Kipling, and Kipling knew.[19] But Baden-Powell overcame this particular disability, and later reached both national and international fame as the founder of the Boy Scout movement.

The British also put new commanders in the field. Lord Roberts, Wolseley's rival, was called in to take command of the troops in South Africa, replacing Sir Redvers Buller. Herbert Lord Kitchener (hero of Khartoum and later of World War I) served as his second in command. John French (later Lord French of Ypres) made his name as a cavalry commander. His subsequent performance as commander of the British Expeditionary Force in Europe in 1914–15, was lamentable, but as a cavalry leader he was impressive. Speed and surprise were his watchword. At Klip Drift, for instance, he was faced by Boers strongly entrenched on low hills that commanded a two-mile-long valley. French knew, however, that the Boers were weak in artillery. He also counted on the fact that a large body of horsemen moving at high speed in that country would raise so much dust as to make his cavalry almost invisible. His division lined up by brigades, each brigade formed into two lines, with a five-pace interval between files and a half-mile between brigades. They were to ride straight forward at a gallop, turning aside for nothing. Successively, his two brigades charged—French, his staff officers, and all. The Boers were taken aback. What they beheld was an awesome sight—one about to disappear from warfare—a huge, fast-moving cloud from which came the ominous thunder of hooves. This was followed by another cloud, and yet another, until the whole valley was a maelstrom of dust, resonant with the sound of galloping horses. The Boers recovered and kept firing into the charging ranks. Their fusillade had little effect, however, for their target not only was moving at great speed, but also was so spread out that most shots missed their mark. Here and there a horse fell headlong or a rider dropped from the saddle. But nothing could stop the mounted avalanche in khaki. The Boers made off, and at the cost of fewer than a dozen casualties French had opened the road to Kimberley.[20]

By 1900 the war seemed nearly over. The British relieved their besieged garrisons. They captured Bloemfontein and Pretoria and took numerous prisoners. But for two more years the Boers kept up the attack, turning now to mounted guerrilla warfare, damaging railway communications, isolating small posts, and seizing convoys, while avoiding contact with pursuing columns. In a way, their struggle was the first of the modern-style "liberation" wars in Africa. It found widespread sympathy abroad and even in Great Britain, where sentiment of that kind was rarely accorded to black guerrillas.

But in Kitchener, the man who had to cope with these hit-and-run tactics, the Boers met an opponent very different from the brave, amiable incompetents who had previously filled so many high positions. A former Royal Engineers officer, Kitchener was considered one of the best organizers in the army. He had conquered the Sudan, defeating the Dervish state created by the Mahdi in the decisive battle of Omdurman (1898).* Kitchener assumed supreme command in South Africa in late 1900, when Roberts returned to England. He first

---

*The Sudan was later to benefit from Kitchener's interest in academic development, an interest that belied his tough, bulldog-like appearance. He was the moving force in the creation of Gordon Memorial College in 1903, financed initially by public subscription in England and later fused with the Kitchener School of Medicine into the University of Khartoum.

set himself the task of making railway communications secure by setting up blockhouses, by turning the area of operations into a wasteland, and by burning farms. The so-called concentration camps of the Boer War were established as a humanitarian measure to protect Boer women and children from hardship and African hostility. The internees suffered heavily from disease and overcrowding, but in principle the Boers welcomed the camps as relieving them of responsibility for their dependents. And indeed once Kitchener recognized the military utility of these camps to the Boers, he banned further admissions. Meanwhile, he kept the enemy on the move by mobile columns that were pushed out along the lines of blockhouses. There were a few reverses, but the system worked with inexorable efficiency. The Boers could not rely on privileged sanctuaries for food and ammunition; neither could they afford to subvert the African masses.

Finally the Afrikaners could no longer resist, and in May 1902 they signed a peace treaty at Vereeniging—a place whose name, ironically, means union. The British terms were generous. They paid the burghers £3,000,000 in compensation for their farms, an unheard-of concession in a century when the vanquished, rather than the victor, was wont to pay reparations. But the British victory ultimately proved barren, except in purely military terms. The British Army learned some valuable lessons in the art of deploying large numbers of troops overseas, and both the minor tactics and marksmanship of the British soldiers vastly improved. As a result, when World War I broke out, they were ahead of the Germans in some respects: German infantry was still inclined to "bunch" in attack, and the cavalry was still reluctant to dismount in combat.*

Politically, the war turned out to be a disaster. If the conflict had only limited objectives, the British would have been well advised to make peace after the occupation of Bloemfontein and Pretoria, before partisan warfare had poisoned relations between Briton and Boer. In-

---

*There were also important organizational reforms. These began in 1904, when the so-called Esher Committee had completed its findings. The post of commander-in-chief was abolished and replaced by an Army Council, chaired by the secretary of state for war and responsible to the Cabinet. In 1907 War Secretary Richard Burdon Haldane (later First Viscount Haldane of Cloan) instituted a General Staff. The old voluntary home defense organization was superseded by a comparatively well-trained territorial army. The British Expeditionary Force that landed in France in 1914 was a disciplined, well-organized force. Unlike the formations that had departed for the South African theater of war, the major divisions of the BEF had been trained together, and mostly remained under their peacetime commanders. The British Army, however, suffered from an overemphasis on mounted warfare; too many of its senior officers were cavalrymen, ill-prepared for the problems of combat in Europe.

stead, the protracted struggle contributed to a new rise of Afrikaner nationalism, with a literary renaissance and even a new missionary inspiration. If, on the other hand, the objective was total victory, Britain's subsequent administration of the region ought to have been consistently of the military type, with no concessions made. The British gained considerable strategic and economic advantages that stood them in good stead in two world wars. But in the end they lost political control. Only a few years after the South African War, the British restored self-government to the Orange Free State and the Transvaal, and local power passed from the British-dominated cities to the Afrikaner-dominated countryside. In 1948, less than half a century after the peace of Vereeniging, the Afrikaners gained by ballot what they had failed to win by bullets—a precarious supremacy over the whole of South Africa.

African Military Responses

Seen in retrospect, African resistance was bitter, skillful, and long-lasting. It took the British more than 25 years to pacify their possessions in West Africa after the Scramble began in the 1880's. The French were still fighting in the Ivory Coast in 1916, and the Portuguese in Mozambique until 1912. Many large kingdoms fought, and so did many chiefless societies. In some cases the Europeans faced large armies, as the French did in Dahomey and the British in Rhodesia; but often resistance came from small villages, clans, and tribes.

The struggle was not as uneven a contest as some writers have claimed. The Africans had a great superiority in numbers, a thorough knowledge of the terrain, a limited immunity to some local diseases, and sometimes even modern rifles, supplied by rival European countries. But the colonial powers had technical superiority: machine guns and artillery. Above all, they had trained troops. Most Africans were farmers or herders; only a few were professional soldiers supported by a king or chief.

European commanders came to respect their African opponents, for the process of conquest and pacification was neither easy nor quick. Yet some questions remain: "Why African military resistance was not more effective, why some states resisted and others did not, why some states were able to adapt their armies to deal with the military strategies of their European opponents, why others fought entirely in traditional terms."[21]

For the people of Western Europe these wars in Africa were exciting events, with heroes emerging in almost every campaign. Accounts of the conquest of Africa poured from the presses in books, newspapers, journals, novels, and children's fiction. The white hero slashing away at black "savage" hordes became the stock character in European fiction. Pierre Mille in France and G. A. Henty in Great Britain captured thousands of readers. Accounts of wars against the Ashanti or the Zulu stimulated the adult reading public. Today little or nothing remains of the memories of most of these heroes; the death and destruction and the scale of heroism and battles of World Wars I and II have made events in Africa seem minor to the people who experienced the battles of Ypres or the Somme, or the sieges of Leningrad and Iwo Jima. Still, for their time and scale these were bloody, fierce engagements with high casualties and great destruction. Yet the roll call of the European combatants, though illustrious—Archinard, Baden-Powell, Gallieni, Gentil, Kitchener, Lugard, Wolseley, and Wissmann—is largely unremembered.

European invading forces were usually small and were generally greatly outnumbered by the African forces opposing them. The Nigerian town of Sokoto was captured by 600 British troops who were resisted by about 30,000. The Dahomeyan army had 12,000 men facing 2,000 in the French Army. Jameson sent little more than 1,000 men against Lobengula's 12,500-man army in the Ndebele war of 1893.* Against Samori, however, the French had to marshal almost an equal number of troops before they could defeat him.

After a few bad experiences in Ashanti and Senegal, where European troops too often sickened and died or had to be invalided home, all colonial armies shifted to African troops led by European officers and NCOs. White troops were decimated by climate and disease—malaria, yellow fever, dysentery; 40 to 50 percent became noncombat casualties unless they were led by a commander such as Wolseley who enforced strict medical rules. The British also used West Indians and native troops from India. But in the long run the indigenous fighting man proved better adjusted to the exigencies of Africa, a lesson that the British forgot to their cost when fighting General Paul von Lettow-Vorbeck's askaris in the East African campaign during World War I. Black troops were also cheaper, knew the local topography, and were less susceptible to local infections.

European technical superiority made up for the great disparity in

* Jameson's forces in the Ndebele war of 1893 consisted of 672 whites and 378 African levies and Cape Coloreds. But Jameson had eight machine guns and two field pieces, whereas the Ndebele had no heavy arms of any kind.

numbers, a superiority that rested on superior weapons and superior tactics, discipline, and logistics. The coming of the machine gun—the Gatling, and later the Maxim—gave the Europeans a great advantage in firepower. The light Maxim gun could be used in the front lines and, with a firepower of 660 rounds per minute, could stop most charges. The development of lightweight maneuverable artillery, such as the Gardener and Nordenfeldt pieces, also helped.

A trained military unit had substantial advantages in discipline and drill over almost any tribal levy. Special routines taught the colonial troops to deliver concentrated, accurate fire on a target, and the British square formation, with rapid-fire rifles supported by machine guns, smokeless powder, and light artillery, proved invincible. Most African forces used spears and arrows, or highly inaccurate muzzle-loaded guns with rocks and pieces of metal serving as shot. Samori sent his people to enlist as *tirailleurs* to learn the new tactics and skills. He also tried to recruit men who had served in European forces. Kano tried to enlist trained soldiers. Such men proved to be most formidable opponents when they joined rebel forces or rebelled themselves, as shown by the Sudanese troops in Kenya and Shona policemen in the Rhodesian rebellion.

Even when Africans did manage to get hold of the newer weapons, they failed to use them to full advantage. For example, they often fired breech-loaded rifles from a standing position, as they had done with their muzzle-loaders, fair game for an opponent who had learned to shoot lying down, thus giving the enemy a smaller target. African warriors like the Zulu and the Ndebele, who were trained to fight in regular tribal formations, were apt to neglect the art of ambush and preferred to charge full on, a tactic often linked to the belief that some special magic would deflect the enemy's bullets. This was an irrational creed that entailed grave consequences. Except for a few successes won by surprise, such as the destruction in 1891 of a German column commanded by Baron von Zelewski in East Africa or the better-known Zulu victory at Isandhlwana, the result of sudden rushes was usually devastating. More often than not, the attacking Africans were mowed down, and the colonial forces carried the day by vigorous counterattacks.

Other Africans, though, fighting guerrilla-type wars of movement and surprise attack, traveling light and living off the countryside, had the colonial armies at a clear disadvantage, and long-drawn-out campaigns resulted. The Europeans, if they hoped to win, then had to adjust to local conditions. The process of adaptation was hard. Clothing and equipment had to be lightened, units had to be reduced in size, and some heavy artillery pieces had to be abandoned in order to create a disciplined, fast-moving, and self-sufficient force capable of living off the land. Among the colonial forces, the German Schutztruppen was best at adjusting its forces to this pattern, with the King's African Rifles a distant second, followed by the Tirailleurs Sénégalais and the Force Publique in the Belgian Congo.

The ambush or surprise attack was the Africans' best tactic, be it in the jungle, bush, or desert. Since colonial units almost always had to travel through bush and forest strung out in single file, they were highly vulnerable to ambush. Surprise assaults at dawn or dusk also worked well in the desert, where visibility was limited. Colonial forces learned to prevent such tactics by sending out scouts in front and on either side of the column, and by using local men as scouts and auxiliaries. Some also acquired considerable expertise in night operations, a form of warfare avoided by many African tribes for fear of evil spirits.

African armies varied greatly in size, composition, and equipment. They fought with the weapons and methods they had evolved in facing traditional enemies, and usually they were not able to change rapidly enough to face the different strategies and weapons of their European opponents. Even a leader like Samori, for all that he managed to reorganize his forces and military operations to meet the new threat, was handicapped by the same major technological weakness as all the African forces: a lack of modern rifles and suitable ammunition. Before 1890 Africa had been a dumping ground for outmoded European weapons, but then the colonial powers clamped down. After 1890 they prohibited their nationals from exporting weapons to their possessions in West Africa, though European traders continued to sell guns in their rivals' colonies. African forces now had great difficulties in resupplying their arsenals. Keeping their existing arms in working order was equally difficult; few Africans were skilled in the art of repairing modern rifles. Unless trained in European armies, African soldiers did not know how to handle machine guns or artillery. The bulk of African fighting men had to make do with spears, swords, lances, arrows, and muskets, the weapons of a preindustrial age.

Few African states had standing armies, and none of the decentralized societies could support professional soldiers. Villagers were expected to rally to the defense of the clan or tribe in time of war, and men usually received some training in weapons and tactics. Raiding societies like the Zulu and the Ndebele raised regiments of young men who were specially trained and housed in regimental towns, but this was the exception, not the rule. The king of Dahomey had a regular force of Amazons; Samori had a kind of police guard; the Ashanti had militia regiments. But in most African societies the professionalization of war had not gone very far. Soldiers had to equip and supply themselves. The African army lived off the land, and the wives accompanied the men on campaigns—a practice continued by the Africans in the Colonial armies, who also lived off the countryside, their spouses marching alongside them.

Almost invariably, the African tribes failed to unite against the Europeans. True enough, they often stood together in their dislike or fear of the white strangers. John Ainsworth, a pioneer administrator in British East Africa, recalled how women and children used to scream at the sight of a European when the whites first made their appearance in the country. Some thought that Europeans ate little children; others believed they were responsible for the appearance of human disease, cattle sickness, and locust swarms, or for phenomena such as an eclipse of the moon.[22] But black people often saw other Africans as greater threats to their independence than the Europeans. The conquest of Africa would have been much more difficult had Africans not assisted the European powers as soldiers or as allies in wars against their fellows. Between 1895 and 1904 the Masai, who cooperated with the British by serving on punitive expeditions against other tribes, were rewarded with cattle, sheep, and goats, and thus were enabled to rebuild the herds devastated in "The Disaster" of 1884–94. Such raids brought them many thousands of animals; they received a share (up to as much as one-half) of 2,150 cattle in 1895, 3,466 cattle and 29,306 sheep in 1900, and 26,213 cattle and 36,205 sheep in 1905.[23]

The other colonial powers were no less quick to exploit existing rivalries than the British. Thus, just as the British used the Fante against the Ashanti and the Masai against the Nandi, so the French used the Bambara against the Tukulor and the Tukulor against Mahmadou Lamine (a Muslim leader of the Upper Senegal). Frequently, moreover, European leaders merely led an African group against its rivals, thus managing to conquer those who resisted them piecemeal at relatively small cost in European lives. To be sure, some native rulers managed to build alliances for the purpose of rebelling against white rule. Many Shona and Ndebele communities combined in the 1896 revolt against the British South Africa Company's regime in Rhodesia. Likewise, during the great rebellion in German South-West Africa (1904–7) the Nama joined their erstwhile enemies, the Herero, in order to do battle against the Germans. But African resistance was far from universal. There was no sense of a common African interest. Indeed the very words "Africa" and "African" were European imports to a continent where Nandi and Masai, Shona and Ndebele, thought of themselves as members of separate communities. African tribal units or kingdoms shared few feelings of common race—much less of common nationality—with their neighbors. On the contrary, they were often antagonistic—farmers against herders, animists against Muslims, raiders against cultivators. Thus, in all recorded rebellions many indigenous groups preferred to remain neutral, or attempted to use the occasion to settle accounts with long-standing opponents, a policy that involved military cooperation with the whites.

Among those groups that chose to resist, the most successful were the ones that learned how to fight guerrilla wars, to evade set battles, and to avoid operating from fortified townships or villages. Pastoral peoples like the Somali and the Nama proved particularly adaptable to partisan warfare. Their herds gave them a steady, reliable source of food, and their training as herdsmen, rovers, and raiders was ideally suited to turn them into mounted guerrillas. There was protracted resistance from many Muslim peoples in the Sudan as well, and also from the Baoule in the Ivory Coast, who fought against the French. But the insurgents lacked the cohesion afforded to most modern guerrillas by centralized organization, rigid political discipline, and commitment to an abstract cause transcending local loyalties or personal fealty to some great captain. Neither agricultural nor pastoral peoples, moreover, could fight without herds or crops. The whites learned from indigenous warriors how to keep an enemy on the move and how to shatter his economic support by seizing herds, ravaging crops, and burning huts.

In planning their counterinsurgency strategy, the whites did not develop elaborate theories comparable to those worked out by French theoreticians attempting to cope with Indochinese or Algerian rebels after World War II. Yet the European practice in fact shows a surprising correspondence to the counterrevolutionary concepts of a later age. In 1958 Jacques Hogard, a French soldier, attempted to reduce counterrevolutionary warfare to set rules. One fundamental, he argues, is that the incumbent government must never negotiate on equal terms with a revolutionary group. This was also a fundamental for the Europeans in Africa, none of whom ever accorded full legitimacy to any preliterate indigenous kingdom. Cecil Rhodes might have been willing to negotiate with insurgent Ndebele chiefs in the mountains of Matabeleland, but no Ndebele embassy would ever have been granted undisputed diplomatic status in Europe.

Most of Hogard's other rules also reflect the policies or at least the inclinations of the colonialists of an earlier day. He insists, for example, that the success of counterrevolutionary war depends on the close linkage of all civil, military, social, cultural, and economic resources, with a view toward holding or recapturing enemy support— a rule that was sometimes ignored, but that certainly accorded with the views of soldiers like Marshal Lyautey and General Joseph Gallieni. Again, final victory over the revolutionary forces, Hogard proposes, can be achieved only by the destruction of their leadership— an assumption that was clear to every settler in Rhodesia intent on hunting down the "witch doctors" responsible for the great rising of 1896–97. Irregular forces, according to Hogard, do not need to be defeated in battle, but can simply be "suffocated" by being deprived of material and moral support in a hitherto friendly region; guerrilla formations must be worn out physically and morally by tracking them down with units suited to the purpose, operating in familiar country; the safety of communications and vital points depends not on static defenses, but on the ability of the security forces to create a state of constant insecurity for the guerrillas.[24] All of these points were perfectly well understood by soldiers of the Victorian era.

The Europeans succeeded primarily because their actions generally met with little criticism at home. Opponents of colonial expansion might condemn overseas enterprises on the ground that such ventures were expensive in blood and treasure, or that they might involve clashes with another European power. There was widespread sympathy for the Boers, a white people. But few Europeans preferred the Zulu to the British, or the Herero to the Germans. Not even Marxists believed that African insurgents represented a new and more advanced social order. The colonial powers were accustomed to clash with their rivals in Africa; but they were not accustomed to giving material support, much less permanent sanctuary, to rebels operating in a neighbor's territory. Public opinion in the metropolis might condemn individual excesses, but rarely questioned as a whole the human cost of counterguerrilla warfare against Africans and Asians. As Churchill put it in connection with the Northwestern Frontier in India:

I invite the reader to examine the question of the legitimacy of village-burning for himself. A camp of a British brigade, moving at the order of the Indian Government and under the acquiescence of the people of the United King-

dom, is attacked at night. Several valuable and expensive officers, soldiers
and transport animals are killed and wounded. The assailants retire to the hills.
Thither it is impossible to follow them. They cannot be caught. They cannot
be punished. Only one remedy remains—their property must be destroyed.
Their villages are made hostages for their good behaviour. They are fully
aware of this, and when they make an attack on a camp or a convoy they do
it because they have considered the cost and think it worth while. Of course
it is cruel and barbarous, as is much else in war, but it is only an unphilosophic
mind that will hold it legitimate to take a man's life, and illegitimate to destroy
his property.[25]

To almost all African groups, resistance in the end seemed fruitless
and bloody. The Europeans had technical superiority and the ideological initiative. Even the Muslims—whose creed forbade submission to
Christians and who fought skillfully and tenaciously—had little faith
in their ability to resist forever. The feeling spread that the whites
and their black soldiers were invincible. The price paid for resistance
was high for subsistence economies: villages burned; fields destroyed;
cattle, sheep, and goats confiscated; flight and death, with the captives
left to the mercies of African auxiliary troops who went to war—as
in traditional times—for slaves and booty. Casualties on the African
side were heavy, and guerrilla warfare seemed only to prolong the
inevitable.

Conquest and Pacification: Policies and Costs

The Europeans in Africa, few in number and in no position to deal
with a united African rising, counted on their moral superiority and
on absolute obedience to their command to cow the African masses.
Prestige alone, it was felt by administrators, kept the Africans in check,
and prestige in turn depended on the Africans' believing that no order
could be disregarded with impunity. This attitude is shown, for example, by Meinertzhagen's response to insubordination: hit swiftly
and punish severely, or small acts of defiance will grow into big ones.
To put it in Indian Army terms, a shot in time save nine. Both the
military and the civilians seem to have agreed with this principle of
punitive expeditions, of hammering African peoples for any act of defiance or disobedience.

Fear was plainly one factor in this policy. Another, perhaps less
obviously, was the military's search for glory and promotion. Sir
Charles Eliot, high commissioner of the British East Africa Protector-

ate, criticized the soldiers' enthusiasm for expeditions: "If there were no decorations there would be fewer of these little wars."* But to be fair, many soldiers felt that it was the civilians, and not they themselves, who wanted tribal groups punished for every small offense.[26]

The wider role of the military as distinct from the civilians is harder to disentangle in the British than in the German or French possessions. In the French and German colonies the military normally formed the cutting edge of occupation. Remote districts were administered by soldiers, and only the more-developed areas by civilians. There were some British parallels to this system. In East Africa, for instance, the British initially established "military districts" in the interior and "civilian districts" along the coast. But the British ruling class was more homogeneous than its German or French equivalent, and a civilian might be asked to perform military tasks. Administrators passed easily from military to civilian status.

There remains the question of how far the availability of military force provoked the very violence it was meant to prevent. The evidence is contradictory. In 1891, when the British Central Africa Protectorate was formed, Johnston had a small police force at his disposal. With his military commander, Captain Cecil Maguire (brother of Rochfort Maguire, Rhodes's private secretary), he at once set out to "make our protectorate a reality to the unfortunate mass of people who are robbed, raided and carried into captivity to satisfy the greed and lust of bloodshed prevailing among a few chieftains of the Yao race."[27] The sequel was one little war after another. To Johnston the course seemed clear. For instance, Kawinga, a powerful Yao chieftain, was told that he must accept the queen's sovereignty, pay taxes to the administration, buy gun licenses, and renounce slave-trading and witch-hunting. Kawinga was willing to sign a treaty. He sent ivory and cattle for his gun licenses, but made known his determination to continue selling slaves. Given Johnston's governmental assignments, he had little alternative but to fight, and in retrospect it is hard to censure him. The British crushed the Yao and wiped out the slave trade, with the result that many Yao—deprived of their previous employment—enlisted in the very forces that had defeated them.

The military unquestionably placed a heavy burden on rural econo-

---

* Sir Charles Eliot, *The East African Protectorate* (London, 1905), p. 2. Between 1902 and 1910 British expeditions in East-Central and West Africa were issued 34 clasps of attachment to the African General Service Medal (Donald Anthony Low, *Lion Rampant: Essays in the Study of British Imperialism*, London, 1973, p. 436n).

mies, especially on the poorer ones, where men, food, and beasts were scarce. Villagers were forced to supply the required porters, provisions, and ancillary services. In some cases, moreover, the colonial armies resorted to traditional patterns of violence. The British paid the Masai raiders well for their efforts against the Nandi. Until 1900 or so, the conquerors in many parts of French Africa recruited soldiers and African tribal auxiliaries by promising them they could *razzia*—that is, go on a raid and capture slaves and other booty.

Differences in the treatment of Africans had little to do with the civilian or military status of administrators per se. Johnston was a civilian by background and an intellectual by inclination. He wrote a whole shelfful of books, including a novel (*The Gay-Dombeys*). Yet he was also a man of autocratic temperament, who never hesitated to use military force when circumstances seemed to indicate a show of strength. On the other hand, Colonel Colin Harding, a police officer, resigned from his position in Northern Rhodesia because he did not like the British South Africa Company's policy of burning the huts of tax defaulters. He subsequently served with distinction as a district commissioner in the Gold Coast.

The difference between civilian and military approaches was to be found not merely in individual personalities, but also in different systems. I. F. Nicolson, in his excellent study on the administration of Nigeria, gives an extensive account of the differing ethos of a civilian-minded and a military-minded administration in Southern Nigeria. Under Sir Ralph Moor's administration (1896–1900), the British advanced their influence in ten stages. They first sent out small, peaceable expeditions and reported on the economic production of the area; councils of chiefs were set up in friendly towns. They then completed route surveys, concluded treaties, and considered complaints. Subsequently, they began to patrol waterways, opened land routes, did away with tolls, protected African travelers, and finally established permanent posts, native courts, and native councils. This process was likened by French administrators to the policy of the "spreading drop of oil." It aimed at the peaceful development of commerce, but did not always go smoothly. District officers sometimes had to flee ignominiously from a town that they had entered with confidence. But the British knew how to make haste slowly:

There was nothing in the terrain or in the organization of the people which permitted the speedy deployment of mounted infantry on punitive expeditions; there was no room for the rapid exemplary humbling of power which the open spaces of the North permitted Lugard to administer to the Emirs. The desperate, dangerous work of the early pioneers in the South, on the other hand, produced a service in which cheerful resourcefulness and a sense of humour were more valuable than impressive personal dignity.[28]

Lugard relied instead on military prestige and military force. His basic policy was militaristic—"Thrash them first, conciliate them afterwards." He insisted on careful ceremony based on rank and precedent, described with loving detail in his *Political Memoranda*. When he met resistance or felt that his gubernatorial dignity had been affronted, he was apt to use force, a policy that corresponded to his autocratic temperament. Whereas in the south the flag slowly followed trade, in the north it went well ahead of commerce. Indeed, the British colors were displayed in such a way that traders were discouraged from following in their wake. Military opinion regarding the peoples of Nigeria was oddly similar to that in India, where Lugard had received his training. There was the same stress on the splendor of great Durbars, and that same tendency to divide Nigerians into "martial" and "nonmartial" races. The north was regarded as "martial" and the south as "nonmartial," a division corresponding broadly with the types of government established by the British in India. As Nicolson puts it:

Military empire thrived best in open country where the horse could be used to advantage, rather than in the forest, creek and estuary, where every tree and every bend could conceal a dozen "unsporting" enemies, ready to launch a concealed and "cowardly" attack. At any rate, the military conquerors in Northern Nigeria, as in Northern India, were in no doubt as to their own preference for the open country and its inhabitants, and in no great hurry to "spoil" their sturdy military virtues and simple loyalty to their officers by too much education.[29]

Sentiment apart, there was the simple issue of how many soldiers were in fact available. Lugard's force was relatively numerous; he was physically able to fight when he wanted to do so. The British South Africa Company in Northern Rhodesia, on the other hand, could only rely on a scratch force of less than 800 men—who were expected to police a country nine times the size of England. Northern Rhodesia's early ethos of government was civilian, determined above all by the need for economy and by the shareholders' unwillingness to spend money. Despite the company's bad reputation among humanitarian circles, the history of British penetration into Northern Rhodesia was comparatively peaceful. Company officials preferred to get their way by treaty-making and by gradual inroads. A short military campaign against the Ngoni of Northeastern Rhodesia in 1898 necessitated the deployment of a few companies from the Central Africa Protectorate. There were a few petty police actions against Bemba, Lunda, and Lovale. But, in the main, district commissioners managed to enforce their authority with little more than strength of character, a gift for diplomacy, a small force of police, and—in much of Northwestern Rhodesia—an ability to turn to their own purposes the subimperialism of the hitherto dominant Lozi people. Harding recorded how he toured the outlying districts of Loziland, sat down in public meetings on an old whiskey box, and played a wax-cylinder phonograph on which King Lewanika had recorded a message.

The effect was indescribable. . . . The voice which came from the box was the voice of their own ruler who, not without dubious forebodings, had been induced to record his kingly voice on one of the spare cylinders. He told his subjects . . . to treat me with all kindness and respect. [The voice] went on to say with a premonitory accent, "Send all your arrears of taxes due to me without further delay, or the White Man, who now visits you, will mete out the punishment you deserve."[30]

Among the Nandi of British East Africa, on the other hand, conquest was a long-drawn-out and violent process. The difference was not due solely to the presence of settlers; after all, white colonists also found homes for themselves among the Tonga of the Northern Rhodesia copper belt, which was occupied peacefully. The difference was determined in part by the availability of military force and also in part by the disposition of men like Meinertzhagen, determined to fight over any provocation. From the Nandi standpoint, traditional tactics did not usually succeed against the Europeans. During one foray the Nandi thought they could surprise Meinertzhagen with a ruse they used against tribal opponents: their warriors hid in trees expecting to catch passing columns unaware. Meintertzhagen's scouts spotted them and warned the main column, which then calmly picked them off.

The cost of military conquest and pacification can only be guessed at. It clearly differed a great deal, depending on the recuperative capacities of the societies involved and on the type of white opponent they faced. In Matabeleland, for instance, the total population during the 1890's was said to number about 150,000 (in all likelihood a serious underestimate). The war casualties in 1893, as we have seen, have been assessed at 3,500—or about 2 percent or less of the population. But the Ndebele must have suffered a good deal in addition from indirect effects of war—sickness, exposure, and hunger. During this war, as in many other conflicts—colonial and precolonial—villages were burned, cattle, sheep, and goats were seized, and crops were destroyed.

The list of African casualties is further lengthened when account is taken of the destruction of human life associated with porterage—providing carriers to supply army and police units. These demands could be enormous. The Marchand mission of 1896, for instance, used 25,000 porters to carry supplies from Gabon to Chad, yet Marchand's forces numbered only about 250 men. To supply the French Army in the Sudan and Chad taxed beyond limits the people living along the line of March. Whole areas were abandoned as villagers fled the oppressive demands of porterage or paddling. The death rate of porters was high in French Equatorial Africa—20 percent in the dry season and 40 percent in the wet. To give some idea of the scale of the pressures on an agricultural society, we cite the figures of the military administrator of Bangui for workers during the period 5 April to 31 October 1900: for government and concessionaire use, he had to provide 4,400 paddlers and 6,500 workers. According to the local French administrator, the Mandjia people, who provided a large proportion of the laborers required to supply Chad, declined in population from 35,000 in 1900 to 18,000 in 1905.

The full story of the effects of porterage on African societies remains to be written, but it was an incredibly costly institution. In East Africa porterage was a long-established profession. With the coming of war the increased demand for carriers had catastrophic effects, with porters poorly cared for and often unpaid. Lettow-Vorbeck used tens of thousands of porters to defend German East Africa; deserters were shot. The British admitted to using over 200,000 by 1917. The death rate was high, estimates running from 10 to 20 percent. But porters did not just carry supplies and equipment. In peacetime they were used to build roads, railroads, and public works. Here, too, their working conditions and lack of medical care led to death rates as high as 25 percent.[31]

Added to these costs of military conquest and administration were the losses suffered from the forced growing of crops or gathering of rubber. Police and military units ensured obedience to government demands, with death and destruction the fate of those who failed to comply. The horror stories of the Congo Free State and the concessionaires in French Equatorial Africa are well known; the British were never quite as ruthless, not even in Rhodesia, where European settlers competed with the inhabitants for a sizable proportion of the land.

No adequate statistics exist on the numbers of Africans killed in protracted guerrilla wars. In all probability, however, African losses in many of these campaigns were higher than the losses incurred in the head-to-head confrontations of campaigns such as the Matabeleleland war of 1893. Certainly, more people were killed by the indirect effects of war—famine, disease, and demoralization—than by enemy guns. The Maji-Maji rising in German East Africa in 1905 supposedly took 75,000 or more lives, though no one can be certain. Even the so-called small wars must have proved devastating in their effect on the small-scale societies involved.

Colonel Meinertzhagen left a graphic account of a small war against the Nandi of Kenya in 1905–6. In a three-week campaign a force of about 1,100 King's African Rifles cost the Nandi 10,000 head of cattle, 70,000 sheep and goats, and 500 warriors killed; the number of wounded is unknown.[32] In 1906 the KAR was instructed to drive the Nandi from their land into a reserve area. Meinertzhagen led a small patrol in this campaign, with orders to destroy all crops, to burn all villages and huts, and in general to lay waste the countryside so they would have to move. His patrol's record: 917 huts, 239 granaries, and 46 stock enclosures burned; 145 acres of standing crops destroyed; eight Nandi captured and 51 killed. Let these figures be multiplied many times over to account for the efforts of other patrols and one has some idea of what the Nandi suffered. They moved, but no provision was made to feed them, and how many died in their new land is unknown. In desperation, some of them broke out—only to be run to ground by Meinertzhagen. So ended the Nandi war.[33]

Against the losses from conquest and military administration, and the burdens of porterage and forced labor, must be weighed the beneficial effects of pacification. The conquerors learned from their mistakes and were not afraid to say so. The lengthy struggle waged by the British against the Tiv—a farming people in south-central Nigeria —largely derived from British ignorance, wrote a Resident shortly before the outbreak of World War I. But in the long run, he added, the British would never be able to govern the blacks through fear or physical force alone. Junior officers who considered a military escort an indispensable mark of prestige were of no use in the province. British influence must depend on the ability to settle local feuds by arbitration, by stopping wars, by opening markets, building roads, and promoting trade.[34] In the short run, pacification engendered a good deal of violence, but eventually colonial conquest put an end to inter-tribal wars and slave raiding. The new rulers established for themselves a quasi-monopoly of armed power. Indigenous armies were disbanded. Indigenous warlords were put out of business. Indigenous traders could travel in areas that had once been closed to them. Labor migrants were able to traverse huge regions without fear of being robbed of their cash.

In spite of the small wars and campaigns of pacification, the imperial authorities essentially brought peace—often the first peace imposed over large areas. As one old Nigerian woman put it to a British officer: "Salutations and blessing and peace! For in my young days we knew nothing but fear, peril and continual fighting. White men alone have brought safety and peace to our land."[35] That blessing was heard from many Africans throughout the continent.

For the European invaders were conquerors with a difference. Unlike Ndebele, Zulu, or Masai warriors, the Westerners brought an entirely new system of economic production, a system that made the white victory inevitable for a time. According to Hilaire Belloc:[36]

> Whatever happens, we have got
> The Maxim gun, and they have not!

But Maxims and Mausers were themselves merely the product of a highly complex industrial, technical, and scientific culture, a culture that also produced railways, clocks, quinine tablets, charts, and bully beef—all equally essential instruments in the conquest of Africa. Ultimately, the material well-being of Africans increased, as indicated by the demographic explosion that followed the colonizing period. But the era of population growth did not begin until wars—large and small, colonial and precolonial—porterage, and forced labor ended. Conditions improved significantly after 1910 throughout most of the continent, though World War I, with its heavy demands for porters, recruits, and supplies, bore heavily on traditional societies as the Allied colonial powers sought to conquer all German-held territory.

The Social Impact of the Armed Forces

The military was one of the most influential agencies in molding the new colonial societies. Colonial armies provided the physical force required to conquer Africa. They helped to shape the territorial units that were created by the colonizers, units later elevated into sovereign states in the wake of empire. In some ways armies resembled mission stations. Both served as agents of a kind of Westernization. Missionaries and officers were teachers of sorts, salaried employees who spent much of their time instructing Africans in specialized skills. The quality of the new colonial armies depended, above all, on the quality of their European officers. Between the officers and their men there was a social chasm wider even than the gap that separated an officer and a gentleman in Wellington's army from the slum-born private under his command. Nevertheless, the officers, with their peculiar sense of honor cemented by class pride, technical efficiency, and—above all—collegiate solidarity, provided the kind of leadership few tribal warriors could equal. Barracks and mission stations alike created new social groups. They attracted ex-slaves and the poor, and trained them in various trades, providing many with a modest means of advancement. Both regiments and missions had their specific customs and ritual. They were among the first wage employers and among the first to cope with labor unrest, be it on the part of underpaid mercenaries or discontented converts.

The role of colonial armies as purveyors of skills should not, of course, be overestimated. The African soldiers who did duty in Nigeria, Cameroun, or Kenya were first and foremost infantrymen trained to port arms and clean their boots. All the same, soldiers learned how to handle simple military tools. They became acquainted with nuts, bolts, screws, and other appurtenances of an industrial civilization unknown in a backwoods hamlet. They learned to live outside tribe and clan and to look to officers and NCOs, not to chiefs, for leadership and rules of behavior.

The returning ex-soldier had traveled and learned new customs and new skills. Like the mission stations, the army insisted on the virtues of punctuality, order, and obedience, qualities prized by European employers. Many an ex-sergeant thus became a government official, a farm foreman, a gang boss, or a supervisor in a Public Works Department. Some made good as traders. In many cases the demobilized soldier had become somewhat estranged from the values of his community. He had gained a measure of prestige apart from and outside his clan or village. At times he had more money or more knowledge of the white man's ways than the village elders. The ex-soldier, like the migrant porter, the itinerant hawker, the "mission boy," or the convert to Islam, was often a solvent that weakened the structure of traditional society.

The psychological impact of the army is hard to assess. There was doubtless a great deal of dislike and contempt for the native troops, a dislike that found expression in the reluctance of the better-educated African "to go for a soldier." On the other hand, current and former members of the colonial forces took a great deal of pride in their calling. In Nyasaland, for instance, there were many Yao villages where retired members of the KAR proudly put up notice of their rank and military decorations outside their huts. Like the missions with their hymns, the army spread a new kind of music, especially since the various colonial regiments all had trained African bandsmen. The army also provided impressive spectacles, parades, and flag-hoisting ceremonies that gave evidence not only of the white men's physical power, but also of the social stratifications within white colonial society.

In both German and British East Africa, in fact, some ordinary Africans incorporated the Europeans' military order into their ceremonies. These ceremonies, built around the *mbeni* dance, first appeared in German East Africa, with principals bearing the titles Kaiser, Kaiserin, Hauptmann, and so forth. A similar ceremony came into being in Nyasaland during the 1920's, patterned on the British model. Its central figure, a man called the Governor, disposed a full army, with differently ranked generals, a colonel, a captain, and so forth down to the rank of private. The dancers wore helmets, whistles on lanyards, appropriate badges fashioned out of lead, and occasionally even Sam Browne belts. In observing the Europeans at Zomba, the Nyasaland capital, Africans were clearly struck by the rigidly fixed hierarchy, with a set of distinctive uniforms and public ceremonies that seemed to advertise the social position of each person. The appeal of the mbeni dances lay in the African's vicarious participation in a social relationship from which he was excluded, but one that impressed him. Some may argue that these dances were satirical, the African's way of expressing his hostility to the ruling group. But Clyde Mitchell, whose research is summarized here, has found no evidence that any satire was intended.[37] To the laborers, truck drivers, tailors, and housewives who participated in such dances, their role represented a wish-fulfillment. Indeed, the popularity of the ceremony perhaps represented the most subtle and insidious victory won by European arms in Africa.

FIVE

The Colonial Governor

The British administered their possessions through a bewildering group of dignitaries and systems of governance. At the beginning of the twentieth century the Indian empire was headed by a viceroy, surrounded by royal splendor and answering to the India Office in London. In Canada and Australia the Crown was represented by a governor-general who, to all intents and purposes, carried out the duties of a constitutional monarch in a self-governing federal state. The Cape Colony had almost attained dominion status by this time, but its governor's powers, though vast in theory, still bore a largely ceremonial character; in practice he was not a ruler in any real sense. The non-self-governing colonies fell into three main categories: the Crown colonies, under the aegis of the Colonial Office; the protectorates, most still at this point under the Foreign Office, but soon to be put under the Colonial Office; and the chartered-company, also theoretically under the Colonial Office but only loosely supervised at best.

Most of the men in charge of these non-self-governing colonies were called governors. Some bore different titles at various times and in various parts of the empire—Jamaica at this point had a captain-general, Southern Nigeria a high commissioner, Zanzibar a resident, Swaziland a resident commissioner, and Uganda a commissioner—but they were governors all the same, which is to say, chief executives, responsible for the day-to-day administration of their territories. By this definition, there were 32 colonial governorships in the empire in 1900, 18 of which were in Africa.

The Governor's Functions and Emolument

The duties of a British governor were both formal and informal; they were written down in various rules and regulations and developed through his relations with the Colonial Office. He was appointed by the sovereign on the recommendation of the colonial secretary after consultation with the prime minister, and before leaving for his post he was received at Buckingham Palace.* At the time of his appointment, he was given three documents: a commission in the form of Letters Patent; Royal Instructions; and the *Colonial Regulations*, which in effect were the directions of the secretary of state for the guidance of governors. On his arrival in the colony, the oath of office was administered to him by the chief justice, a formality essential to his legitimacy as governor.

In a non-self-governing colony the governor was both the most prestigious and the most influential official. As personal head of the government, he acted as the sovereign's representative, and formed the kingpin in a system of governance foreign to all theories of divided legislative and executive powers. He initiated policies, shared in their implementation, and presided over the executive council—a kind of cabinet. As head of the executive, he supervised the work of all departments and scrutinized all matters of importance. He acted as president of the local legislature—called a Legislative Council in its embryonic stage and a Legislative Assembly in its fully developed form. He was expected to shoulder all responsibilities under the Royal Instructions issued to him, and every act of government was done in his name. He alone communicated with the colonial secretary, and to signal the importance of his communications in the bulky files, he wrote them in red ink. He usually held the title of commander-in-chief, but was not empowered to command imperial troops based in his colony, though they could only move with his permission. Local troops, however, such as the KAR and the WAFF, were under his direct control. By direct delegation from the Crown, he was invested with the power of life and death and could exercise the royal prerogative of mercy. In effect, by Anthony H. M. Kirk-Greene's definition, he was king, prime minister, speaker, and head of the civil service.[1]

In theory, a governor's powers were rigidly circumscribed, and his position one of strict subordination to the Colonial Office. The colonial secretary had to approve any important legislation a governor wished to enact. Likewise the secretary's consent to all appointments to the permanent staff was required, and he was in no way bound to follow the governor's recommendations in filling senior posts. The governor was obliged to keep the Colonial Office fully informed of his policies.

*Queen Victoria was very interested in colonial affairs and wanted to see all important dispatches. She took an active interest in the appointment of governors, being anxious to keep them independent of Parliament and political parties.

And not least, the annual estimates of each colony's financial needs had to be sanctioned by the colonial secretary. MP's could, and occasionally did, raise questions in the House of Commons or Lords concerning the expenditures or policies in a particular colony or area, but the colonial secretary—not the governor—was answerable in all cases. Unlike the German Reichstag, Parliament had no budgetary oversight over the colonies. Nor did the British voters have any say in colonial matters. In theory Parliament was supreme. In practice the House of Commons had no power over the appointment or dismissal of any governor, let alone over his legislation.

Most governors, however, enjoyed a good deal of de facto independence from the Colonial Office. As Sir Hesketh Bell, a Uganda governor, noted in his diary:

I was given to understand, at the Colonial Office, that I would be allowed a fairly free hand, but that I could expect short shrift if I made a mess of it. It is indeed wonderful to find myself, at my age, in such a position. I have complete authority over nearly three and a half million of people and a territory larger than Spain . . . and almost everything still remains to be done to develop the administration and trade of the country.[2]

With communications so slow, the Colonial Office usually hesitated to meddle with the man on the spot on matters in which local administrators were better informed than their London colleagues. The office may have been anxious to prevent a governor from overspending or overlegislating within his colony. But London was reluctant to censure, snub, or overrule a governor lest his authority should be undermined. Above all, there was a good deal of trust. The British ruling class was more homogeneous than its continental counterparts. There was nothing like the separate corps, each with its own tradition, ethos, and rivalries, that divided the higher reaches of the French bureaucracy. There was nothing comparable to the *inspecteurs d'état*, with their formalized power. There was a good deal of informal give-and-take between imperial and local authorities, strengthened by the ties of Public Schools, church, clubs, and associations like the Royal Empire Society (previously known as the Royal Colonial Institute and later the Royal Commonwealth Society). Sometimes the Colonial Office was almost afraid of a strong character like Lord Lugard. But as long as a governor did not create a public scandal, a parliamentary crisis, or a financial deficit, his position was unassailable.

A governor's effective power, however, differed a good deal from time to time and place to place. Much depended, for instance, on the length of his tenure. Perhaps the most powerful governor of all was

Sir Reginald Wingate, a professional soldier who served as governor-general of the Sudan from 1899 to 1916. He was supervised to a certain extent by the British consul-general of Egypt; otherwise his authority was limited neither by representative bodies, public opinion, nor the Foreign Office. Wingate, who combined a brilliant record in intelligence with a penchant for ceremonial splendor, was thus able to act almost like an independent potentate, his power enhanced by his 16-year tenure. During his extended stewardship he was able to impose his own military style on the administration and to develop the country's economic resources as he saw fit.

The British South Africa Company likewise allowed Sir William Milton to run Southern Rhodesia for some 16 years (1898–1914). The average British governor, however, like his German colleague but unlike the average French or Portuguese governor, rarely stayed in office for more than five years or so.* This was certainly long enough for a man to familiarize himself with the local situation, and if he was a man of strong character, to put his stamp on the administration; but did not leave him much room to enforce his policies down to the provincial or the district level.

Most governors were called "His Excellency" (the British South Africa Company's administrator in Rhodesia was addressed by the humbler title of "Your Honor"), lived in "Government House," and were entitled to a 17-gun salute. But they were far from equal in importance, status, and salary. There were four grades of governorship that descended all the way from the largely ceremonial governor-generalship of Nigeria (worth £7,500 a year with allowances in 1909) to the relatively humble post of governor of Gambia (at £2,500 or only one-third as much).

The most dignified appointments—those carrying no administrative responsibilities—were the best remunerated. The governor of the Cape Colony in 1909 received an official salary of £8,000 a year, whereas the salaries of "working governors" varied from about £2,000

---

*Governors were first appointed for six years; later the term was reduced to five years with possible two-year extensions. Some, like Sir Gordon Guggisberg, served eight years (Gold Coast, 1919–27); others had their terms extended twice (Sir Edward Twining and Sir Philip Mitchell). Outstanding men were sometimes chosen for successive appointments; a few, such as Sir Arthur Richards, Sir Hesketh Bell, Sir Alan Burns, and Sir Hugh Clifford, held four or five governorships. There were wide variations. Between 1874 and 1912, 11 governors held power at the Gold Coast; between 1886 and 1906, five at Lagos; 1891 to 1913, four commissioners and two governors in Nyasaland. For details, see David P. Henige, *Colonial governors from the Fifteenth Century to the Present: A Comprehensive List* (Madison, Wis., 1970); and A. Kirk-Greene, "On Governorship and Governors in British Africa," Chap. 8 of L. H. Gann and Peter Duignan, eds., *African Proconsuls: European Governors in Africa* (New York, 1978).

a year to £4,000.* By and large, however, the British governors were among the best-paid people within their own colonies (and indeed, as we shall shortly see, within the British civil service). They were also the highest-paid officials in any of the European colonial services (see Table 13). Their importance was emphasized through a wide "spread" in official salaries, which saw the next-highest-ranking official in each colony receiving only about half the governor's salary (see Table 14). In 1924, before copper mining had created great new fortunes in Northern Rhodesia, the governor was not only the most powerful local resident, but also the wealthiest—the only person able to entertain on a fairly lavish scale, so that Government House remained the apex of the social pyramid, where anyone of any social pretension hoped to be invited to some suitable function. His annual income was £3,000, and he had a representation allowance of £1,000.†

As Table 15 shows, the remuneration paid to governors compared favorably to the income received by successful men in the army, the civil service, and the judiciary. Indeed, on the eve of World War I, the governor-general of Nigeria made substantially more than his putative superior, the colonial secretary, and more than twice as much as the army chief of staff, even discounting his £1,500 representation allowance. The resident commissioner of Basutoland received as large a salary as the director of military operations at the War Office. Within the British hierarchy, therefore, a governor occupied a higher position than his counterpart within the French or German establishment.‡

But for all this, many governors had financial problems. Most appointments, as we have seen, were for a period of five or six years.

* Note that this salary range is for Africa. There were lower-paying posts elsewhere in the empire. The governor of the Falkland Islands, for example, made only £1,200 at this time. Moreover, the highest-ranking post in Africa did not approach, in pay or prestige, the governor-generalship of India, which carried a salary of £17,500 even in the nineteenth century. Nyasaland and Uganda, like Gambia, were at the low end of the salary scale, at £2,000 and £2,200 respectively. The governors of British East Africa and the Gold Coast were at the top of the "working" governors' scale, at a salary of £3,000 plus £1,000 in allowances.

† The spread in salaries within the colonial administration was still as great as ever at this time. In 1924 the chief secretary—the principal civil servant in Northern Rhodesia after the governor—received £1,200 and a stores clerk made about £300. The gap, however, began to narrow after World War II, and by 1953, whereas the governor's official salary had risen only slightly, to £3,500, the chief secretary's pay had almost doubled, to £2,200, and the clerk's had almost tripled, to £815.

‡ This gubernatorial preeminence continued well beyond World War II. In 1947 the colonial secretary was paid £5,000 subject to all taxes, whereas the governor of the Gold Coast, Sir Alan Burns, received a tax-free salary of £6,000. The prime minister at that time received only £10,000, but he too had to pay all taxes, so that some governors were in fact better paid than the head of the British government.

TABLE 13
Comparative Annual Salaries of European Governors in Africa, c. 1913
(In £)

Post or rank	Salary
Great Britain	
Governor-general, Nigeria	7,500[a]
Governor, Gold Coast	4,000[a]
Governor, Nyasaland	2,000
France	
Governor-general, French West Africa	2,469[a]
Governor, 1st class	1,235[a]
Governor, 3d class	823[a]
Portugal	
Governor-general, Angola	2,200
Governor, Mossamedes	267
Belgium	
Governor-general	2,058[a]
Vice governor-general	1,646[a]
Germany and Italy	
Governor, German East Africa	1,893
Governor, Somalia	1,070[a]

SOURCE: *Colonial Office List, 1914*; Reichstag, *Verhandlung . . . XIII Legislaturperiode*, 1 session, band 303, Anlagen, "Die Kolonialverhandlung der europäischen Staaten," Aktenstück no 1356 (Berlin, 1914), pp. 2633–2780; SPA 123. Divers. Archives Africaines, Brussels.

a Including allowances.

TABLE 14
Annual Salaries of Governors and Other Colonial Officials of Sierra Leone and the Gold Coast, 1880 and 1934
(In £)

Position	Sierra Leone		Gold Coast	
	1880	1934	1880	1934
Governor[a]	3,500	4,000	3,500	5,000
Chief justice	1,800	1,900	1,500	2,400
Colonial secretary	700	1,680	1,000	2,160
Colonial treasurer	600	1,420	700	2,400
Other				
Colonial surgeon	591	1,680[b]	—	—
Teachers/school officials	—	—	12–100[c]	1,620[d]

SOURCE: Henry L. Hall, *The Colonial Office* (London, 1937), p. 194.

a Of all West Africa.   b With a large staff, including 20 doctors.

c Six teachers in all; five of them earned £50 or more.   d With a large staff.

TABLE 15
Comparative Annual Salaries of British Officials in
London and Africa, c. 1910
(In £)

Title	Salary
Archbishop of Canterbury	15,000
Archbishop of York	10,000
Governor-general of Nigeria[a]	7,500
Bishop of Durham	7,000
Secretary of state for the colonies	5,000
First lord of the treasury	5,000
Justice of the King's Bench Division	5,000
Governor of British East Africa[b]	4,000
Chief of the Imperial General Staff	3,000
Governor of Gambia	2,500
Commissioner of Metropolitan Police	2,500
County court judge	1,500
Director of military operations, War Office	1,500
Resident commissioner of Basutoland	1,500

SOURCE: *Whitaker's Almanac* (London, 1912).
a Salary tax free and includes duty allowance.   b Includes duty allowance.

The maximum pension for a governor, however, was granted only after
10 years; hence a man was under some pressure to secure a second
governorship without regard to health, age, or general fitness.* Power
came late in life. Governors were normally appointed after many years
of colonial service, in their late forties or early fifties. Young governors
—such as Geoffrey Archer, appointed to British Somaliland at the age
of thirty-two—were a comparative rarity. The social requirements of
their office were expensive. Governors and their wives were expected
to entertain on a scale commensurate with their position, and visitors
of all kinds arrived to be wined and dined at Government House.
This was true even in the Spartan days that followed World War II.
When Sir Edward Twining was governor of Tanganyika, his journal
for 1950 listed the social occasions of a fortnight: 17 civilian and 16 military guests, with a host of receptions, presentations, and lunches, plus
a state dinner party for 40, and a garden party for 500. As a result,
most men retired with limited funds to live on, and many had to find
new occupations. Governors thus gained prestige and sometimes fame,
but rarely material wealth.

*This qualification was set forth in the Governors Pension Act of 1865, which also
provided that the pension be calculated on the last three years' salary. This rule caused
hardships and sometimes tragedy. For example, Guggisberg had served only eight years

The Governor's Ceremonial Life

Governors, as we have seen, combined the position of sovereign, prime minister, and head of the civil service with the leadership of a colony's social life. The British, moreover, believed that the "native races" were as much impressed by the pomp and circumstance of British authority as British expatriates themselves. There was great emphasis on the symbols and ceremonies of office. Accordingly, governors were expected to look and dress their part. Within his own colony, a governor was second only to the sovereign on a state visit. Even a British prime minister was required to defer to the governor in his capacity as the personal representative of the Crown; while staying with Sir James Robertson in Nigeria, Harold Macmillan each morning gave to his host the bow reserved for royalty. Just as with the sovereign, His Excellency always had to sit behind the chauffeur, so that no one might appear to be honored by sitting at the governor's right hand.

A guard of honor greeted His Excellency each time he left and returned to Government House; senior officials, and later cabinet ministers, were expected to see him off on major tours and to welcome him on his return. The Union Jack flew over Government House when he was in residence, and the national anthem was played whenever he appeared at a public ceremony. Protocol was strict, starched, and stratified. Questions of precedence were treated with great solemnity and everyone knew the local pecking order and who should be seated where. Signing the visitors' book by the gates of Government House was essential protocol—especially if a newcomer wanted to be invited to "H.E.'s" functions.

A governor in full uniform was an impressive sight. He had two basic uniforms: one white, with white and red plumes in his helmet; one dark blue, with a cocked hat and white plumes. These were topped off by gold and silver gorgettes, epaulettes, buttons, and frogging, and an elaborately decorated sword. These outfits were expensive—as late as 1946 Twining paid £350 for a second-hand full-dress uniform—and they were uncomfortable. Yet every governor was expected to sweat in his resplendent dress of heavy English cloth even under a tropical midday sun.*

---

and therefore took another governorship in order to qualify for a higher pension. He died a few months before he would have retired at the highest possible pay.

*Corona Club dinners were started in 1901 by Joseph Chamberlain. They were held in June, and he would address the 300–400 members of the colonial service on leave in Great Britain. Subsequent secretaries kept up the custom. On those evenings the governors in their dress uniforms, medals, and decorations lit up the head table.

There was also a good deal of residential splendor. Once the frontier period was over, most local administrations put up a stately Government House where, according to the *Colonial Regulations*, "every day he [the governor] flies the Union Jack from sunrise to sunset." Life at Government House was not to everyone's taste; Mary Kingsley, who did not like colonial administrations, once described it as "a coma punctuated by fits." But life was certainly dignified. In Uganda the governor lived in a great double-story edifice surrounded by a fine veranda, the kind of building that would have appealed to a nineteenth-century California railway magnate. Government House at Zanzibar was resplendently Moorish in style.

They were not always comfortable, however. Two of the Government Houses along the West Coast—Cape Coast Castle and Christianborg Castle—were old slave forts. The governors of Lagos lived in a Victorian iron building—an "iron coffin," according to Sir Richard Burton, "with generally a dead consul inside." The occupants spent sleepless nights going through the corridors in search of a cool breeze. Lady Glover, the wife of one governor, described her husband's nightly wandering in the following fashion:

His Excellency, as was his wont, having tried in vain to rest before the break of day, compromised the matter of sleeping either indoors or out by lying down with his head and shoulders in the passage and the rest of his body in the room. The dusky constable on duty as guard came across the Governor in that position and attributing it to a physical inability to move [i.e., that he was scandalously drunk] and alarmed lest his condition should become known, shook him mightily by the shoulders . . . till he thoroughly roused him up, and sleep for that night was impossible.[3]

Whatever the discomforts, Government House in a Crown colony was usually impressive, with a magnificent hall adorned with African weapons of all kinds, finely fashioned wooden furniture, and good carpets. In tropical areas, governors often had up-country lodges where they could escape the heat and bustle of the capital. Official quarters came rent-free. The local administration also supplied the governor with an impressive domestic staff, a majordomo, stewards, chiefs, chauffeurs, houseboys, gardeners, and laundrymen—sometimes as many as 30 people.

In settler Africa, Government House and the protocol of government tended to be somewhat simpler. Sir Harry Johnston, the first commissioner and consul-general of the British Central Africa Protectorate, picked Zomba as a site for the capital. With its beautifully laid-out garden on a lovely site, Government House was rebuilt in a composite Public Works Department style: an odd blend of castle, mission station, and municipal hospital. Johnston appreciated the blessing of living at some distance from the Scottish traders and preachers at Blantyre.

Farther to the south, in Rhodesia, the administrator lived in a pleasant, simple, whitewashed cement house on a tree-lined avenue along the northern edge of Salisbury. Other senior civil servants, professional people, and successful businessmen soon made their homes in the area near the polo grounds. Social life was agreeable to those with a taste for cricket and polo. There was also a Salisbury Hunt Club, whose members aimed at "the promotion of fox-hunting in Rhodesia" but rode to hounds in pursuit of jackals. At first there was little ceremony; Sir William Milton, one of the early administrators, was content to demonstrate the dignity of his office by having his bicycle painted in royal red. In Northern Rhodesia, on the other hand, the official residence was a hell-hole. Livingstone, the early capital, was situated in the Zambezi Valley, where the weather was hot, mosquitos plentiful, and fevers rife. Government House—an old hotel roofed with corrugated iron—caught the sun's rays and turned into an oven. Inside, His Excellency conducted the country's affairs from the former billiard room, while his private secretary had his office in the old bar.

A governor on tour was a formidable sight, and a great logistic problem for the people he deigned to visit. About 1906 Hesketh Bell toured Uganda in regal style: 200 porters carried his tents and equipment; 12 servants attended him; 40 constables protected him as he moved by mule, chair, and occasionally bicycle. Robert Coryndon, the resident of Barotseland in Northwestern Rhodesia (and future governor of Uganda and Kenya), preferred a more Spartan style; he traveled on horseback accompanied by one servant, and shot the game he required for the pot.

A governor seldom had an opportunity to meet ordinary African people except on formal and highly stylized occasions. He was, however, the effective head of local European society. If he cared to, he could act as arbiter of local fashions, deportment, and cultural attainments. Like a great landowner "at home," he was expected to take an active interest in good causes—philanthropic, educational, and religious. He belonged to the gentry ex officio. Whatever his personal mode of life, almost every governor received a knighthood during or after his term of office, a degree of social recognition inconceivable in German or French Africa. Service in British Africa came to be associated in particular with the Order of St. Michael and St. George,

and the Most Excellent Order of the British Empire. Each order had
several ranks. One could be a Companion (CMG), Knight-Commander
(KCMG), or Grand Cross (GCMG) of the Order of St. Michael and
St. George; a Member (MBE), Officer (OBE), Commander (CBE),
or Knight (KBE) of the British Empire. The governor's presence at any
public function was thus a much sought-after privilege. At every official
concourse, he was the last to arrive and the first to leave. It was a bold
man indeed who dared to scoff at His Excellency.

The Machinery of Government

British colonial policy favored decentralization, in both the administrative and the legislative sense. Theoretically, the power of Parliament was supreme; in practice its power was used sparingly, and the
British legislature rarely interfered with the details of colonial governance. Subject to Parliament, the Crown was empowered to legislate
for the colonies by Orders in Council, which were used to lay down
major lines of policy—for instance, to create local constitutions for the
colonies. The Crown's right to make laws by means of Orders in
Council did not normally lapse once a legislative assembly had been
established within a colony.

In the British possessions, unlike those of all other colonial powers,
day-to-day legislation regulating the normal work of government originated in local legislative bodies—known as legislative councils in their
earlier stage of development—whose enactments were known as ordinances. Occasionally these ordinances were disallowed by the colonial
secretary, but only when they conflicted with some major principle
of imperial policy or law. The composition of the various legislative
councils varied from colony to colony. But their evolution followed a
similar pattern. Initially, "official members," meaning the governor as
president and his senior officials, held most of the seats, and selected
a few "unofficial members" from the ranks of influential settlers to
serve with them. In time the number of unofficial members—professional men, merchants, planters, and even missionaries—increased.
Still later in the process nominated members came to be replaced by
elected members, chosen at first on a narrow franchise, which was
broadened in the later stages of colonialism as the "unofficials"
gradually acquired a majority on the council until they came to dominate the legislature. The governor ultimately became a constitutional
monarch; power was exercised by a ministry composed of councilmen
able to command a majority in the legislature.

During the "classical" era of colonialism, however, legislative councils were conceived merely as a means of giving representation to powerful local interests. A determined governor was expected to dominate his council, just as he dominated his administration. Under the conciliar system, senior civil servants were obliged to defend their politics in public; ordinances and budgets were discussed, and the debates were printed. Most of them make dull reading. But they were published in the form of *Hansards*; they were reprinted in local papers—and they were read. (Even a backwoods newspaper like the *Livingstone Mail* in Northern Rhodesia carried almost in full the proceedings of the Legislative Council, to be read over the breakfast table by the local white pioneers and some black mission graduates. Their reading habits sharply contrasted with those of a supposedly better educated generation in years to come.) Colonial governance, accordingly, became an intelligible process to the educated, not a mystery inaccessible to all but the initiated.

In running his colony, the governor was assisted by an Executive Council, whose composition was laid down in his Royal Instructions and which served as his cabinet. Under Royal Instructions, he was required to consult this council on all matters of importance. However, its role was purely advisory; sole power rested with the governor, who was entitled to reject his council's advice. In most cases, the council consisted only of the governor's most senior officials: the chief secretary or the colonial secretary, the attorney general, and usually the treasurer. Sometimes, in the more-developed colonies, it also included a few nominated unofficial members.*

The governor's principal assistant was the colonial secretary, who headed the local civil service. He was in daily touch with the governor, all communications to His Excellency passed through his hands, and he acted as deputy in the governor's absence. Sir Hugh Clifford, a distinguished British proconsul and governor of Nigeria from 1919 to 1925, put it well:

The Colonial Secretary . . . occupies, vis-à-vis the Governor, very much the same position as the Commander of a battleship in relation to her Captain. Thus it is to the Colonial Secretary rather than to the Governor that heads of departments and prominent members of the local public go in the first instance for assistance, . . . and where the system is working, as it was de-

*By 1914, for instance, the Executive Council of Nigeria consisted of the governor-general, the administrative heads of the three main territorial divisions, the attorney general, the director of railways and works, the commandant of the Nigeria Regiment, the treasurer, the director of marine (the Shipping Department), and the comptroller

signed to work, the Colonial Secretary is in such close touch with the Governor
. . . that in the majority of cases he can deal on his own responsibility with
questions brought before him.[4]

Under the colonial secretary was the secretariat, the nerve center
and the memory of government, and the vital connecting link between
the central administration and the outlying districts. Secretariats differed in their organization and power. During the early days of the
British East Africa Protectorate, for instance, the secretariat was
staffed by junior officials and could not give much direction to the
provincial commissioners. But as the pioneering period drew to its
close, the power of secretariats universally increased; so did the rift
between the secretariats, with their bureaucratic tradition, and the
provincial and the district administrators, with their ethos of independent action. "Secretariat wallahs" were expected to work reasonably
hard. Theo Williams, arriving at Livingstone in 1912, found he was
expected to attend the office from 8:00 A.M. to noon and from 2:00 P.M.
to 4:00 P.M.; these hours were closely observed.[5]

Work at the secretariat appealed to the kind of administrator who
realized that the road to promotion increasingly led through the central
organization. Many a chief secretary attained gubernatorial office. One
of these was Alfred Claud (later Sir Claud) Hollis, whose career serves
as an excellent case study. He was the son of a London barrister,
was privately educated in Switzerland and Germany, and went to
British East Africa as a trader. In 1897, at the age of twenty-three, he
joined the administration as an assistant collector (assistant district
commissioner). He was seconded to Dar es Salaam in German East
Africa as vice-consul. Subsequently he returned to East Africa as
private secretary (PS) to Governor Sir Charles Eliot. This position was
an important stepping-stone to a gubernatorial appointment; Alan
Burns, George Stewart Symes, and Bernard Bourdillon—all of whom
were later raised to knighthood and governorships—each served as PS.

The PS was expected to do all kinds of work to facilitate the governor's life and make things run smoothly at Government House, especially the social life. To fail in this position could be fatal for a career
officer—he might wind up in some godforsaken station specially re-

---

of customs. The 20-man legislature consisted of seven official members, the governor-
general and six senior administrative staff; three unofficial members named by the Lagos
Chamber of Commerce, the Calabar Chamber of Commerce, and the Chamber of
Mines; "four European members nominated by the Governor-General representative
of Commerce, Shipping, Mining and Banking"; and "six Native members nominated by
the Governor-General representative of the native population of the Coast and Interior."

served for such offenders, the glory of Government House only a memory. But Hollis did well. In 1902 he took direction of the newly formed secretariat in British East Africa and proved to be a capable administrator. He was the kind of man the Colonial Office liked. A fine linguist, studious, he wrote widely on anthropology and allied subjects, including books on the Nandi and the Masai. He sided with the "negrophilists" and incurred the dislike of European settlers, who castigated him as a reactionary, anxious to create vast African reserves where no white man might settle.[6] By the time he was transferred he had built up the power of the secretariat until it played a key role within the colony's administrative framework. In 1912 he became colonial secretary at Sierra Leone; subsequently he served again in East Africa in various capacities, including a stint as resident at Zanzibar, and wound up as governor of Trinidad and Tobago.

In the average secretariat a certain amount of routine work was delegated to assistant secretaries, but any business requiring a decision by the governor was embodied in a Minute Paper. British colonial governance hinged on these Minute Papers, which originated in many ways—through a report from a district officer, a petition from disgruntled villagers, or a development scheme put forward by the head of a technical department. In case of urgency a Minute Paper could be transmitted directly to the colonial secretary and then to the governor. Usually, however, it circulated among various departments, so that the so-called Paper grew into a substantial file filled with detailed notes from different officials. Properly designed Minute Papers were expected to contain the whole history of a subject, together with all relevant reports on the matter at issue. In this fashion, nothing went before the governor except with a recommendation from the colonial secretary, and nothing was placed before the colonial secretary without a recommendation from a more junior officer.

This system placed a premium on regularity and formality, on accumulated experience and bureaucratic expertise. It required also a relatively large number of clerks, including African clerks, to run it. The colonial government accordingly was among the first institutions to employ mission-trained Africans, able not only to read and write English, but also to file reports under their proper classification, to retrieve Minute Papers, and to understand the workings of the administration. By local standards these clerical workers were quite well paid. In the Gold Coast in 1910 fourth-class clerks earned between £80 and £100, and second-class clerks from £100 to £150 a year. The government translator in Sierra Leone in the 1880's—T. G. Lawson, an African—received a salary of £350. Given the prestige of these clerical posts, competition for government employment was intense:

No ordinary resident of Great Britain can gain any conception of it. It is the ambition of every educated young man, not possessed of other special qualifications, to enter the Government clerical service, if not by one of the permanent posts, then at least by one of the numerous incidental posts that are from time to time presenting themselves.

In spite of the elaborate efforts that are made to appoint and promote the best entitled men, the aspirant has a firm conviction that the appointments and promotions are made by personal influence, and that if he can only induce some important official to write a personal letter on his behalf his future is secure. No young man in such a country who succeeds in attracting the personal interest of any important official—whether through a literary society or some form of sport or other social co-operation—fails to apply to the official in due course to use his personal interest to secure an appointment or promotion in the clerical service either for himself or for one of his relations.[7]

The secretariat—with its powers of appointments, transfers, promotions, and dismissals—thus wielded extraordinary powers over both the British and the locally appointed African officials. It molded a new "administrative bourgeoisie" that, in time, shared the reins of power with the politicians.

The governor's relations with the outside community could be stormy in settler areas like Kenya, Northern Rhodesia, and Tanganyika. Kenya whites were especially hard on governors; they marched on Government House in 1908, threatened a civil war over the Indian question in 1922, and demonstrated to get the governor to resign in 1952. Missionaries, too, could be formidable opponents by bringing pressure to bear through Parliament and the Colonial Office. Protecting Muslim peoples from Christian proselytization was a major source of friction, as was the colonial governments' supposed toleration of "pagan vices": polygamy, child-pledging, domestic slavery, female circumcision.

Many governors were authoritarian and paternalistic. Sir Gordon Guggisberg thought of himself as a cross between a paterfamilias and the captain of the school team. Most were proud of what they had accomplished during their tenures, even with limited resources. For example, Sir Philip Mitchell (governor of Uganda, 1935–40) encouraged higher education, and Guggisberg—an ex-Royal Engineers officer—built the harbor of Takoradi and founded Achimota College. All governors tried to develop their colonies; but in times of financial stringency, little could be done, and many lacked the vision or technical skills to modernize. Some were disappointed; Sir William MacGregor felt that Lagos did not appreciate men of peace, but only men of war, and Robert Coryndon could not get the Colonial Office or the local people to work toward his goal of economic cooperation in East Africa.

The Governor: A Social Profile

British governors were a varied lot. Some were aristocrats, like Clifford, a Catholic and scion of an ancient family made famous by a member's participation in the Cabal, the ministry that had once wielded power under King Charles II. A few were of humble origin, such as Johnston, who began his young manhood as an impecunious art student. There were military men like Lord Lugard who retained in their civilian career much of the army's training and outlook. And there were men like Sir Henry Belfield, governor of East Africa during World War I, who was so unmilitary in outlook that in a wartime speech he disgusted British fighting men by deploring the way in which his colony had been dragged into a conflict not of its own making. A fair share were ex-officers of the Royal Engineers, a group that included a number of distinguished civil servants whose social origins did not quite correspond to those of the conventional British establishment, notably Sir Matthew Nathan (Natal, Gold Coast) and Guggisberg, both of Jewish descent, and Sir Percy Girouard (Northern Nigeria, British East Africa) of French-Canadian extraction. A fair share, too, came from the consular service, the Cinderella of the British bureaucracy, which throughout the nineteenth century was reserved for the private patronage of the foreign secretary. Consular appointments went to an extraordinary variety of men: dandies and soldiers on half-pay, scholars, men of letters, and explorers like David Livingstone, Richard Burton, and Henry Kirk.

Quite a few governors were accomplished stylists. Clifford and Johnston wrote novels. Sir Ronald Storr's (Northern Rhodesia) autobiographical reflections *Orientations* figured in the catalogue of the Readers' Union. Sir Charles Eliot, a product of Jowett's Balliol, was a writer of merit and a fine linguist. His first posting in the diplomatic service was to Saint Petersburg, where he compiled a pioneer Finnish grammar. Later, stationed in Constantinople, he wrote *Turkey in Europe*—a minor classic distinguished for its insight and humor, and for its author's willingness to take up unpopular positions: he believed that the Christians were too quarrelsome to make common cause with each other and too incompetent to drive the Turks from Europe. Eliot was not only interested in the Masai and Nandi languages, but also in Swahili and Chinese; he wrote a three-volume work on *Hinduism and Buddhism*, his magnum opus. He was equally conversant with marine gastropods; between 1899 and 1917 he compiled over 40 papers on the Nudibranchia, culminating in a standard monograph on the subject.

In many cases, chance took a hand in the selection of governors. The right man might happen to be on the spot when a new protectorate was set up or when a new territory began to develop under chartered company governance. But the method of choice gradually fell into a routine. Candidates were selected from lists prepared in the Colonial Service Division of the Colonial Office, using the annual confidential reports submitted by every colonial governor concerning his staff. List A held the names of serving officers considered eligible for promotion to governor; List B named men thought suitable to be chief secretary.

When a governorship was to become vacant, a small committee of Colonial Office officials drew up a short list of names, and this list worked its way up to the colonial secretary. The procedure was relatively easy in the early days—in 1909 the secretary and the permanent under-secretary simply chose governors in secret session. By the 1930's governors normally were appointed from the career colonial administrative service, and few military or political men were chosen. The qualities sought were of the kind stressed by the Public Schools: leadership, character, and a good name, along with the virtues of a strong will, courage, a sense of duty, and the ability to act fairly and firmly. In addition, a good deal of weight was attached to experience, such as previous service as provincial commissioner or chief secretary, and to seniority.

In the nineteenth century, especially, many military men were chosen. The Colonial Office favored using ex-officers "who had either proven themselves in a colony, or who they thought would make good, and members of the Royal Engineers were in great demand, because of the nature of their training, and their experience of different parts of the world made them excellent administrators."[8] Soldiers, moreover, were used to personal hazards, an important consideration at a time when climate and disease still took a heavy toll of life. One newly appointed governor to West Africa who asked whether his fare home would be paid on the expiration of his term of office was told that the question had never previously arisen.* After the turn of the century, however, health conditions began to improve, and better medical conditions helped to speed the de-militarization of the service. The Colonial Office, moreover, often had a prejudice against appointing soldiers to civil administration, for military men were unacquainted with its rules and independent traditions.

By the end of the nineteenth century the professionalization of Colonial Office senior officials had gone a long way. In 1871 seven of the 26 colonial governors in the empire were military men, nine were political appointees, and 10 were professionals; by 1901 there were no longer any political appointees, and about half of the governors (15 of 32) were professionals. None of the African governors at this stage had been appointed from the military. There was still a good deal of vocational diversity. Just before World War I the British gubernatorial staff included several ex-diplomats, two former medical doctors, 10 former Colonial Office clerks, a considerable number of regular soldiers, a few sailors, an ex-inspector of the Royal Irish Constabulary, and six members of the Indian civil service. Many of these men had organized military expeditions to Africa or set up colonial police forces. Others had made their mark in civilian administration. †

Though most British governors were Protestant Englishmen, the group included Scotsmen, Irishmen, and Canadians, Catholics and Jews. These appointees, however, like most of the candidates for office, tended to be men of the gentry or upper middle class.‡ Many of the colonial governors were younger sons of gentlemen not entitled to inherit the ancestral estate. Many more were the younger sons of professional men (often country clergymen) who could only afford to give an expensive education to the eldest son. This generalization applies to both the nineteenth century and the twentieth.[9]

According to the Marxist interpretation of history, the colonial sys-

---

* Edwin Williams Smith, *The Golden Stool: Some Aspects of the Conflict of Cultures in Africa* (London, 1926), p. 193. One in nine men died in the colonial service in East Africa before 1914, and seven of 20 administrators died between 1897 and 1907. Eight governors and three of their wives died in Freetown between 1805 and 1887.

† Over half the 103 men who served as governors between 1919 and 1939 had started their careers in the colonial service; 28 had begun in the army, and seven had served in South Africa before joining the colonial service. Fifty-five were university graduates. (Kenneth Robinson, *The Dilemmas of Trusteeship: Aspects of British Colonial Policy Between the Wars*, London, 1965, pp. 45–47.)

‡ Almost all the men who served as lieutenant-governors and governors between 1830 and 1880 (260) were from these classes, including 21 noblemen. Fifty-four had gone to university; 139 were English, 34 Scottish, and 33 Irish. About half the group had had careers in the army or navy before joining the colonial service. (Henry L. Hall, *The Colonial Office*, London, 1937, pp. 88–89.)

tem was a capitalist invention, designed to enrich merchants and industrialists. They were supposed to have sent their sons out to rule the empire. Or conversely, the rulers of the empire were but the employees of monied men, chosen to serve the wealthy. In fact, British colonial governors rarely had any links with the instruments of production or finance. Sir Drummond Chaplin, administrator of Southern Rhodesia under the British South Africa Company (1914–23), was in some ways an exception. By training a barrister, Chaplin worked for a while as *Times* correspondent on the Rand, and later for the *Morning Post* in Russia. In 1900, having made a favorable impression on Rhodes, the young journalist received an offer to manage the Consolidated Gold Fields of South Africa. Rhodes's hunch proved right. Chaplin made an outstanding name for himself in the industry, and acquired numerous directorships. In politics he was an uncompromising imperialist of the Milner school, and represented the mining interests—first in the Transvaal legislature, and later in the parliament of the Union of South Africa. Despite his industrial experience, Chaplin was very much a pukkah sahib, born of Gloucestershire gentry, an Old Harrovian and an Oxford man, welcome in every English country house.

But even the British South Africa Company did not normally appoint businessmen. Southern Rhodesia's first administrator, Archibald Ross Colquhoun, was a former imperial official in Burma, who at one time doubled as *Times* correspondent for the Far East and fell foul of his superiors by criticizing them in the press. Accordingly, he had to look for another job, and in 1899 accepted with much pleasure an offer from Rhodes to run the colony of Mashonaland. A professional civil servant firmly wedded to the niceties of administrative procedure, Colquhoun did not last long in a boisterous frontier community. He was replaced by Leander Starr Jameson, a young Edinburgh physician who had emigrated to Kimberley, where he built up a good practice in the fast-growing mining center, and where he met Rhodes, who was highly impressed by the young doctor's charm and ability. Jameson thus became involved in administration and politics, the first of a run of medical men—like Godfrey Martin Huggins (later Lord Malvern), James Maxwell, and Hastings Kamuzu Banda—who later took a prominent part in Central African public affairs. But Jameson blotted his copybook in the raid on the Transvaal that bears his name.

The chartered company, anxious to clear its reputation and institute far-reaching administrative reforms, then called on William Henry Milton (later knighted) to take over the affairs of Southern Rhodesia.

Milton was the son of an English parson who had emigrated to the Cape, and had all the traits that colonial officials looked for in a man. He joined the local civil service, made a name for his honesty and competence, and rose to be permanent head in the department of the prime minister and native affairs. He enjoyed the complete confidence of Rhodes, who also had been born in a parsonage. In 1896 he left for Southern Rhodesia, where he reorganized the administration and remained in charge until 1914.

Rhodes was an uncrowned emperor in Rhodesia, who normally had his way with senior appointments. In a certain sense, his appointments were all political. In the colonial service in Africa, however, the element of personality and political choice was not very important. According to the folklore of British radicalism immortalized in Hilaire Belloc's verse, the British ruling class was in the habit of sending off its undeserving offspring to rule the more remote dependencies.[10]

> We had intended you to be
> The next Prime Minister but three:
> The stocks were sold; the Press was squared;
> The Middle Class was quite prepared.
> But as it is! . . . My language fails!
> Go out and govern New South Wales!

Belloc, however, took insufficient account of colonial realities. Jobs in Government House at Livingstone or Freetown were not particularly desirable. The ideal patronage position was one where the work was neither arduous nor technical, where leave was plentiful and local society was cultured, where the hunting was good and distances from "home" not too great. Such posts were not to be had in Africa. The so-called "cuckoos in the nest" (political appointees) were mainly sent to Australia and New Zealand, later to pleasant island colonies like Trinidad or the Bahamas, or to Kenya with its magnificent climate and its "White Highlands" society. The high commissioners for South Africa, of course, were also political appointees, but they were carefully selected for their assignments in a key post of empire. Lord Milner assumed office in the Cape as high commissioner (1900–1905) to take a stern line against the Boers and later to consolidate British conquests. His successor, the Earl of Selborne (1905–10)—a Liberal Unionist and formerly a First Lord of the Admiralty—was dispatched as high commissioner and governor of the Transvaal and the Orange Free State to conciliate the Afrikaners. In tropical Africa the most important political appointee was Lord Lugard, who was personally selected by Joseph Chamberlain as high commissioner of Northern Nigeria (1900–1906); in 1914 he became the first governor-general of a united Nigeria, the most populous colony in Africa.

But men like Lugard were exceptions. Of the 214 governors studied by Colin Hughes and I. F. Nicolson, only 14 were "cuckoos in the nest." The remainder owed their position to promotion through established channels—that is to say, through a mixture of seniority, real or reputed ability, and good luck. Nearly all of them derived from the so-called middling ranks of society. Whereas the Germans initially appointed mainly noblemen to gubernatorial positions, the British were more likely to choose untitled men. Hughes and Nicolson could find less than a dozen scions of the nobility in their study of the years between 1900 and 1960. An aristocrat like Clifford was exceptional in the British service, unlike a Count Julius von Zech or a Duke Alfred Friedrich zu Mecklenburg. The progenitors of governors included plenty of soldiers and sailors; but tinkers and tailors, beggarmen and thieves, were conspicuous by their absence. MacGregor (governor of Lagos, 1899–1904, and then of Newfoundland and Queensland) was exceptional in being of working-class origin. But, as Hughes and Nicolson point out, MacGregor was Scottish, a Highlander, proud of his nationality and of his royal clan. He also had unusual qualifications. He held a doctorate in medicine, and another in science; he had served as resident physician in the Royal Lunatic Asylum at Aberdeen before going out to serve in the colonies; and he was also a Watson Gold Medallist (that is to say, the holder of a high British medical distinction).

The average governor was the son of a civil servant, a military officer, a squire, or some kind of a professional man or a parson. Of the 95 governors whose religious affiliation Hughes and Nicolson were able to discover, no fewer than 34 were the sons of Anglican clergymen. There were at least six Catholics and three Jews among those of known origin, but not a single son of a Nonconformist or Free Church minister. The Anglican-born vicarage boy normally advanced through a minor Public School, commonly with the aid of scholarships or with financial aid extended specifically to sons of clergymen. From there he went to one of the smaller colleges in Oxford or Cambridge; thence to a life of service abroad; and eventually to a knighthood.

This pattern was so pervasive that even the British South Africa Company, with its City connections and South African links, soon came to employ the same kind of man who would have risen high in the colonial service. To the Colonial Office, "London Wall"—the

company's headquarters—was somewhat suspect, the home of par-
venus and wealthy miscreants. But service with the British South
Africa Company also attracted many "improvers." When Milton left
for Rhodesia to reorganize an administration discredited by the
Jameson Raid and disorganized by a great African rising, he was more
disturbed by the amateurish incompetence and the favoritism extended to well-connected speculators. "Everything official here is in
an absolutely rotten condition," he disgustedly wrote to his wife. He
had constant trouble with "titled understrappers." Matters would not
improve "until we can clear out the Honourable and military element
which are rampant everywhere, and are evidently expecting a reward
with fat billets after the war."[11] Milton set up a regular civil service
patterned on the British Cape tradition, introduced a variety of reforms, and remained in charge of the country for 18 years.

The Education of a Governor

The great majority of British governors came from the southeastern
part of England or were educated there—the portion most in touch
with London and with the universities of Oxford and Cambridge, the
geographical core of the British ruling class. Whereas the French recruited many of their best colonial administrators from more remote
areas like Corsica or Brittany, and the Germans relied heavily on the
rural regions of Silesia, Pomerania, East Prussia, and the more backward parts of southern Germany, the British colonial rulers usually
had a variety of links to London and the Home Counties. The Mid-
lands and the North were underrepresented. So were Ireland and
Scotland except for the Anglo-Irish and the Edinburgh Scots. Moreover, the Protestant gentry from Ulster provided a disproportionately
high percentage of military officers. According to Hughes' and Nicolson's findings, no more than 17 "outsiders"—men not of English
birth and background, not educated at English Public Schools, or at
Oxford or Cambridge, or at one of the residential colleges maintained
by the armed services—became a governor. Most of these outsiders
spoke with a Scottish "burr" instead of an Oxford accent, and usually
had taken their degrees at Edinburgh or Aberdeen.

The background of the majority of governors was strikingly similar
to that of the soldiers discussed in Chapter 3. Eighteen of the Hughes-
Nicolson sample were educated at Eton, Harrow, or Winchester, and
21 at Charterhouse, Merchant Taylors, Rugby, St. Paul's, Shrewsbury,
or Westminster. Eighty came from smaller Public Schools not widely

known outside England, such as Sedbergh near Carlisle, and five from recognized Public Schools outside England. Thirty-two obtained their education in well-established grammar schools.* The ethos of these establishments, and of the "prep schools" that prepared candidates for admission to Public Schools, has been described by many authors, but nowhere better than in the excellent work on George Orwell by Peter Stansky and William Abrahams.[12] We shall therefore confine ourselves to reprinting the "Ten Commandments of a Public School Boy," as enunciated in a semi-facetious fashion just before the outbreak of World War I.[13]

   I. There is only one God; and the Captain of football is his Prophet.
  II. My school is the best in the world.
 III. Without big muscles, strong will, and proper collars there is no salvation.
  IV. I must wash much and in accordance with tradition.
   V. I must speak the truth even to a master, if he believes everything I tell him.
  VI. I must play games with all my heart, with all my soul and with all my strength.
 VII. To work outside class hours is indecent.
VIII. Enthusiasm, except for games, is in bad taste.
  IX. I must look up to the older fellows and pour contempt on newcomers.
   X. I must show no emotion and not kiss my mother in public.

The cult of athletic prowess, courage, and endurance grew apace. It went with an unrelenting, albeit a losing, struggle against juvenile onanism, a pastime held accountable for a multitude of afflictions. By 1880 or so the mania for games had come to dominate all Public Schools. At Harrow the government of the houses was passing from the studious to the physically fit; at Rugby, where the athletes did not rule officially, they acquired unofficial power as the monitorial system began to decay.[14]

Contemporary evaluations of the Public School differed widely. To the average Anglican vicar in the country parish, the Public School was God's chosen instrument for building "character," that odd blend of patriotic loyalty, skill in ball games, respect for tradition, contempt for intellectuals, and the cultivation of a stoic dignity. Empire builders

---

*Of the 110 governors appointed between 1940 and 1960, 78 came from the colonial service and 17 from the army. Eighty-two were university graduates (Oxford, 40; Cambridge, 27), and 82 had been to Public Schools. (John Michael Lee, *Colonial Development and Good Government: A Study of the Ideas Expressed by the British Official Classes in Planning Decolonization, 1939–1964*, Oxford, Eng., 1967.)

like the pioneering administrator of Northern Rhodesia Robert Codrington looked on the Public School as an institution ideally suited
for the purpose of training colonial administrators. Radicals were more
likely to regard the Public School as a successful device for fusing the
landed gentry with the new bourgeoisie sprung from commerce,
banking, and industry. Kipling, the prophet of the "younger sons"—
the middle-class young men who looked for fame or fortune overseas
—idealized the Public School product; yet he castigated the system
with a bitterness never equaled in British literature. The Public
School, he wrote in "The Waster," was a prison where the English
filled their children with useless social prejudices that made them unfit
to compete with Jews and Scotsmen, who brought up their boys in a
more sensible fashion.

In recent times the charge has been picked up by Norman Dixon,
a distinguished psychologist with a military background, and by Correlli Barnett, a fine military historian, among others. Dixon considers
that the Public School had a deleterious effect on British generalship
by helping to shape authoritarian personality patterns, casting men in a
conventional and inflexible mold that was ill-suited to the needs of
high command. However, a large proportion of the great British
generals and military thinkers Dixon admires—Liddell Hart, Mont-
gomery, O'Connor, Wingate, Allenby, Plumer—were products of the
great Public Schools. Progressive schools like Dartington Hall, mindful
of Freudian psychology, have as yet made no comparable contribution
to British leadership. And children of liberal-minded parents, anxious
to bring up their offspring in a permissive fashion, have also been
known to have blinkered minds. Barnett's criticism of the Public
Schools goes even further than Dixon's. The Public Schools, and Oxford and Cambridge, he argues, artificially separated aristocratic and
upper-middle-class youngsters from the bulk of the nation. The system
placed little value on science, either pure or applied. It taught nothing
about technology, or business, or economics, or sociology, or military
strategy, or indeed the realities of power in general. British merchants
and manufacturers were encouraged to ape the gentry; their children
were taught to despise the world of the laboratory and workshop. Not
surprisingly, British technology and business methods became increasingly obsolescent; the British ceased to be aggressive, dynamic, and
competitive. Even the Royal Navy lost its technological preeminence
over the more efficient German High Seas Fleet. The Public Schools
were poorly designed for the purpose of training ruthless men determined to hold on to what they held. Instead, their pupils were filled

with abstract notions concerning higher morality that merely put British rulers at a psychological disadvantage vis-à-vis their more educated subjects.[15] All in all, the Public School has been held co-responsible for an astonishing variety of ills, ranging from the inefficiency of British industries and the incompetence of British generals to an acquired taste for sodomy.

Moreover, according to some, the British managed to pass on their prejudices to their subjects. As a Nigerian government report put it toward the end of the colonial era: "The literary tradition and the university degree have become indelible symbols of prestige in Nigeria; by contrast technology, agriculture and other practical subjects, particularly at the sub-professional level, have not won esteem. It is small wonder, then, that training for qualifications other than degrees, especially in technology, is not popular."[16]

We cannot, however, accept these conclusions in their entirety. True enough, Great Britain did experience a relative decline in relation to Germany during the three decades that preceded World War I. But it is doubtful whether the Public Schools and their values bore the main responsibility for this. Educational stratification in Germany was no less rigid than in Great Britain. Wealthy German manufacturers like the Krupps were no less anxious to acquire patents of nobility and dwell in baronial mansions than their opposite numbers in Great Britain. There was somewhat more social mobility in France than in either Germany or Great Britain; yet France lagged behind in industry. The British, moreover, acquired considerable indirect benefit from a relatively cohesive ruling class. The gulf between civilian and military officeholders in Great Britain, for instance, was nothing like as wide as in Germany, and even within the German military itself. The German Navy was technically efficient, but its officer corps was sharply segmented into several layers—Deckoffiziere, Seeoffiziere, and so forth—a division that contributed to the subsequent collapse of morale in the High Seas Fleet in 1917, a political breakdown from which the Royal Navy remained exempt.

As administrators of empire, the British Public School boys did what was expected of them. They built an ethos of mutual confidence that helped to make the empire's colonial administration into one of the least corrupt in history. They won the admiration of French and German experts, apt otherwise to sneer at the British. They created a pattern of social excellence that probably had a greater impact on colonial Africa than any form of missionary endeavor. These former Public School boys, used to cold, drafty rooms and poorly cooked food, combined the good manners of the upper classes with the hardihood of the poor. They provided a plentiful supply of all-around-men for a colonial administration designed primarily to provide no more than an elementary degree of physical security and a fairly rudimentary infrastructure. There is no evidence that the British would have speeded development, or endowed their subjects with more industrial skills, or prolonged colonial rule if they had selected their civil servants from the ranks of marine engineers trained at Glasgow or economists graduated from the London School of Economics. British gentlemen were also apt to be more sympathetic toward Africans than the sons of British workers and shopkeepers trained in elementary and secondary schools. (Sir Ralph Furse, one of the makers of the British colonial service, thus rightly contrasted in later years the racial attitudes of Public School–bred officials in Northern Rhodesia with those of British foremen and technicians, much to the latter's disadvantage.)

Critics have raised similar objections regarding the proconsuls' lack of familiarity with the social sciences. The majority of British officials in the colonies were unacquainted with works on economics. Sociology was hardly regarded as a respectable pursuit at Oxford and Cambridge. Academic anthropology had not as yet come into its own as a powerful discipline. (In the decade preceding World War I the British appointed a few scholars to conduct ethnographic inquiries in the colonies, including C. G. Seligman in the Sudan, but anthropology only made a serious impact after the war.) Even historians were apt to emphasize the remoter past. Few proconsuls had read much history at school or college beyond the period of the French Revolution. Greece and Rome played a larger part in their historical consciousness than the contemporary history of their own island. But there is no evidence that these biases in any way disqualified them from an efficient discharge of their duties. A thorough acquaintance with Caesar's conquest of Gaul or with the causes of the Peloponnesian War may have been a positive advantage, as opposed to excessive familiarity with the minutiae of some obscure British trade dispute.

A more serious criticism applies not only to the British Public School, but to all higher educational institutions in Europe designed to turn out colonial administrators—the lack of practical training.

In my life is an ever-present regret [wrote a British colonial administrator] to think of the time wasted on Latin, Greek, German and Higher Mathematics, of which I really learnt but little and remember nothing now. If I had spent all those long and tedious hours in learning the elements of the arts of the blacksmith, mason and first-aid, they would have been of everlast-

ing value to me. . . . At different times I have had to act as carpenter, blacksmith, armourer, mason, doctor, midwife, gardener, shopkeeper, policeman,
architect, planter and surveyor, but fortunately, never in the course of my
work in Africa have I been called on to make Greek verse or enunciate the
binominal theorem.[17]

Skills of a more practical kind could be acquired at the Deutsche
Kolonialschule at Witzenhausen, designed to train settlers. American
administrators in the Philippines also had a reputation for their manual
and technical know-how. Such capacities were relatively uncommon
among the British, except among former Royal Engineers officers. The
Royal Engineers in fact supplied an impressive number of empire
builders. A few have been mentioned—Guggisberg, Nathan, and
Girouard. But there were many others, including Sir John Chancellor,
first governor of Southern Rhodesia, Sir Hector McCallum, an early
Lagos governor, and such renowned figures as Goldie, Gordon, and
Kitchener.

Whatever its weaknesses, the Public School instilled sufficient confidence in its pupils to permit their tackling the most improbable assignment. There was nothing of the guild spirit that adjured youngsters
not to tackle a task unless it could be finished to perfection. And the
Public School ethos was pervasive. It filtered down to grammar (day)
schools, situated in provincial towns proud of their local traditions,
where sons of local gentlemen would sit next to the sons of well-to-do
butchers and master bakers. But rugby was played hard; prefects stood
no nonsense from Third Formers. Troublemakers were duly caned in
the headmaster's office, preferably waiting their turn in a row on Saturday morning; Latin irregular verbs were memorized without fail;
morning prayers were compulsory; and a conscientious headmaster
might use the Scripture period to teach Saint Thomas Aquinas's five
proofs for the existence of God to an unbelieving Upper Sixth.

No matter whether he was a grammar school or a Public School
graduate, the average governor was well-educated. At least 127 of
the Hughes-Nicholson group had been university men, another 136
had some kind of military training in place of—or in addition to—their
university training; 36 had legal qualifications. Quite a few won academic distinctions at a university, a gold medal in mathematics, or a
Bacon scholarship in law. Once admitted to the civil service, they
sometimes made their reputation as private secretary to an influential
minister. More often than not, however, they worked their way up
from district officer to provincial commissioner or, most frequently,
they gained experience as chief secretary, learning how to control the

administrative nerve center of one colony before taking over the governance of another. Within the service, they were apt to form part of unobtrusive, little-recognized connections, subsystems that linked together men who had gotten to know one another within particular parts of the empire—say, the Cape or West Africa—or who were held together by common interests or common service in the same military unit.

For an example, Robert Edward Codrington, the pioneer administrator of what later became Northern Rhodesia and scion of an old Gloucestershire family with a great naval tradition, had knocked around the world before going into government. After trying his luck in Virginia, he made his way to South Africa, where he joined the Bechuanaland Border Police, a great preparatory school for Central African administrators; one of his colleagues in the ranks was another future governor, Sir Robert Coryndon. Codrington's promotion was quick; at twenty-four he was a sergeant. He distinguished himself in fighting against the Ndebele, then left the police and joined Harry Johnston's pioneer administration in Nyasaland. Johnston had very strong convictions about the kind of people he wanted—men with Indian experience and sons of consular and diplomatic officials, not adventurers or applicants from the self-governing colonies "without a proper governing class."[18] Codrington fitted this mold. He now had experience; he was a member both of a Central African and a South African "network"; in 1900 he was promoted to be administrator of Northeastern Rhodesia. In this capacity he reorganized the local administrative service on Johnstonian lines. And he took particular care to recruit young, rugby-playing schoolmasters from minor Public Schools—known locally as "bumswitchers"—on the assumption that men capable of disciplining English schoolboys could not fail to subjugate tribesmen.

British governors, then, were men of many parts drawn from a variety of backgrounds. Typically they were of English origin and Protestant persuasion, though a goodly number were neither. But they were invariably white, and they looked on Great Britain as "home." By and large, they were gentlemen both in the sociological and the ethical meaning of the word. They were, on the whole, incorruptible and well educated; there was no British equivalent to that minority of French governors who, during the pre–World War I period, had come up from the ranks without even having completed a secondary education. They were never besmirched by financial scandals. Colonial governors were rulers of a peculiar kind: autocrats within a limited sphere, wedded to a secular cult of "improvement," but without the legal powers or military means to govern as despots. For better or for worse, they reflected the qualities of the Victorian and Edwardian British upper classes, with their weaknesses but also with their manifold strengths.

SIX

The District Officer

When the British embarked on the Scramble for Africa they had numerous advantages over their competitors. They dominated much of the trade in sub-Saharan Africa; and they could draw on a larger reservoir of men with tropical experience than any other nation, men already in the colonial service as well as "odd men out": big-game hunters with a love of Africa, ex-employees of chartered companies, soldiers sick of garrison life, physicians with a bent for scientific exploration and a distaste for a regular provincial practice, missionaries eager to save black souls, clerks anxious to leave their counting houses, and young men of good family intent on adventure and on drawing a salary in the bargain.

The staffing system for the quickly expanding empire was unsystematic. Men were recruited at home, locally on the spot, and by transfer from other African territories. At the center of the empire in London all the appointments were at first made by a youthful assistant private secretary in the Colonial Office, helped by an unpaid colleague and subject only to the minister's formal assent. The names, qualifications, and credentials of applicants were entered into large leather volumes labeled "Administrative," "Legal," "Medical," and "Treasury, Audit and Customs." Candidates were also interviewed. Those who made a good impression on their youthful interlocutors received consideration as vacancies arose. "I don't think we made many mistakes," wrote the civil servant in charge of this operation, "and I shouldn't wonder if the system worked as well as another."[1]

Selection at the periphery at first was equally haphazard, with the result that pioneer administrators were an extraordinarily mixed group. Many joined the colonial service locally after being in a chartered company or in an army or police unit in Africa. The Imperial

British East African Company provided numerous officials for the colonial administration of British East Africa when the company lost its charter. Some were not educated or able men and saddled the Colonial Office with second-rate officers; others, however, became outstanding colonial officials. Similarly, the British South Africa Company in the Rhodesias supplied the colonial service with a larger number of able recruits.

There was also a missionary-humanitarian strain, perhaps best represented by the Reverend John Mackenzie, who served as government agent and later as deputy commissioner in Bechuanaland toward the latter part of the nineteenth century. In the eyes of many settlers and of the British South Africa Company's directorate, Mackenzie was the archetype of the meddlesome cleric, with stern mien, "negrophilist notions," and Scots diction.

The grant of a royal charter to the British South Africa Company in 1889 was resolutely opposed by Mackenzie, who was convinced that direct imperial governance in southern Africa would uplift the heathen and protect the blacks against white ruffians. He compared the situation in the "far interior" of southern Africa to that in the American west before the Civil War. As Mackenzie saw it, the future of Bechuanaland and Rhodesia depended on the question of whether the new territories should be "Free Soil" or "Slave States." Only the imperial government would preserve African rights against chartered speculators and settlers.

Nevertheless, Mackenzie, the crofter's orphan from Morayshire, and Cecil Rhodes, the vicar's son from Bishop's Stortford, had a surprising lot in common. Both had an unshakable faith in Great Britain's imperial destiny. Both believed that the rush of white settlers into the interior was inevitable. According to Mackenzie, there was no place inland for Boer raiders or British adventurers; but a loyal and contented class of colonists would be a source of strength to the British connection, as were the colonists of the eastern Cape. Like Rhodes, he believed that British miners and farmers had as much right to be in the Transvaal as Boer and Bantu pastoralists.

In defending his brand of humanitarianism, one reminiscent of David Livingstone's, Mackenzie proved a formidable lobbyist. Like Livingstone, another prominent member of the London Missionary Society, Mackenzie knew how to plead his cause in missionary meetings and lecture halls, in private gatherings and public concourses. He would buttonhole editors and argue with members of Parliament. He also managed to gain the confidence of the Tswana rulers—realistic men who looked to Christianity as a road to salvation, as a means of acquiring Western skills, and as an instrument of diplomacy capable of strengthening their position against the Boers.[2]

The great majority of pioneer administrators, however, lacked both Mackenzie's ideological fervor and his London connections. Though they were a varied group they had some things in common—they were tired of a sheltered existence at home, and they had widely traveled abroad. T. H. R. Cashmore gives a fascinating picture of the civil servants who ran the British East Africa Protectorate.[3] Francis Hall, later a prominent administrator, was a nephew of Lord Goschen; A. C. W. Jenner was the son of a baronet and a barrister by training. John Ainsworth, a tough and ruthless pioneer, derived from a more modest social stratum. He was the son of a Manchester trader and was brought up in north Wales. He joined a British mercantile firm, then went overseas and spent five years trading in West Africa and the Congo. Stricken by a fever in the Congo, he left the area to seek employment with the Imperial British East African Company and later the colonial service. D. J. Wilson had come from India as a superintendent of telegraphs; J. J. Anderson, an engineer from Norway, had resigned from a minor civil service post because he objected to a Radical ministry.

There were gentlemen of private means, such as F. J. Jackson, who had been educated at Shrewsbury and at Jesus College, Cambridge. There was a substantial contingent of military men at a time when a plentiful supply of subalterns on half-pay still roamed the world in search of interesting employment. Lugard was one of these; so was Girouard. Others were ex-policemen, among them G. H. L. Murray, whose experience oddly combined employment in the General Registry Office at Somerset House in London with a lengthy spell in the Natal Mounted Police. Some had been to North America: H. R. Tate had ranched in North Dakota before coming out to Africa; C. P. Isaac had farmed in California. There was a former master mariner, a former Church Missionary Society lay artisan, and a seaman who had been beached after the loss of his ship. There were ex-naval officers, a classics master, a bank clerk, and a tea planter. And above all, there were parsons' sons, including J. R. W. Piggott, a strict and "zealous churchman" who married a lady missionary.*

Many officials in East and Central Africa came from South Africa.

---

* Still, Colonel Meinertzhagen, then a junior officer in the King's African Rifles and a harsh critic of his fellow men, was not much impressed with the group as a whole. Many of them lacked education, he wrote in his diary (1904). One of them was illiterate. But even Meinertzhagen found civil servants whom he respected and liked. See his *Kenya Diary, 1902–1906* (Edinburgh, 1957), *passim*.

The war of 1899–1902 played an especially important role in this transfer by whetting the appetite for African life in men from the United
Kingdom, Australia, New Zealand, and Canada who had seen service
in that part of the continent. Perhaps 10 percent of the officials in
the administration of British East Africa before 1914 had come from
South Africa, and the Rhodesian and Nyasaland colonial services were
similarly heavily staffed by men who had been born in the south or who
had served there in the army or the police.

An example was J. H. Osborne, the son of a Sheffield clergyman
who managed to send his youngster to Cambridge. Failing the entrance examination for the Indian civil service, he entered the Sheffield Steel and Iron Works as a clerk, and when war broke out he
joined the Imperial Yeomanry. The war experience spoiled him for life
in Sheffield. He tried his luck as a farmer in Canada and then as a
schoolmaster before coming to the protectorate, aged twenty-nine and
still a bachelor.

Such men found England a depressing place, apt to produce a sense
of claustrophobia among those who longed for the freer life in the
bush. Kipling put this sentiment into a poem about a private soldier
who was unable to settle down at home after having fought on the
South African veld:[4]

> Me that 'ave been what I've been,
> Me that 'ave gone where I've gone,
> Me that 'ave seen what I've seen—
> 'Ow can I ever take on
> With awful old England again,
> An' houses both side of the street,
> An' 'edges both side of the lane,
> An' the parson an' "gentry" between,
> An' touchin' my 'at when we meet—
> Me that 'ave been what I've been?

The Systematizing of Recruitment

As the supply of candidates increased and as health and transport
in the tropical colonies improved, the recruiters—whether employed
by the Colonial Office, the British South Africa Company, or the Sudan
political service—became increasingly selective. There was more discrimination against locally recruited men, including both European
settlers who had not obtained a Public School education and educated
Africans. The colorful pioneers were replaced by sons from the profes-

1. Royal Colonial Institute, London.

PIONEERS

Left: 2. Lord Lugard, high commissioner of Northern Nigeria, 1900–1907.

Below: 3. Sir Cecil Rhodes (seated third from left), with Sir Harry Johnston, commissioner of Nyasaland, 1891–96, to his right and A. R. Colquhoun, resident commissioner of Rhodesia, 1890–91, to his left.

RESIDENCES   *Above*: 4. Palace of the regent of Zanzibar.

Below: 5. Government House, Bulawayo, Southern Rhodesia.

IN THE INTERIOR   *Above*: 6. William Edward Maxwell, governor of the Gold Coast, 1895–97, on tour up-country, 1896.

Below: 7. British officers in talks with Kumasi chiefs, Gold Coast, late 1890's.

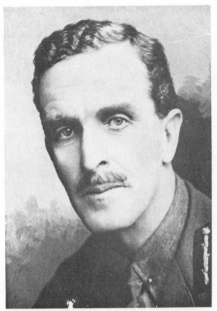

GOVERNORS   *Above left*: 8. Sir Gordon Guggisberg, Gold Coast, 1919–27. *Above right*: 9. Sir Matthew Nathan, Gold Coast, 1900–1904; Natal, 1907–9.

Below: 10. Sir Leslie Probyn, Sierra Leone, 1904–11, with staff.

AFRICAN   *Above*: 11. Mungo High School, Sierra Leone, 1906. Founded by the Christian
EDUCATION   Missionary Society.

Below: 12. Faculty and students of Fourah Bay College, also founded by the Society and later affiliated to the University of Durham.

13. British officers and Hausa
NCO's, Southern Nigeria, 1896.

14. Nairobi police, Kenya, ca. 1900.

Below: 15. Postmaster James Carmichael Smith (seated third from left)
and staff, Sierra Leone, early 1900's.

SPECIALISTS   *Above*: 16. Survey caravan, West Africa, ca. 1899.

Below: 17. Railway building camp, Uganda, ca. 1899–1900.

SPORT   *Above:* 18. A lion kill, 1906.

Below: 19. Entebbe hockey team, Uganda, ca. 1911.

20. Freetown, Sierra Leone, ca. 1890.

sional classes, properly trained and furnished with approved university diplomas. British administrators, unlike their opposite numbers in the German and French service, had graduated in a variety of subjects —classics, mathematics, history. As a group they were never as rigidly specialized as their German confrères, whose training as Referendar and Assessor emphasized legal and administrative questions.

The recruitment of colonial servants was influenced also by the prestige of the Public Schools and by the admiration for their graduates evinced by many of those who had never attended one—and who would have fared badly had they got there. Sir Harry Johnston's father, for example, was the respectable secretary of a large insurance firm and a leading member of the Catholic Apostolic Church, a strange amalgam of Calvinist theology and Catholic and Eastern Orthodox practices. Johnston went to Stockwell Grammar School. He was a gifted boy, studious, plump, with a high-pitched voice, given to fits of hypochondria and theological ruminations—not the kind of man to get into a rugby First Fifteen.

These disqualifications did not prevent him from becoming a great empire builder; he played a major role in subjecting Nyasaland and Northeastern Rhodesia to the British Crown. He was convinced that sons of the British ruling class who had been to a Public School would make the best colonial administrators. He showed a distinct preference for men with Indian experience rather than those whom he styled local "adventurers"; he favored the sons of consular and diplomatic officials and disliked candidates from the self-governing colonies devoid of a "governing class." He was particularly determined to keep out South Africans, whom he considered to be "without any conception of justice where natives were concerned." He soon found, however, that though he could get good men to come out for almost nothing in order to see the country, it took good salaries and pensions to keep them. Thus, in 1897, he set up a regular civil service, with different grades and a stepped promotion system in which all candidates had to start out as "assistant collectors."[5]

The Nyasaland system was extended into Northern Rhodesia by Robert Codrington, a Public School boy from Marlborough who had served under Johnston. Codrington also asked for men trained at Public Schools and at one of the great universities, and in 1901 he set up a regular, graded civil service. The chartered company, a commercial body, was at first by no means satisfied with these arrangements, which involved fixity of tenure and pensions, but it accepted the system and benefited in the end by getting competent administrators and few resignations. By 1914 all probationers in the company's service north of the Zambezi had to be university men, and the "imperial" type of administration had come to stay.[6]

In Southern Rhodesia, on the other hand, a university education was not obligatory except in the technical services, and civil servants could be promoted to senior positions from the clerical ranks—an arrangement reflecting the more egalitarian patterns of a settler-dominated society.

For the recruitment patterns in British East African we turn again to Cashmore's valuable study. Approximately 200 men joined the administration between 1895 and 1918. There is little or no information for a third of the officials, but Cashmore makes the following estimates: at least one-third had been to a university, and half had attended a Public School; one in five had served in the armed forces; one in five were sons of parsons;* one in 10 had come from South Africa, where they had been soldiers, settlers, or civil servants; one in 20 became a colonial governor; and one in nine died in the service.

These figures are not comparable to those in the West African colonial service because so many men who joined the Imperial British East African Company had motives different from those who had joined the colonial service directly. For example, the level of education would be higher for members of the colonial service than for the staff of chartered companies. Probably even more parsons' sons joined the colonial service than went to work for business concerns such as the Imperial British East African Company; in the Sudan political service about 33 percent of the members were sons of parsons, against only 20 percent in East Africa.

When the Colonial Office took over the administration of British East Africa, recruitment was tightened, and fewer local men gained entrance to the service. The colorful variety of the earlier days largely disappeared after 1907. The administration looked instead for men who had obtained a university degree or a regular commission, or who were qualified as barristers. Governor Girouard thus insisted in 1910 that he wanted only university men—no more "cowpunchers." †

---

*T. H. R. Cashmore, "Studies in District Administration in the East Africa Protectorate, 1895–1918," unpublished doctoral dissertation, Cambridge University, 1965, pp. 21–30. Other family backgrounds were: 12 sons of army or navy regular officers; nine sons of businessmen; seven sons of gentry; five sons of doctors; five sons of lawyers; four sons of civil servants; three sons of peers.

† In 1911–12 three of eight recruits came from Oxford and three from Cambridge; the youngest was twenty-two and the oldest thirty-one. All were bachelors and most engaged in sports.

The pattern followed by Johnston under the Foreign Office, by Codrington under the British South Africa Company, and by Girouard in
British East Africa was applied also by the Colonial Office throughout
the rest of Africa. The growth of the British colonial administration
paralleled the development of the older British universities, in particular Oxford and Cambridge. The reforms effected at Oxford improved the lecturers' position and led to the rise of a regular resident
faculty. Schools and degrees multiplied; the number of graduates
increased, and the universities took a more active part in finding jobs
for their B.A.'s. In 1892 Oxford set up the Oxford University Appointments Committee headed by the Reverend M. B. Furse, a Trinity
College man who later rose to be bishop of Pretoria; the committee
acted as a placement office and soon expanded its contacts from education to business and government.

Under the new dispensation aristocratic and ministerial patronage
gave way to a system in which the Colonial Office relied on the great
universities to produce trained candidates. By 1910 the Colonial Office
had two full-time assistant private secretaries for appointment work.
One of these was R. D. Furse, himself a graduate of Oxford and a
nephew of the original head of the appointments committee. Except
for his military service in World War I, Furse remained responsible
for colonial service recruitment until 1948. As Robert Heussler puts
it in his classic study, "More than any single man, he *made* the C. S.
[colonial service] and is deservedly spoken of as its father. His personality, his outlook on life, and his conception of the qualities which
colonial officials ought to have were stamped indelibly on the character
of the service."[7]

Furse himself was the epitome of what he wanted the colonial
service to be. An Old Etonian, descended from a county family with
long-standing Oxford connections, he came to Balliol College in 1906,
played rugby and cricket with some distinction, and in 1909 passed
out with a Third—still a good degree at a time when any Oxford man
belonged to an elite and received the intellectual training appropriate
to an elite institution. His contemporaries at Balliol included such distinguished men as Julian Huxley, Ronald Knox, and Lewis Namier.
Balliol's ideology, in so far as a college could be said to have an ideology, was one of public service tempered by paternalism and good manners—the kind of good manners that went down fully as well in eti-
quette-conscious societies like those of the Bemba and Fulani as they
did in English country houses.

Balliol, and Oxford as a whole, was profoundly affected at the time by the work of T. H. Green, whose creed became the university's accepted philosophical tradition during the years preceding World War I. Green's idealist philosophy, developed in opposition to men like Mill and Spencer, rehabilitated—not exactly Christianity—but a religious approach to existence. It inculcated in its adherents a strong sense of obligation to subordinate personal interest to what Green believed to be the common good. As a political theorist, he emphasized social solidarity and claimed a larger sphere for social action than most utilitarians had been willing to allow. His work seemed to discredit the optimistic beliefs of an earlier generation that free competition was the surest way to obtain universal happiness. Green encouraged an interventionist approach to the economy and was supported in his views by other Balliol dons like A. D. Lindsay and Richard Tawney.

The Balliol men of Furse's generation took these notions very seriously. As a group they were oriented toward public service, and took only a minor share in business or the science-based industries. They had largely ceased to become Church of England parsons. Overwhelmingly, they made their careers in law, the public services, education, and the army—occupations where the service motif predominated and where ambitious men commonly believed, without justification, that a livelihood derived from fees and salaries was somehow morally superior to an income founded on commercial or industrial profits. Almost to a man they were willing to risk their lives for their country. During World War I a high percentage volunteered for military service; 22 percent of those who served lost their lives, double the national average; many more were seriously wounded, as was Furse. A cynic might suggest that Balliol men used their background and social connections to obtain comfortable staff positions for themselves. But the record shows that the overwhelming majority, like Major Furse, became front-line officers, mainly in the infantry.[8]

In the Colonial Office, Furse, like Johnston and Codrington, wanted the kind of cadets who had been prefects in British Public Schools, who had played cricket and made it into the rugby First Fifteen. The outdoorsman with not too many brains and a great deal of common sense was the ideal. Public Schools supposedly developed the concepts of honor, fair play, and duty, as well as a sense of snobbishness and superiority. Athletic prowess in recruits was perhaps emphasized most strongly of all in the Sudan, but by 1914 even British East Africa had engaged four "Blues" (men who had played for an Oxbridge university team). According to Governor Geoffrey Archer, "For native administration the qualities of scholarship and academic attainment are not to be prized so highly as the leadership of men. Brilliance in debate can hardly equal the initial advantage gained in youth by having led in the field a body of well trained and disciplined young men of similar age."[9]

Furse did not look for intellectual brilliance. Men with Firsts were more likely to go into the Indian civil service or into the academic profession than into colonial employment. He did want men who had learned the elements of what he called leadership; men who were detached, self-disciplined, and self-reliant, who were well-spoken and possessed of reasonable culture, and—above all—who were gentlemen.

To a considerable extent he succeeded. Under his tutelage, the typical colonial administrator came to be much like his superior, the governor, in background. Well-educated—at least 80 percent of the men who served between 1900 and 1914 had attended a Public School or a university—"most of them came from 'good' country families; they obeyed a rigid code of manners; and were punctilious about shaving. They believed quite genuinely that those 'lesser breeds without the law' who had been gathered into the British fold were remarkably lucky."[10] They tended to be young—reflecting the Colonial Office's preference to recruit men who were under twenty-five.

The "local men" all but disappeared from higher posts in Colonial Office territories. "Cowpunchers," hunters, and soldiers of fortune ceased to find jobs available to them; and Africans, who previously had filled a number of senior posts in Sierra Leone and the Gold Coast, could no longer rise to high positions. By and large, the plums of the service went to the "home-born," to men recruited in the United Kingdom and educated at Oxbridge, at a good Public School, at a military school, or in law. The new-style colonial service was not staffed by a "ruling class" in the Marxist sense. Poor relations and overdrafts were familiar companions. A good family background and social connections made no difference in getting an applicant promoted to the higher ranks. The plums of the service instead went to men with a distinguished bureaucratic record. But the service did attain a considerable measure of uniformity in ethos and life-style. The course was set, and the "gentlemen" took charge.

Motives and Men

What made so many British gentlemen take up a colonial career, a way of life that not only entailed considerable hardship and risk but

also meant semi-permanent expatriation? For one thing, service overseas was socially acceptable. Few British applicants for colonial service
were ever deterred by their relatives or teachers or employers in the
way in which young Frenchmen and Germans were frequently discouraged by their elders. A Wilhelmian paterfamilias might have been
a loyal supporter of colonialism in theory, but he was still apt to look
on the German colonies as a refuge for scoundrels and ne'er-do-wells,
not the kind of place where his own son should serve. Such was the
experience of Heinrich Schnee, a governor of German East Africa, and
many of his contemporaries.

A British father was likely to look on a colonial career as an honorable
pursuit, especially if he had forebears, brothers, or friends associated
with the colonial empire. To quote Sir Alan Burns:

I was practically born into the Colonial Civil Service. My grandfather and my
father were both members of that Service, and most of my childhood was
spent in the colonies, where many of my father's friends were also civil
servants. My father's sister was married to a colonial judge. I cannot remember
ever having thought seriously of any other possible career. With all its draw-
backs, it offers great possibilities to a young man for a pleasant life and a useful
one and if I had the chance to begin again I do not think I should choose any
other. I realize that I have been more fortunate than the majority of my colleagues, chiefly because I have been blessed with good health, and that the
prizes of the Civil Service go to very few, but notwithstanding this I still
believe that the Colonial Service offers a great deal that is worth while to those
who are prepared to face discomfort and the possibility of prolonged separation from home and family.[11]

Service in the empire was often less a matter of glory and wealth
than a call to duty and a means of service to mankind. Lord Curzon,
in explaining what constituted the "true" imperialism, noted that
England had been invested with wealth and power, with control of
distant lands, for a great and important purpose. It was the Englishman's duty to carry civilization, humanity, peace, good government,
and Christianity to the ends of the earth.[12] Many Englishmen felt the
same way. To them, colonial service afforded an opportunity to serve,
a personal proving ground, a career that gave a man a purpose greater
than himself. The young Winston Churchill expressed it as well as
anyone:

What enterprise that an enlightened community may attempt is more noble
and more profitable than the reclamation from barbarism of fertile regions and
large populations? To give peace to warring tribes, to administer justice where
all was violence, to strike the chains off the slave, to draw the richness from

the soil, to plant the earliest seeds of commerce and learning, to increase in whole peoples their capacities for pleasure and diminish their chances of pain —what more beautiful ideal or more valuable reward can inspire human effort? The act is virtuous, the exercise invigorating, and the result often extremely profitable.[13]

For not a few applicants Africa itself was the magnet, a land of pure myth. For some it was a dream of gold and of hunting lions and elephants; for others the return to natural man and an escape from European civilization. To many it was the last frontier, a place to gain fame, glory, or profit. Colonial service in Africa appealed also to the eccentric, to the individualist, and to those who wanted personal power. The pay was poor, and the death rate high, but it promised adventure and independence, or "escape from narrow convention and the sound of bells."[14]

In general, officers were discouraged from marrying while young; the Colonial Office—like the army—was apt to consider that an officer married was an officer marred. Promotion was slow; living conditions were usually hard. Material compensation differed considerably among the various colonial territories; the British East Africa Protectorate had difficulty obtaining suitable men until 1912, when the conditions of service were improved. Yet colonial service provided middle-class young men of modest means with both an acceptable career and a secular mission. The majority of parsons in the Church of England, for instance, had large families and small stipends; their sons were well educated—often with the help of scholarships—but they still had to earn a living. In the colonies they might do good among the heathen, as their parents were doing among English country folk. This was an important consideration, especially for the numerous contingent sprung not only from parsonages, but from the homes of military officers and civil servants. The service motif was even more significant at a time when professions requiring an academic diploma had not yet proliferated. The colonial service thus attracted men who wanted adventure; it also appealed to men with a sense of mission to improve the world, the kind who—two generations later—would have joined the Peace Corps or taken up a career in social service.

Some had thought only to serve overseas for a period of years with an organization like the Imperial British East African Company or the Bechuanaland Border Police, and happened to be at the right spot at the right time when an area became part of the British Empire. Others had never considered anything except an expatriate career. One of these was L. A. (later Sir Lawrence) Wallace, a Natalian who was a

civil engineer, who had built railways in Argentina and who later came
to Northeastern Rhodesia as a big-game hunter. Under Robert Codrington's administration he rose to be chief surveyor; when Codrington
died he took over the job. An administratorship in the service of the
British South Africa Company did not compare with the greatest of
prizes available in Wallace's profession. But it was not a post to be
despised.

As Heussler points out in *Yesterday's Rulers*, competition for attractive civil service positions at home and abroad intensified in Great
Britain during the early part of the twentieth century. Even before
the outbreak of World War I there was an incipient class of newly
poor. Land had ceased to be the principal basis of wealth or influence;
hence the sons of landed or formerly landed families, or of families
with gentry aspirations, came to depend increasingly on civil service
and military positions as a guarantee of continued family status.[15] The
most highly qualified men, in an academic sense, joined the Indian
civil service or the British home service, where applicants had to pass
stiff examinations. Volunteers for the colonial service, the Sudan political service, or the British South Africa Company's administration, on
the other hand, were not required to pass competitive tests. Hence
they were apt to attract men with Lower Seconds or Thirds, well-
educated in elite institutions, but glad to find jobs that did not entail
additional training of a formal kind.

Other men went to Africa to pursue the same career they followed
in England but with—they hoped—more scope and a greater sense of
achievement among black tribesmen than among London schoolboys
or Manchester dockers. Doctors, engineers, and schoolteachers entered the colonial service. Herbert Irvine Arabin Wimberley, for instance, was educated at Kings School, Canterbury, and Keble College,
Oxford; he was headmaster of Northampton Grammar School when he
obtained a position in 1903 as inspector of schools in Lagos. Another
teacher was Selwyn Macgregor Grier, a parson's son who went to
Marlborough College and to Pembroke College, Cambridge. He
taught at Berkhamsted School from 1901 to 1902, and from then to
1905 at Cheam. In 1906 he joined the colonial service and was posted
to Zaria province, Northern Nigeria.

The lure of literature was strong—novels, journals, and newspapers.
Events in Africa caught the imagination: the explorations of Livingstone and Stanley, the Emin Pasha Relief Expedition, the conquests
of the Ashanti and the Ndebele or the defeat of the Mahdi, attracted
the adventuresome and the robust. During the Victorian and Ed-

wardian eras there was no separate youth culture. The adventure
stories of Edgar Wallace, H. Rider Haggard, and G. A. Henty were
read with equal relish by most of the boys who went to Public Schools
and to grammar schools, and by many of their elders. Their influence
was considerable. So was the influence of journals. *The Boy's Own
Paper*, edited from 1872 to 1912 with indefatigable enthusiasm by
G. A. Hutchinson, regaled its readers with tales of daring deeds in
exotic lands. It also provided moral instruction: cads and cowards
came to a sticky end; boys practicing "secret vice" in bed at night lost
their manhood and risked eventual insanity.

Even more important was the influence exercised by Kipling. Rudyard Kipling was more than a bard of empire. He was also a critic
of genius, one who spoke for the up-country pioneers, for the common
soldiers, the sergeants, and the subalterns, for the railway builders,
the engineers, and the district officers in some forlorn bush station.
He voiced the concerns of the "younger sons," the men in the lower
and middling ranks of empire, the "Sons of Martha," those willing to
tackle any task, however humble, rather than the "Sons of Mary," the
governing class proper, the generals and the viceroys, who simply
accepted wealth and power as their natural due. In his way he was as
bitter a critic of the Establishment as Karl Marx, with whom, oddly
enough, he had certain features in common. He lambasted incompetence and irresponsibility in high circles. He despised nepotism (as in
the poem "Public Waste"), the moral cowardice of the military establishment ("Stellenbosch"), the inanities of a decadent Public School
creed, the stupidity and pretentiousness of "The Old Men." He saw
the tragedy of job-hunters who took the "Exiles' Line" to India:[16]

> Bound to the wheel of Empire, one by one
> The chain-gangs of the East from sire to son,
> The Exiles' Line takes out the exiles' line
> And ships them homeward when their work is done.

Kipling had a striking degree of sensitivity, as in the tragic pre-
monition of the Jewish tragedy expressed in "The Rabbi's Song" and
"The Prayer of Miriam Cohen." He had a true sense of the common
humanity that united the members of a lower-middle-class Masonic
lodge in an Indian outstation:

> We'd Bola Nath, Accountant,
> An' Saul the Aden Jew,
> An' Din Mohammed, draughtsman
> Of the Survey Office too;

There was Babu Chuckerbutty,
An' Amir Singh, the Sikh,
An' Castro from the fittin'-sheds,
The Roman Catholick!

He even had a weak spot for the outsiders, the casualties of empire who fell by the wayside, the "Broken Men" exiled for domestic misdemeanors, in some remote Central American republic; the army deserters, the "Wilfully Missing"; and the "Gentlemen-Rankers," the disgraced sons of good family who sought oblivion in a barracks room.

His powers of observation led Kipling into an odd form of cultural relativism that became part and parcel of many an empire builder's mental equipment. He put it in a pseudo nursery rhyme entitled "We and They":

Father, Mother, and Me,
Sister and Auntie say
All the people like us are We,
And every one else is They.
And They live over the sea,
While We live over the way,
But—would you believe it?—They look upon We
As only a sort of They!

All good people agree,
And all good people say,
All nice people, like Us, are We
And every one else is They:
But if you cross over the sea,
Instead of over the way,
You may end by (think of it!) looking upon We
As only a sort of They!

Above all, Kipling stressed the service motif. The rulers of empire must shoulder deprivation, hardship, and danger in strange lands. By doing so they not only would give to backward peoples the blessings of peace and modern government, but would receive in return a sense of purpose, acquiring a meaning to their own lives that could no longer be found in some humdrum City job in England.

One of those on whom Kipling cast his spell was Sir Bryan Sharwood Smith, who saw service in West Africa, but whose first and abiding interest, thanks to Kipling, was India. As he put it:

Enchanted, while still young, by Kipling's *Kim*, I had begun to experiment with other authors who drew their inspiration from that eternally fascinating country. Soon my interest became almost an obsession, and I eagerly devoured every book on which I could lay my hands which was in any way connected with India and its peoples. Most of all it was the fabled North West Frontier, and what lay beyond, that attracted me.[17]

He resolved to gain a commission in a frontier regiment, and then to transfer to the Indian political service. Adult life nearly came up to schoolboy expectations. During World War I he joined the Royal Flying Corps and served on the Northwest Frontier. He then entered the colonial service and obtained a posting to the Southern Camerouns, and later to Northern Nigeria, which resembled most nearly the India he had known.

The colonial service attracted most young men because it promised them a sense of personal responsibility, with power and freedom from domestic constraints. "I have been delighted with life in Mwinilungo," wrote Theo Williams, a young assistant native commissioner in Northern Rhodesia in 1913:

I like the sun and the breeze. I like the open air life. A year ago I was reading Tacitus and suffering the ever-lasting consciousness of miserable Schools [the final examination at Oxford]. Now I lead a varied life. I have to deal with office matters, supervise the building of my house, concern myself with boundary commission problems, look after a herd of livestock, superintend the station garden, go on tour to identify a copper mine, help a trader with a labour contract and what not.[18]

Many a young man bored with life in London or Oxbridge thus sought escape in faraway places from the dullness of unrewarding jobs. They heard the call of an unknown African continent that appeared from books and journals to be an exotic, romantic place full of adventure and danger, and they felt the desire to play an important part in its history. They also responded to the appeal of open air life and of physical recreation easily obtained. Sports were important. in the empire—especially polo, horse racing, and the hunt. Where there were no foxes, something was found to hunt—in Rhodesia, as we have seen, the Salisbury Hunt Club rode to hounds after jackals. And where proper polo mounts were lacking, donkeys, camels, ostriches, and oxen were made to serve. According to Lord Cromer, race courses and golf greens were almost the first things Englishmen built in the colonies.

Precise data on the psychological characteristics of these empire builders cannot be assembled at this late date. But there is evidence that quite a number may have been introverts rather than the jolly, rugby-playing fellows who performed so many deeds of valor in Victorian novels. Men afflicted with a stammer, often attributed to anxiety or some other underlying psychological disorder, seem to have been no rarity. George Grey, a born leader of men and one of the pioneers of copper prospecting in Northern Rhodesia and of the Swaziland land settlement, stuttered so badly that his subordinates got into the habit of not staring him in the face when talking to him lest his embarrassment become insupportable. Edward Tyndale-Biscoe, the officer who first hoisted the Union Jack at Fort Salisbury in Southern Rhodesia, had been invalided out of the Royal Navy on account of a severe speech defect.*

Taciturn and self-contained men, such as the young George Orwell who served with the imperial police in Burma, were probably better able to cope with isolation and hardship in lonely outstations than a cheerful "Rugger Blue," who might crack when removed for too long from the gregarious and ritualized existence of a male fraternity in a school "House," a club, or an officers' mess. In fact, the colonial service probably attracted the more self-sufficient type, a man who was resilient and self-reliant and not put off by isolation and loneliness. It took all kinds to rule an empire.

The Conduct of Administration: Direct and Indirect Rule

British administration in Africa was marked by extraordinary diversity, reflecting a process of empire building in which totally different lands and peoples were absorbed with little attempt at centralization. Authority was at first divided among several entities—the Colonial Office, the Foreign Office, and chartered companies. But the differences extended far beyond this. Each colony had its own service with a unique ethos and traditions; it was not until the 1930's that there was a united colonial service with standard conditions of employment.

A description of the various territories would fill a volume by itself. We shall therefore emphasize the administrative problems of Nigeria, Great Britain's most populous colony in Africa. In Nigeria the civil service at Lagos stood a world apart from Kaduna in the north.[19] Lagos had a commercial tradition of long standing. African cultivators and African middlemen between them had built up a substantial export

*Tyndale-Biscoe later distinguished himself in the Boer War. Grey, like a hero of Victorian fiction, died with his boots on; he was killed while lion-hunting on horseback.

trade, which was firmly linked to Liverpool and to England's industrial north, with its free trade and Nonconformist tradition, with its moral earnestness, its reluctance to incur wasteful expenditure and high taxation, and its pacifism. Lagos governors like Sir William MacGregor tried to please north country British businessmen by emphasizing the needs of trade, communications, and public health, by avoiding wars and punitive expeditions, by their reluctance to impose direct taxation, and by their determination to maintain a policy aimed at "peaceful penetration" and commercial development. They also, as a matter of policy, employed a substantial number of Africans in senior positions. The British colonial officers in Lagos did not live in messes, much less in tents, but in their own houses. They wore civilian garb, not semi-military uniforms. They mingled with the commercial society of Lagos. They did not seek unnecessary discomfort, and were strangers to the belief that there was a positive virtue in enduring hardship or in excelling at athletic exercises.

Northern Nigeria differed in almost every particular. It was a borderland, and its trade was meager. Its society was shaped by a peculiar variety of Afro-feudalism and Islam. In this region the tone of administration was military; the British ruling group was linked to London and the Home Counties rather than to Lancashire; traders—British as much as Fula and Ibo—were regarded with suspicion if not disdain. The northern administrative ethos was shaped by Lord Lugard, whose administrative gospel blended muscular Christianity with a military puritanism that exalted the virtues of physical fitness, self-denial, and "character." Government emphasized prestige instead of profit, hierarchy in place of diversity.

Originally, Nigeria was divided into three separate entities—Lagos, Southern Nigeria, and Northern Nigeria—which were only amalgamated in a gradual fashion.* Military force was used to conquer the greater part of this immense region. But given the size of the territory and its population, the British could not have ruled its people in a "direct" fashion. White officers were few in number; sickness took too heavy a toll of administrators and soldiers. Roads were few or nonexistent; most of the rivers were inaccessible to navigation.[20] Necessity, therefore, made Britain—like every other colonial power—depend on

---

*In 1900, after the charter of the Royal Niger Company had been revoked, the Niger Coast Protectorate was turned into the Protectorate of Southern Nigeria, and its supervision was transferred from the Foreign Office to the Colonial Office. In 1906 it was amalgamated with the colony of Lagos into the Colony and Protectorate of Southern Nigeria. In 1914 the protectorates of Northern and Southern Nigeria were united into the Colony and Protectorate of Nigeria.

Africans and indigenous political systems to help them rule their empire, just as they had relied on African soldiers to conquer and to pacify the new colonies.

European officers did not know the local languages or customs; they would have been isolated and numerically insufficient to govern local African societies. Ignorance of local ways produced resentment and rebellions; displaced local leaders were apt to plot. The British, therefore, attempted to govern through traditional rulers, councils, and local institutions—with some changes to satisfy the needs of the new colonial government. The system came to be called "indirect rule." But there were different forms of indirect rule in Northern Nigeria, Southern Nigeria, and Lagos, and indeed in the rest of Africa.

The Lagos protectorate had been acquired more by treaty than by military means. The administration there sought to ensure the cooperation of the Yoruba rulers and their councils by recognizing their authority. Imperial control expanded only gradually. Residents and district officers were posted with the local administrations set up by the colonial rulers supposedly on traditional lines. The British at first acted only as advisors to the *obas* and their councils. In 1899, however, MacGregor strengthened the system in Yorubaland so as to gain more control over the councils. New residents and traveling commissioners were sent to tour, organize, and supervise native authorities. In the colony of Lagos and in the protectorate, MacGregor's "Native Council Ordinances of 1901" set up provincial and district councils and a central Native Council to advise the British authorities on Yoruba traditions and to carry out day-to-day governance. All native councils were regulated in great detail. MacGregor thus made use of traditional rulers, laws, and customs to rule Yorubaland. But if the traditional rulers refused to do his bidding, he replaced them. European ideas and practices were thus gradually introduced into African societies through the native councils.

Colonial officials in Southern Nigeria were also aware of the necessity of cooperating with traditional rulers. Sir Claude Macdonald and Sir Ralph Moor created native councils and courts to settle disputes. The native councils, composed of chiefs sitting with a British officer as president, administered for the colonial government; in Northern Nigeria the resident was only a council member, not president. In a proclamation of 1900, Moor more fully defined the powers and responsibilities of native courts; he also set forth their jurisdiction in language that was to be repeated everywhere in Africa: courts were to be guided by native laws and customs in so far as these were in accordance with natural law and morality, as understood by the British. All courts were subject to the supervision of a local British Supreme Court; in this fashion new laws could be imposed and practices considered unjust or barbarous by the British could be eradicated.

In southeastern Nigeria the chiefs had little power. Their functions therefore had to be increased if they were to be useful to the British. The "house" system of political control (based on powerful families that operated as both political and economic units) was strengthened in the hope that this would give chiefs more authority. The British also had to decide who was to sit on the courts. This was a difficult problem, for in the interior of the protectorate villages were small and authority was diffused among elders, age-sets, secret societies, and kinship groups. The first British officials did not understand this system and looked for "chiefs" to act as power brokers. The local Africans were fearful and suspicious and did not identify their leaders; instead they put forward "criminals or people of no special consequence . . . to go and see what this was all about."[21]

The British gave these people a "warrant" as a symbol of their authority. "Warrant chiefs" thus came to rule the people of southeastern Nigeria because they were mistakenly thought to be traditional rulers. They received executive and judicial authority, and many abused it. From 1891 to 1929 the local population suffered under their rule until riots broke out, and an investigation revealed the flawed foundations for their appointment: they lacked traditional authority; their position derived solely from British warrants.[22] After 1906 the different local governments continued to operate in the Colony and Protectorate of Southern Nigeria, except that the various administrative units were brought more fully under the control of the Supreme Court, and the Yoruba obas allowed the Supreme Court to have jurisdiction over their principal towns.

Local rulers were used even more extensively in Northern Nigeria, where Muslim conquerors had established a number of relatively powerful emirates governed under Koranic law. Lugard had only a few officers at his disposal. Communications were poor. British military resources were limited. He thus had no choice but to rule in an "indirect" fashion. He reorganized the traditional systems of government, establishing five grades of chief with different salaries and insignia of authority. On the top of the scale were the emirs; at the bottom were the village leaders. The powers and duties of each grade were set forth in a "Native Authorities Proclamation." Though the chiefs and native authorities were based on traditional usage, Lugard appointed each chief and stressed that his nominees owed their position to the colonial government and could be removed for various offenses.

Attempts were made by the ruling British cadre to reform and modernize traditional institutions, cut corruption, eliminate harsh punishments, and remove inefficiencies. In the north there were the British courts as well as the native courts, each governed by its own system of law and customary usage. In order to promote development through native authorities, in 1904 Lugard introduced a system of direct taxation—a single tax to replace the variety of taxes formerly assessed by the emirs and the chiefs. The British took about one-quarter to one-half of the tax revenue; the remainder was used to pay the emir and his staff and to provide local services. The emir could, in fact, spend the money as he wished, for under Lugard the emir's share of the revenue was not audited. Only after Lugard's time (1911) were regular native treasuries instituted; these became the pillar of the indirect rule system, for the Northern Nigerian budget could seldom be balanced, and the British Treasury between 1900 and 1912 had to contribute over £3,000,000 toward the cost of administration.

Whether in Nigeria or Kenya, the British tried to pursue a policy of pragmatism, caution, and compromise. They ruled through obas, emirs, chiefs, or whatever other dignitaries they could find. For the time being they also accepted domestic slavery; to have brought it to a precipitous halt would have created chaos, disrupted trade, and alienated African rulers. Only gradually did the British move these territories from the status of a protectorate, which recognized existing customs and laws, to that of a colony designed to closely supervise native authority and to modify traditional values.

In allying themselves with the traditional authorities, the British managed to strengthen their rule with a minimum of force. Administrative consolidation was furthered also by improvements in communications and public health, and by clearing creeks and building roads and bridges. Railways, river traffic, and trade helped to bring peace, and to diffuse new crops and new skills. Modern communications also enabled the British to move their troops more quickly and to enforce their pax with relatively small forces.*

By 1914 armed African resistance had all but ended in Nigeria. The new system of colonial governance was largely accepted by the people. Passive resistance of a kind continued in some traditional societies, but political opposition and criticism of colonial rule was now dominated

* By 1909 the Lagos administration had built a 320-mile rail line to Jebba on the Niger.

by the new men—the educated elite of clerks, lawyers, doctors, journalists, and merchants. In newspapers and magazines, in legislative councils and improvement societies, these men urged more self-government for Africans and a variety of reforms. But few, if any, challenged the right of the British to rule, or doubted the benefits of colonial governance as such.

In areas settled by whites—notably Southern Rhodesia and Kenya—"direct" rule was used more widely. This did not exclude the use of chiefs and councils, but less effort was made to find the "natural" rulers or to transform existing institutions for the purpose of ruling Africans. Government under direct rule was also simpler. The administrations at first limited their role to keeping the peace, collecting taxes, and putting direct or indirect pressure on African cultivators to enter the labor market by working for pay under private employers, or to render "free"—that is, coerced—labor for communal purposes, or to do compulsory paid labor for the state. In Kenya "native headmen" were used after 1902 to transmit instructions from the administration to the people. In 1912 they were given power to arrest criminals and to issue minor regulations. But native courts were not recognized until 1913; they had limited jurisdiction and could be overruled by the district commissioner. Native councils were not established until 1924.

The District and Provincial Commissioners

Diversity in the functioning of British governance went with a goodly measure of uniformity in formal structure. The colonial system was thus devoid of powerful territorial administrators such as the French prefect and the German Regierungspräsident. The chief factotum was the district commissioner (DC; called the native commissioner in the Rhodesias and the collector in territories under Foreign Office sway), whose job first came into being in nineteenth-century India, where the local title of collector rightly stressed his financial functions. DCs did not appear in Africa until the 1880's and 1890's, when government moved off the coast and into the interior; their position was unknown in the administration of England—the product of a parliamentary system with a strong tradition of local self-government under the auspices of gentry and burgesses.

The DC exercised far-reaching administrative, judicial, and police powers within a defined geographical area. He was aided—or often hampered—by one or several assistant district commissioners, who received on-the-job training. Districts were grouped into provinces headed by a provincial commissioner (PC), whose function was purely supervisory; he saw to it that the DCs followed government policy—if there was any—and that they submitted correct returns, collected taxes, and carried out the law. The distribution of de facto powers between the PC and the DC varied considerably from time to time and region to region. An exact description would reveal a bureaucratic maze. Suffice it to say that in the early days, where central organization was weak, as in the British East Africa Protectorate, the PCs wielded extensive power and, to some extent, played the role later assumed by the secretariat. Their power diminished as the territory became more developed and as the central administration was able to have a more effective say. This generalization also applies to Rhodesia, where the provincial system was abolished in 1913. The rise in the numbers of DCs is evidenced in Table 16.

The DC's work schedule reflected the changing nature of colonial society. The conventional DC of colonial fiction governed backward peoples with little regard for central authority, a rural image that was by no means always correct. At the beginning of the twentieth century, before Lagos joined with a larger unit of government, the city government provided public health services on a par with those of British cities. Lagos, the commercial capital of Nigeria, was also the administrative headquarters; the largest government departments were those connected with commerce, communications, and public health. Government in the provinces was in the hands of DC's, assisted by a certain number of technical officers. They looked to Lagos. Their job was to promote peaceful economic development at a minimal expenditure.

As the African empire expanded, however, the typical DC was apt to become a backwoods administrator interested almost exclusively in rural problems. An official in a lonely *boma* (government station) in Northeastern Rhodesia during the 1890's was largely thrown on his own resources. Communications were poor, supervision from headquarters was scanty if not nonexistent, and an administrator could usually avoid filling in returns and making up lengthy reports. Indeed, even a resident was sometimes able to ignore the forms sent his way, as R. T. Coryndon did during his tenure in Barotseland (1897–1907), much to the anger of the high commissioner in Cape Town.

A frontiersman like Robert "Bobo" Young, a pioneer official in Northeastern Rhodesia, lived in conditions not very different from those of an African chief. His headquarters consisted of pole-and-

TABLE 16

Numbers of Provincial and District Officers in British East Africa and the Gold Coast, 1897–1913/14

Area	Provincial commissioners	District commissioners	Assistant district commissioners
British East Africa			
1897	4	7	11
1903	7	19	20
1910	6	30	45
1913	6	33	51
Gold Coast			
1897	0	17 [a]	—
1905	4	15 [a]	—
1910	4	9	15
1914	4	12	26

SOURCE: R. S. T. Cashmore, "Your Obedient Servant," unpublished manuscript, Afr. S. 1034, Rhodes House Library, Oxford University; *Colonial Office List* for the years 1897–1914.

a Includes assistant district commissioners, who are presumed to account for at least half of the group.

dagga huts built in the African fashion; his retinue was composed of a small number of armed African policemen. He was expected to do battle against Swahili-speaking slave traders, to arrest evildoers, collect intelligence, and open up communications, and to raise some revenue. Taxes and duties initially were paid in kind—in ivory, livestock, or even chickens and grain—so that his position was apt to resemble even more that of a traditional warlord.

The system put a premium on the skills of an outdoorsman, a big game hunter, a police sergeant, or a military officer—men used to roughing it and accustomed to command. Given the relatively small amount of armed force available to the average administrator, prestige was the cornerstone of government. As explained in the section on the military, most of the pioneers were convinced that they had to scotch trouble quickly lest it spread. The use of force—provided it was followed by kindness—was widely supposed to have the same effect on a rebellious African community as a birching on an insolent British schoolboy. Officials saw nothing wrong with corporal punishment, though they flogged Africans a great deal less than the Germans. With their limitations in manpower, however, the British were anxious not to alienate their subjects too far. Letters from early administrators were full of phrases like "a good whacking," a "sound walloping," or the "parental slipper"—phrases that had done duty in British homes and in prefects' studies. The most popular administrators were always

those who knew how to "manage the natives," whose proceedings provoked neither expensive wars nor questions in Parliament.

Duties varied in the district office. A DC in Nigeria in the course
of one day hanged seven men and married five couples. In effect,
the DC was a governor in miniature, as Sir Charles Eliot noted: "In
practice a young man of between twenty-five and thirty finds himself
in sole charge of a district as large as several English counties, and
in a position which partly resembles that of an emperor and partly
that of a general servant.[23] Until the telephone, the telegraph, and
finally the automobile brought the DCs gradually under control, they
ruled semi-independently of Government House as "kings of the
bush." At first they lived under hard, primitive conditions; loneliness
was great, as was the pressure of living surrounded by tribesmen who
were often hostile or sullen. Boredom, sickness, and isolation from
other Europeans took a heavy toll; the happiest men were those with
hobbies, and especially the naturalists. Sir Ralph Williams, in *How I
Became a Governor*, wrote that "the only reason that the officials of
this colony [Bechuanaland] remain alive is that there are no trees in it
high enough to hang themselves upon."

Still, there was no other profession where a junior man could wield
as much influence as in a military or administrative career in the colonies. The newly conquered parts of Africa were an open frontier for
middle-class young men, who had a sense of forming a vanguard.
Kipling put their feelings into verse:[24]

> There's a Legion that never was 'listed,
> That carries no colours or crest.
> But, split in a thousand detachments,
> Is breaking the road for the rest.

The "Lost Legion" operated under conditions where men were thrown
back to a very large degree on their own resources, and where both
their good and their bad qualities tended to be magnified.

The political service of the Sudan, set up in 1899, stands out as an
example.* Civilians—recruited by preference from Oxbridge candidates with a good physique, a pleasant personality, and a Second- or
Third-class degree—were given responsible assignments at an early
stage in their career. They supervised the northern Sudan with its
Islamic population, while the soldiers ran the distant south with its
predominantly "pagan" peoples. Even greater powers were bestowed
on military officers, who were generally posted to quasi-administered

---

*The Sudan was under the Foreign Office, not the Colonial Office.

TABLE 17

Comparative Annual Salaries of British District Officers in Africa (Including Allowances) and Government Employees in London, 1910

(In £)

Title	Salary
COLONIAL POSITIONS	
Gold Coast	
Provincial commissioner	800
District commissioner	480–500
Assistant district commissioner	300–400
Nyasaland	
Resident, 1st grade	450–600
Resident, 2d grade	350–450
Resident, 3d grade	250–350
LONDON POSITIONS	
Chief clerk, Office of the Receiver, Metropolitan Police	800
Staff clerk, Department of Works and Public Buildings	300–400
Assistant, 1st class, British Museum	350–500
Assistant, 2d class, British Museum	150–300

SOURCE: *Colonial Office List 1911; Foreign Office List 1911; Whitaker's Almanac* (London, 1912).

territories in the Sudan, or to districts bordering on independent tribal areas. At a time when communications were poor, the military men—known as the Bog Barons—were exceptional in their ability to ignore orders. Whereas the administration in Khartoum identified itself with the Islamic north, the Bog Barons refused to learn Arabic, remained aloof from their superiors in the capital, and tried to uphold the cause of the local population. Service in southern outstations attracted the self-sufficient kind of officer, the man who could shoot for the pot, who did not depend on the companionship of the mess, who was not afraid to enforce his own pax in swampy and pestilential lands inhabited by warlike peoples distrustful of government and all its works.[25]

Colonial administrators got comparatively modest salaries (see Tables 17 and 18). In 1910 a PC in the Gold Coast, in charge of a territory as large as a European duchy, made no more than a chief clerk in a major British government department. A resident second grade in Nyasaland, equivalent to a DC in other areas, earned no more than a first-class assistant in the British Museum. His financial position might be made worse by the high cost of living and the expense of educating his children in England. Working hours for the DC were long; in Nigeria he was supposed to be at his office from 7:00 A.M. to 2:00 P.M., but these officially designated times meant little in practice, for a political officer had to do everything:

You see him as the prosecuting counsel and defender, as well as judge in the Provincial Court, sometimes the hangman too—Coroner and deputy sheriff and keeper of the gaol. Also he is policeman, postmaster and supplier of transport, sub-treasurer and keeper of that remarkable invention, the revenue suspense account, wherein recorded on fair paper are the details of a quaint collection of rubbish, called tax in kind, which lies in the mud-built store; such things as bags of cowries, ivory and iron, strips of cloth, or bundles of guinea corn. How we have wrestled with it, that suspense account, till with reeling brain we have been driven to multiply the corn by cowries or deduct the cloth from gutta-percha, to find out why there is a loss on realization to cash.

The list of duties is not ended, for the political man is the doctor of himself and others, sanitary officer and town planner. He collects tsetse flies, and samples of native products such as fibre, silk, and seed, reports on cattle, cotton, or shea butter, answers questions which are legion: on how best to segregate lunatics and lepers; the reason why the children do not care for European education; if the people are willing to be vaccinated; why the taxes are in arrear; when he will get them in—almost in fact "Where do flies go in summer time?" He assesses and collects the taxes on land and cattle; he counts the cash, divides it with the Chief; he ropes in slave dealers, stamps out wizardry and *bori* dancing. Further, he makes roads and bridges of a sort, drains marshes and trains bullocks to draw carts, builds houses, fixes boundaries both of districts and of provinces, makes maps, lays out markets, supervises the working of the native administration in all its branches. Experiments with this and that, fails and succeeds, paves the way in fact, for all the experts who shall come in later years to damn his work or alter it. A Jack of all trades, there to be shot at, blamed when things go wrong, but, if such be unction to his soul, alluded to at far off public dinners as a nameless one of the gallant band who fly the flag at Empire's farthest outposts.*

Some civil servants acquired an interest in their adopted country, in its people and their culture, in its geography, its fauna and flora. Scores of great tomes filled with hunting stories and sketches still attest to the popularity of the African chase. It had the attractions of a sport but was utilitarian in its ability to provide food for the hunter and his ser-

---

*Archibald Charles Gardiner Hastings, *Nigerian Days* (London, 1925), pp. 90–91. It is hard for contemporary readers to realize how varied a DC's work was. Mothers inquired concerning the whereabouts of their sons; officials asked the local DC to get errant husbands to pay their alimony; various kings and emperors of Europe wanted wild game captured; London desired specimens also; two vultures might have to be captured for a Cairo zoo; transferred officers demanded that their effects be forwarded; a citizen of Ipswich called for £5 of local postage stamps. In 1899 a British ship lost one of her torpedos while cruising in East African waters; all coastal DCs were asked to look for it. In some areas the district officer had to arrange the execution of criminals—in Kenya by shooting before 1906, by the gallows after that. And headquarters was always sending circulars or asking for information on tribal customs because some learned society had requested it.

TABLE 18

Comparative Annual Salaries (Excluding Allowances) of Officials and Staff
Members of the European Colonial Administrations in Africa, c. 1913

(In £)

Post and/or rank	Salary
Great Britain	
Colonial secretary, Gold Coast	1,440
Provincial commissioner, Gold Coast	700
District commissioner, Gold Coast	400
African clerk, 3d class	100
France	
Assistant administrator, 1st class, Dahomey	469
Chief assistant, 1st class, Dahomey	386
Agent, 1st class, Dahomey	222
African head clerk, 2d class	82
Portugal	
Secretary-general	667
Secretary, Congo district	191
Belgium	
State inspector	1,368
Commissioner-general	782
District commissioner	665
Agent, 2d class	235
Germany	
Chief secretary, German East Africa	568–724
District commissioner	393–563
Colonial secretary	256–369
African clerk, 3d class	99

SOURCE: See Table 13.
  NOTE: The Belgian figures represent starting pay. For comparative governors' salaries, see Table 13.

vants, and to familiarize newcomers with the bush. It was also socially
desirable to expatriates who came from an island kingdom where hunting and shooting had become largely the preserve of a social elite.
Hunting continued as an outdoor venture until the deadly combination
of high-powered rifles, expanded farming and herding, and barbed-
wire fencing destroyed much of the wildlife on the veld.

Writing was another outlet. Most British administrators had a solid
literary training in the classics. Whereas French civil servants, with
their legal background, published little—least of all their own reminiscences—British officials were usually quite ready to put pen to paper.
The shelves of libraries concerned with Africa are full of books written
by colonial officials, with titles like *Far Bugles* and *In Remotest Barotseland*. But other works attained a considerably higher level. Harry
Johnston's autobiographical novel, *The Gay-Dombeys*, was thought
worthy of a preface by H. G. Wells. Frank Worthington's *Chiromo*,

the Witch Doctor, and Other Rhodesian Studies is still worth reading because of its vivid character sketches. Then, too, there are numerous important scholarly works by administrators such as R. S. Rattray and Sir John Milner Gray.

The most famous novelist to write about the DC was Joyce Cary, who served in Nigeria from 1913 to 1919 and incorporated his experiences in fictionalized accounts during the 1930's. Cary immortalized three different types of administrator. Rudbeck in *Mr. Johnson* believes in progress and in "opening up the country" by building roads; Bewsher in *An American Visitor* is a "paper man," determined to keep out traders, missionaries, and ranchers. Bradgate in *Aissa Saved* differs from the other two in that he has no overriding desire either to develop or to preserve; he simply prides himself on "knowing the African" and understanding his ways like *Sanders of the River*, the ideal DC.

Some DCs also made their reputation as ethnographers, though most of them lacked professional training. Their work was without theory, their interpretations seldom rigorous, and their conclusions sometimes flawed. (Chinua Achebe, the great Nigerian novelist, has some brilliant pen portraits of British DCs—honest men, but sometimes pompous and obtuse.) Nevertheless, they were careful observers; their field notes were based on first-hand knowledge over long periods of time. They usually had a sense of identification with "their" people. They were shaped by a culture that valued objective research. No other conquerors in history ever conducted more research on the history and cultures of their colonial subjects than did nineteenth- and twentieth-century Westerners. Perhaps the best-known of the British DC anthropologists was Charles Kingsley Meek, who wrote on Northern Nigeria. Other administrators who made valuable contributions to ethnography before World War I were Charles William Hobley (the Akamba, 1910), Sir Claud Hollis (the Masai, 1905, and the Nandi, 1909), and Sir Harold MacMichael (the Kordofan peoples, 1912).[26]

The literary DC, of course, was an exception. But once the frontier fighting days ended, and once the money economy began to spread into the backwoods, all DCs were increasingly required to put pen to paper for administrative purposes. A major departure was the introduction of taxes payable in cash; money imposts required a census, copies of which had to be sent to headquarters, and detailed returns became necessary. Colonial governments, always anxious to keep down expenditures, insisted on careful spending of funds, on accurate returns, and on strict accounting of stores and cash.

More paper work was added when courts and the legal system grew more formal, when administrators ceased to be simple arbitrators or autocratic local lords and were expected to adjudicate cases according to British legal procedure. In Northwestern Rhodesia, for instance, the Law Department began to demand monthly accounts of all cases; it sent out advice to district officers on legal points, proudly reporting in 1910 that it had filled 1,200 pages in letter books during the year. The administration began to regulate the recruitment of labor, and district officers became responsible for giving some protection to immigrants. New problems arose with laws concerning land titles, credit sales, mining, and a host of other economic activities. At the same time, the imperial government became more anxious to acquire information for the purpose of answering its parliamentary critics, for statistical analysis, or for the sake of providing data to learned societies and entrepreneurs.

To deal with the increase in clerical work, typewriters came into use, and by the outbreak of World War I their employment had become almost universal. The typewriter, however, created a new kind of work: carbon copies could be reeled off and circulated to other offices where they had to be read and acknowledged. The art of filing grew ever more important. As a result offices acquired a permanent memory embedded in their records; administration became more impersonal. Statistics—sometimes accurate, more often compiled by guesswork—began to play a larger part in the evaluation of government. Connoisseurs of paperwork will find in the reminiscences of W. R. Crocker, a retired administrator, a list of 60-odd reports— weekly, monthly, quarterly, half-yearly, and yearly—that had to be submitted by a Nigerian district officer. The list covered every conceivable subject, from reports on typewriters and locusts to records of judicial floggings.[27]

Officials were also expected to promote economic progress by building roads and bridges—usually with obligatory labor. They were asked to advise on crops, even to vaccinate men and their cattle. And this frequently while waging an unending battle against an unsympathetic secretariat, an over-censorious audit department, or the judiciary. In the East Africa Protectorate, for instance, many DCs had "goat bags," secret funds accumulated from unrecorded court fines, from the proceeds of cattle or goat sales, or even from a district officer's private purse that were used to supply items the government would not or could not supply—a house, water tanks, a village dispensary, a stable, even salaries for African carpenters and masons in the DC's employ.

"Goat bag" accounts had to go when a regular bureaucracy was established and the secretariat audited all station accounts.*

In Kenya, for example, pacification was only completed in 1906, when the Nandi submitted. Once the caravan routes were secured, roads were built and a protected transportation system was established. Railway and telegraph lines appeared. Administration away from the rails and roads was minimal—peace-keeping and collecting taxes. There was a more positive program of administration after 1906, but there were too few officials to carry out much development. And the colonial official with little or no training was expected to be many things: builder, soldier, policeman, judge, engineer, agricultural expert, and doctor.[28]

Such a man was John Ainsworth, PC of Nyanza (1907–10), who desired to improve both white and black agriculture and to develop new cash crops, experimenting with wheat and barley, cotton and sisal, simsim and groundnuts, as well as with improved strains of maize. He was a great administrator, one of many who ably ruled the African colonies. The villagers responded to his program, and new roads carried the expanded production to the rail line. In the five years between 1908 and 1913 Nyanza's export trade more than tripled in value, from 287,640 rupies to 987,623 rupies. Europeans criticized Ainsworth for reducing the need of Africans to work for the whites, but Africans praised him. His major agricultural innovations were not limited to Nyanza, but affected the whole of Kenya.[29] Ainsworth's impact was far-reaching, as Bethwell A. Ogot observes: "The new maize seed in particular, which was universally accepted, soon revolutionized not only the people's food habits, but to a large extent their way of life as well."[30]

As the revenue of a colony grew so did its staff of technicians— engineers, doctors, and DCs. Thus, for example, whereas in 1901 in Northern Nigeria there were only two residents and seven assistant residents, about seven medical men and no agricultural department at all, by 1913 there were 135 residents and assistants, 47 medical men, and five agricultural technicians.[31] As a result, the DC's work became even more bureaucratic in nature. As early as 1909 Frank Melland, one of the ablest of administrators in Northern Rhodesia, complained that DCs were growing more like accounting, transport, and postal clerks with every passing year. They no longer had as much time to

---

*In 1899 John Ainsworth was reprimanded for using his "presents to chiefs" for famine relief (R. S. T. Cashmore, "Your Obedient Servant," mss. Afr. S. 1034, Rhodes House Library, Oxford University).

tour and to talk to Africans about matters small and great. More work had to be delegated to chiefs and to African officials—messengers, clerks, and interpreters.

In retrospect the era of the *ulendo*, the safari, "the tour," or whatever it was called, seemed to old-timers the best period of colonial government, the golden age between the troubled days of pacification and the emergence of modern nationalist movements. Good footwear became more important than good musketry. In East Africa, for example, officials were expected to spend about three months a year traveling through their respective districts; one such official traveled 1,000 miles in three months and wore out two stout pairs of boots in the doing of it. Their actual performance varied; only a few officials continued to cover their whole district each year, but those who did got to know their districts and their people; their influence was more direct.

A district officer on tour headed a small caravan. His retinue included at least a cook, a policeman or two, a clerk, "several houseboys," one or two gun bearers, eight hammock-men, a dozen or so porters to carry kitchen supplies, tent equipment, general stores, and the like. On arriving in a village, the cook routinely took over a hut for his kitchen. Village women brought chickens, eggs, and groundnuts for sale; others gathered firewood. The DC's retinue itself provided an itinerant market and a source of cash, as well as information concerning the outside world.

The clerk collected the taxes, gave out colored receipts, and entered the names in the tax book; it was the DC who decided whether an impecunious or disabled villager should get a tax exemption. Then formal court was held in the center of the village. The DC sat at a table adorned with the Union Jack, assisted by his clerk—dressed for the occasion in a white uniform and fez. The policeman—erect, arrayed in a dark blue jersey, khaki shorts, and black fez, with his bare legs oiled and shiny—acted as usher, lending added dignity to the proceedings. A Nyasaland district officer's case load might include charges of adultery and manslaughter, a land case brought about by a river that had changed its course, and an accusation of witchcraft.

When the court session was over, the DC might lecture the assembled villagers on the need to keep the village clean so as to protect themselves against disease; or tell them to give their children milk instead of feeding it all to the calves. He might present them with cotton seeds or soya beans to grow in their gardens, and give them injunctions of a more general moral nature.[32] In addition, a DC on tour was expected to inspect store ledgers and cash accounts, to take a look at townships, stations, police camps, and prisons, and to comment on the state of the local economy, on the promotion and posting of staff, on wild animals and ruffians.

Another kind of officer was the resident who governed indigenous states—such as C. L. Temple, posted to the Emirate of Kano in Northern Nigeria. He supervised a number of political officers who were enjoined to respect the power and prestige of the emir. Headmen were discouraged from dealing directly with whites, and administrators were not to handle the villagers' complaints directly but were to act only through traditional authorities. A resident's job thus depended on his ability to maintain good relations with the local head of government and his officials. He helped to determine policy; he also supervised native courts, inspected prisons, audited the local revenue, kept account of prices, of trade figures, and other such items.[33]

The qualifications to be a good resident were many. He had to have sympathy with and a liking for Africans and their way of life. He had to have a sense of proportion—to know when to act firmly and when to defer criticism; and when to reform African institutions and customs. Perhaps his most important ability, said Temple, was to supply eggs, corn, and horses to the military.[34]

In Kano the emir was assisted by a judicial and executive council that acted as the highest court of appeal and administered Koranic law. The British maintained the authority of the court, whose decisions they respected. They permitted the emir to raise his own revenue, derived from court fees, from an inheritance tax, and—above all—from a land tax derived from rent for the use of agricultural and pastoral lands. The land tax was a fixed license to farm, so to speak, and one that bore no relation to the true value of the land, a system that—according to Temple—discouraged the cultivation of more specialized crops. The British saw to it that the emir's officials received regular salaries in an effort to do away with a system whereby the native officials depended on the payment of presents from their subjects.* According to Temple, the old system really worked like a graduated income tax, since the rich paid more than the poor. In its stead, the British created a new bureaucracy.

The work of government forced administrators to make basic policy

---

* Under the new dispensation the *waziri*, the emir's chief assistant, received £1,000 a year; the *alkali*, £300; junior officers known as *limans*, £72; and *mallamis*, £24. Night watchmen got £12 a year; skilled workers received 6d. a day; and unskilled workers were paid 500 cowries and their food.

decisions. In theory, they were enjoined to treat their people sym-
pathetically. As governor of the East Africa Protectorate, Girouard
instructed his officers to know their people and the local laws and customs, and to work to procure the contentment and satisfaction of
their district.* To the Colonial Office the ideal DC was the man who
treated "his people" in a friendly fashion, whose conduct prevented
unrest, expensive punitive expeditions, and unpleasant questions in
Parliament. In practice a DC had to reconcile the opposing needs
of "his people" and the needs of government. When settlers entered
a colony, the newcomers often clashed with the indigenous people
over labor and land. Officials in the East Africa Protectorate and
Southern Rhodesia then tried to do their duty, as they saw it, to both
peoples, but could not easily resolve the contradictions between opposing policies. In both places land alienation was a major source of
friction between Africans and the government. While settlement was
encouraged, and the settlers received vacant or supposedly vacant
land. To work their new estates, the whites demanded African labor,
and sometimes sought to restrict the Africans' development of their
own reserves. Labor laws and taxes payable in cash forced Africans to
seek employment, and the government forcibly recruited labor for
public works, especially in road and rail building.

DCs, accordingly, were forced to arbitrate between different European pressure groups—traders and farmers, farmers and mine recruiters—as well as between European interests and African. On the
local level these decisions were often complicated by issues of a personal kind. The DC and the European residents in some forlorn outstation might have bitter, long-lasting quarrels, occasioned by some
petty slight and aggravated by isolation and boredom. Officials and
farmers also frequently clashed regarding specific aspects of government policy. But on the whole the DC and the better-off settlers
came from a similar background. They played tennis together, and
they played bridge. The home of the DC was often the most convenient place to meet for a drink. Hence European officials could not
help being affected by settler sentiments. But the settler influence did
not operate in an illegitimate fashion. We have not come across any

* Girouard felt his administration lacked esprit de corps, was ruled by the "old gang,"
and was prone to factiousness. A Colonial Office minute noted "the rage for uniforms
and precedence which appears to characterize the E. A. P. officials." Visiting cards continued to be left in East Africa long after this had stopped being a common practice in
England. Settlers commented often about officials with their court swords and helmets.
The *East African Standard* regularly attacked officialdom for its love of pomp and uniform and lack of action (see, for example, the issue of 19 Feb. 1903).

instance, in any colony, of British officials accepting bribes or other financial inducements to sway their decisions. Most officials differed vigorously with the settlers concerning many aspects of native policy. But the district officers and the European entrepreneurs formed part of the same society. European officers in general were quite unaware of this dilemma, of having to reconcile their role as protectors of "their people" with their role as governmental agents. Indeed, the details of daily administration left them little leisure for such reflections. In the early days there were no policy outlines; each district improvised as best it could. Even the governor and the chief secretary had little time and less inclination to contemplate their own work or the consequences of their regulations; administration tended to run on ad hoc decisions framed in a spirit of parochialism.

The majority of officials remained part of white society. But there were exceptions. In British East Africa, for instance, a few officials became converts to Islam. One of them was Kenneth McDougall, a former employee of the British Imperial East African Company, who ended his career as chairman of the Coast Arbitration Board and a recipient of the Star of Zanzibar. Another was J. E. Stephenson— "Chirupula"—administrator in Northern Rhodesia under the British South Africa Company, who was sent to burn down a village in arrears on its taxes. When the chief sent in two lovely maidens to help him take his bath, the girls begged him to spare their people, and Chirupula confessed he could not deny such beautiful emissaries. The girls stayed the night. He eventually resigned because, like Colonel Colin Harding, he objected to the company's practice (later discontinued) of burning down the huts of persistent tax defaulters. He then settled in the bush, successively married three African wives drawn from the most aristocratic lineages, developed his land with the help of labor furnished by his in-laws, begot numerous progeny, and acquired the reputation of a great magician. He lived to an old age, the very image of a British scholar and gentleman, with a well-trimmed white goatee, a beautifully modulated Cambridge accent, a dignified bearing, and a gentle voice—but boycotted to the end by the settlers' wives as the embodiment of a reprobate.

Such men, however, were unusual. The average British administrator stuck to his own kind. As a rule, however, the colonial officers acquired a greater measure of tolerance and respect for their subjects than they had possessed at the outset of their careers; and some even discovered an element of superiority in indigenous over imported institutions. The Nigerian resident Temple was impressed by the adaptability of Muslim administration in Kano. Faced with a rising crime rate, the local emir made an interesting innovation. He drew on the services of the local ratcatchers, who plied their calling at night and were thus familiar with the Kano thieves. The ratcatchers were enlisted as night watchmen, a service for which they received £1 a month. But whenever a burglary took place they had to pay 2s. 6d. to the person robbed. Crime dropped rapidly, and the night watchmen were rarely required to pay compensation.[35]

Administration depended on wits and instinct as much as on logic. The frustrated or angry official was ineffective. C. H. Stigand commented in 1910 that "it is no good ever getting angry with natives, as they then pretend that they are hopeless idiots and understand nothing you say."[36] Administrators worked out their own methods— bluff, humor, aloofness, enthusiasm. Each community reacted differently, but all of them knew whom they could trifle with and whom they could trust. One DC, A. Aldington in Kenya, found that when he requested porters the local chief would produce an old woman, who would take three or four days to carry the load. But when Aldington put the load in a mail sack and covered it with official seals, he was besieged by young Nandi warriors eager to carry the load in a single day for little pay.[37] John Ainsworth got the Kamba to be his porters by holding dance competitions at his campsites. He would announce a competition for the next day and invite them to come along. They willingly carried his loads.

Health and Housing Conditions

·Along with his copy of the *Colonial Regulations*, the new colonial officer received an "Introduction to District Commissioners" and "Simple Medical Directions" to inform him of the most common diseases in his area; there were 22 listed for West Africa. Under food and drink, the new DC was told the safest alcoholic drink was Scotch whiskey, and was warned that wines and beers were far from good for his health. He was also warned to avoid depression by getting up different forms of amusement and was advised to make others happy instead of retiring to his room and grumbling about the lot that had placed him in West Africa.

How did the district officers face the realities of a colonial existence? Life in the bush of East Africa or the bogs of the Sudan could be oppressive and even fatal. Letters home and diaries give some idea of what it was like in the pioneers days. The diary of Alfred Harry

Sanders portrays the suffering of one early officers. He was posted
from Cairo in 1902 to the 15th Sudanese Battalion and was to act as
civil commissioner for the district as well. His job was to cut wood
for steamers going upriver from Khartoum to Wau and to clear and
keep the river free of *sudd* (thick weeds).

Sanders became ill soon after he left Khartoum. He had to struggle
hard to get his men and supplies up the shallow river. He was in the
water much of the day pulling and pushing boats, cutting wood, and
clearing the weeds from the river. At night he slept wet out in the open
exposed to hordes of mosquitos. When the river dried up he had to
carry three tons of supplies forward. Then at his base camp he had to
clear a parade ground, build huts for his men, cut wood, and clear
the sudd. He and his men kept coming down sick. Sanders himself
was stricken with fever, and the work of cutting the sudd repulsed
and sickened him. Yet he continued his daily routine in spite of a high
temperature, headaches, dizziness, and an inability to hold down his
food. In December 1902 he became violently ill. He died the following
May of blackwater fever while on his way home on leave.[38]

Nor was there any romance in the district station described by Joyce
Cary in *Mister Johnson*, a novel dealing with Nigeria:

The barracks, across the parade ground from the fort, are four rows of neat
huts, like nursery counters arranged for a game. The Union Jack, just outside
the guard-room, hangs upon a crooked stick, shaped like one of those old gig
whips with a right-angled crank-turn in the middle.

The office, . . . the center of Fada government, lies beyond the parade
ground in a bare patch of its own, like a small wart of mange grown out of a
huge, dried scar, polished brown. It is a two-roomed mud hut with a mud
stoop and half a new roof. On the mud stoop between the two door holes a
messenger and an orderly are asleep. The orderly's blue fez has fallen off.

He [the new arrival] looks round at the huge bush houses, each alone and
unprotected in the scrub, like sulky and dangerous beasts, at the guard-room
with its crooked white eyelash, at the rag of pink and blue hanging over it,
at the mysterious pattern of the barracks, and his flesh shivers. He steals away
from the incomprehensible, terrifying place, as from devils. This brings him
again to the town road and the store.

The Fada Company store, a tin-and-wood shack with the usual laborers'
compound behind, stands on the river close to the town gate. Since it is almost
part of the town, natives do not fear it like the station in the bush, with its
bush devils. Since it belongs to a white man and has an English-speaking
clerk in a cotton suit, it is regarded as part of the government.[39]

Many a lonely outstation in the bush was still more unprepossessing.
Even the hardiest Public School boy—used to the discipline, the poor-

ly cooked food, and the damp cold of an English winter intensified by perpetually open windows—might well have been intimidated on arriving in his new quarters.

Housing was usually very poor, for the Colonial Office lacked the funds and the imagination to build and furnish proper quarters. The colonial secretary was shocked in 1910 by the conditions under which administrators lived, but little improvement was made before 1945. Governor Girouard complained in 1909 that almost all government offices and houses in Kenya were in a disgraceful and dilapidated state. One of his officials described his house as designed for curing bacon rather than for human habitation, and two others, living in Kitui, shared a two-room shack with no ceiling or floor. There were, of course, no refrigerators and no electricity for most bomas until after World War II. Food usually came out of tins or, where game abounded, was whatever could be shot locally. Fresh fruit and vegetables were limited to a few weeks a year.

Bachelor Englishmen not used to caring for themselves suffered to a greater or lesser degree from chronic malnutrition and ill-health. In this respect the Public School ethos of indifference to food and physical comfort probably made the English poor pioneers. A young boy sent off to school at seven or eight, brought up away from a mother's care, was ill-fitted to care for himself in Africa. Some continued to stay in buildings that any French or German official would have scorned. The French were shocked at the way British officials lived and ate, with few or no creature comforts to sustain their minds or bodies. Maurice Delafosse, when touring in British West Africa, was dismayed at the hovels in which the British lived, and at their ineptness and lack of skill in building comfortable stations. Few British Public School boys ever acquired any sort of craft skills, and cold or badly prepared, monotonous fare did not bother them—it was what they were used to. A DC sitting in his windowless, doorless house, wrapped in his overcoat and bathrobe and eating an unsavory dinner, was not an unusual sight. During hot weather they suffered even more, for they did not know how to build spacious rooms that created a sense of coolness and shadow.

"Activity was essential, for the great enemies of these men were loneliness, sickness, drink and death," notes R. S. T. Cashmore.[40] Staying healthy was a major problem. Between 1901 and 1910, 11 administrators died in the British East Africa Protectorate alone. Though medical conditions were not as bad there as in West Africa, sickness constantly drained off men from the staff, and put stress on an always short-handed administration. Up to 1914 the average death rate per 1,000 European officials in West Africa was 17.1, in East Africa 13.6; the average invaliding rate per 1,000 was 28.8 in West Africa and 18.4 in East Africa. It was estimated that a pensioner, on the average, lived only two years after his 20 years of service.*

Major causes of death were disease, accidents involving wild animals, murders, and suicides. Blackwater fever, caused by repeated malarial attacks treated with uneven dosages of quinine, was the greatest killer. The diaries and letters of administrators tell of almost daily illness. Common complaints included sores, ticks, earaches, sore throats, colds, toothaches, dysentery, neuralgia, prickly heat, boils, worms, stomach pains, headaches, and—an omnibus term—fever. Suicides are hard to document, for they were usually covered up by the administration. Several stations in East Africa had bad reputations, including Kisumu, where three men took their own lives in one year. Africa in the prewar period, then, was not a place for men with melancholy temperaments or for those who were concerned about their personal comfort. The mosquito, loneliness, depression, careless eating habits, and liquor took a heavy toll in sickness and death.

Isolation and lack of companionship often led to heavy drinking. The Colonial Office handbook for officers going to East Africa read: "Heavy drinkers should not go to East Africa. . . . Moderate drinkers should be very moderate there and total abstainers should remain so."[41] Some officers had to be retired for alcoholism; Cashmore cites three for British East Africa before 1914. The average administrator, however, controlled his intake. But there were always men like E. W. Kelt, a supervisor of customs at the Gold Coast, who lost out to liquor, allowed his work to deteriorate, and publicly disgraced himself at a concert, where he got so violent that an African had to keep him quiet with a revolver.[42] Others went on drugs, such as Dr. Blair Watson, an administrator in early Northern Rhodesia, whose profession as a physician gave him easy access to narcotics.

With small staffs throughout British Africa, many one-man stations had to be established. Sir Charles Eliot, high commissioner of the East Africa Protectorate, warned about them in 1901: "One man cannot properly administer these large districts, where the natives have no machinery of Government which can be utilized and every village requires individual attention. Also a solitary existence, sometimes five

---

*In West Africa between 1903 and 1920 there were 623 deaths in a staff that ranged from 1,259 to 2,687.

to six days' journey from every other white man, is not conducive to the well-being of Europeans or to the vigorous performance of their duties."[43]

The isolated DC developed a great sense of his own importance and resented orders from the secretariat. He also tended to quarrel easily with the people he ruled or with his fellow officers, and to take the law into his own hands. Eliot also commented on this: "When on out-station work there is often a temptation to inflict irregular punish-ments. It isn't a case of sadism. . . . In most cases the infliction of irregular or excessive punishments has nothing to do with lust or any other sort of pleasure; it arises from anger and exasperation."[44]

Many contemporary writers described "furor Africanus"—a sudden anger that drove administrators, settlers, and even missionaries into violent and unwise acts. The beating of Africans was often explained as a result of furor Africanus; even Bishop James Hannington, for example, thrashed his men when they irritated him while on safari. One young DC kicked a European minister in the behind because the man tried to hide some tax dodgers, and because his choir practiced at night near the DC's tent. The bishop of Mombasa and N. E. Noel-Buxton took the matter before the House of Commons.

Illness coupled with a *bwana mkubwa* complex—a sense of self-importance—probably caused the petty quarreling among officers. But the DCs seem to have quarrelled with everyone—the military, the railroad, the police, the settlers, and especially the judiciary. For the courts sometimes reversed the judgments of the DCs, and this revi-sion was resented as undermining their authority and prestige. From the point of view of the courts, however, some officers seemed to be guilty of autocratic rule.

Field officers usually had a difficult time in satisfying the often conflicting orders and rules of government. As R. W. Hamilton, the presiding judge of the Kenya court, wrote in 1909 on the question of forced labor: "The Government has brought pressure to bear on the District Commissioner; he in turn has brought pressure to bear on the Government headman who had instituted a system of kidnapping, flogging, and fining to find labour."[45]

The medical officer Wordsworth Poole commented on the symptoms of the Nyasaland DCs:

There is a peculiarity about men who have been in Africa some time. They can't get on with anybody else. You get into a groove of your own and can't bear anyone else to be running the show with you. . . . One's temper must become ruined. It is noticeable with every head of out-stations; they are all bears in one way and brook no interference. I see that one must make enormous allowances for people out here. The circumstances are so adverse.[46]

Men became increasingly individualistic in their outstations. They ruled through the force of their personalities, but once they were gone the replacement had to start anew. Eliot noted this defect, too: "The only fault of the administration of up-country tribes is that it hangs too much on the personality of officials. A tactful Collector by long residence will gain great personal influence among a tribe, and when he is moved his successor will have to begin afresh, and it will probably take him many months of uphill work to gain the goodwill of the people."[47]

The DCs' work also made them parochial. They spoke of "their people" and "their district," and their loyalty was to their people, not to the government. "For the good officer, the District and its people became a projection of his inner self."[48] Not only did most officers have a favorite tribe, but they tended to have a specific enthusiasm: road building, latrine digging, water supplies, agriculture, health measures, touring, gardening.*

The bush administrator's loneliness and illnesses sometimes produced eccentric behavior. There seems to have been a full measure of eccentrics in Nyasaland during Johnston's administration. One man wore nothing but glasses and a bath towel; another dressed himself in dilapidated knee-length drawers, patched with string and wire; still others appeared in bizarre colors and evening clothes. One officer brought rhino dung to Government House for lunch, and another planted his garden with canned peas. But there were eccentrics in every administration. The DC of Kisii in East Africa went to his office in chief's robes and dancing pumps; when he thought someone was lying, he would hit him over the head with his pumps. Another DC was found on safari in formal clothes. Still another, also in East Africa, challenged his neighboring DC to a duel with armies made up of an equal number of Masai.

---

*Africans often gave nicknames to the officers who ruled them. R. S. T. Cashmore compiled a list for the Central Nyanza District in East Africa: "the orphan," "the arm swinger," "long neck," "bull neck," "hard hitter," "the thin one," "the ladies' man," "fiery eyes," "the tall hen," "omniscient," "the leopard's son," "the woman," "quick decisions," "keeps to himself," "stammers," "slow speaking," "red eyes," "can a leopard ask questions?," "he jumps at me," "chief of Kisii," "bent shoulders," "doesn't waste words," "the dove in the crocodile's house." Cashmore also cites the story of the new DC, proud owner of an automobile, who came to Nyere in 1914 to find only one road in the district, and who left it with 150 miles of motorable roads a few short years later. ("Your Obedient Servant," pp. 82, 83.)

Reassignments were frequent. They were caused by staff shortages, ill-health, and gaps caused by home leave. One district had 10 DCs in eight years. This involuntary mobility discouraged colonial officials from learning local tongues. Even though bonus pay was given and promotions came to depend on language skill, it was difficult to become proficient in African idioms. There was neither the time nor the source material (grammars, dictionaries) to master them. In East Africa few officers (perhaps six) knew any language other than a little Swahili; figures for 1910 show that only 41 of the 81 officers had passed even the Swahili examination. As a result the administrators could not understand the Africans, nor could they explain their policies to them except through interpreters. Much of the friction and misunderstanding between the indigenous peoples and government officials sprang from this lack of a common tongue. If interpreters failed to be competent, honest, or impartial, injustices would abound.

As we saw, a Kenya DC's error in sending a policeman who did not speak Kikuyu to make an arrest had tragic consequences. Sir Charles Eliot, one of the most experienced administrators, wrote:

Disastrous and costly misunderstandings have occurred because no one was capable of giving or receiving explanations when trouble was brewing. Hitherto few of our officers have known any language but a little Swahili, and except for a few intrepid spirits the absence or inadequacy of textbooks has made the acquisition of all others a practical impossibility. . . . In practice the difficulty is to *insist* on a knowledge of any language but the lingua franca, Swahili, because the others are mostly spoken in comparatively small districts, and it is impossible to restrict the officer's service to one linguistic area, or to require him to learn Masai when he may any day be removed to a Somali-speaking area.[49]

The British South Africa Company's administration in the Rhodesias had better success in finding skilled linguists among people who had lived in South Africa and who knew Zulu or Sotho. Furthermore, its commissioners tended to stay put for a period of years. A man had a chance to learn the language of his district, and indeed to spend his entire career in the colony. By and large, however, the district officers were men on the move, and for better or for worse, their rule remained governance by outsiders.

The Judges

The Europeans came to Africa not merely as conquerors, but as lawgivers. Almost every Briton was convinced that British governance alone would supply to the indigenous Africans "security of life and property, freedom from the tyranny of the witch doctor . . . an impartial and trustworthy justice."[50] The difficulties in attaining this objective, however, were immense—much harder than the victors had imagined. British imperial policy—as expressed, for example, in the text of the charter granted to the British South Africa Company— insisted that the rulers should pay "careful regard to the customs and laws [of the indigenous tribes], especially with regard to the holding, possession, transfer and disposition of lands and goods and testate and intestate succession thereto and marriage, divorce and legitimacy." African law, however, had nowhere been codified; even had the British tried to do so, they would have found the task overwhelming. Native law was therefore apt to be defined so as to accord with the senior administrator's notion of what native law should be, leaving considerable leeway to the executive. But there was no uniformity about European justice either—even in the formal sense. Roman-Dutch law, not British, applied in South Africa as well as in Southern Rhodesia, a colony regarded by legislators as a "white man's country." The "tropical dependencies," on the other hand, were subject to British common law, modified by statute law; but the interpretation of these laws in the colonies allowed vast scope for differences of application or even for the personal idiosyncrasies of individual judges.*

More difficult still was the problem of reconciling conflicting European and African ideas of justice. No compromise was possible between trial by a poison ordeal and trial by European rules of evidence. No compromise could be made between evidence elicited by the throwing of the diviner's wooden slats and evidence of the kind acceptable to British courts. No compromise could be allowed between European and African modes of punishment. The olden-times monarchs of Barotseland had seen nothing wrong in throwing convicted

---

*Whenever a territory was acquired as a Crown colony or protectorate the government promulgated an Order in Council specifying, among other things, the laws to be in force from the date of the order or from a stated future date, and providing for the establishment in the territory of a supreme or high court and a system of subordinate courts. A typical example would be the East African Protectorate Order in Council of 1897, which provided that the laws to be in force were certain specified Indian applied acts, the Acts of General Application in force in England on a named date, and where no other provision was made, the common law of England and the practice of the courts in England in force on a specified date. The "native law" and custom prevailing among people living in a tribe or in a tribal area would be in effect, provided that these were not contrary to "natural" justice or repugnant to the practice of civilized peoples. (Sir David Edwards, "H. M. Colonial Legal Service, 1900–1960," mss. Brit. Emp. S. 307, Rhodes House Library, Oxford University.)

criminals to the crocodiles in the Zambezi or having miscreants slowly eaten by fierce ants. A Bemba ruler thought he was serving the aims of justice by chopping off an evildoer's hands. The British, on the other hand, humanized law and humanized punishment in a manner that shocked the upholders of African tradition.

The British also tried to introduce their own notions with regard to individual choice. Adultery ceased to be a major crime; tradition-minded Africans, not surprisingly, condemned the British as agents of permissive immorality. African villagers, like villagers in sixteenth-century England, felt fully justified in detecting witches by arcane means and ridding the community of clandestine evildoers. Modern Englishmen objected to both practices and were embarrassed when Africans defended their own customs by reference to the Laws of Moses. While making the practice of witchcraft illegal, the British at the same time prohibited anyone from accusing his neighbor of exercising the black arts. Africans therefore believed themselves to be bereft of official protection against the clandestine witch. Neither were they secure against the man who, possibly unknown to himself, was possessed of the "evil eye" that injured others. Understandably, discontented Africans might imagine that the whites were in secret alliance with the witches, or at least permitted witches to wax in numbers by dint of criminal negligence.

The Europeans, moreover, manufactured a vast array of new offenses unknown to ancient African lawgivers. Breaches of labor contracts, transgressions against forestry and game laws, violations of firearm regulations, all became offenses in the eyes of the law. The new courts operated not merely in an alien tongue, but according to incomprehensible rules. As Lord Hailey, the greatest colonial scholar of the classical period of empire, phrased it:

[African] procedure may be contrasted with that of the European court, where evidence is given according to rule and is conveyed to the magistrate through an interpreter; linguistic difficulties, often very great, the restrictions of free discussion, the lack of contact with the presiding magistrate, and even the need for standing in the box may well give the accused a feeling of helplessness and oppression not always relieved by the fairness of the judgment. The rules of evidence must often seem to the African to have been designed to hinder the discovery of the fact. Again . . . the court cannot avail itself of those forms of oath which have special force in Africa.[51]

African feelings with regard to British courts were therefore ambivalent. Educated blacks looked to British justice for protection against the power of the chiefs. Chiefs did not understand the remoteness and complexity of the system. Unlettered men were apt to be fearful and suspicious; often they also looked on the whites with a contempt that was quite unsuspected by the imperial overlords. They remarked on the Europeans' apparent lack of manners; they noted with disdain the seemingly brazen way in which white children spoke to their parents and a white wife to her husband. More seriously, Africans understood only too well that the Europeans often enforced an uneven kind of justice, punishing whites for crimes of violence with less severity than blacks. Europeans, as skilled workers or managers, were not subject to the "Masters and Servants" ordinances, whose rules were applicable only to unskilled hands.

But when all is said and done, European and African notions of justice and rightful conduct also had something in common. European courts may have treated white men more leniently than blacks; but the courts did punish offenses committed by white men as well as by black. Africans may have had their doubts about the quality of "white" law, but they increasingly appealed to British courts. European pioneer administrators, for their part, soon realized that Africans, far from being the "prelogical" savages of contemporary anthropology, had certain clear rules of morality and definite notions of "reasonable" conduct and dignified demeanor that were as acceptable to white men as to black. There was, however faint, a common notion of natural law that helped to tie African justice with European notions of justice.[52] The early European bush administrators supplied the connecting link between traditional notions of informal and familial justice and European concepts of formalized law, recorded in statute books and linked to Western notions of individual responsibility and individual property. At first the pioneer officials dealt in an informal manner with disputes brought before them. They possessed neither a legal nor a formal anthropological training; but they did have common sense and a thorough knowledge of "their" districts, acquired by many years of touring. Their judgments were probably not very much out of tune with the ideas of justice they acquired from Africans.

Political officers who lived and worked among the people probably made better judges than a trained legal person who lived apart from the people he tried. The colonial judge lived in a bungalow removed from the town or carefully sited in a healthy, segregated part of the town. In his job he was surrounded by other officials, and they alone made up his society. He went daily to the center of town to try cases, and passed Africans in the street; but he could not speak to any, for he did not know their language. He returned home every 12 months to recover and to refresh himself with things English. Though he might know the law, he knew little about Africans. The political officer, in contrast, came in daily touch with Africans and their affairs; he knew their customs and laws and sometimes their language, and he usually had years of experience before he became a provincial court judge.

As the cash economy advanced, and as the administrative machine and the cases brought to court became more complex, the judicial system became more formalized. Each major British territory set up its own high court, from which appeals could be directed only to the judicial committee of the Privy Council. The high court thus wielded great powers. It served as court of appeal, with original jurisdiction in all major civil and criminal cases, and was empowered to issue prerogative writs of habeas corpus. These courts were staffed by professional jurists, drawn from the ranks of British barristers, incorruptible, competent, and enamored of their dignity. They essentially derived from the same social group as the senior administrators—normally educated at the great Public Schools, followed by Oxford or Cambridge, eligible for the best clubs in London and *Who's Who*. They were a tiny elite, proud of their independence from local pressures, men who moved from colony to colony, and sought to make their reputation in the legal world more than the colonial world. Their social position within the British Establishment was much higher than that of their German colleagues, top-medium bureaucrats rather than gentlemen ex officio. A chief justice in a British colony, however undistinguished, could expect a knighthood, just like a governor.

Leicester Paul Beaufort may be regarded as a worthy representative of these lesser legal lights. He was born in Warburton, Cheshire, the son of a country parson but well connected through his mother's side to the minor aristocracy. He was educated at Westminster and at Oxford, and subsequently became a barrister at the Inner Temple and a member of the London School Board. In 1889 he accepted a position as government secretary and judicial commissioner for British North Borneo. He transferred in 1901 to Northeastern Rhodesia, where he helped to set up a rudimentary judicial system, ending his career as chief justice of Northern Rhodesia and being knighted for his services. Judge Beaufort did not write any books; his entry in *Who Was Who* lists his recreations as shooting, fishing, and golf. Several of his confrères, however, made their mark as authors of legal studies or major commission reports.

Men like Beaufort held a special position within the colony or protectorate in which they served. The chief justice ranked in the "Table
of Precedency" immediately after the governor, because he represented the sovereign in the latter's capacity as "Fountain of Justice."
He deputized for the governor in the governor's absence. Neither the
chief justice nor the other members of the judiciary were in any way
subject to the executive. They did not form part of the administration
properly speaking, but rather were meant to act as a kind of check.
Judges often presided over major commissions of enquiry. The chief
justice, alone among senior officials, had direct access to the governor
without having to apply first to the chief secretary. He was consulted
by the governor on most matters affecting the judicial establishment;
he might also be requested to comment on general policy. He issued
circulars to magistrates. The high court reviewed all cases tried by the
lower courts lest these had exceeded their authority or acted with
excessive harshness. The chief justice, moreover, submitted to the
colonial secretary, through the governor, an annual report on each
member of the judicial establishment. A so-called registrar was responsible for the daily operation of the legal machinery and for corresponding with various government departments. The attorney general
served as legal adviser to the governor and the different administrative
departments.

Lesser crimes were heard by district officers in their position as
magistrates. British practice did not follow Montesquieu's cast-iron division into judicial, administrative, and legislative functions. British
administrators were represented in the colonial legislatures; they likewise acted as judges in the lower courts. These were presided over
by a variety of officers—resident magistrates (the highest category),
or administrative officers ranking as first-, second-, or third-class magistrates. Initially the DC, sometimes even the assistant DC, acted as
judge, prosecutor, policeman, jailer, and executioner. Gradually the
judicial functions became more specialized. Grave crimes came to be
heard by the Supreme Court or High Court, sitting with a jury when
trying whites or with African assessors when trying blacks. Other offenses were heard by a district court or a magistrate—who might
be a fully qualified, full-time lawyer, a magistrate, or a PC. The DC's
magisterial powers were slowly reduced, and eventually he had to pass
a law examination to judge cases requiring imprisonment or fines
above a certain amount.

The resident magistrates had wide powers to try civil and criminal cases; they were full-time members of the judicial establishment and had to be members of the bar, but their numbers were limited before 1914. The number of African lawyers in West Africa increased so rapidly after 1906 that Lugard forbade the use of counsel in provincial and district courts in 1914, for these courts did not have trained lawyers as judges. It seemed intolerable to Lugard that black lawyers should know more than the white judges. African intellectuals in Lagos pointed out the injustice of a system in which Africans were tried and condemned by a judge who often had no legal training, without a jury or access to counsel.

African courts were also regulated; the cases they could try and the punishments they could inflict came to be tightly controlled. Appeals were permitted to higher "native" courts and even to the high court, though none but the most highly educated Africans who understood this procedure could profit from it. Indigenous courts, regulated or operating in a kind of official limbo, continued to deal with the everyday affairs of African life—disputes over cattle or bride price, adultery, breaches of contract, slander, and such. In Muslim areas, religious courts dealt with matters affecting marriage, divorce, inheritance, and succession, according to Islamic law. Between them these lesser courts continued to serve as the "maids of all work" within the judicial establishment of empire.

The Women in Their Lives

In Victorian missionary and imperial imagination, Africa often figured as a land of lust. Evangelical journals printed many accounts depicting the black man as a heathen who lived a slothful and lascivious life, sustained by the sexual favors and physical work of his several spouses. Soldiers who had seen service in Africa brought home tales of exotic amours, tales that lost nothing in the telling. According to the mythology of a more modern kind, imperialism had its sexual component. Young Englishmen were supposedly attracted to service in Africa by the prospect of easy liaisons in the bush, among other things. The realities of empire were nothing like as picturesque. Young gentlemen with pleasing manners and a few pound notes in their wallets were not sexually marooned in Victorian England. On the contrary, they encountered no exceptional difficulties in starting an affair with an impecunious shop girl, a dressmaker's assistant, or—if the suitor was shy or in a hurry—one of the many harlots who played such an im-

portant part in the underworld of nineteenth-century England. Ronald
Hyam doubts this interpretation, however. He sees imperial expansion
deriving not from the export of surplus capital, but from the export of
surplus emotional or sexual energy.[53] His thesis, though interesting, is
not persuasive.

There may have been more emotional opportunities for sexual satisfaction overseas than in Victorian Britain, but the motivation of many
of those who served in the colonial service can hardly have been due
to a search for sex rather than for overseas service. Perhaps it is more
correct to say that empire building was a sublimation or alternative to
sex. This seems to partially explain a Gordon, a Kitchener, or a
Rhodes, who remained lifelong bachelors, and governors like Milner,
Baden-Powell, and Lugard, who married late in life.

There were plenty of chances for sex in England, though the middle
and upper classes paid a high price for offenses against morality. Life
overseas, away from family and friends, may have presented more opportunities or pressures to be promiscuous; officials had great power
over the people they ruled, and black flesh may have seemed attractive merely because it was forbidden or was thought to be more "natural." The reports of liaisons between officials and "native" women
brought regular warnings and confidential memorandums from the
Colonial Office or the colonial secretary, but no examples have been
found of officials who were charged with homosexual relations with
Africans (or indeed with other Europeans). Unlike the Middle East,
where homosexuality was common, tribal Africa did not condone the
practice.

The sexual mores of colonial Africa derived from their local African
setting. The district officer's lonely existence and the lack of white
women in Africa led to a widespread practice of taking native concubines. Junior officers were not encouraged to marry, and wives'
passages to Africa were not paid in any case. Not every DC took an
African mistress, but some evidently did so. The DC at Nandi was
believed to have had a harem. At Nyeri in 1907 an inquiry into a scandal disclosed that two officers had paid bride price to the local chief
for Kikuyu girls. One of the men was posted away, but his wife refused
to go with him. The other officer fought with an African policeman
over the policeman's wife, whom the white man had abducted; he
then arrested the offended husband. It was the abuse of his official
position that shocked the Colonial Office, not his concubinage. One
London official noted: "It must be borne in mind that the practice
of cohabitation with native women has been and is extremely common

throughout West and East Africa; indeed I am informed that of the unmarried white officials there is only a small percentage who have abstained entirely from the practice."[54]

Such tolerance was shattered when the government and Parliament learned of the case. A confidential circular was issued by the secretary of state in January 1909 condemning such unions; copies were sent to all officials in British Africa, warning them that concubinage would be punished. This did not stop the practice, but it was enough to ensure that cases in the future would be hushed up locally to avoid trouble and scandal.[55]

Statistics, therefore, are hard to come by; civil servants were apt to keep quiet about the peccadilloes of their colleagues, and even more so about their own. Details found their way into official files only when there was a scandal. Early in Northern Rhodesia, for instance, there was the case of one R. A. Osborne, who took an African "wife" and illegally flogged and "fined" his cook when he found him sleeping with his paramour.[56] Osborne was sacked from his post, but liaisons of this kind continued there as elsewhere, only diminishing when more white women came to the colonies and enforced their own notions of respectability.

Such was the experience of Walter Mayes, who had advanced from the lowly state of a "Distressed British Seaman" to that of a successful transport officer in British East Africa. One evening, wrote Colonel Meinertzhagen,

he rushed into my house, hair dishevelled and in frantic excitement. . . . He screamed out: "a terrible thing has happened; my wife has arrived and upset everything! For Gawd's sake give me a bottle of whisky." . . . Apparently Mayes deserted her in Mauritius . . . and she finally found out where he was and suddenly appeared. It is all a bit difficult, as Mayes has half a dozen Nandi concubines in his house. I left them to fight it out among themselves.[57]

In the Sudan political service a higher moral tone appears to have prevailed; it was imposed by Governor-General Wingate and his wife, and men who took African mistresses or wives were socially ostracized and sometimes even dismissed.

The change in British colonial sexual practices is revealed by a story that went the rounds in West Africa about 1910. With improved conditions, colonial officials had begun to take their wives with them to live up-country. One DC brought his new spouse to his boma late at night and promptly went to bed. About four in the morning his cook walked boldly into the room, lifted the mosquito net sheltering the exhausted sleepers, soundly slapped the lady on her bottom and said, "Leave now, missi, time to go back to village."

Normal sexual practices were widely supposed to be paralleled by, or supplemented with, activities "unmentionable among Christians," according to Victorian parlance. "Kitchener, Lugard, Stanley, Raffles, Rhodes, Burton, Speke, Emin," chuckled the old-timer in the mess, "you name 'em; you got 'em. They were all queers." Our own findings do not support this unconventional wisdom. The British services presumably contained their component of sexual deviants. But social disapproval of homosexuality was universal, and social disapproval was probably strong enough to keep waverers in line. Personnel reports marked "secret" or "not to be handled by native personnel" relate to all manner of misconduct in remote outstations. But *le vice anglais* was not widespread among the English out in the bush. A taste for young men or little boys was more easily gratified in the anonymity of a great metropolitan city like London than in the bush, where Africans detested homosexual practices with the same fervor as the bulk of white colonials.

Male peer pressure was reinforced by the British officer's wife, a most influential person in colonial society. Official wives rarely got a good rating in colonial literature. Writers like Somerset Maugham made much of the memsahib's social snobbery and lapses into marital infidelity. Above all, white women were far from popular in the man-centered world of pioneer officials trained in Public Schools. With the women came the dreadful era of respectability, as an old-timer from Northern Rhodesia told one of the authors. Men were expected to wear starched shifts, to stop swearing in public, and to put away their African mistresses. It was the cheap steamship ticket for women that put an end to racial integration. Still, as Laura Boyle, wife of a DC in the Gold Coast, noted in her diary:

The majority of men out here . . . don't believe in women coming out to the Coast . . . they don't want them; they'd only get ill and be a nuisance. Even if they do come out, as I have . . . they are politely received but always with the sort of suppressed view, "Poor beggar, it's a pity she is here, but, come on, let's be kind to her." In the coast towns . . . it is different, for they can be packed off home easily . . . but even then they are not so far really wanted.[58]

No scholar has ever gathered data on the social origins of the wives of colonial service officers. Knowledge concerning the exact status of young Mrs. Somebody-or-other has disappeared, though the PC's wife and the colonel's lady were wont to be well informed regarding such details. From what information we do have it appears that colonial administrators wedded their own kind. They were married to the sisters of colleagues or to the daughters of military officers or clergymen; quite often it was to girls they had known from childhood or whom they had met on leave.

Many of these young women had gone to boarding schools run along lines similar to the great Public Schools—establishments where hockey was played to teach toughness and team spirit, where cold showers were regarded as a sovereign aid to morality. They mostly belonged or pretended to belong to that world where servants were supposed to know their place, and where even youngsters knew well who was and who was not "our kind of people." They shared the same culture, oddly blending the Book of Common Prayer and the poetry of Kipling with the operettas of Gilbert and Sullivan where—come love, poetry, or witchcraft—the social order is always triumphantly restored in the last act. They took pleasure in the same kind of amateur dramatics, party games, and charades that empire builders carried to the remotest cantonments.

The code of manners followed by a well brought-up young lady is described by Lady Bellaire's *Gossips with Girls and Maidens*, a late-Victorian work that provided guidance to cultivated females. Here are some specimens of "what to avoid":

> A loud, weak, affected, whining, harsh, or shrill tone of voice. Extravagancies in conversation—such phrases as "Awfully this," "Beastly that," "Loads of time," "Don't you know," "hate" for "dislike," etc.
> Sudden exclamations of annoyance, surprise, or joy—often dangerously approaching to "female swearing"—as "Bother," "Gracious!," "How jolly!"
> Yawning when listening to anyone.
> Talking on family matters, even to your bosom friends.
> Attempting any vocal or instrumental piece of music that you cannot execute with ease.
> Making a short, sharp nod with the head, intended to do duty for a bow.
> Crossing your betters.
> All nonsense in the shape of belief in dreams, omens, presentiments, ghosts, spiritualism, palmistry, etc.
> Entertaining wild flights of the imagination, or empty idealistic aspirations.[59]

This code of manners, tough and rationalist, conformed to the spirit of an age that saw the start of feminine emancipation. Before Queen Victoria ascended the throne, women who worked for cash were found mainly on farms, in domestic service, in workshops connected with fashion wear, and in prostitution. The expansion of industry proved an unmixed blessing to Victorian women. Cheap manufactured products —soap, iron bedsteads, inexpensive underwear—made a major contribution to domestic hygiene. So did the gradual disappearance of picturesque, thatched-roof cottages or shacks, and their gradual replacement by houses and apartments built of brick and stone, covered by solid roofs, and served by piped water. Machines provided new jobs in factories; typewriters furnished new employment opportunities in offices. (The census of 1881 mentioned upward of 330 occupations followed by women.) Victorian ladies also played an important part in evangelical pioneering. Missionaries' wives, nurses, and aides went to the remotest parts of the empire. Many of them raised large families under conditions that were often unbelievably hard. Their hardihood and resourcefulness belied later campus stereotypes concerning Victorian middle-class women—a breed very different from the prim, sex-starved females of subsequent feminist mythology. An equally important part was played by the wives of British administrators, for whom the frontier experience likewise often meant a measure of social liberation.

Even poverty-stricken brides usually came from an "acceptable" background—like Vyvien Hart-Davis née Bishop, whose reminiscenses survive in the stacks of Rhodes House Library at Oxford.[60] Vyvien had a hard life as a child. Her father was a man of artistic bent and ill-suited to provide for a family of thirteen. Her mother was good-looking, bad-tempered, and quarrelsome, with the result that young Vyvien always felt herself unwanted. Her parents managed to send her to the Slade School of Art, an eminently respectable institution; but when she was sixteen her father died in an accident, and she had to get a job with a theatrical dressmaker, a tough, businesslike woman with an improvident husband—just like Mama's. Vyvien found lodgings in a girls' hotel, where she had to get by on 15s. a week, an unskilled worker's wage.

Nevertheless, she was middle class: her father had been a captain in the Cheshire Regiment; her friends were mainly students; and she spoke nicely. And one fine day fortune beckoned. She met a young colonial officer on furlough, Charles Hart-Davis, who came from a military family just like hers. He was educated at Eton and at New College, Oxford; he had served in the South African War—and he was handsome. It was love at first sight, and after a suitable interval the two married, with their families' consent.

Though Mrs. Hart-Davis was a woman of spirit, the life that awaited her at the Gold Coast might well have terrified the toughest person. In 1908 the young couple took a steamer to the West Coast, disembarked at Cape Coast Castle, and departed the next day for Charles's station at Salt Pond. Vyvien was carried by four porters in a hammock, an uncomfortable way to travel. At Salt Pond an African delegation received them in state in correct London dress, with tall hats for the men and satin veils for the women.

People were friendly enough, but living conditions were harsh. Their home consisted of a few rooms above the government offices, furnished in Spartan fashion by the Public Works Department—two tables, a dozen bentwood chairs, two rusty iron bedsteads, a sit-in bath, and a couple of zinc pails. Everything smelled of mildew, and everything dripped. The food was poor, the chicken stringy, the eggs minute, and the butter oily. Refuse was everywhere, since the indigenous villagers had no notion of European-style hygiene. There were flies and decay and fever-ridden mangrove swamps.

Mrs. Hart-Davis contracted malaria, but medical help was unavailable, for the doctor had gone mad and fired his rifle on sight at all comers until he was taken away. When her husband went on tour Vyvien stayed with the PC's wife, and they entertained themselves by sewing flags for different tribal communities. In the end she could stand these conditions no longer and—having become pregnant—returned to England, where she stayed for a time with her husband's parents. Fortunately Charles was later posted to Fiji and then to Cyprus, where he reached high office before retiring to Somerset. Vyvien managed to adjust herself successfully to these service conditions and brought up three children.

Another venturesome woman was Olive MacLeod, who made a name for herself in Africa. Olive's fiancé, Boyd Alexander, a great ornithologist, explorer, and writer, was murdered in the Sudan in 1910. She made a pilgrimage to recover his belongings and to learn more about the circumstances of his death. The press of England was moved by the tragedy. Newspapers avidly reported her 3,700-mile trip through Africa with such headlines as "Come Bid Me Farewell in My Lonely Grave" and "Sweetheart's Pilgrimage." At Zungeru in Northern Nigeria Olive dined with the British resident C. L. Temple. Two years later he followed her to England, and they were married.[61] Olive joined Temple in Northern Nigeria and traveled extensively, studying the area and compiling a book edited by her husband and entitled *Notes on the Tribes, Provinces, Emirates and States of the Northern*

Provinces of Northern Nigeria (1919). She also made notes on natural history, forestry, agriculture, plants, animals, insects, birds, fish, and reptiles in the region.

The majority of colonial service wives adapted themselves to life in Africa, more like Mrs. Temple than Mrs. Hart-Davis. The bush appealed to young women who liked an open-air existence, who took an interest in plants and animals, who liked to see strange sights and to meet strange people. The successful DC's wife, in the early days, had something of a Girl Scout, something of an amateur anthropologist, and something of a maid-of-all-work in her makeup. By 1914 conditions had improved considerably, and Laura Boyle clearly enjoyed herself. Indeed, she considered herself lucky to get engaged, "with the chance of learning to know and appreciate the Ashanti people, the Hausas, and other races." [62]

When she arrived in Nigeria most of the towns along the coast had a fair complement of European wives; there was the same routine of life in the club and the Sunday church service, the same cult of empire and respectability, that marked all the empire's little expatriate communities, from the banks of the Niger to the shores of Borneo. But "north of the Coomassie area," Laura Boyle records, "many of the Districts had never had a white woman as a permanent resident, and I was inwardly very proud, though perhaps slightly nervous, that I would be living in one which had not been so favoured since the Ashanti war." [63]

Officials brought out their own food and supplies for at least nine or ten months.* Fresh food and vegetables were purchased locally or cultivated in their own gardens, but most colonial officers bought their other supplies, ranging from soap and candles to tinned fruit, butter, sausages, jams, tea, and coffee, at Fortnum & Mason in London. The young Boyles had to arrange for train and carriers to get them and their supplies up-country.

After an 11-hour train ride and a week-long trek through the bush,

---

*A man going to the Crown colonies was supplied with an advance and an outfit allowance. The Crown agents also provided him with various pieces of camp equipment, including two pillows, a mattress, a bed bag, and a camp bed with mosquito netting; a table and camp chair; a portable bath and washstand; a Pasteur-Chamberlain filter; two hurricane lamps; and a bucket and two chop boxes. Military uniforms could be bought at Humphrey's & Crook, and clothing for the tropics at Isaac Walton & Co., Ltd., or Way & Everett Penn, Ltd. MacSymon's Stores, Ltd., offered everything one might need: tropical outfits, groceries, camp equipment, clothing, boots, sports goods, and George Waugh's Farmer Real Scotch Haggis. They even shipped baggage and automobiles, and did taxidermy work.

the Boyles reached their post. Her husband had prepared his town and bungalow for his new wife. An avenue of Flamboyant trees lined the road to their house, and red and yellow Pride of Barbados stood in front of the "low bungalow raised off the ground, with a garden of flowers and fruit trees, a tennis court, and behind it the kitchen and servants' quarters." [64] She was a guest for dinner that night at one of the young officers' quarters, and as she noted in her dairy, it was an excellent meal, full of good conversation, with records of Wagner and Beethoven, the men in white mess jackets with bright yellow cummerbunds and she in a cool white dress. The bush pioneer days were over. A new era had begun.

Mrs. Boyle accompanied her husband on tour, and she took an active interest in his judicial activities. She did welfare work; she went hunting with her husband; and she was not the kind of person who was easily rattled. One Sunday afternoon she and her husband were walking through the bush when she heard her gunbearer suddenly say "Bad cow! Bad cow!" She looked to her right and saw a dun-colored horned cow running straight at her. Darting across the road, the cow in pursuit, she took cover behind a small tree. The beast charged and nearly gored her. She fled around the tree and doubled back to the road, then tripped and fell headlong in the grass, expecting a pair of great horns to plunge into her back. But they did not, and somehow she picked herself up and managed to climb a tree. Her husband took her home, where a whiskey and a hot bath soon restored her natural good humor.

Mrs. Boyle had more than sang froid. She was a good manager who knew how to improvise. On arriving at her husband's station she had arranged the rooms, checked the unpacking and storing of their food and supplies, ordered meals, allotted different duties to their servants, and supervised the builders who were adding an extension to the house. The Boyle household rose early. There was no plumbing; hot water was brought up in cans carried by convicts. At six in the morning the Boyles had fruit and tea on the veranda in their pajamas, and then set the gardeners to their tasks before dressing themselves.

One of her main jobs was household management. By the standards of the time, the staff employed by the Boyle household was modest; even so it contained an orderly, a cook, a cook's helper, a valet, a maid, an undermaid, and about a dozen men who served as hammock porters or gardeners, as circumstances might dictate. In addition, Laura was expected to go to market, to entertain, to maintain an interest in her husband's work, and to keep up their proper station in society. She was unusual in that she learned Hausa, and she read a good deal about the country's history and ethnography.

Servants were the bane of most wives' lives. They were cheap, and thus plentiful around most officials' homes. The main problems were how to get them and how to keep them after they were trained. But it was how to ensure their moral and physical well-being that most often tried a white mistress's soul and temper. Dealing with men servants—"boys"—was the most difficult task, for one had to be somewhat indulgent and not too authoritarian. To obey a woman was not usually part of an African tribesman's system of values. The white "missus" had not only to manage the servants and household, but to tend them when they were sick. Every boma had its special cures and medicines, including a few from England: calomel, tartar emetic, laudanum, and quinine. Otherwise the household had to depend on local herbs and remedies. Partly for health reasons, few officials raised their children in the colonies; at eight or nine they were packed off to school in England.

Women like Laura Boyle did not have an easy time, even when their husbands were posted to larger urban centers, as hers was to Accra. Fever was still rife. Comforts were few. The dining room of her Accra bungalow looked dreary and drab, like a waiting room in a railroad station; it had grimy walls, green painted doors, four plain wooden chairs, and a square table in the center. For all her domestic staff, there was little glamor in being a DC's wife. Yet these women had an important role in maintaining colonial society. Their advice on matters political and administrative did not always go unheeded. An intelligent wife would play her part in getting her husband promoted or posted to a more agreeable district. Above all, a capable woman was required to change her husband's life-style.

As noted earlier, British bachelors stuck out in lonely stations often were ill-equipped to cope with the petty and not so petty concerns of everyday life. They rarely knew how to cook or to mend their clothes, or even how to keep their homes tidy. Mrs. Boyle described the existence led by the typical single man in an isolated spot:

The tablecloth is left on all day; in the middle of it there is a bottle of Worcester sauce, a glass jar of brilliant yellow butter, various receptacles with pepper, salt and mustard together with at least two whisky-advertisements-inscribed ash trays. The very chairs are cobwebby, the stores are kept in old boxes in a big room with no table or shelves to put them on, and in fact none of the modest refined comforts of life are available or apparently even required.[65]

Decima Moore, a musical-comedy actress and singer in London, met and, after a whirlwind courtship, married in 1905 Captain F. G. Guggisberg of the Royal Engineers, on leave from his survey work at the Gold Coast. Both had been previously married; she had a son, and he had two daughters. She delighted in Africa on her first tour. She took an interest in everything, was joyful and flexible, resourceful and simple. Her later days were not as happy; she had regrets about leaving her career and London's pleasures.[66] She seemed a strong, energetic, ingenious woman, who managed to cope well with the formidable problem of living in the tropics, and who wrote an interesting account of her early years in Africa.[67] Her heart fell when she first saw her new home just outside of Accra—it was the abandoned officers' quarters of the inspector-general's staff. Dirty wooden walls, and no flowers or trees to greet her. She had the walls scrubbed down, and since the government made no furniture issue, put out the few furnishings she had found and cleaned. Her prize was the officers' huge wardrobe chest. Soap and water and chintz transformed the old pieces, and she set an African carpenter to work to make what else she needed. The old billiard room with four glass doors and six windows jutting out into a shady veranda became her living and reading room. Water was sometimes rationed, so she revived an old creeper with bath water; it burst into delicate mauve and orange flowers.

At first she was terrified of her ten "boys," but she soon learned to cope with them and forgive them their lies. Once a week she bought a supply of frozen meat, game, ice, and butter from the outward-bound mail steamer, which was stored in a large sea chest and kept fit to eat. Snakes, scorpions, and jiggers added to the usual trials of life, as did vicious native ponies. The major problem was to keep clean —the red dust played havoc with light-colored dresses, and washing was hard on all her wearing apparel. Sports were a major part of the Guggisbergs' lives; they laid out a seven-hole golf course around their cantonment and invited their friends to play. Decima believed in keeping fit, and she scorned those idle Europeans who would not play cricket, polo, or tennis.

Her day started at 5:30 in the morning: breakfast an hour later, then mending, writing, and looking after the house until 11:30, when her husband returned for lunch. He left again at 1:00 and worked until 4:00. Twice a week they went to Accra—"everyone" went to the European Club at 6:00 P.M. The club had a reading room and library, billiards and cards, a bar, and a veranda where the bachelors retreated. Golf was popular; polo was played on Tuesday and Friday, and cricket on Saturday, and each year home-and-home matches were played with Lagos in both sports. The Africans took up only cricket and had their own leagues.

Pioneer conditions were no easier for women in East Africa than in West Africa. The surviving reminiscences of Madeleine La Vie Platts provide an interesting insight into the life of a DC's household in the East Africa Protectorate.[68] Madeleine was born in Ireland in 1883, a doctor's daughter. On her mother's death she went to live at Oxford with an uncle, the Reverend R. N. Charles, a fellow of Merton and later archdeacon of Westminster. She took a B.A. from Trinity College, Dublin. In December 1909 she met W. A. F. Platts, her future husband, then home on leave after a tour of duty as an assistant DC in British East Africa. Platts's background was similar to her own. He had been born in 1881 at Oxford, attended St. Edward's School and then Balliol, where he rowed, won a Blue, and obtained his M.A. In 1907 he joined the colonial service.

The young couple were married on 8 March 1910, and sailed immediately for Mombasa. They disembarked and took the train to Nairobi, but still had 180 miles to travel, a three-week trek by foot and mule to Meru, where Platts was to serve as DC. All their stores, supplies, and personal luggage had to be carried by porters. What roads there were, were bad; they gave out entirely beyond Fort Hall. The fierce tropical rain, the tremendous thunder and lightning storms on the veld frightened the young bride. The party got lost during one such storm; they crossed eight rivers on rickety bridges and slippery trees; once their cart rolled off the road, and another time Madeleine fell off her mule.

The Meru station had only two other Europeans, Platts's assistant DCs, one a young man from Oxford, the other from Cambridge. Her house was a "homemade" two-story affair, with mud floors and leaky walls and roof. A kind of ladder led to the upstairs drawingroom, 44 feet in length, set off by an enormous mantelpiece. The climate was cool and rainy. Wild animals abounded, but Madeleine managed to keep a garden and provide her own fresh vegetables, mangoes, and bananas. They ate mutton, chicken and guinea fowl, and tinned food. The recreations of the couple and their colleagues were exchanging dinners, golf—500 local girls "cut the grass on the course"—bridge, and reading. There was an Indian bazaar a few miles away; and the local doctor, who gave them excellent medical attention, was Indian. A constant stream of European male visitors brightened their lives, but Madeleine saw only one white woman during her first two years in Africa. By 1912 she saw four bomas with white women in them.

Even though there was a lot going on, Madeleine often felt depressed, ill, frustrated, and anxious. Ants, jiggers in her toes, tides of fleas and flies, were an everlasting torment. The worst time was when her husband was on tour—he usually was gone 10 days a month. "The nights were both melancholy and terrifying" alone in her big house and hearing eerie noises outside in the darkness. Savage storms and lightning made her fear for her husband's safety in his camp tent.

When she was to have her baby, her husband sent her down to Nairobi. She traveled most of the 180 miles accompanied only by African servants, since Platts could not leave his job for long. Some of the way she rode in a two-wheeled cart, pulled by one of the African men; but she usually walked or rode a mule, once again over muddy roads and slippery paths, crossing rivers without bridges, and literally having to crawl up the steep stony hills, helped only by holding onto her servant's rifle barrel—"*Kamata bundiki memsahib.*" It took 13 days to reach Nairobi; her baby was born three weeks later.

Social life in capitals such as Kampala or Freetown was lively after women arrived. Government officials in Freetown, for health reasons, lived on Hill Station outside of the capital and took the train down to work each day, returning at 3:30 to their bungalows for tennis, badminton, or croquet. On Saturdays there were cocktail parties and music, then a bath before dressing to dine at a friend's home or as host. If a military band was available on Sundays, there was always a concert. Dances were held regularly in the evenings at the regimental messes. In town, officials' wives reproduced the life they had known in English villages: tea parties, visits, church, gardening and flower arranging, sewing, and charitable work. The library and the newspaper, together with literary clubs and dramatic societies, sustained their intellectual needs. Colonial society mirrored the metropolitan society, with many of its conventions and taboos, its games and diversions. Picnics and walking, horse racing and talk, croquet and archery —all were successfully transplanted to Africa, and there was plenty of shooting up-country for those who wanted it.[69]

The DC and his wife, like other whites in the colonies, felt they had to set an example for the "natives." And those who did not conform or who gave white people a bad name were censured and socially boycotted. The social rules were strict, reflecting the mores of the gentry and the parsonage in England itself. Mixed marriages were not approved. In Sierra Leone one Major Ross had married an African woman and had had to resign his commission. For 40 years he lived in poverty and seclusion even after his wife died; the local Europeans took up a subscription for him each Christmas but never again accepted him in their society. The few white women who married black men were similarly ostracized. Mary Gaunt, a traveler, met one in Bathurst, Gambia, in 1912; though there were only a dozen white women in the town, the lady with a black husband was shut out.

For all a DC's prestige and social position, and for all the paraphernalia that he dragged around in the bush, his life was harsh. As a bachelor he was apt to live in conditions resembling those of a slum, and might easily be undernourished in the bargain. Married women were important in ensuring the health and comfort of their husbands (married men seldom got blackwater fever), and thus played a modest though unrecognized part in maintaining the stability of British rule. They also helped to perpetuate those social distinctions of English life in the bush that have survived the waning of empire.

SEVEN

The African Assistant

The nineteenth century was a great age of British commercial and territorial expansion. Afro-British contacts were closest in West Africa, where they had far-reaching consequences. Thousands of Africans served in British forces, which became both an instrument of conquest and a school of Western forms of discipline, values, and customs. Tens of thousands of Africans became porters, railroad builders, and district police. Anglo-African trade and missionary enterprise also helped to produce a new African—the Afro-Victorian, English or Afro-English in speech, Protestant in religion, African in many of his customs, and African in his kinship links.

A most important center of British influence in West Africa was Sierra Leone, where after 1787 liberated slaves, demobilized black loyalist soldiers from the New World, and African newcomers helped to create a new pioneering society centering on the port of Freetown. British and African merchants developed an export trade in palm oil, palm kernels, and groundnuts, commodities increasingly useful to European industries. British teachers and clergymen built up a relatively developed system of education, from village schools to more advanced institutions. Contrary to conventional wisdom, British cultural assimilationism in West Africa turned out to be a more effective force than French and Portuguese assimilationism, both of which lacked comparable educational establishments.

A major educational institution was Fourah Bay College in Sierra Leone, founded in 1827 by the Church Missionary Society and later affiliated (1876) with the University of Durham, England. Fourah Bay became the first—and for a long time, the only—institution of Western higher learning in West Africa, and its graduates were quick to benefit from these educational advantages. The Sierra Leone creoles,

English-speaking Africans, pushed outward along the coast and inward into the hinterland as missionaries, teachers, clerks, and government employees, and sometimes as traders, farmers, and professional soldiers, becoming—so to speak—middlemen of Western civilization in Africa. By the late 1850's the creoles—the colony-born descendants of free black Nova Scotians (the highest class among the original settlers), the black poor, and the liberated Africans—had emerged as a distinct cultural group, whose values were to a considerable extent those of middle-class Victorian England. Well-to-do merchants built substantial houses; they dressed themselves in dignified frock coats and their wives in crinolines; they attended church bazaars, drank the queen's health on festive occasions, and patronized the poor. They believed, by and large, in the blessings of British governance. They also maintained cultural and trading contacts with other countries, especially the West Indies, and had a taste for certain things American—tobacco and rum, kerosene and cotton goods. The creole community provided a small but profitable market for Yankee merchants.

The British also controlled part of the Gold Coast's Atlantic littoral; their influence resting on commerce. They were wont to appoint members of the merchant community as magistrates and officials. Africans and mulattos were not excluded on principle, and by the middle of the nineteenth century a mulatto held the post of acting governor and three of his sons served as commandants of towns. Africans served in higher administrative positions in the central organs of government; others made their way in law, medicine, and journalism.

British traders, aided by African middlemen, also acquired a powerful foothold in Southern Nigeria. Their commercial stake increased as Western industrialists found a growing range of new uses for palm oil, a product of special importance to Nigeria, where rivers, creeks, and lagoons provided a natural network of communications long before railway tracks and roads penetrated the interior. The Niger delta, with its unique river system, its concentrated stands of oil palm, and its trade-oriented African state system, dominated the palm-oil trade. Southern Nigeria was commercially linked to Liverpool and especially to Manchester with its traditions of free trade, its humanitarian heritage, and its conviction that Africa's future lay with "Commerce and Christianity."

As time passed, educated Africans secured a slight measure of representation on the legislative councils set up by the British within their West African colonies. In 1914 the Gold Coast Legislative Council included two African members. More important, a number of educated black men advanced into the British colonial administration. One of the most prominent was William Fergusson, governor of Sierra Leone from 1844 to 1846—an Afro–West Indian and the only African to hold the rank—who had qualified as a medical doctor at Edinburgh University and was then commissioned as an officer in the British Army. James Bannerman, a prosperous merchant with a Scottish father and an African mother, rose to be lieutenant governor of the Gold Coast. Another distinguished Afro-Victorian was James Africanus Horton (1835–83), a Sierra Leonian. Like Fergusson, he obtained his medical degree at Edinburgh, then one of the best medical schools in Europe, and subsequently obtained a commission in the British Army, where he held numerous appointments and finally retired with the rank of lieutenant colonel. As a man of substance engaged in various commercial adventures in Freetown, he opened a small bank to provide advances for local entrepreneurs, and joined in the granting of scholarships to allow promising African youngsters to go abroad for their studies.

Horton had a good deal in common with David Livingstone, a fellow physician. Both had acquired their education by dint of hard work and study. Like Livingstone, Horton served the British empire in various official positions and combined an ardent belief in Great Britain's civilizing mission with an indomitable faith in the future of the "native races." Like so many other mid-Victorian imperialists, Horton—who gloried in the African past and held high hopes for the continent's future—saw no contradiction between imperial power and home rule. Indeed he had very clear notions of how self-government should work: in a self-governing Sierra Leone, for instance, the language of government should be English, and the country should be ruled by a bicameral legislature and a popularly elected monarch, whose principal objectives should be to annex the neighboring territories and to protect the merchants, and thus to protect and increase the national revenue. Just as the Franco-African merchants of Senegal stood for a "Senegalese imperialism" designed to protect and expand commerce in peanuts while strengthening the French connection, Horton represented an Afro-British variety of empire building. Thus he firmly rejected the notion that "the existence of British rule was a curse to this part of the [West] Coast; that the country was infinitely superior, commerce much more advanced, and life and property safer in the hands of the superseded native governments than under the sovereignty of Great Britain." On the contrary, Horton asserted, British governance "was the greatest blessing that could ever happen to Lagos and the whole of the Yoruba or Aku tribe."[1]

Africanus Horton was one of many Victorian physicians who turned their powers of observation to a large variety of subjects, medical and general. His medical writings essentially followed the traditions of a time when tropical medicine was in its beginnings, when the art of therapy had made only limited progress, and when medical problems were widely seen in terms of Victorian middle-class morality. He adjured newcomers to Africa to avoid hot dishes and spicy condiments, lest these should have "an injurious effect on the passions." For the same reason, newcomers were enjoined to avoid the company of persons accustomed to "licentious indulgences." But in practice he was a sound diagnostician and was much preoccupied with preventive medicine, and the public health questions—sewerage, municipal drainage, water supplies—that were of such paramount importance to mid-Victorian reformers.

Again like Livingstone, Horton was a competent ethnographer and a sound observer, quite unaffected by the racist lore that was seeping into much contemporary ethnology. He shared the Victorians' optimistic belief in science and technology, looking to the day when the printing press, the steam engine, and the telegraph would enable the more favorably placed parts of West Africa to vie with Western Europe in the advancement of civilization. In more general terms, even though he was a professional soldier, Horton was representative of an essentially civilian elite of African traders, teachers, preachers, and civil servants who looked to the British empire for protection, for expanding opportunities in civil employment and commerce, and ultimately for self-government.

Another Afro-Victorian administrator, albeit on a lower level of government, was Thomas George Lawson, the son of a chief in Little Popo on the Gold Coast. He was on his way to England to be educated, but stopped off in Freetown in Sierra Leone and remained there. During the 1830's he became a trading agent employed by the British firm of John McCormack. He aided his career by making an advantageous marriage to a girl descended from one of the royal families of the Koya state. Knowledge of Western business methods, together with his kinship ties, enabled him to operate in many parts of the hinterlands, where he made a name for himself as a reliable trader and accomplished linguist.* In 1846 he entered the Sierra Leone government as an interpreter, and rose to become a man who wielded great influence in the Aborigines' Affairs Department, with a salary of £350

* Governor Kennedy said of him, "[Lawson] is one of the most trustworthy and useful men in the settlement" (Great Britain, Public Record Office, CO 267/319 v. 5, disp. no. 1862, 20 Jan. 1872).

—higher than most white officials. He held office until 1886, when he was forced to retire owing to ill health and old age.

After 1870 the British became increasingly ambivalent in outlook with regard to the "educated natives," who often came to be seen as troublemakers. In 1886 A. W. L. Hemming, a London official, noted in a Colonial Office minute that "the educated native such as Messrs. Bannerman, Brew, &s, is the curse of the West Coast." And in 1909 Sir John Rodger commented that the English busily educated brown and black Englishmen, only to curse the finished product.[2]

On the other hand, opportunities for government employment increased after the early 1870's once colonial administration began to move into the interior. As governor of the Gold Coast, J. Pope Hennessey (1872–73) actively sought to employ educated Africans, though Lord Kimberley at the Colonial Office refused some of his recommendations. But as the area under British control increased along with the scope of government, more Africans had to be hired; they were cheaper than whites and better able to withstand local diseases. By 1883 Africans held nine of the 43 highest posts in the Gold Coast.[3] Governor William Brandford Griffith (1885–95) saw the economy in promoting them, and started a modest training program. He sent a young clerk, George Ekem Ferguson, to England for a year's study to become a surveyor. On his return Ferguson mapped large portions of the Gold Coast and negotiated numerous treaties that changed the shape and size of the colony.[4]

The position of the colony's chief medical officer went to an African in 1892, when Dr. J. F. Easmon came to the Gold Coast from Sierra Leone; but the jealousy of another African doctor led to his suspension, and a European got the job. A new unofficial policy followed, limiting the rank of "Native Medical Officers" so that no European doctor would be under an African.[5] This exclusion of Africans from important posts in the Gold Coast began around 1897. Higher requirements were set, training schemes like those instituted by Griffith were not expanded, and as Africans retired or died in office they were replaced by Europeans.

Before the turn of the century, then, the door to African advancement into the higher ranks of West African administration began to close—though it was never shut entirely. Post-colonial historians have since explained the change in terms of racial prejudice. Racial considerations certainly played their part, though their importance can be overestimated. Increasing preference was given to British-born administrators because educational requirements rose so as to keep up with a slowly expanding supply of British graduates. According to the new standards, most Africans were seen as inadequately qualified, all the more so once the senior appointments began to be made in London rather than at the coast. In the Gold Coast, for instance, candidates for DC had to be either solicitors or barristers. Africans with that level of legal training, however, were few, and those who were qualified preferred the higher rewards available in private practice. Africans who retired from senior positions—like J. A. M'Carthy, attorney general of the Gold Coast—were mostly replaced by Europeans. By 1908 only five of the colony's 274 officers were Africans, and only one— Judge Frans Smith—held a high post. The African elite complained of this curtailed opportunity and also of the prejudice against their doctors; they had more opportunity in Southern Nigeria and Sierra Leone. In effect, they began to fill only routine jobs as opportunities were closed for promotion and special service—opportunities that once had allowed men such as George Ferguson to rise to the higher ranks of the administration.

Though the restrictions aroused a good deal of opposition among educated Africans, the Europeanization of the upper levels continued. Meanwhile, however, the expansion of the civil service created more and more jobs for Africans in the lowest ranks of the administration as clerks, messengers, telegraphists, carriers, and the like. A certain number of improvements were effected under Governor Sir Hugh Clifford, a conservative aristocrat whose experiences in British Asia, especially Malaya, had convinced him that "educated natives" should fill more government positions. Despite Colonial Office opposition, Clifford created additional posts for African doctors and appointed the first African Crown counsel. But the rank and file of African civil servants were paid at a lower rate than the whites and could not rise into senior positions.

By 1914 in the Gold Coast and Nigeria there was a virtual dichotomy between the higher ranks of the service—almost entirely reserved for whites—and the "native subordinate service" filled by black applicants. The same rigid barrier between administrative and clerical posts marked the civil service in Britain, where it mirrored existing class distinctions; but educated Africans resented it nonetheless. They did not reappear as heads of departments in the Gold Coast until after World War II.

Despite the burgeoning of the colonial governments, in 1914 they still employed relatively few blacks. In the Gold Coast, for instance, the district administration had just 89 African clerks, bailiffs, and messengers all told. There were 79 clerks in the Treasury Department and 35 serving the Supreme Court. The Customs department had on its roll 149 Africans as first-, second-, or third-class officers.[6]

A "native clerk" started at £36 a year and could rise to be chief clerk at £280. But even the lower posts of government—clerks and inter-preters—carried prestige and power, commanding almost as much outward respect as lawyers or doctors. For clerks and interpreters had real authority. They controlled access to the British officers; they were able to advise petitioners and litigants about the details of British ad-ministrative and court procedure; they acted as unofficial arbitrators. They had enjoyed the benefits of a Western-style education, and they were the indispensable middlemen of empire.

Educated black men also carved out official careers for themselves in other parts of West Africa, especially Southern Nigeria. These in-cluded both West Indians and Sierra Leonians. The former did well in the West African colonial administration; in fact, they began to replace Africans in important posts in the 1890's. To cite but one example, James Carmichael Smith, who became postmaster of Sierra Leone, was born in the Bahamas of mixed racial ancestry, went into govern-ment service after a career at sea, and was elected to the island's House of Assembly. He served as postmaster from 1889 to 1893. When the postmaster in Sierra Leone was imprisoned for corruption and replaced by an Englishman, Smith was brought to Freetown as assistant post-master in 1896 and was promoted in 1900 when the incumbent died of malaria. He served as postmaster and as manager of the General Sav-ings Bank until he retired in 1911. He was also collector of customs from 1902 to 1903, and was colonial treasurer from 1906 to 1907; but his primary work was to direct the expansion of Sierra Leone's postal services. Under Smith the number of post offices grew from 23 to 58, and postal order offices from none to 33. He lived in Hill Station with other high government officials, and shared fully in the social and polit-ical life of the colony. On retirement he moved to London, where he died in 1919.[7]

Many pioneer officials in Lagos were expatriate Sierra Leonians and Gold Coasters, recruited at a period when the "sound old system was to consider the African an Englishman with a black face."[8] The "sound old system" was urban in orientation, designed to promote an eco-nomic partnership between African producers of tropical crops, black middlemen, and white merchants. It was linked to Lancashire and Scotland, infused with humanitarian sentiments, and civilian in out-look. (At the turn of the century the colony's total military establishment amounted to only one African battalion commanded by 13 British officers. The coercive machinery at the disposal of the government was small; the entire Prison Department had four members. Government centered on technical services and on the collection of taxes and duties.)

Under the Lagos dispensation there were some black physicians in the Medical Department, and an African served as assistant secretary in the secretariat. In 1875 Africans in Lagos were heads of the Police, Post and Telegraph, and Customs departments. Sir William Mac-Gregor's principal medical officer was a West Indian, Dr. W. Strachan; it was he who converted MacGregor to Sir Ronald Ross's theory that mosquitos caused malaria.[9] An African, Henry Carr, was chief clerk, and eventually rose to be head of the Education Department and resident of the Colony and Protectorate of Southern Nigeria. One of his principal functions was to determine the eligibility of schools for government grants; he also acted as an examiner for the civil service, Lagos by this time having become an examination center for candidates for the degrees of B.A. and L.L.B. at London University. The lower ranks of the civil service—clerks, foremen, and such—were filled almost entirely by Africans, most of whom had adopted English surnames.

A description of the Lagos civil service is given by I. F. Nicolson in his excellent book *The Administration of Nigeria*. Entrance at the lowest clerical grade was by competitive examination in a variety of

TABLE 19

The Lagos Civil Administration, 1899

Office/department	Total establish-ment	Subordinate African technical and clerical personnel	Office/department	Total establish-ment	Subordinate African technical and clerical personnel
Governor	5	3	Prisons	9	2
Secretariat	11	7	Medical	16	5
Queen's Advocate	3	2	Sanitary	3	2
Registrar general	4	2	Public works	22	4
Treasury	10	9	Audit	3	2
Customs	42	40	Harbors and marine	17	11
Supreme court			Post office	6	5
(including district			Education	3	2
commissioners)	22	9	TOTAL	183	107
Interior	7	2			

SOURCE: *Colonial Office List, 1900.*

TABLE 20

Annual Salaries of African Civil Servants in Lagos and Some Comparable British Salaries, c. 1898

(In £)

Africans	Salary	British nationals	Salary
Clerk, 6th class	24–36	Typist, Foreign Office	42–62
Clerk, 5th class	42–48	Junior clerk and	
Clerk, 4th class	54–66	private secretary to	
Clerk, 3d class	72–96	permanent under	
Clerk, 2d class	108–150	secretary, Foreign	
Clerk, 1st class	200–250	Office	150
Chief clerk	300	Clerk, Passport Office	250
		Asst. colonial surgeon,	
		Lagos	250

SOURCE: Colonial Office and Foreign Office lists.

practical subjects, including arithmetic, English composition, the format of letters, and the Yoruba tongue. A junior clerk could expect to receive about the same salary as a typist in England at the time. In Lagos, as in Britain, there was a great pay differential between junior and senior clerical employees, but able men could advance. Promotion to the middle rank of the service depended on a further examination in typing and shorthand. To be accepted into a senior clerkship, an African civil servant had to undergo further examination in accounting, in the drafting of letters, in the docketing and scheduling of dispatches, and in the knowledge of local laws.

Promotions were centrally regulated; they depended on merit rather than seniority, and on an official's proven ability for "self-improvement." The more senior positions carried rights to tenure and to three months' paid vacation; their holders enjoyed both a considerable degree of social status, and a good rate of pay, with salaries in excess of those paid to some of the more senior white officials and roughly equal to British clerks in the metropole (see Table 20). The spirit of administration was commercial; even the working hours in government offices (8:00 A.M. to 11:00 A.M. and 1:00 P.M. to 4:00 P.M.) were designed to correspond to those of the Bank of West Africa.

The process of imperial expansion and consolidation, however, eventually worked against the interests of the African civil servants here as it had in the Gold Coast. When Lagos came to govern the whole of Southern Nigeria in 1906, the senior Yoruba and other African officials were no longer as favorably placed as before. They faced

all manner of difficulty in getting transfers, in educating their children
at the more remote outstations, in finding accommodations among the
more backward peoples with different standards of living and sanitation, communities that were in fact often more willing to accept a white
man than an African belonging to a different ethnic community.

Then, too, black civil servants lost prestige due to some well-pub-
licized scandals. The Bannerman family became involved in a number
of irregularities.* Judge Frans Smith, posted to the western province
of Sierra Leone, was charged with favoring the clients of his barrister
brother-in-law. There were more and more complaints that senior African officeholders used their posts to benefit their own kin. British
officials, without local family ties, had no incentive to commit such
misdemeanors. †

Above all, the military expansion of empire shifted the balance of
power in the various West African colonies from the coastal cities, with
their Christian, Western-educated African elites, to the more backward hinterland—especially in Nigeria, where the British had to deal
with powerful Muslim emirates. Inland expansion weakened the older
administrative connections between the coast and the free-trading
merchants of Lancashire. Power began to center on the British administrative and military Establishment, oriented to London and the
Home Counties, and on the Public Schools and the great British military academies.

The African coastal bourgeoisie had no ties whatever with these
groups. An African medical man, for instance, had no chance of being
employed in a Muslim emirate or in a remote outstation where a physician was expected to look after Europeans, including British Army

---

*C. J. Bannerman had started his career as a clerk in the 1880's in the Gold Coast.
He and three other clerks accompanied Governor Sir Samuel Rowe on a peacekeeping
mission to Prushue to treat with emissaries of the king of Ashanti. Before the meeting
the governor refused his usual morning glass of egg and rum and said to the servant,
"Give it to the clerks." Bannerman was a total abstainer and refused. When the glass
was returned empty to the governor, his big voice boomed out, "That's right, Bannerman! You are from Mr. Macy's school, eh? Band of Hope Society. I'm glad you didn't
drink—keep to it." Bannerman did remain an abstainer, and became an important
barrister and member of the Legislative Council in the colony. See Lady Clifford, ed.,
*Our Days on the Gold Coast; in Ashanti, in the Northern Territories, and the British
Sphere of Occupation in Togoland* (London, 1919), pp. 117–19.

†According to the British *Colonial Regulations*, all salaried officials were prohibited
from "directly or indirectly holding any local investments, speculating in the shares of,
or being connected with any company, occupation or undertaking, which might bring
their private interest into real or apparent conflict with their public duties." Expatriate
British officials without local links could comply with these regulations much more easily
than local men, who, in the phrase of Lord Malvern, a white Rhodesian prime minister
of a later era, "went home every night and not every three years."

officers. He could not live in the same quarters with whites, who commonly questioned his professional competence and rejected his claim to social equality. African doctors, able to find congenial jobs on the coast, had not the slightest incentive to serve, say, on a river expedition, where they would have to face both the perils of a campaign and the slights of white men.

The improvement in health services that began in the twentieth century encouraged the employment of expatriate Englishmen, for their rate of mortality in the tropics began to decline. Moreover, the Public School ideal worked in favor of civil servants recruited from "home" as against the employment of locals, black or white, men who had not enjoyed the real or assumed advantages of having attended Harrow or Haileysbury, and for whom the pattern of trust implicit among English Public School graduates was not assumed. At the same time, academic anthropology, based on an evolutionist view of human society, increasingly imbued Europeans with the notion that mankind was divided into "advanced" or "higher" races and "lower" and "more primitive" races.

Discrimination in Southern Nigeria became more severe in 1890, when Governor Alfred Moloney's term of office came to an end. Moloney had given every possible encouragement to educated Africans; G. T. Carter, his successor, pursued a very different policy. Opportunities for educated Africans by no means disappeared, but Europeans consistently obtained better salaries and better jobs. Henry Carr, a highly educated man, was long denied promotion. Other Africans—for instance, Herbert Macaulay, a qualified engineer, and James Obadiah Johnson, a physician—likewise experienced racial discrimination. Once Northern and Southern Nigeria had been amalgamated under Lord Lugard, discrimination grew even more systematic, for Lugard had little faith in educated Africans. After the end of World War I the African clerical staff was regraded into a lower division (in which the salary range was £48 to £128 a year) and a higher division (with a salary range of £80 to £400 a year). Candidates for the African clerical service had to pass a simple qualifying examination for the lower division and a more difficult one for the higher division. East and West Indians employed by the service obtained special terms.

Official discrimination created a widespread sense of grievance among the educated. Promotion prospects were limited; many African public servants therefore indulged in magical practices to remove their superiors from office. The lack of opportunities in the technical branches of the service discouraged them from getting qualified in careers like accounting and engineering; the ambitious turned instead to medicine and law, where they could satisfy their aspirations without having to look to official employment.[10]

When the British came to East and Central Africa they were unable to draw on the assistance of well-educated Africans of the kind that had served the imperial cause so well in Accra, Freetown, and Lagos. In Uganda, for instance, the missions initially taught only local languages; hence their graduates learned neither English nor Swahili. This placed them at a great disadvantage in competing for government jobs, since at first they were unable to understand British administrative methods. The influence of Swahili-speaking Muslims was considerably less in British than in German East Africa. The Germans made extensive use of Arabs and Swahili-speakers as clerks and local administrators, and established schools to train African government officials. Moreover, they were in a better position to conciliate Swahili-speaking coastmen than their British competitors. Thus the servants of the queen could not depend on the former Muslim ruling class to anything like the same extent as the servants of the kaiser.

The anti-slavery lobby was much weaker in Germany than in England, and the Germans were slower in eliminating domestic slavery. The British, without this labor pool, had to draw on a large number of expatriates from India to fill subordinate administrative positions. Some were Goans—Roman Catholic by religion and thus less apt to arouse the hostility and suspicion of white settlers than Hindus. Whole families from Goa took to government, and names like Fernandes, de Souza, Lobo, Pereira, and Pinto came to fill the clerical staff lists. Goa, however, was unable to supply the growing demand for junior administrators and technicians, with the result that the Indian share continually increased.[11]

By 1900 the civil service of Uganda and East Africa was organized on a racially determined three-tier system. British administrators stood at the top; Indians and Goans occupied the skilled and middle-level positions; and Africans worked as unskilled manual laborers, without civil service status. Government stations were usually manned by a British officer, a Goan clerk, some Asian artisans, and an Indian sub-assistant surgeon. Asians therefore occupied a peculiarly important position within the East African power structure. At a time when the British lacked both the manpower and the resources to train the indigenous people, Asian immigrants knew English, had experience in British administrative methods, and were satisfied with lower salaries than British employees. They soon filled most of the middle-rank government positions, dominating all departments of the central and provincial administrations and the Ugandan railway.

Goan clerks were particularly popular with the British. They acquired a reputation for efficiency, loyalty, and honesty. Whereas Indians tended to use the civil service as a stepping-stone to commerce, the Goans stayed on at the clerical level. Of 39 clerks appointed in 1913, only two were non-Goans. This near monopoly is not hard to understand: the Goans were Westernized Christians and so were more acceptable to the British. The lives of both groups centered on British-type clubs, on dancing, drinking, music, and sports. Goans could thus socialize informally with the British in a way that Africans and Indians could not.

Initially, few Uganda Africans were trained to handle skilled manual or clerical work. In 1902 only the Printing, Marine, and Public Works departments had trained Africans on their staffs. They began to appear as chauffeurs after 1908, and in 1910 the Public Works Department employed 30 Africans and 12 Indian artisans. The government was forced to meet a growing need for clerks and interpreters, even if it meant using poorly trained Africans, and the number in government employ increased steadily after 1910 as mission schools began to teach English and arithmetic. In 1912 an official memorandum for the first time laid down plans for establishing an African civil service and a government school to train African clerks. Chief Secretary H. R. Wallis opposed the reforms, but he was overruled in a committee meeting in 1913–14, which created the Uganda Native Civil Service, with designated terms of service, pay scales, and job requirements. The first civil servants were appointed in 1915.[12]

In other parts of East-Central Africa the British likewise recruited an ever-increasing number of mission-trained Africans as messengers, detectives, interpreters, clerks, telegraphists, stores supervisors, craftsmen, laborers, and porters. In Northeastern Rhodesia an economy-minded administration insisted on employing Africans—many of them alumni of Scottish mission schools in Nyasaland—in all the lowlier government posts in preference to more highly paid Europeans. By 1904 black clerks typed all the letters in the secretariat; black employees did the bulk of the clerical work in the Transport and Stores department.[13]

The junior African civil servant, who was one of the most important pioneers of empire, rarely got a good press. Many post-colonial historians seemed to regard him as suspect, a collaborator in imperial

exploitation. To the imperialists the African clerk was often the proto-
type of the parvenu, with his flawed English, his malapropisms, and
his unacceptable pretensions. British officials were inclined to deplore
his real or assumed inefficiency, and his actual or supposed proclivity
to take bribes and to favor his own kin. Africans who preferred secular
employment, with its higher pay, to mission posts were resented by
the churchmen who had educated them. Settlers frequently objected
to educated Africans, even though white farmers and traders themselves had no compunction about hiring black foremen, clerks, and
shop assistants. But whether the Europeans liked African clerks or not,
colonial administration could not have operated without this substantial body of office personnel—the noncommissioned officers of empire.
Equally important were the educated Africans who held local office by
serving in the employ of chiefs, transacting business with the whites
on their superiors' behalf and thereby providing an indispensable in-
termediary between the local rulers and their white overlords.

These early African administrators, interpreters, and clerks rarely
wrote their memoirs, yet their life stories were sometimes fantastic
odysseys. One of the first inland Africans in Tanganyika to be educated
in a mission school was Sameni, a member of the Kwavi people. According to his own account, related with biblical simplicity, Sameni (c.
1878–1954) was born in Lushoto in the Sambaa country long before
Europeans had penetrated the interior. At the age of seven he was
captured by roving Masai warriors, but managed to escape. Life
among the Masai, however, does not seem to have been overly arduous, for a year later, when the Kwavi released an elderly Masai
prisoner, Sameni was eager to go back to live among the Masai; he
asked the man to take him along, and the Masai elder agreed. In 1890,
however, catastrophe struck the Masai: their herds were decimated by
rinderpest, and many died of hunger; many more were killed in internecine quarrels over cattle. Sameni now sought refuge among the
Chagga, who took pity on him and allowed him to stay in their midst.
About 1891 he was accepted by an English mission school that had
been established in the area before the Germans took over the government. The boy was baptized and given the name Justin Lemenye.
He completed his studies, became a mission teacher, traveled widely,
and even managed to meet President Theodore Roosevelt during the
latter's visit to East Africa. In 1911 he returned to the Kwavi, where
the local *laibon* (head) asked him to assist in administration. Justin, a
literate man, became a personage of some local influence, and when

the British conquered the country in World War I, they decided to make use of his services. He retired as headman in 1947.[14]

Another servant of empire was Martin Kayamba of the Bondi tribe, who—like most educated Africans of the time and, indeed, like most frontiersmen—knew how to put his skills to many different uses. His father had been educated by the Universities Mission to Central Africa and had even studied in England. In 1885 the older Kayamba became a teacher at St. Andrew's College in Zanzibar, where his son was born in 1891; he resigned in 1895 to become a clerk in the Uganda Rifles, and worked for the government until 1926—his last post that of a headman. Martin was raised strictly and severely in a Christian family. He attended various mission schools and became a protégé of Bishop F. Weston, principal of Kuingani College, who administered "six of the very best" to boys who failed their exams. In 1904 Martin, though still only a boy, was made an assistant teacher, but he did not like the work and left after two years to go to work in the Mombasa Telegraph Department. He continued in government service until 1914, transferring twice—to the Public Works and Stores departments. He then left to try his hand at trading in German East Africa, only to be imprisoned during the war. After 1918 he became an interpreter and clerk for the Uganda administration, was promoted to head clerk in 1923, and later served on local government committees.[15]

The intermediate stratum to which Justin Lemenye and Martin Kayamba belonged consisted almost entirely of mission-trained men. Most substituted biblical names for their African ones; many were Protestants, since Protestant missionaries—with their emphasis on Bible-reading—at first valued literacy more than the Catholics did. These "new men" were among the earliest African wage workers. A large number—though by no means all—were labor migrants, willing to switch employers and their place of work. Some completely cut their links with the ancestral village, becoming what was known in Nyasaland as *machona*, the lost ones. But the great majority of educated men maintained more or less close links to their families, kept a stake in the land, and assisted their relatives with cash and counsel.[16]

Socially and politically, their position was ambiguous. They depended on the empire for their living and their social prestige, but they were excluded from the white society that they served, and were among its earliest literate critics. They grouped themselves into new associations of their own, often known as native welfare societies, improvement associations, tribal unions, or native associations, formed for both social and cultural reasons. These societies both supported and criticized the imperial administration. The North Nyasa Native Association, a small Malawi body, rejected the revolutionary violence that broke out in Nyasaland during World War I, but was also vocal in its call for reforms, decrying, for instance, the fact that African petitioners were sometimes flogged or imprisoned when they attempted to put their complaints to the local officials.[17]

In a formal sense, these humble and usually respectful clerks wielded little power, though they had a great deal of prestige in African circles. But in the actual conduct of administration their influence was tremendous. Black office personnel tended to stay in the same stations longer than their superiors, and were apt to be more familiar with local languages and customs than white men. A DC was helpless without "native messengers" to deliver orders, collect intelligence, and arrest evildoers. Court interpreters played a crucial role in the conduct of a case: the fate of the accused often depended on what advice he received from an interpreter before the trial started, or on how the interpreter translated the testimony of the witnesses and plea of the prisoner. A sympathetic interpreter could sway the court in favor of the man on trial; a hostile one could get him sent to prison. An interpreter's advice was frequently sought by officials charged with laying out a "native reserve," with framing a local police order, or with imposing a road-building corvée.

At the same time, educated Africans in government gained a variety of new skills. A clerk was expected to assist in ordering supplies, checking stores, keeping accounts; he learned how to operate two essential instruments of modern government, the card index and the filing system; he became skilled in typing letters, thus acquiring some familiarity with the white man's system of government—the kind of knowledge inaccessible to the ordinary cultivator.

Not surprisingly, the "new man" held numerous advantages over his unlettered countrymen. Clerks worked for the same employer for much longer periods than labor migrants in unskilled jobs. They were among the first specialized African workers, hence they drew higher wages than farm hands. Early in the twentieth century a highly skilled African worker or clerk made up to 15s. a month in Nyasaland, whereas a farmworker got only 3s. plus board and lodging. The "new class," however, did not at first subsist solely on its wages. Some clerks and mission teachers practiced agriculture on the side, working their land in their spare time or through hired hands or relatives. Others engaged in a certain amount of private trading. They had many opportunities to use their governmental positions in order to add to their extracurricular revenue. A knowledgeable clerk could sell information obtained from confidential files to an interested third party; he could demand a reward for arranging a special audience with a DC, and his family would expect him to favor his kinsmen in obtaining government jobs. In such ways, many clerks became men of influence.

Their position was evidenced by a semi-European life-style. They wore European dress. They exchanged the traditional pole-and-dagga hut for a brick cottage covered with a roof of corrugated iron and filled with European-style furniture. They saw their superior position recognized by the Europeans themselves in a variety of ways; they received better rations than the unskilled, and even better treatment in prison. Africans learned that the man who wielded a pen stood above the man who cleared the bush and raised corn. The path of ambition led through the office door.

Generalizations with regard to the social and ethnic origins of this "new class" are hard to formulate. At first they were the products of mission schools—government schools came after 1900—and these mission graduates consisted principally of two groups. Kingdoms like Lesotho and Botswana favored white missionaries for their religious message and for reasons of diplomacy, as well as for their technical expertise; in states where the rulers accepted the gospel, the educated at first came from the highest social ranks. In stateless societies, or in communities unwilling to come to terms with white missionary influence, the first converts commonly came from the ranks of the refugees, the outcasts, and the slaves. Justin Lemenye did not quite fit into any of these categories, but he too had been uprooted at an early age and became one of the intellectual pioneers willing to embark on a new venture.

Wherever they came from and whatever their personal loyalties, the mission-educated men found themselves in an ambivalent position toward the colonial government. They acquired a firm conviction that in the future no indigenous ruler could afford to govern without an understanding of the white man's administrative techniques. In 1893 Micka Nxobbe, an expatriate evangelist of Ndebele descent, put the matter in halting but forceful English in a letter to Lobengula, the Ndebele king soon to be overthrown by British arms: "Better for you must want a clerk and put them in an office to make your right [law]. . . . I am one of them. . . . Then you let the people build a big house

for office and coming work. . . . If you get a high case with the nother
[another] people, you send the case to England. . . . If you do not
than you lose your country indeed."[18]

The vast number of Africans who worked for government, however,
were illiterate and followed a variety of careers: porter, laborer, askari,
trader, policeman, forest guard. The career of Rashed bin Hassam,
cited by Margery Perham, provides one case study. Born a Bisa in
Northern Rhodesia, he was captured as a boy by Angoni raiders and
sold as a slave in Zanzibar to a woman for whom he worked for a number of years. The sight of porters spending money, drinking, and
gambling inspired him to sign on for expeditions into the interior of
East Africa. After a few years he became an askari, moved on into trading for a time, then returned to being a police askari. In 1903–4 he
tried hunting, and became a forest guard. He was too old to fight in
World War I.

The future lay more with men like Martin Kayamba than with the
Rashed bin Hassams; but the support of both was essential to sustain
British rule. Without their help the whites could not have governed a
vast empire with their small numbers and limited force; neither could
modernization have gotten under way.

EIGHT

The Transportation Network

In every colony the first priorities were communication, transport, and medical care. Railroads were built wherever economically feasible to promote agricultural or mineral exports, or to facilitate the movement of soldiers and policemen. Post offices, telegraphs, and telephones gradually formed communication networks that helped to tie together various administrative units of the colony. Major roads were laid out, both to assist the military and the administrators and to promote trade and the marketing of crops. In the Gold Coast these roads above all benefited the African cocoa farmers; in Nyasaland, the white planters.

Among the first government units established in a territory were public works departments for the construction of government buildings, bridges, roads, harbors, and the like. In most places a transport section was attached to the departments. In a few there was a separate Transport Department. All these units routinely handled the forwarding of goods and supplies; some were also responsible for mail services, water supplies, and electricity. In British East Africa there was a division that ran the railway, the port facilities, and the steamship services. Steamers played an even more important part in the Sudan, where river craft were essential to British conquest.

Printing departments or government printers became responsible at an early stage for the publication of laws, ordinances, regulations, and such. Agriculture, forestry, and livestock all required their own administrative arrangements, however rudimentary, and governments became responsible for the essential work of providing surveys. By 1914 all the British African dependencies possessed a basic infrastructure of specialized services, the most important of which was the creation of a modern transportation network.

Throughout the early colonial period the lack of roads and other facilities, high transport costs, and great distances seriously retarded economic development. Given the prevalence of disease, animal-drawn carts could rarely be used successfully. The whites tried all manner of animal transport—elephants, oxen, donkeys, bullocks—but all failed due to the animals' susceptibility to disease. The Germans even tried—unsuccessfully—to breed a hybrid Wunderzebra. Both merchants and administrators were thus forced to rely on human porterage, which had been a prestigious occupation in East Africa even before the colonial period. Colonizers at first employed carriers on a large scale; until the railway reached Lake Victoria in 1902 the only way to send goods inland was on the heads of Africans. To regulate such porterage, caravans were inspected, and officials controlled their loads and rates of pay; they insisted on medical screening, on vaccination, on the provision of rest camps, medicine, blankets; they arranged for setting up carrier reserves. Porters remained indispensable to the economic life of most tropical colonies until the advent of the railway and the development of backwoods roads.* The demand for paddlers, however, lessened considerably in West and Central Africa when flat-bottomed, light-draft steamboats began to ply the rivers and lakes, greatly reducing the cost of transporting bulky goods by water.

Porters still did a great deal of work in the backwoods even after the main railway lines had been built. Sir Alfred Sharpe, on a journey through Ruanda, observed thousands of porters carrying hides and goods to Lake Victoria, where they could connect with the train to Mombasa. In one instance, in Western Uganda, African cultivators had to carry their crops 179 miles in order to find a buyer; since they had to buy and carry their own provisions for the trip, their efforts earned them little profit. The demand for carriers continued after porters ceased to be employed for long-distance caravans. They were used to link outlying areas to the railroad. Ex-porters worked as mailmen—often an adventurous occupation in lion-infested country—and took part in building the railroad, which in many instances followed old caravan tracks that they knew well. They served on survey parties, worked as interpreters, became policemen; when not carrying supplies for construction gangs, they were sometimes used for grading road-beds or making bricks and lime.[1]

We have spoken previously of the caravan porters, but their role

---

*As we have noted, the 1914 war created enormous demands for porters; an estimated 500,000 men served as porters during World War I in East Africa. The French in West Africa conscripted in one year 125,000 carriers just to transport 4,000 tons of foodstuffs.

was of such importance as to warrant repetition. They were among the first Africans to work for wages; they were among the first to be exposed to the new ways of colonialism; their profession brought new hardships as well as new opportunities in its train. They made new contacts. They broke out of the limitations imposed by village life. They acquired money and goods; they traveled and learned new things, and they transmitted to their fellow villagers some of their experiences. They were also among the most numerous government employees, needed by administrators, police, and military units on tour, and by the transport division of the central government.

Transport Departments

The best example of transport operations is the Gold Coast Transport Department, one of the few separate departments in the colonies.[2] It was organized by Chamberlain in 1901 as a general forwarding agent from Cape Coast, and functioned until 1919, when its duties were taken over by the Public Works Department and the Northern Territories administration. Its first and only head was Frederick William Hugh Migeod, who had a small permanent staff of four Europeans, some African clerks, mechanics, drivers, and messengers, and about 300 carriers.* Illness, invaliding, death, or promotion caused frequent changes in the European staff. Until the railway was completed in 1903, the department was simply a transfer company, employing gangs of carriers to take supplies inland. After that, it primarily provided labor for the mines in areas served by rail. It also supplied carriers to the Northern Territories and Ashanti; it organized motor transport, moved mail to and from railway stations, furnished carriers to private firms, and ran the boat services.

Migeod set the carriers' load weights and pace—60 pounds per load, 20–25 miles per day—and their salary—1s. a day plus 3d. for subsistence. His terms were not generous; he called for an end to subsistence pay on Sunday since it was a day of rest. He objected to open competition for labor in the colony and wanted all recruitment to be controlled by his department. On the plus side, he made every effort to protect the porters and laborers in the department's employ. Rest

---

* Migeod was born in 1872 in England. He was educated privately at Folkestone and in 1890 entered the Pay Department of the Royal Navy. He resigned to join the WAFF in Northern Nigeria. He moved into the transport job from a position as supervisor of customs at Accra, a post he had taken in 1900. Migeod was a fellow of the Royal Anthropological Institute, the African Society, and the Folklore Society. He wrote Mende and Hausa grammars and books of anthropological interest.

camps were maintained along the main routes, and food, wages, and conditions of service were carefully regulated. He developed a system to protect labor, and his carrier crews—mainly Mende and Krepi from Sierra Leone—usually renewed their contracts and served for many years.*

Cars and trucks came into use as better roads were built. The first car in the Gold Coast belonged to Governor Sir Matthew Nathan (1900–1904). It was purchased on Chamberlain's suggestion in an experiment to try out the roads near Cape Coast and Accra. A Gardner-Serpallet paraffin-fired, steam-driven car was purchased and used by Government House until 1908, when a local French trader bought it for £5. He could not maintain it, and the car eventually was hauled away by the sanitary authorities and dumped into the sea. The original plan had called for a gasoline-driven car, but the shipping company refused to carry the necessary fuel because it was reported that gasoline was of "an exceptionally dangerous nature."

While Migeod was on home leave, the colony's chief mechanic exchanged a new Ford he felt lacked power for a new yellow Overland, a big car that rode better.[3] In his opinion, the Transport Department should have the best car of any government department. The fact that the division had no funds in the budget to pay for the car caused him some concern, as shown in letters he wrote Migeod about ways of hiding the purchase from Accra.

Automobiles and trucks became more numerous in Africa after 1909–10. By 1912 Nairobi had two garages to care for the growing number of vehicles. The first East African governor to own a car was Sir Percy Girouard (1909–12). Some officials purchased their own automobiles to work in their districts, but for the remote, roadless areas of the African colonies simpler means continued to be used until the

---

* In 1910 Migeod prepared a new code for workers from the Northern Territories. He instructed his staff to use African recruiting agents, to give physical examinations to applicants, to vaccinate new hires before they left home, to advance them money for food until they got to their employers, and to encourage them to take their wives. He also insisted that the workers should have houses to live in; these should be clustered by tribal grouping, and their condition should be checked by labor inspectors. The Transport Department itself employed up to 14 carrier gangs (of 24 men each); seven gangs served Ashanti and seven served the Northern Territories. They were provided with pots, food, water bottles, cutlasses, badges, uniforms, and housing while on the march. Their daily food ration consisted of one and a half pounds of rice, cassava, plantains, or yams and one-half ounce of salt. In addition they got a quarter-pound of meat or fish two or three times a week. The department also had to provide carriers for European officials on tour—four men per official—and for infantry companies; a company of 300 men required 637 carriers. In 1905 the department carried 17,609 loads and supplied 3,635 carriers for officers and troops, and 1,219 for other government services.

1930's—camel, horse, mule, bicycle, sedan chairs, hammocks, and feet. Though the private sector took readily to the use of cars and trucks, the Colonial Office before 1914 discouraged their use; they thought motor vehicles impractical for Africa.[4]

Another kind of transport section was found on coasts, on lakes, and along rivers. The Nigerian Marine Service was founded in 1893 in order to provide a vessel for the imperial commissioner to visit different ports on the coast. In 1895 it acquired several small launches for transport through narrow creeks. From 1894 to 1911 the Marine Service took part in punitive operations and kept a semi-naval character as it helped the military to conquer Nigeria. As the colony was occupied, the department directed its attention more to commercial transport and administrative uses. The Marine Service grew steadily; in 1906 there were 63 European staff members operating one coastal vessel and 40 steam and motor launches and pinnaces.

In the north the Marine Service developed to communicate with the coast by the Niger, the Benue, and branches of the delta. Its main function was to provide transport for officials, government personnel, and stores. It took 14 days to cover the 566 miles from the coast to Zungeru; four transfers into shallow-draft craft were required. The service's work was considerably increased by the building of the railway from Baro to Kano in 1907; on its completion, however, the use of the river for transport was substantially reduced.

One important part of the Marine Service's work was the surveying, charting, and marking of the numerous creeks and rivers of the delta. But by far its most important work after 1903 was clearing waterways to allow merchants to get timber and produce down to the coast. Most of this work involved blowing up trees and other obstructions from the waterways.[5]

Railways and Railwaymen

The most important requisite for the economic penetration of Africa was the construction of railways. Steam power saved an extraordinary amount of labor, and trains revolutionized the techniques of administration and warfare by permitting the quick transport of policemen, soldiers, and civil servants through the country. For the first time mining companies could move heavy machinery to the interior and export their ores; great armies of wage laborers could be recruited; city populations could grow unchecked once there was an assured supply of food.

There were unintended economic consequences of a far-reaching character. Railway construction opened a market for local goods and services. The development of new industries was stimulated; in order to operate, railways required trained personnel and repair shops. In most parts of Africa the railway was thus the first harbinger of the Industrial Revolution. It stood for fundamental social change. Steam transport, Lord Salisbury explained to a public meeting in Glasgow,

kills every other mode of locomotion that formerly held the same ground. . . . It costs two or three hundred times as much to bring goods by caravan as it would cost to bring them by railway. Of course, when once a railway existed, caravans would become a matter of antiquity. . . . I do not see that any slave dealer who presented himself with a body of slaves to be carried on trucks to the coast would be very civilly received.[6]

In sub-Saharan Africa the era of railway construction began at the Cape with the discovery of diamonds, and received added impetus from the development of gold mining and the growth of great urban centers like Johannesburg. By 1913 the Union of South Africa could boast of more than 8,000 miles of track, an impressive achievement in logistics for what was still a backward country largely dependent on the production of a few raw materials. But considerable progress was also made in other British colonies and protectorates, which by the outbreak of World War I had more than 6,000 miles of rail. (See Table 21.)

The great majority of these railways, including the South African lines, were planned by the state, run by the state, and owned by the state. The Nyasaland and Rhodesian railways were exceptional in that they were built by private enterprise. In Nyasaland the government provided the builders with all manner of incentives—land conces-

TABLE 21

Railways in the Principal British African Territories
(Excluding the Union of South Africa), 1914

Territory	Miles of track	Territory	Miles of track
Northern and		Sierra Leone	310
Southern Rhodesia	2,357	Gold Coast	208
Sudan	c. 1,500	Nyasaland	129
Nigeria	975	TOTAL	6,081
British East Africa			
Protectorate and			
Uganda	602		

SOURCE: *The Statesman's Yearbook, 1916.*

TABLE 22

Capital Expenditure and Cost per Mile of Selected Railway Systems
in British Africa, c. 1924

(In £)

System	Capital expenditure	Cost per mile
Rhodesia	16,977,304	6,896
South Africa	111,769,666	10,327
Uganda	9,636,358	11,350
Gold Coast	6,469,742	16,279

SOURCE: *Report by Brigadier F. D. Hammond, CBE, DSO, on the Railway System of Rhodesia* (Salisbury, Rhodesia, 1925).

sions, subsidies, and other advantages. The promoters, however, embarked on the project for imperial rather than commercial motives, and the railway-building venture involved its supporters in losses despite government help.

The Rhodesian railways started under somewhat more favorable auspices. Constructed in financial association with the British South Africa Company, in every sense they formed a "miners' railway," having been built mainly to serve the needs of the mining industry both south and north of the Zambezi. The trains mostly traversed the high veld; later this turned out to be an unexpected boon to white farmers, who found much of the coolest and healthiest portion of the two Rhodesias served with transport.

These railways represented a tremendous capital outlay. Service had to be provided to the small population of a large country—more than four times the size of the British Isles—in the middle of Africa. To avoid heavy engineering works, the line went up along the watershed. Earthworks were light; stations were spaced at great distances. But to make up for these disadvantages, Rhodesia managed to obtain its railways at low cost. The British South Africa Company and its associated interests enjoyed the benefit of unified financial control and managed to raise capital at a favorable rate. Hence Rhodesia spent much less per mile than South Africa and most other British African countries. (See Table 22.)

Outside Rhodesia and Nyasaland those railways that were not constructed by or on behalf of the colonial governments were constructed by the military. Railway-building and railway management were tasks in which the British Army excelled. Not even the railway Abteilung in the Prussian General Staff could compete with the Royal Engineers in the logistics field. Only the British could have brought off in 1867 the feat involved in assembling all the materials needed for a short-track railway in the port of Bombay and transporting these impedimenta— complete with engines and rolling stock—across the Indian Ocean to the Gulf of Aden to build a railway line that would keep the tiny port of Zula clear of confusion and clutter. The British did equally well in the Sudan, where the original Wadi Halfa–Saras line, with its subsequent extensions to Akasha and Kerma, served no economic purpose but was built by the Anglo-Egyptian Army for purely military reasons. During a period of more than 40 years (1884–1925) the system was run by Royal Engineers officers. It served as a training ground for general administrators with a technical background, as well as for military railway managers. Girouard served as director of railways in the Sudan between 1896 and 1897, and then built railways in Nigeria and Kenya. Men with Sudanese experience were always welcome in Northern Nigeria, where military considerations likewise played a major part in railway construction.

State management represented a remarkable departure from British domestic experience, where private corporations both built and operated the lines. But the construction of colonial railways was inspired by economic, administrative, humanitarian, and above all, strategic considerations. Not surprisingly, private firms were reluctant to step in on their own. Western European systems had been built to serve densely populated industrial areas or rich farming country in proximity to each other; in Canada and Australia the railways opened new land and attracted settlers, who were expected to provide the lines with traffic. In Africa, these economic attractions were uncommon. Railway builders had to cope with fevers, with difficult terrain, with tropical rainfall, sometimes with inaccessible mountain country or jungle, and even with man-eating lions. Building and operating costs were great, distances were vast, and indigenous populations were relatively small. Land concessions were not much of an inducement unless the land could be sold to immigrants with savings. Mineral concessions did not by themselves guarantee the railway companies sufficient revenue to warrant the required capital expenditure.

The East African railway project (1895–1902), for instance, was regarded as an uneconomic venture right from the start; the government was expected to face an annual deficit for many years. The line was not built to make money, but was undertaken merely to placate a variety of military, missionary, and imperial lobbies. One of Sir William Mackinnon's most cherished dreams had been the completion of a line into the interior; a railway, he believed, would secure Britain's military position in the Sudan should the Suez Canal ever be closed in wartime. A new line would safeguard the British position against the Germans and would assist the work of missionaries in Uganda; it would serve as an important weapon in the battle against the slave trade and promote African cash farming. The notion of making the line pay by encouraging white settlement in Kenya came as an afterthought. The radical MP Henry Labouchere mistakenly lampooned the project in a poem penned in 1896:[7]

> What it will cost, no words can express;
> What is its object, no brain can suppose;
> Where it will start from, no one can guess;
> Where it is going to, nobody knows.

> What is the use of it, none can conjecture;
> What it will carry, there's none can define;
> And in spite of George Curzon's superior lecture,
> It clearly is naught but a lunatic line.

In the Gold Coast, on the other hand, the construction of railways owed a great deal to mining interests. The government built a railway from Sekondi to Tarkwa in order to benefit gold producers; the line had the added military advantage of improving communications with the recently subdued Ashanti region, and a similar combination of economic and strategic interests led to its extension to Kumasi in 1903. The line in Nigeria from Port Harcourt to Enugu facilitated exploitation of Nigerian coal deposits; it later was extended to the tin mines on the Jos plateau.

Construction of these railways was a major technical achievement. All building material had to be imported from abroad, even the crossties. The problems of tropical forests, bad weather, sickness, and mosquitos, combined with all manner of supply difficulties and harsh living conditions, necessitated short tours of service and constant staff changes. There were also severe financial problems. Funds for railwaybuilding were supplied originally by Chamberlain with cheap loans from the imperial government, advanced at a rate of 2.75 percent. As time went on more money was needed; local government had to resort to the London money market to secure loans on ordinary commercial terms. Nevertheless, the various obstacles were overcome, and the railways were completed, albeit at considerable cost.*

---

*The initial cost in Sierra Leone was only £4,316 per mile, compared with £7,064 in Lagos and £10,314 in the Gold Coast. The differences in cost reflected both topographi-

In itself, railway-building supplied a boost to the local cash economy, with laborers remunerated in coin and construction works opening new markets for local produce. It also gave impetus to the building of feeder roads, which in turn encouraged the use of bicycles and trucks.

In East and Central Africa the construction of railways was fully as difficult as in West Africa. The line extending from Beira in Mozambique to Umtali in Rhodesia was known to white foremen, crew chiefs, and technicians as the "man-a-mile" line, for a life was lost for every mile on the way. The 584-mile East African railway, completed in 1902, required even more heroic effort; it was built at a cost of over 25,000 Indian casualties. The terrain was largely unknown. Inland communities remained unsubdued, and raiding was widespread. Disease was an ever-present problem, as were the depredations of wild animals. Above all, workmen, victuals, and supplies all had to be brought in from abroad and transported over great distances.

The men chosen to deal with such difficulties were pioneers of a peculiar stamp. From the ethnic and cultural standpoint, the most diverse group was found in the Sudan, where the structure of railway management reflected the shifting power relationships within the territory as a whole. The first Sudan railway, built in 1875, was an Anglo-Egyptian enterprise under Egyptian administration and technical management. The line was the property of the Egyptian government; Egypt supplied loans for its development and an army battalion for its construction; the first three directors were Egyptians, and so were the clerks and accountants, affectionately remembered by the historian of the railway as ample, majestic men, bespectacled, dignified, omniscient.[8] The senior technical experts were British; the artisans were Egyptian, Maltese, and Greek; the laborers were Nubian.

Subsequently, during the period of the Mahdist wars, the railway came to be dominated by the Royal Engineers of the British Army, assisted by naval officers who ran the river transport service. It was not until 1900, after the track had been extended to Khartoum, that British civilians began to take the place of soldiers in the higher grades of the administration; but not until 1925 was the first British civilian general manager appointed. The artisans continued to be both ethnically distinct from the governing British strata and heterogeneous in national composition, with Egyptians, Syrians, and Greeks doing most of the

---

cal difficulties and markedly different rates of pay for unskilled workmen. The daily rate for unskilled labor in Sierra Leone was only 10d., against 1s. in Lagos and 1s. 3d. in the Gold Coast.

skilled work. The Sudanese slowly made their way into the technical hierarchy as traffic inspectors, clerks, and locomotive foremen in a manner that would have been unthinkable in the early Rhodesian railway system, where civilian management was run by local whites.

In Rhodesia all unskilled work was done by Africans, but there were at first no skilled African workers. All skilled and managerial work was done by immigrants, mostly of British origin. George Pauling, the greatest of Rhodesian railway builders, was the very archetype of the pioneers of this "heroic" era. His father originally had served as an engineer on the Indian railways and had intended his son to join the Indian civil service. But the senior Pauling's health broke down, and his son's scholastic career came to a premature end; at fourteen he was lucky to get a job in a drafting office in England. He later made a brilliant career for himself in Africa, where he became responsible, among other things, for building most of the railroads in Southern Rhodesia. For a time he also served on the Rhodesian Executive Council as commissioner of public works and mines, and looked after postal communications. He was a man of tremendous physical strength—he once carried a pony around a billiard table for a bet—and proved to be the right sort for the tough frontier community of early Rhodesia.

The man chosen to build the railway in East Africa was George (later Sir George) Whitehouse, the first chief engineer and general manager of the railway. His experience was impressive. The son of an English clergyman, he decided against his father's career and went to King's College, London, to study civil engineering. Subsequently he became part of what might be called the Victorian railway-builders' International. He worked on the construction of lines in Natal, Mexico, Peru, and India, and after pioneering the East Africa railway, he ended his career as chief engineer of the Central Argentine railway (1904–9).

In Africa Whitehouse drew heavily on his Indian experience and connections. After lengthy negotiations with the government of India, he secured the services of two Indian officers of the Public Works Department, who in turn recruited some 2,000 coolies and a number of masons, carpenters, smiths, clerks, surveyors, and draftsmen. Once the project got well under way, 15,000 of the 16,000 workers were Indians. Their labor did not come cheap. The cost per man ran to 30 rupees (£2) a day, including the expense of import and repatriation, wages, rations, and medical expenses.* The most urgent immediate

---

*The Indian connection with British East Africa was close in every way, not just in the matter of railroad-building. The East Africa Protectorate kept an agent in Bombay to buy government supplies. Troops were sent from India to put down rebellions in

task was to construct huts for the men, depots for stores, and port facilities for the steamers that would bring railway equipment from overseas. Local timber supplies could not be relied on, hence crossties had to be imported from abroad. In the face of a shortage of potable water, Whitehouse improvised his own distilling machinery. Work could not proceed without an adequate survey, but the coastal strip was thrown into a state of turmoil by a widespread Swahili revolt, and the government could not always supply troops to protect surveying parties. And as the workmen hacked their way through the bush they were sometimes attacked by lions; the danger proved so great at one point that work stopped for three whole weeks until the most dangerous beasts had been shot.

In purely engineering terms, the project was fraught with extraordinary difficulties. The line was essentially a mountain railway constructed with a 3.28 gauge, its gradients 1 in 50 and 1 in 60. From Mombasa it crossed to the mainland over a half-mile-long bridge. It then ascended a plateau until it reached the edge of the Great Rift Valley—a height of 6,200 feet above sea level—went down across scarps and ravines bridged by viaducts to the valley floor, then climbed the Mau escarpment to a height of 8,321 feet. In the last 100 miles to Kisumu the level again sank to 3,728 feet, the altitude of Lake Victoria.*

But bad as the engineering problems were, still worse were those posed by disease. Whitehouse's work force soon resembled a gigantic hospital on the move. Every European employed on his staff was laid low at one time or another by fever. The Indian workmen seemed to have somewhat greater powers of resistance; even so, between 1896 and 1897 more than half of the Indian laborers sickened from malaria, tropical ulcers, and jiggers.[9] The beasts of burden were even more susceptible to the local conditions than the men. Camels and horses used to supply the earthwork gangs perished quickly; oxen could not

---

1895, 1897, and 1898. The protectorate's law came from Indian regulations, its courts used the Indian penal code, and its first legal adviser was an Indian lawyer. The clerical staff of government was largely Asian, and most medical and technical specialists were recruited from India. The Indian mint even coined the local currency. See Robert G. Gregory, *India and East Africa: A History of Race Relations Within the British Empire, 1890–1939* (Oxford, Eng., 1971).

*Mervyn F. Hill, *Permanent Way: The Story of the Kenya and Uganda Railway* (Nairobi, 1950). The total cost of the project was £5,331,000 or about £9,500 per mile. Between 1911 and 1912 additional branch lines were built. By 1926, 25 years after the first locomotive had reached Lake Victoria, the rail and harbor revenue of Kenya stood at £2,058,000 and expenditures at £1,216,000.

be used because of the tsetse fly. Donkeys were the only animals that proved satisfactory, but they were in short supply.

The railway-building enterprise in East Africa created a new hierarchical society, with the general manager at the top and ranging downward from chief engineers, superintendents, and accountants to warehousemen, engine drivers, foremen, and crew chiefs. It was a society based on wage contracts. This was one of the few colonial institutions that initially included a substantial number of white foremen and artisans who were familiar with trade-union organization and who were not subject to the military discipline that constrained white sergeants in the colonial armies; as a result, railway enterprises were to see some of the first modern wage struggles in Africa.

In response to criticisms voiced in the British Parliament about rising costs, the East African railway authorities in 1900 decided to effect economies by reducing the privileges and allowances of lower-level white staff members. The immediate reaction was a strike of white employees in Mombasa. Then, as reported by the official history of the company, "a few agitators got out of hand and persuaded some Indian coolies to follow their example. Some damage was done to railway property; rails were pulled up and work came to a standstill."[10] The strikers, however, lacked proper organization. There were no unions to provide strike pay. There were no alternate jobs for men thrown out of work. There were no supplies except those that the company provided. Workers in one center downed tools while their colleagues elsewhere continued to work, leaving each pocket of rebellion isolated. Whitehouse thus was able to take resolute action. He dismissed the militants and settled the grievances of the more conciliatory men. When unrest was settled at the coast, the up-country centers returned to work, and the strike was over.*

Pioneers like Whitehouse represented a system in which a colonial government, anxious to build a railway, let the job out to private con-

---

* Modern trade-union organization did not apparently come into being on any British African railways until World War I, when wartime shortages strengthened the bargaining position of the European workers who manned the engines and served as skilled artisans on the Rhodesian lines. In 1916 the Bulawayo firemen went on strike. Their demands were met, and engineers and other firemen then joined them in forming the Rhodesia Railway Workers' Union. The union rapidly spread to all important centers, including the Northern Rhodesian depots, so that white railwaymen became a pressure group of some importance in the territory. In East Africa the bulk of skilled jobs soon passed into the hands of Indian workmen; and in the Gold Coast and Nigeria Africans rose to be engine drivers, stationmasters, and even captains of great river steamers. For both groups, the opening of these jobs represented a chance for rapid promotion, so that black and brown unionism lagged far behind its European equivalent.

struction firms in London, which then worked through a manager on the site. The system was well adjusted to backward territories whose public works departments were too small to undertake extensive projects, but it met with a good deal of opposition. The original estimates, framed at a time when local conditions were little known, were almost invariably exceeded; there was no check on the materials or on the quality of the work done. The system was said to be costly, even though the work was admittedly done in a solid fashion. Governments, moreover, feared free competition for African labor. Critics claimed that African workmen would fare better under the government's political staff than under a private contractor, who "necessarily enters as a competitor against other employers, including the State itself." State employment therefore was assumed to have "a potent educative effect among primitive people." The same assumption was used in defense of government ownership of the Nigerian coal mines, where the advent of competing employers "would inevitably create difficulties in connection with the labour supply."[11]

In Northern Nigeria the so-called system of departmental construction originated in the first decade of the twentieth century under Girouard, who was himself an engineer with a firm and well-founded belief in his own technical abilities. Under the new system the government itself became a railway builder; it selected its own consulting engineers, appointed its own construction staff, completed its own surveys, made its own agreements with subcontractors, recruited labor, and adopted whatever construction standards it saw fit.

At the same time, government railways settled down to a uniform, hierarchical system, run by a general manager with the assistance of railway officials recruited from Great Britain and, to a lesser extent, from the "white dominions." Though these railway officials did not enjoy the same social prestige as the district administrators, they were generally remunerated on a somewhat higher level. The general manager of the East African railway, for instance, drew a salary substantially superior to that of the chief secretary and second only to the governor's; the chief engineer earned more than a DC; and the workshop superintendent earned more than an assistant DC. (See Table 23.)

Policy decisions were made by the general manager, a person of considerable consequence; in East Africa he was an ex officio member of the Legislative Council. He was answerable directly to the governor, who reported on railway matters to the Colonial Office, which in turn dealt with railway affairs through the assistant secretaries for East and West Africa, respectively. The effect was that the various colonies

TABLE 23
Comparative Annual Salaries of Members of the Railway and Political Staffs of British East Africa and Nigeria, 1914
(In £)

Political staff	Salary	Railway staff	Salary
	EAST AFRICA PROTECTORATE		
Chief secretary	1,100	General manager	1,650–1,950
District commissioner	440–540	Chief engineer	700–970
Assistant DC	250–400	Workshop foreman	350–550
	NIGERIA		
Secretary, central gov't	800–1,000	General manager	1,350–1,500
Resident, 2d class	720–820	Chief engineer	960–1,160
Assistant DC	300–400	Workshop foreman	300–350

SOURCE: *Colonial Office List, 1915.*

operated in isolation from one another, and there was no unified railway service for the colonies as a whole. The system had other disadvantages. A committee of inquiry explained in 1924 that general managers had insufficient powers; their staff consisted of civil servants subject to colonial regulations, so the general manager could not easily get rid of an incompetent man. The railway budget, moreover, was drawn up as part of the territorial budget as a whole; and railway profits could be skimmed off to support other services.

The general manager was assisted by a deputy, who helped in overseeing the various technical departments. In Nigeria the central staff numbered some 35 accountants, office assistants, and supply clerks. There was a Ways and Works Department under the chief engineer, with an equal number of engineers, foremen, and draftsmen. Transport operations were handled by the Traffic Department, headed by a superintendent concerned with rates, timetables, and the operation of the various stations, which were supervised by nine district stationmasters, each with his own subordinate staff. The Traffic Department in Nigeria also administered the colliery, the first mining enterprise operated by the state.* A locomotive superintendent looked after the technical side of operations and was responsible for about 30 superintendents, foremen, and draftsmen.

The Nigerian railway had nearly as many senior and medium-grade

* Nigeria was the only African territory outside South Africa and Southern Rhodesia where coal was worked before World War I. The fields, discovered in 1909 at Enugu, could only be developed after a line had been built from Port Harcourt.

officials as the entire district administration, and played a major part in the country's rapidly expanding economy. The railway became an important employer of African labor. By 1917, in addition to 124 European officers, there were 809 African artisans, crew chiefs, interpreters, and junior administrators, and 17,687 laborers on the payroll.

The state-run railways operated with a reasonable degree of efficiency. In giving evidence before the aforementioned inquiry commission, the merchants themselves could not agree whether they preferred private or state enterprise; some of the West African entrepreneurs wanted private enterprise, but the Manchester, Liverpool, and London chambers of commerce all opposed the transfer of management from the state to private firms.

State management of the railways—and in Nigeria, of the coal-mining industry—represented a major departure from the principle of private enterprise. This was pragmatic in inspiration; it did not derive from an *étatiste* philosophy, but still was fraught with far-reaching consequences for the future. The physical feat of building some 6,000

TABLE 24

Growth of Railway Traffic in British East Africa, the Gold Coast, and Nigeria,
1903/4–1912

(Revenue/expenditures in £)

	1903	1912
East Africa		
Number of passengers transported	68,662	500,304
Freight (tons)	16,371	172,694
Revenue	131,567	489,231
Expenditure	190,468	280,185
Surplus (deficit)	(58,901)	209,046
Gold Coast	*1908*	*1912*
Number of passengers transported	109,641	361,905
Freight (tons)	46,190	83,202
Revenue	148,097	253,202
Expenditure	91,465	84,800
Surplus	56,632	168,402
Nigeria (Lagos-Ilorin-Jebba-Minna)	*1909*	*1912*
Number of passengers transported	—	125,443
Freight (tons)	—	202,883
Revenue	203,558	394,919
Expenditure	131,820	236,280
Surplus	71,738	158,639

SOURCE: F. Baltzer, *Die Kolonialbahnen mit besonderer Berücksichtigung Afrikas* (Berlin, 1916), pp. 155, 162, 172.
   NOTE: The monetary amounts for East Africa have been converted from the rupee amounts provided in the source (at 15 rupees to the £) and rounded.

TABLE 25

Comparative Transport Costs on the Gold Coast, c. 1914

(In shillings per ton)

Means of transport	Cost per mile	Means of transport	Cost per mile
Cask rolling, palm oil	14s. 5d.	Headload	30s. 6d.
Cask rolling, cocoa	23s.	Truck	20s.
Handcart	22s.	Railway	11s.

SOURCE: R. Szereszewski, *Structural Changes in the Economy of Ghana, 1891–1911* (London, 1965), pp. 54–55.

miles of track through mountains, bush, and rain forest was also a major technical achievement.

Railways had a major economic impact. The 584 miles of the Uganda railway vastly increased the amount of goods carried, and diminished both the costs and the time taken for shipping merchandise to its destination. Before its completion, it took 35 porters, each balancing 56 pounds on his head, approximately three months to transport about one ton of material from the coast to Lake Victoria. Estimates vary on the precise savings gained. According to one estimate, a 56-pound load cost £3 10s. to carry along this distance. When the railway had been completed, the price of transporting a pound of merchandise fell from 7s. 6d. ($1.80) to 2.5d. ($0.05). By another estimate, the cost of bringing a ton of goods to Uganda from the coast before 1900 amounted to £250. By the 1920's the expense had dropped to £6. Road-building was stimulated by railway construction, and by 1913 Uganda had 360 miles of all-weather roads, and 800 miles able to carry light cars, carts, and wagons at all times save the rainy season. By then it also had 370 miles of waterways that were regularly served by steamers. It was the railway that made possible the production and sale of cotton by peasant producers in Uganda.

The economic impact of railways was also significant in other parts of Africa. The extension of rail and road communications in the Gold Coast by 1911, with the completion of the Sekondi-Kumasi line, opened the main gold fields to exploitation; provisions as well as mining machinery could be sent up-country. The utilization of other natural resources such as timber was facilitated. Improved roads allowed for a primitive method of transport, but one serviceable in remote areas—workmen rolled cocoa or palm oil in round casks on their surface. Truck drivers and trucks later took the place of cask rollers with great benefit to the cultivators. Improved transport services began to

TABLE 26
Selected Skills of African Adults in 29 Towns of the Gold Coast, 1911

Professional and clerical		Commercial and industrial	
Clerks	2,349	Blacksmiths	298
Doctors	3	Bricklayers, masons	557
Engineers	2	Carpenters	1,445
Lawyers	27	Coopers	183
Photographers	31	Electricians	1
Printers	16	Engine drivers	15
Surveyors	6	Fitters	40
Teachers	130+	Mechanics	40
Telegraphists	12	Painters	37
TOTAL	2,576	Sawyers	87
		Shopkeepers	161
		TOTAL	2,864

SOURCE: R. Sereszewski, *Structural Changes in the Economy of Ghana, 1891–1911* (London, 1965), p. 59.

vanquish distance and to make resources more useful and usable. Exports from the Gold Coast expanded enormously, with gold and cocoa having the greatest share (76 percent) of value in 1911 (compared with 12 percent in 1901).

More investments, more Europeans, and more laborers came into the Gold Coast as the railway took hold. The mines employed 19,000 men in 1911; government construction employed several thousand workers, and the expanding cocoa industry used about 37,000,000 man-days of labor in that year, or an estimated 185,000 people. More new skilled jobs developed. In Sekondi by 1904 there were six sawmills and six brick and tile factories. Thanks to the boom induced after 1901 by railway-building and mining, entrepreneurs began to develop timber-processing, construction, light consumer goods industries, and repair and maintenance industries. Auxiliary services such as hotels, lighting, and newer transport appeared. Increasing numbers of Africans entered the skilled trades and the professions. (See Table 26.) More money flowed into the colony. By 1911 the capital investment in construction, railways, machinery, and cocoa alone amounted to £13,800,000; new commercial and industrial companies grew up, and gross capital formation in the Gold Coast reached £3,420,000. The basic infrastructure and the range of economic activities were established by that year. There was little further structural change in the economy until the 1960's.[12]

Transport grew very much cheaper than it had been. According to the calculations of Kurt Hassert, a German economic geographer, a single railway carriage could carry as much as 10 oxwagons or 300 carriers. Long-distance trade ceased to be confined to the traditional traffic in goods of small bulk and high intrinsic value—gold, ivory, and kola nuts. Timber, minerals, and coal acquired a new economic value when they could be taken over long distances at reasonable cost. Without railways, the mineral wealth of the Gold Coast, of the Northern Rhodesian copper belt, or of the Enugu coal fields in Nigeria would have remained inaccessible assets. The Nigerian export trade in tin, coal, cotton, and groundnuts actually was created by the railways; and the export of palm oil and palm kernels, cocoa, and hides was enormously expanded.

In social terms the railway impact was equally revolutionary. The train station—usually built in brick, covered with a corrugated iron roof and surrounded by a great veranda—became a major center of local life, a point of departure and a point of return for labor migrants, merchants, and private travelers. Trains were often uncomfortable and overcrowded, and journeys were slow and infrequent, but people, goods, and ideas began to circulate in a manner inconceivable to men used to the pace of porters. The villagers' ability to travel in comparative comfort and safety vastly increased. Isolation began to break down and accelerated change transformed village life. The growth in passenger traffic shows this. (See Table 24.)

A nineteenth-century German nobleman, discussing the effect of railway-building in his native land, had lamented that the steam engine had turned into the hearse that carried the old order to its grave. Marx, on the other hand, had rejoiced that the railway immensely facilitated means of communication, and drew all, "even the most barbarian nations," into civilization.[13] Both observers turned out to be equally right.

NINE

The Specialist

Early Victorian England was one of the least-administered countries in Europe. Except for defense, diplomatic relations, postal services, and the collection of revenue, there was little that a Frenchman or a Prussian would have recognized as administration. A large part of the national revenue was absorbed by the National Debt; an even higher proportion—£26,000,000 of £41,000,000 in 1860—went to maintain the Royal Navy and the army. A great variety of services—educational, charitable, and such—was furnished by private or semiprivate associations, churches, philanthropic undertakings, or local government. The great British technical departments of state are mostly of modern vintage. The Local Government Board, for instance, an ancestor of the present Ministry of Health, was only set up in 1870.

The British carried this tradition to Africa. The colonial administrative apparatus was slender. In 1914 the enormous regions under the aegis of the Colonial Office—the East Africa Protectorate, Uganda, Nyasaland, Gambia, Sierra Leone, the Gold Coast, and Nigeria, an area embracing more than 900,000 square miles—were managed by fewer than 600 British administrators, and were run on a shoestring, primarily from income generated within the colonies themselves, supplemented by occasional loans and subsidies from London. The provision of social services at first was largely left to the private enterprise of the missionaries. Evangelical societies, financed by the subscriptions of private benefactors, laid the foundations of most modern social services—educational and medical—in colonial Africa.

The rulers believed that their first responsibility was to maintain "law and order," put an end to internecine warfare, and raise revenues. Secondarily, they were determined to develop communications, improve health services, promote the production of raw materials, and expand the cash economy. In order to attain even these limited ends, they could not rely solely on the endeavors of missionaries and merchants. Willy-nilly, the British were forced to employ a slowly growing specialist staff. At the outbreak of World War I the number of government servants with advanced technical training—educators, physicians, entomologists, engineers, veterinarians, and such—was still small, under 900. Even so, the colonial state had become more than a mere constabulary organization, and the specialists now substantially outnumbered the district administrators (See Table 27.)

The colonial rulers faced formidable problems in trying to develop Africa. Men and animals were sickly and suffered from scores of debilitating and killing diseases. Little was known before 1900 about the parasites and insects that attacked men, plants, animals, and soils. Resources in manpower and money were lacking to do much scientific research. But there were some important beginnings; departments and institutes were started, and research teams were organized to study ways to make Africa a more productive and healthier place.

The development of India also had at first been left to private foreign capital. But development by the state, or by Indians assisted by the state, became the prevailing mode of operation near the end of the nineteenth century. Economic development in West Africa, as envisaged by Chamberlain, and the Crown agents, was influenced by the Indian experience. Hence the British in Africa pioneered state capitalism long before the metropolitan state began to operate industrial enterprises. An outstanding example is Nigeria, where as we have seen, the state owned and ran railways, collieries, and harbors; it also had its own limekilns and tile works.[1] To develop the colonies, colonial administrations had to teach Africans what to do and how to do it, to provide an infrastructure of roads, railways, and schools, and to establish research laboratories and experimental stations to determine what could be done. Before 1914 the principal technical services provided in the colonies were health care, agriculture, education, and communications. These formed the essential infrastructure for development.

The Work of the Metropole

The Colonial Office gave little support to scientific work in the empire before 1895. A number of medical men collected information; a few metropolitan institutions tried to advise the colonies. The Colonial

TABLE 27

Senior Technical and Administrative Staff in the British African Colonies Under Colonial Office Governance, 1914

Branch	East Africa Protectorate	Gambia	Gold Coast	Nigeria	Nyasaland	Sierra Leone	Uganda	Total
Education (director, inspectors, senior schoolteachers)	8	—	18	41	—	11	—	78
Railways (engineers, telegraph engineers, etc.)	13	1	14	23	—	15	10	76
Surveyors (director, surveyors)	33	1	13	31	3	2	14	97
Agriculture (advisers, specialists—i.e., entomologists, biologists)	6	—	6	18	5	3	9	47
Veterinary (surgeons, pathologists, etc.)	12	—	1	2	3	1	3	22
Forestry (curators, assistants, specialists)	5	—	5	34	2	4	2	52
Medical (physicians, technicians, sanitary inspectors)	32[a]	6	67	116	12	25	—[a]	258
Marine (steamer captains, officers), transport department	17	2	3	35	4	2	2	65
Public works (district/sanitary/road engineers, architects, inspectors)	17	—	55	70	4	10	10	166
Total number of technical officers	143	10	182	370	33	73	50	861
Total number of district administrators (provincial commissioners, district commissioners, assistant DCs, etc.)	117	4	44	252	40	29	52	538
Combined total	360	14	226	622	73	102	102	1,399

SOURCE: *Colonial Office List*, 1915.

NOTE: These figures are for the official establishment only. They do not include the specialists employed by mission societies or by the larger private companies engaged in mining, railway transport, and similar activities.

[a] Combined figure for the East Africa Protectorate and Uganda.

Office occasionally issued a circular on a subject such as animal husbandry; but any real initiative rested with the local officials. Governor
Alfred Moloney of the Gold Coast tried to introduce new crops; other
colonial administrators also tried to encourage agriculture by supplying
seeds and seedlings, grading produce, opening markets, and perhaps
even building some roads. But they had few means at their disposal,
and their efforts had limited effect.

Botanical gardens played one of the greatest roles in scientific pioneering. Few such gardens existed in the African colonies themselves
before 1900, but there were many famous ones in other parts of the
empire, notably in Singapore, Ceylon, Mauritius, Jamaica, and British
Guiana. The Trinidad Botanical Garden, in particular, helped various
African territories by supplying new crops and seedlings and by fur-
nishing trained agriculturists. The most important institution, however, not only for the African colonies, but for all the British possessions, was the Royal Botanical Gardens at Kew, which trained colonial
staff members and supplied the colonies with advice and plants. The
directors of Kew from 1846 to 1900 were Sir William Hooker and his
son, Sir Joseph; it was through their work, and periodic reports and
bulletins, that Kew became the empire's botanical center—classifying
plants, studying crops, and supplying information to colonists. From
Kew came cloves, nutmeg, cinnamon, palm oil, castor oil plants, coffee, the quinine-yielding tree cinchona, and Para rubber. In 1900 the
director of Kew Gardens received the official title of botanical adviser
to the Colonial Office.

Another institution that played an important role in the early colonial period was the Imperial Institute in Kensington. Founded in 1887
as a memorial of Queen Victoria's Golden Jubilee, it was jointly financed by the national and colonial governments. Professor W. R.
Dunstan was the director of the institute for many years. Though research was not intended to be its primary focus, the institute soon after
its founding began to carry out major investigations regarding the
qualities and possibilities of colonial products. Cotton and tobacco
were given their start in many territories as a result of studies and
advice from Kensington. Dunstan encouraged colonial research, and
investigated many specific economic and scientific problems for the
colonial secretary. He was one of the first to push for an agricultural
training school for colonial officers and for the full-scale organization of
colonial research. Whenever minerals were found in the colonies, the
institute sent out officers to survey and examine the deposits. In this

way coal came to be worked in Nyasaland, tinstone and iron in Northern Nigeria, and lead and coal in Southern Nigeria.

The work of these older bodies was not sufficient, however, to satisfy the growing needs of empire. Under Chamberlain, scientific research came to be applied more systematically as part of a wider policy of development. As previously noted, Chamberlain followed a consistent scheme: British security and prosperity required assured access to essential raw materials. Great Britain therefore had an obligation to develop its colonies to the fullest. The development of new crops and resources would provide new wealth to the indigenous peoples, open new markets to British industrialists, supply more jobs to British workmen, and furnish colonial governments with additional revenue. Colonial development required a transportation and communications network. But it also required the improvement of medical services, the study of human, animal, and plant diseases, and the investigation of the problems of forestry, geology, and related subjects of both theoretical and practical significance.[2]

Chamberlain originally had not been much concerned with scientific questions, but under the influence of Daniel Morris (agriculture) and Sir Patrick Manson (medicine) his interests widened. Manson, the "father of tropical medicine," had been responsible for the vital discovery that infectious diseases could be transmitted to human beings by animals; in 1879 he had shown the role of mosquitos in filariasis. His influence became pervasive when he was appointed medical adviser to the Colonial Office in 1897: he standardized medical reports from the colonies and made sure that the more important documents were published; he helped to reorganize the West African Medical Service. Most important, he persuaded Chamberlain to establish a school of tropical medicine in London. It opened in 1899, the same year that saw the opening of the Liverpool School of Tropical Medicine. Starting with a three- to four-month course, the London school grew from six students to 292 within three years. Both schools, however, did more than teach; they conducted research and sent out medical expeditions. Under Manson's urging, Chamberlain encouraged the work of a committee studying malaria. This became the Tropical Disease Committee, charged with research on sleeping sickness as well as malaria, and supported by Colonial Office grants. Chamberlain also induced the colonies to contribute to a newly established Tropical Diseases Research Fund, and over £3,000 was provided annually.[3]

In addition, Chamberlain encouraged the application of science to agriculture. In 1902 the British Cotton Growing Association was founded as part of his effort to develop cotton cultivation within the empire, thereby making British textile firms less dependent on American suppliers at a time when prices were going up. Headed by Sir Alfred Jones, the West African shipping magnate, the association was a private concern, but it received steady Colonial Office support; it held its monthly conferences at the office itself, and took a special interest in Africa. The British West African colonies agreed to pay the salaries of cotton experts sent out by the association, and under a new agreement in 1904, Sierra Leone, Lagos, and Southern Nigeria paid £6,500 to the association to run three experimental plantations. The Gold Coast and Northern Nigeria joined the program in 1906–7. Its main work, however, was not experimental; the association sought to increase cotton acreage by providing seed, lending money and tools to cultivators, and then buying the crop and providing ginning facilities. Results were good; cotton production in the colonies doubled between 1906 and 1913. After 1910 the British government made grants to establish ginning and buying centers, and to provide free seed.

In Uganda cotton became an important peasant crop. Exports rose from 96,000 pounds in 1903 to 12,000,000 pounds in 1911, making Uganda the leading British cotton-growing colony. The colonial administration, in cooperation with the association, had directed this production. Free seeds were provided, and botanical gardens tested the best varieties until the Department of Agriculture took over this task. Through experimental stations and careful seed selection, quality and quantity improved. Coffee became another good crop for Uganda, thanks largely to the work of C. C. Gowdey of the Imperial Bureau of Entomology.

Such efforts had far-reaching effects. More colonial jobs became available for British physicians, veterinarians, foresters, and botanists. Professional support for the imperial cause widened, and the occupational structure of the colonial establishment was significantly modified. The British Empire was the world's largest, and employed more technical officers than any other. Chamberlain's policies were continued by the Liberals when they attained power in 1905. Sir Lewis Harcourt, who took over the Colonial Office in 1910, did perhaps more than any of his successors to develop the empire through scientific research and grants, but all were interested in medical investigations. Other groups involved in tropical medicine were the Army Medical School at Netley, the University of London, the Quick Laboratory at Cambridge, the Wellcome Bureau of Scientific Research in London, the Lister Institute, and the Society of Tropical Medicine and Hygiene of London. The Imperial Bureau of Entomology (1913) grew out of various committees organized to study blood-sucking insects.* Experts such as James T. Simpson were sent out to the colonies to survey insects, and reports were issued in the *Bulletin of Entomological Research* (1911).

After 1910 the Imperial Institute produced a series of handbooks on the principal commercial resources of the tropics. They furnished descriptions of the occurrence, cultivation, and uses of such products as cotton and other fibers, cocoa, rubber, oil seeds, and tobacco. The handbooks were meant to be of use to the tropical agriculturists and colonial officials, as well as to merchants and manufacturers at home. The institute also offered a short course in tropical cultivation and products that was mandatory for all colonial officers posted to the area. It was based on a commercial geography of the West African colonies, written by Gerald C. Dudgeon, a former inspector of agriculture in West Africa, that covered the rainfall, soil, and main crops of each colony.[4]

The Physicians

The most pressing problem that faced the white pioneers throughout colonial Africa was to preserve their own lives. Malaria was endemic in most parts of the continent and struck down many strangers who had not acquired at least a partial degree of immunity. Blackwater fever, a consequence of repeated and improperly treated malarial infections, was an even more deadly killer.[5] Unless properly cared for by a nurse or a physician, the disease was almost invariably fatal. Its victims were plagued by a high fever, shivering, severe headache, depression, nausea, and back and kidney pains. Their skin and eyes became jaundiced, and their urine turned dark red; in some cases the skin even turned black. Attacks could last for two weeks or so. The end was grim and sad.† Another terrible disease was yellow fever, also spread by mosquitos. Beyond this, there were waterborne plagues, infections carried by lice, flies, and fleas, and a host of other afflictions, including all the common killers such as tuberculosis, pneumonia, smallpox, and syphilis. Before the second half of the nineteenth cen-

---

*Though the bureau's work helped agriculture in the control of plant insects, the government did not establish a bureau specifically devoted to agriculture until the 1920's. The Development Commission, a body established in 1909 to promote research on agriculture in Great Britain, did, however, fund some projects that benefited the colonies.

†The risk of blackwater fever is reduced if a person takes good care of himself. It is significant that the disease was largely restricted to bachelors, who did not have the domestic advantages of the married men.

tury, European physicians were almost as helpless in coping with sicknesses as African medicine men. Pioneers like Livingstone learned how to observe certain elementary precautions; he developed the prophylactic use of quinine, and was one of the first to make extensive use of the clinical thermometer, to employ arsenic against sleeping sickness in animals, and to link relapsing fever with ticks. In an age when medical men knew little about the impact of nutritional deficiencies on health, Livingstone also noticed the connection between an ill-balanced manioc diet and night-blindness.[6]

Nevertheless, tropical medicine was slow to develop into a separate discipline. And health conditions in tropical areas for long remained grim. In 1898, for instance, the Lagos *Standard* commented:

There is no doubt that something should be done to relieve [the grave-diggers] from the strain of work to which they are continuously subjected. The demand of a constantly increasing death-rate, which has caused the cemeteries to be enlarged, makes it necessary that the number of grave-diggers should be increased. No holidays. At it from 6 am to 6 pm, every day, Sundays included, for the Grim Reaper is ever busy.[7]

The *Standard* was not exaggerating. In the 1890's, 46 of the 150 Europeans in Lagos died in a 15-month period; in Accra 46 of 200 whites died in six months. (Compare this to 1919, when only one European died of malaria in the whole of British West Africa.)[8] There was, moreover, a considerable time lag between medical discoveries and their practical application. As late as 1907, when the cause of malaria was known to all, many European communities in Africa still suffered heavily. At Kalomo, then the headquarters of Northwestern Rhodesia, the death rate for white men in 1906 was 12.8 percent, against 6 percent per annum in Northeastern Rhodesia.

The position of the Africans was no better, though they were more likely to die from diseases other than malaria, to which most had developed some resistance. In any case, there was little statistical information to guide investigators. In the words of an official report: "In regard to natives [of West Africa], trustworthy statistics do not exist. In Freetown and Lagos there is registration of deaths, but the causes are only in a small percentage certified by medical men. In Freetown the deaths are no index as to which parts of the town are most unhealthy. . . . In Lagos only the street is given. There are no numbers of blocks or of houses."[9]

The medical revolution in British tropical Africa dates only from the turn of the century. The first real successes were attained in the field of preventive medicine, where vast progress was being made in Europe. The "new imperialism," in fact, coincided with the development of new urban and industrial health techniques in the West. Until the early 1870's, for instance, the Birmingham City Council had still opined firmly that sanitary inspectors were unconstitutional, un-British, and apt to violate the sanctity of a British home. But later, under Chamberlain, it was Birmingham that helped to pioneer municipal improvements. Municipal and industrial notions of health and efficiency were soon applied in the outposts of empire. Lagos, Accra, Freetown, Mombasa, Entebbe, and Nairobi all had public health departments to enforce ordinances on sanitation, water purity, yellow fever, and plague control.

Humanitarian concern had allied with business interests to establish the Liverpool School of Tropical Medicine. Prominent citizens of Liverpool and Manchester had pushed for better communications and health measures in West Africa. They supported the Liverpool University Institute of Commercial Research in the Tropics and the British Cotton Growing Association. They sent delegations to the Colonial Office, where their influence paralleled the impact of reform-minded governors anxious to build ports and railways and to deal with problems of public health. Sir William MacGregor, for example, was a model administrator and did much to improve the public health in his domain. His medical training had given him a striking grasp of public health problems, and he warmly supported educated Nigerians. He formed a Lagos Ladies League to work among the children; he established the Lagos Board of Health; he had hygiene courses taught in the schools with lectures by medical officers, many of whom were sent to London and Liverpool for work in parasitology and antimalarial measures. MacGregor gave the Department of Public Health enough money to reclaim the Lagos swamps and to dig a canal across the island to drain the land.[10]

MacGregor was also one of the staunchest backers of Ronald Ross's antimalarial campaign. Ross and his supporters placed considerable pressure on the Colonial Office, and Chamberlain took up their cause. The work done by Ross and others was consolidated and extended by the schools of tropical medicine in London and Liverpool, by the Tropical Diseases Research Fund, and later, by the Colonial Office's own Advisory Medical and Sanitary Committee for Tropical Africa, established in 1909. Had the high losses due to disease—comparable to those of an army in battle—continued, stable administration would have been out of the question.[11]

Attitudes toward health care for Africans changed dramatically after

1901–2, when an epidemic of sleeping sickness in Uganda took an estimated 200,000 lives. Two commissions were sent out to investigate; and later two doctors from the Royal Army Medical Corps were assigned to deal with the high incidence of syphilis in the same area. In Great Britain the Sleeping-Sickness Bureau was created in 1908; it became the Bureau of Hygiene and Tropical Diseases four years later, supported by funds (£7,500) from the colonial and home governments. Two monthly journals were published, the *Tropical Diseases Bulletin* and the *Bulletin of Hygiene*.

An outbreak of plague in the Gold Coast in 1908 brought Professor (later Sir) W. J. Simpson to survey sanitary and medical conditions in West Africa. He found that the only towns with a public water supply were Freetown and Calabar; the rest depended on shallow wells, waterholes, ponds, and rain barrels and tanks. These, of course, harbored anopheles mosquitos, and commonly caused dysentery and other intestinal diseases. Improvements were gradually made in water supplies; the Accra waterworks were opened on 7 January 1914, and conditions in Mombasa were ameliorated after Professor Simpson did a study of the town in 1913.[12]

Most of the physicians who worked in colonial Africa were of a high professional level. Many were military doctors, members of the Royal Army Medical Corps, formed in 1898 by the amalgamation of the army's Medical Staff Corps, responsible for military hospitals, and its Medical Department. The corps soon gained a deservedly high reputation, and gave employment to many a competent young physician unable to buy a practice on completing his medical training. The medical men listed in Michael Gelfand's standard medical history of Northern Rhodesia likewise had solid degrees including an Oxford graduate (J. E. Cole), a Cambridge graduate (F. G. Brown), and two graduates of London University (A. Martin, J. Spillane). Four had taken their degrees at Edinburgh (D. S. MacKnight, H. N. Pelly, J. D. Harmer, R. R. Murray). The high proportion of Scottish doctors, as of engineers, in the colonial services reflected the educational structure of a country where poor boys had a much easier time getting university places than in England, and where the learned professions acted as ladders of social promotion for "lads o' pairts." During the 1860's one Scot in every 1,000 went to a university, as against one Englishman in 5,800. The specialist qualifications obtained by the doctors mentioned in Gelfand's study were excellent; they included diplomas of public health and even fellowships of the Royal College of Surgeons, badges of academic distinction.

These British doctors had studied for their profession at a time when the future of medical science looked bright and no obstacle appeared too great to be overcome. Socially the world of British medicine ranked high in Victorian England. London's aristocracy, for instance, included a number of great consultant surgeons, men of enormous ability and often terrifying eccentricity, who treated patients and taught students for nothing at famous hospitals like St. Thomas's or St. Bartholomew's and who appeared to their inferiors like gods from Olympus stepping down into the ordinary world of medical wards. Men of that stamp sometimes received knighthoods; indeed, it is fair to say that, to some extent, they took over (and passed on to their students) both the prestige and the doctrine of noblesse oblige that used to characterize the landed nobility. They worked hard; they charged their wealthy clients great fees in fashionable consulting rooms in Harley Street, and then went to treat East End waifs for nothing.

Wealthy contributors kept "voluntary" teaching hospitals like St. Thomas's in funds. The British Medical Association possessed nothing like its present powers; nor did the state meddle much with medicine. In exchange for their genuinely honorary services, the great consultants received from their juniors respect and deference to an extraordinary degree. The best of British doctors—men like Godfrey Huggins, a pioneer surgeon in Southern Rhodesia—went to Africa imbued with a sense of professional optimism and of medical paternalism in which the "natives" took the place of the London poor. Huggins rose to fame and fortune, ending his career as Lord Malvern, the longest-lived prime minister in modern British history.

Medical paternalism, like missionary paternalism, could spill over into the political field. One of the most remarkable of "medical politicos" was Norman Leys, son of a Scottish barrister. Norman's father had converted to Catholicism, thereby endangering the souls of his sons in the eyes of their mother's rigidly Presbyterian family. Young Norman and his brother were spirited off to America, and Norman returned to Scotland only when he was old enough to study medicine in Glasgow. He took his degree; but lacking the means to buy himself a practice in Britain, he signed up for government service, first in Nyasaland (1904), later in the East Africa Protectorate. Leys initially was quite convinced that the evils of empire were necessary if Africans were to be lifted from their barbaric state. But he became increasingly dissatisfied with British rule, and the colonial officials' propensity to support the settlers rather than the Africans. Struck down by ill health, in 1918 Leys bought himself a small country practice in England. He turned to socialism to solve the problems of empire, and made a name for himself as scholar, politician, author, and champion of African rights. Leys had a true sense of tragedy—the tragedy of culture change. But, like Marx, he believed that change was inevitable, and that for all its beauty, the old Africa could not survive.

Much more typical of the ordinary district surgeon was P. A. Clearkin, whose career serves as a convenient case history of a young physician's experience in Africa.[13] Clearkin received his medical education in Belfast and worked briefly as a provincial doctor in the north of England; but he did not like general practice and applied to the Colonial Office for overseas duty. At the interview he was sure he had failed. The other candidates were all London doctors, smartly attired in morning coats, striped trousers, and appropriate accessories, while he wore a rough tweed suit and brogues, dress more suitable for the moors of Yorkshire and Durham than the pavements of Whitehall. He was interviewed by several elderly, bearded gentlemen, who made a few inquiries about his amusements, hobbies, games, and the like. He felt his answers were wrong, for he did not like team sports, and stated his preference for athletic pursuits of a more individualistic kind like boxing, rowing, sailing, shooting, and fishing. But he got the job. Later experience proved the wisdom of the committee's choice, for as we have seen, the hearty extrovert and team player was often out of place in the lonely outposts of empire. Indeed, the gregarious type was prone to become a psychiatric casualty or an alcoholic, whereas the individualist content with his own company was better able to survive.

Clearkin joined the Colonial Medical Service in 1913 and was sent to study at the London School of Tropical Medicine before assignment. The school was located on a site where an adequate number of patients suffering from tropical diseases would be available: it was attached to the Seamen's Hospital on the Royal Albert Dock, where vessels arrived from tropical areas. There were 12 colonial officers among the 70 students, each of whom had a study bedroom but never enough coal to heat it. There was a large dining room and lounge for residents. The courses were hard and intense, but these were dedicated students, for they knew that they would have no one to consult in the field, and they were determined to learn as much as possible; their salary was £400 a year to start, with annual increases of £25 up to a maximum of £600.

The lectures on tropical diseases were apt to be depressing, for the professor often concluded by saying, "and in this case, Gentlemen, the patient invariably dies." One of the slide demonstrations showed a train of porters bearing headloads and a European knee-deep in mud and water; it was described as "a medical officer on patrol in West Africa." Clearkin's companion gasped, "My God, I am not going to that sanguinary country." But he did, and died within a year.[14]

After passing the course, Clearkin was posted to Sierra Leone. As he was about to disembark at Freetown, Colonial Secretary Crewe's confidential circular of 11 January 1909 was handed to him. It warned him against sleeping with native women, and of the disgrace and official ruin that would certainly follow any such dereliction of duty.

The young physician found no animal-drawn or vehicular traffic in Freetown in 1914. Horses, mules, and oxen could not survive the tsetse fly. Kru men carried goods and pushed carts from the wharf to the town. People were carried in hammocks or pulled in carts, but bicycles were unknown in the rough and precipitous streets. There was a railway running east and west across the colony, and a tramline was to be built; however, no other means of transportation existed—no roads and no navigable rivers. Freetown did not have electricity, hence there were no fans or ice. In the heat and humidity mold grew on everything, even on shoes left out overnight. The town had no sewage system; buckets were used. But there was a good water supply. As a result, typhoid fever, dysentery, and yellow fever were gone, though malaria was still prevalent.

After a few months in Freetown Clearkin moved to an up-country hospital. His daily routine presented him with cases of malaria, dysentery, filariasis, intestinal worms, skin diseases, leprosy, hernias, sleeping sickness, venereal diseases, injuries, and burns. He had a creole pharmacist to assist him. While he examined each patient, the creole recorded the details.*

The most important work of the medical officer, Clearkin felt, was not curative medicine; his assistant was perfectly capable of seeing patients in hospital, performing minor operations, and handing out medicines. Rural sanitation was the medical officer's urgent task. Many DCs shared his view, sometimes almost to the point of obsession; one DC who made his people keep digging latrines won as his tribal nickname "shit-hole digger." Village sanitation was primitive. Houses and areas within villages were clean, but garbage disposal was crude—offal was cast out in the surrounding bush, where hyenas disposed of it. But the residue bred flies, which were ubiquitous in African villages.

---

*The medical officer was also expected to maintain a small meteorological station, keeping daily records of the maximum and minimum temperature, the relative humidity, and the rainfall.

Patches of bush outside villages were reserved as latrines, but excreta were left uncovered, and flies carried infection into the village. The ground teemed with hookworm larvae. Dysentery and other intestinal diseases were thus rife. Water supplies were often contaminated, so people became infected, for they washed themselves and their clothes frequently.

Clearkin devoted most of his time to traveling from village to village in his district advising chiefs, headmen, and villagers how to deal with the breeding grounds of flies and mosquitos, showing them how to dispose of garbage and how to construct simple pit latrines. Malaria control required more resources than villagers had, Clearkin realized; but intestinal parasites, infections, and dysentery could be eliminated, and the health and stamina of the people improved in order to better resist malaria and become more productive.

In some parts of Africa the British employed a few non-European physicians. Most were relegated to the lower ranks of the service, but there were exceptions. A Parsee physician named Boyce served as surgeon to the first Indian contingent in Nyasaland; he also took an important part in Johnston's early negotiations with Yao chiefs and died as the result of Yao treachery. But for a variety of reasons, the positions of real responsibility mostly remained in British hands. In the Sudan, for example, the British administration was at first of a military kind. Like other specialists, doctors were drawn from the British-controlled Egyptian Army, in which British officers held most of the senior positions; no British officer occupied a rank lower than *bimbashi*, or major. The great majority of junior medical officers, on the other hand, were Syrians and Lebanese trained in Beirut, generally in the Syrian Protestant College—later known as the American University of Beirut—and a few from the French Medical School. These "Syrians"— including many Lebanese—played an important part in pioneering medical work in the early Sudan, and considerably outnumbered their British colleagues. By about 1908 the authorized quota of Syrian medical officers was over 30, compared with six British physicians.[15]

The West African Medical Service likewise emerged from a military background. The service at first was small; in 1864 there were no more than 35 military doctors in all the scattered West African forces—but they included a small number of Africans, most of them Edinburgh graduates.[16] These physicians included men of considerable distinction. Obadiah A. Johnson was one, a Sierra Leonian, son of an ex-slave who had become a horticulturist at Kew Gardens in London. Johnson went to school in Freetown, Lagos, and Kutedi, and then worked as a teacher for the Church Missionary Society in Sierra Leone; later he took classics and theology at Fourah Bay College, where he was one of the first African students to earn a degree. He subsequently followed a medical course at Edinburgh, graduated as Master of Surgery, and at the age of thirty-seven joined the Sierra Leone service as an assistant colonial surgeon. On moving to Lagos, he discovered that Africans were barred from holding such posts; but after a scandal involving three British doctors, the authorities reversed their policy and accepted qualified blacks. Johnson resigned after a quarrel with the chief medical officer and went into private practice. *

Africans like Obadiah Johnson faced ever-increasing difficulties in the civil service after the turn of the century. The Victorian army had been willing to commission native doctors, such as Lieutenant-Colonel James Africanus Horton, whom we mentioned in Chapter Seven. The newfangled civilian organization, however, operated on avowed racial principles. In 1902, when Chamberlain amalgamated the medical departments of the various British West African colonies into the West African Medical Service as part of a wider movement toward administrative rationalization and centralization, African physicians were excluded from the service. In Sierra Leone, for instance, the chief medical officer, Dr. W. Renner, was replaced merely because he was of African parentage. The new policy was linked to military expansion and the shift in Nigeria's center of gravity from the mercantile south to the military north. According to a British report in 1909, European officers could not be expected to serve under the orders of Africans; hence African physicians, even if employed, should not participate in military expeditions. Other documents of the time sounded the same theme. The new policy, however, aroused considerable opposition— not merely on the part of the educated Africans, but also on the part of British colonial physicians and administrators, including Walter Egerton, governor of Lagos (1904–6), and Dr. W. Strachan, a West Indian and the colony's chief medical officer. The official line was not strictly upheld, but it was 1922 before government employment opportunities for black West African physicians improved.

No matter whether a government doctor was black or white, his life was an exacting one. His practice was extremely varied at a time when there was little specialization in the tropics. Primarily, he looked after government officials, policemen, soldiers, prisoners, and laborers in

---

*In 1912 Johnson, by then a prosperous man with an established reputation in medicine and historical scholarship, endowed a Chair of Science at Fourah Bay.

official employ.* The medical officer of a district often had to travel hundreds of miles across his area and at the same time supervise a clinic staffed by an African pharmacist and hospital attendant. Station duties included treating patients plagued by a wide variety of diseases, keeping the books, rendering returns, organizing vaccination campaigns, enforcing sanitary precautions, attending executions, and compiling meteorological observations. There were even cases where the physician had to deputize for the district officer and rule his charges as well as cure them.

On tour in his district the medical officer—like the DC—traveled by horse, hammock, foot, or bicycle; he was expected to attend sick people, carry out vaccinations, supervise bush hospitals, and sometimes supervise the evacuation of villages from areas stricken by sleeping sickness. Not surprisingly, the overworked and understaffed pioneer services had little time for research, and the district surgeon—again like the DC—had to be a jack-of-all-trades. The life of a generalist, however, had many attractions, especially for a man with a taste for outdoor living. Moreover, there were financial inducements. Pay in West Africa was reasonable, and with wise management of his finances a man could save enough money in a few years to buy a small practice in Great Britain. †

Life in the nursing service had no such attractions. Nurses out from Great Britain needed an almost missionary sense of vocation, for the hospitals in the prewar years were often primitive, and the work could be incredibly hard. There was the case of a young British nurse who came out to Accra in 1896, full of high hopes. She arrived on the same ship with Governor William E. Maxwell. On disembarking, she was dumped soaking on the beach by the Kru boatmen and left there by

---

*In Sapele in Southern Nigeria, for example, the doctor had to care for a population of 14 Europeans. That sounds an easy enough job, but in one year he treated 119 cases, many of them serious; eight men were invalided, and five died. Yet by 1914 Governor Hugh Clifford was complaining that nine doctors were too many for the Northern Territories of the Gold Coast colony; he suggested reducing the number to three. (Great Britain, Public Records Office, "Despatch Confidential, 9th April 1914," CO 96/543.)

†Just before World War I a government doctor in West Africa was paid £400 a year with an annual raise of £20 to a maximum of £500. In addition, there were special travel allowances. One could live reasonably well in Nigeria on £200 a year, so that doctors had an opportunity to save a goodly amount. If a physician stayed on for 18 years, he could retire on a "full pension," or nine-twentieths of his last salary. In the Sudan financial conditions were even better; a British medical inspector started at 600 Egyptian pounds a year (the Egyptian pound then equaled £1 6d. in British currency), and could expect to rise to a maximum of 900 Egyptian pounds after 10 years' service. There were also a few more highly paid posts for hospital directors.

the governor's party. After walking a considerable distance, she was met by the hospital cart, and two fellow nurses took her to her room, with a small bed and a single chair—all the furniture it could hold. There were neither sheets nor blankets, let alone mosquito nets. The Colonial Office authorities had told her that linen, crockery, and cutlery would all be provided; hence she had taken along nothing, and nothing could be bought on the spot. The patients were even worse off. European patients did not even receive tea and sugar; the nurses supplied these necessities from their own small hoards. The hospital itself was in a sorry state: "The beds were such as an educated native would not sleep on, . . . all in rags." No grass or trees grew around the hospital. She thought she had come to the most desolate place on earth and was bitten wildly by mosquitos, for she had no net. But she hung on and was still nursing in Accra in 1918.[17]

These physicians and nurses between them at first accomplished little in the struggle against disease. They were few in number. They were apt to be frequently moved from one district to another. They lacked knowledge, money, and resources. By 1914 the Uganda Medical Department's annual budget, for instance, stood at no more than £28,000. Besides, the great majority of tropical diseases was not as yet susceptible to cure. Quinine was available for the treatment of malaria, and new techniques in the form of intramuscular and intravenous injection were being tried. Syphilis and yaws began to be treated with some success as a result of Paul Ehrlich's discoveries. But doctors could do little for patients with such illnesses as dysentery, bilharzia, relapsing fever, typhoid, and liver abscesses. Sleeping sickness loomed like a specter, and anyone who contracted it knew that only by suicide would he escape a terrible, lingering death. Other "imperial diseases" listed in contemporary literature included influenza, bubonic plague, smallpox, tuberculosis, alcoholism, and drug addiction. A certain amount of research was carried on by government and mission laboratories in West Africa and the Sudan. By 1903, for example, a trypanasome was recognized as the cause of sleeping sickness and the tsetse fly as its transmitter. In addition, physicians successfully investigated relapsing fever, guinea-worm infection from polluted water, and yellow fever. The West African Medical Service, working with research centers in Great Britain, acquired an enviable reputation. So did the Wellcome Laboratories in Khartoum, headed by Dr. Andrew (later Sir Andrew) Balfour, which became the single-most-important center of medical research in tropical Africa and helped to make Khartoum one of the healthiest cities on the continent. The period 1890 to 1914, then, was to see one of the most successful attacks on tropical diseases in the history of Africa.

In the field of preventive medicine, the British South Africa Company's administration in Southern Rhodesia took an unusually progressive part. A district surgeon first established the presence of anopheles in the territory in 1899. Immediately afterward, Andrew Milroy Fleming, the medical director, began to take vigorous countermeasures. Government, mission, and private doctors all joined the campaign and gradually began to make some inroads on sickness. The towns grew cleaner and healthier as the ragged-looking pole-and-dagga huts or tin shanties gave way to better buildings. At the same time the authorities began to clean up stagnant pools of water—dangerous breeding places for mosquitos—and to provide better water supplies, thereby helping to do away with the once-frequent outbreaks of typhoid fever. Improvements spread into the countryside as farmers and miners learned how to protect themselves by using mosquito nets, building better houses, and eliminating the breeding areas of anopheles.

The work of Fleming and his associates in some ways was almost as remarkable as the contemporary American success in cleaning up the Panama Canal Zone, for Rhodesian doctors had to cover a vastly larger area and cope with isolated settlers scattered all over the veld. But sickness started to retreat from the first decade of the twentieth century, and medical treatment spread farther afield into the native reserves, where the pioneering was done by mission doctors. More hospitals were built, and from 1911 the Southern Rhodesian administration, acting under pressure from the chartered company's London board, began to set up village dispensaries in African areas. * The company thereby initiated what was to become the first comprehensive medical service for Africans, a service designed to benefit villagers as well as mine workers—a departure far in advance of the policies pursued by a hard-line reactionary like Lord Lugard in West Africa.[18]

The Rhodesian administration at the same time began to take steps to cope with mortality in the mines. In the early years of European enterprise, mine managers imagined that African laborers living in compounds in pole-and-dagga huts and eating the same kind of food as in the village—maize with some occasional meat—would keep as fit as in their kraals. But experience proved otherwise. The sudden influx of large numbers of men, working much harder than before and living

---

* Between 1904 and 1922 the white death rate in Southern Rhodesia dropped from 18 per 1,000 to 8.98 per 1,000. Accurate figures for the overall African mortality in this period are not available, but after a considerable time lag they showed a sharp decline.

under strange conditions without their wives' care, crammed together
in overcrowded quarters with poor ventilation and inadequate washing
facilities, resulted in death rates that shocked the most hard-bitten.
Sanitary conditions remained bad through the end of the century and
after; water supplies were infected, flies contaminated the food, and
dysentery followed. There was usually ample food, but with no one to
collect the herbs used as relish in the villages, it was deficient in vita-
min content, and many men reported sick with scurvy. Pneumonia
was the greatest scourge of all, accounting for well over a third of the
mine workers' deaths in 1903–4.[19]

At one time the annual mortality rate of African miners was over
7 percent, the casualty rate of many an army in wartime, and the
Southern Rhodesian administration thus came under heavy pressure
both from the company's head office in London and from the British
government. At last something was done. The administration appointed compound inspectors to look into health conditions and, after
exhaustive investigations, the government began in 1907 to enforce the
medical screening and proper feeding and housing of African miners.
The small companies, unable to spend as much money on social improvements as the larger concerns, put up some resistance but could
not reverse the trend. In 1911 and 1914 the administration introduced
further regulations that compelled employers to make additional improvements in the workers' diet and provided for one compulsory day
of rest in seven. The small entrepreneurs growled angrily that all the
government wanted them to do was to "feed, feed, feed," but the new
reforms, coupled with the expansion of hospital facilities, soon proved
their worth: mortality rates in the mines began to slump.* After an
initial period of frontier friction in the 1890's the chartered company
thus on the whole established a better record in labor and health matters in Southern Rhodesia than any colonial administration in Africa at
the time. Mine work became more popular among the Africans, and
Rhodesian mine workers were healthier and better fed than their cous-
ins in the villages.

The effect of Western medicine on Africa as a whole is hard to assess.
The Western impact on health was double-edged. By improving com-

---

*The mortality rate dropped from 75.94 per 1,000 in 1906 to 21.68 per 1,000 in 1917.
The influenza epidemic after World War I saw a sudden rise to 113.38 per 1,000 in 1918,
but the rate declined thereafter, falling to 15.39 per 1,000 in 1925. (L. H. Gann, A History of Southern Rhodesia: Early Days to 1934, London, 1965, p. 180. For a more
detailed account, see Michael Gelfand, Tropical Victory: An Account of the Influence of
Medicine on the History of Southern Rhodesia, 1890–1923, Cape Town, 1953.)

munications, the Europeans helped to spread new diseases as well as new ideas. Labor migration introduced a variety of new afflictions, and so did the wars of conquest. On the other hand, the new technology and the new science helped men to preserve their lives to an extent unknown to earlier generations.

Western administration and industry between them probably saved far more lives than Western medical science on its own. Internecine wars and slave raids ended. Cheap soap and cheap textiles were a boon to personal hygiene. Brick huts, covered by cheap corrugated iron, reduced fire hazards and were more easily kept free of dirt and vermin than traditional dwellings. Improved rail transport and modern storage facilities for crops enabled traders and administrators to shift food supplies to drought-stricken areas in a fashion inconceivable in the olden days, when transport depended on the muscle power of porters and canoe-paddlers. Finally, the provision of proper sewage, the availability of pure water, and the elimination of stagnant, mosquito-infested pools did infinitely more good than the curative efforts of physicians. These efforts, however, were no less important, for all that. Smallpox vaccination, for example, became common in all colonies, and medical dispensaries in African areas reached tens of thousands of sick people.

By 1914 Westernization had clearly changed African health conditions for the better. The first beneficiaries were the empire builders themselves—the officials and the settlers. The second group to profit were Westernized Africans. Indeed, family histories of Christian converts suggest that the first generation of African followers may have lived longer than their fellows; they knew better how to protect their newborn children against disease than the illiterate villagers, hence infant mortality was lower among the families of teachers, evangelists, and clerks than among cultivators.* Educated men initially seem to have made no effort to keep down the number of their offspring; the population explosion of modern Africa probably started among the "noncommissioned officers of empire."

As a group, the villagers remained more prone to sickness than the educated, despite a good deal of nonsense that was spread at the time —and since—about happy, healthy, unspoiled Africans. The DCs and assistant DCs continued to draw attention to the poor health of the

---

*Infant mortality statistics for the various African territories leave much to be desired. But in the Gold Coast mortality clearly began to drop after World War I; per 1,000 births, infant mortality declined from 359.6 in 1919 to 293 in 1924–25. (Raymond Leslie Buell, *The Native Problem in Africa*, London, 1965, 1: 845.)

rural people. Living and traveling among Africans as they did, they became a prime source of information on tropical disease and sanitary conditions in the villages. They pressed for dispensaries and free medicines, and most district offices became medical dispensaries to treat minor ailments. The DC often supervised smallpox vaccination; at least this disease was brought under control before 1914.

By World War I every British colony was in a position to provide basic medical services. All had at a minimum government hospitals, dispensaries, and a Medical Department; and all had doctors, trained African assistants, and missionaries to deliver these services. Most of the medical effort was devoted to the care of European and African soldiers and government staff, but Africans were treated in dispensaries, and thousands were treated by missionaries. Medical research had some major successes, and in the interwar years more of Africa's endemic diseases would be cured.

The Agriculturists

The colonial era witnessed a vast and unparalleled increase of agricultural production and trade in Africa. To a considerable extent, this was brought about by the introduction of new techniques and crops and by the development of markets and transport facilities. The clearest indicators of this heightened productivity were the sustained rise in agricultural exports and the growth in population. Infant mortality declined, and life expectancy was lengthened, both signs of improved material well-being.

Opening the export market for tropical goods was a major stimulus to agricultural development and technical change in Africa. Colonies that failed to develop an export crop or mining industry remained poor and backward. The colonizers at first simply introduced new crops and did not attempt to change African agricultural techniques. Only gradually were colonial agriculture departments established to influence cultivation practices.

Cheap transportation facilitated the rapid development of tropical export markets, as sailing ships were replaced by the faster steamships that carried three or four times as much cargo. Macgregor Laird's development of a small, shallow-draft steamboat revolutionized river transport, and opened the Gambia, Niger, and Senegal river valleys to economic penetration. The newly industrialized West called for tropical African export crops—cocoa, coffee, tobacco, palm kernels and oil, groundnuts, cotton, sisal, and rubber. African societies, spurred on by missionaries, by commercial concerns, and by the colonial governments, responded to this demand and increased their cultivation of export crops.

The period from 1880 to 1913 was especially productive. Gold Coast exports grew from £390,000 in 1882–84 to £5,427,000 in 1913, an average annual growth rate of 9.2 percent. Southern Nigeria's economy expanded even faster, with exports rising from £1,608,000 in 1899 to £7,099,000 in 1913—an average yearly rate of 12 percent.

Export crops represented a net increase in farm output. Though production for overseas use of commodities such as cotton, sisal, cocoa, and palm oil was enormously expanded from 1880 onwards, food cultivation kept pace with population growth except in Senegal, where the cultivation of groundnuts led to a decline in food supplies and the importation of rice. The colonial pax, better transportation systems, the introduction of new crops, and the spread of better agricultural methods and tools, along with what we would now call extension work by missionaries and departments of agriculture, improved local food supplies while dramatically increasing export crops. Such a rise in productivity can be credited to changes in traditional agriculture, many of them caused by the imposition of an export crop and its related technology on the existing food economy.

Increasing the productivity of agricultural systems traditionally based on shifting cultivation, however, presented many obstacles. It was difficult to bulk, process, and transport produce raised on small plots for a year or two. Agricultural improvement was not easily achieved on communal land. Plant and soil diseases also slowed development.

Given the colonial governments' limitations of manpower and finance, their approach to increasing agricultural productivity was sound —indeed, it was probably the best way that agriculture could have been improved. Administrators made use of the traditional framework while introducing important technological changes, such as plows, fertilizer, crop rotation, and irrigation, and encouraging the cultivation of new crops. The first impetus for rapid economic change came mainly in the pre-1914 colonial period, an era that also initiated the logistic, administrative, and scientific infrastructure essential to the promotion of change.

Agricultural innovation in Africa first came from the Africans themselves. Unknown and unacknowledged black experimenters adapted to their use a large variety of foreign crops, including maize, manioc, and tobacco, and developed an extensive export trade in cocoa, groundnuts, and palm kernels. European colonists in East Africa introduced a dairy industry, along with the cultivation of sisal, pyrethrum, and coffee; they also imported new breeds of cattle and sheep and practiced selective livestock breeding. Among other things, Europeans brought barbed-wire fences, cattle dips, boreholes, and tobacco barns to Rhodesia. The Basel Mission founded an agricultural station at Akropong in the Gold Coast, where Surinam cocoa was grown experimentally. In Uganda a mission-supported trading company introduced cotton, and in Nyasaland missionaries helped to naturalize the tea plant.

The work of early botanists in collaboration with the Royal Botanical Gardens at Kew played a major part in developing economic colonial crops, as did the work done by the Imperial Institute. But distance and varied local needs and problems forced the colonies gradually to develop their own scientific and technical units. Botanical gardens and experimental farms were usually established first; departments of agriculture followed after 1900. Starting in 1890, the West African colonies began to develop their own experimental farms and botanical gardens headed by curators in government employ, most of them trained at Kew, who were expected to travel widely and to help local cultivators in whatever way they could.* As the governor of the Gold Coast put it in a dispatch to the Colonial Office in 1899: "I propose, as soon as I find a King or Chief wishful of growing either rubber or kola, or any other product, the cultivation of which it has been decided by the Government to push, . . . to send the Curator or Assistant Curator to select suitable sites [and] to give the requisite number of seedlings to the King or Chief, [with the planting to be undertaken] under the direct supervision of the Curator or the Assistant Curator."[20]

The botanic gardens had various functions: to introduce and try exotics, especially those of economic importance; to collect and classify indigenous species, especially useful trees and shrubs, pot-like herbs, and medicinal plants; to distribute plants, seeds, and seedlings; to demonstrate the uses for which plants were suitable—economic, decoration, shade, foliage, flowers; to educate the public in the recognition of the various trees and plants and their uses; and to provide relaxation and pleasure.

The Botanic Gardens, Entebbe, can serve as an example. They were begun in 1898 by Alexander Whyte, M.A., F.L.S. As curator, he

---

*Sierra Leone opened a botanical station in Freetown in 1895. Four years later an experimental farm was opened at Songo Town. Plants that had done well in the botanical station—coffee, cinnamon, kola, and cocoa—were transferred to the experimental farm.

sought to examine and to develop the agricultural resources of the Uganda protectorate. He planted lawns, specimen trees, and flower beds. He laid out plots for commercial crops—rubber, cocoa, oil palms, and fruit trees—and had a large nursery to propagate plants for distribution. The gardens were responsible for the introduction or early experiments with all of the chief tropical agricultural crops, including cotton, coffee, cocoa, sisal, hemp, hevia, and rubber, as well as other marketable plants and fruits. Kew Gardens helped them with seeds and seedlings. After experiments, American upland cotton was doing best by 1904–5, and Africans were taking to the crop. Tea was introduced and had small successes. The staff slowly increased and diversified: a tobacco officer was added in 1907, a cotton inspector in 1908, an entomologist in 1909.

The development of agricultural departments as such was a slow affair. Apart from botanists, the Colonial Office list for 1890 shows only a few posts connected with agriculture. Trinidad, for instance, had a Superintendent of Government Pastures and Examiner of Animals; and in Barbados there was a vacancy for an Island Professor of Chemistry and Agriculture. However, colonial governments began to develop small agricultural departments of their own as part of a wider campaign to develop the imperial estate. Southern Nigeria set up a department in 1902; the Gold Coast, Kenya, and Southern Rhodesia followed suit in 1903; Lagos and Uganda in 1904; the British Central Africa Protectorate and Sierra Leone in 1906.

These departments were staffed with men from many different disciplines. British universities did not provide training in agricultural science until the first decade of the twentieth century. Some of the early specialists held doctorates in science; others were fellows of the Linnaean Society; still others had diplomas from the Royal Horticultural Society or had trained at Kew. Some had no academic qualification whatever, but made up for this deficiency by experience and ability—like M. T. Dawe, who began his career as an assistant in the Uganda Botanical Gardens and ended as the director of agriculture in Palestine. On the whole, the experts fitted easily into the social framework of the administration. They earned salaries broadly similar to those of the administrators,* and they came from comparable backgrounds—Public School, university, and, commonly, the gentry class.

Outside the Rhodesias and British East Africa, the government tried

*In 1914 the director of agriculture in Sierra Leone made £720 a year, slightly more than a PC. His assistants earned between £300 and £400, as much as an assistant DC.

to promote the production of cash crops through a partnership between black cultivators and white merchants. Authorities largely rejected direct government intervention in agriculture in the tropical
colonies, as well as in areas of white settlement. They encouraged
private entrepreneurs, white or black, by providing both technical
and logistical assistance. Uganda, for instance, received cotton, cocoa,
and rubber plants from Kew Gardens. In southern Nigeria both Governor MacGregor and Governor Ralph Moor encouraged experimentation and the testing of plants for their economic value, and supplied
farmers with seed, seedlings, and saplings from the colony's botanical
gardens and experimental farms. Seedlings for coffee, kola, cocoa,
maize, oil palm, citrus, and other fruits produced at Kew helped to
improve the African diet and led to the development of cash crops.
Farmers received instruction in cultivation from government demonstrators. The introduction of steel hatchets made it easier to clear the
bush, and new crops were planted for food and export. Plants and
cattle were brought from the West Indies, and American experts in
cotton-growing and stock-raising came to Lagos. Though many ideas
failed, some succeeded—notably those involving mangoes, tobacco,
firewood plantations, cocoa, kapok, cinnamon, raffia, and kola. The
protectorate experimented also with jute, castor oil, bananas, maize,
and groundnuts.[21]

The Colonial Office created the post of inspector or superintendent
of agriculture for British West Africa in 1905. Gerald G. Dudgeon
held this position until 1910. The main scientific efforts to develop
agriculture in the region went into cotton, cocoa, palm oil, and jute.
The British Cotton Growing Association carried out most of the work
before 1914. Cotton took hold in Northern Nigeria and the Northern
Territories of the Gold Coast, but efforts failed in Sierra Leone and the
Gambia. Thanks to the efforts of the association and the various colonial governments, West African cotton exports rose to 1,500,000
pounds in 1905 and to 4,500,000 pounds in 1912.

The various agricultural departments had to start from scratch and
faced all kinds of difficulties. The research facilities and experience
that were taken for granted in more developed countries were lacking.
There was considerable difference in the organization and function of
the departments, depending on the social policy followed by each
particular colony. Governor Brandford Griffith of the Gold Coast established a botanical garden at Aburi in 1890 and sold cocoa seeds and
seedlings to farmers; by 1892–93 sales were over £400,000. These
seedlings became available when the industrious Akwapim Ridge

farmers were looking for new cash crops, and a great migration of cocoa farmers to the north and west of the ridge took place. The volume of exports mounted steadily: in 1891 they were a mere 80 pounds; in 1895 they were 13 tons; by 1913 they reached 50,000 tons. New trees planted in the 1890's led to a further threefold expansion. Seven more research stations followed between 1901 and 1907, and their work was vital; they learned how to improve plant types and to control plant diseases. Meanwhile, the Agricultural Department encouraged cash-cropping by providing advice and improved seeds and seedlings. The work done by Dudgeon on the insects that attacked the cocoa trees was particularly important in increasing cocoa production, which doubled between 1905 and 1912. Scientific studies were also made on the oil palm; different varieties were imported from the Camerouns, and experimental farms were laid out. Experiments to develop West Africa as an alternate source of jute experiments proved highly successful.

The cocoa farmers of the Gold Coast, like the Kru sailors of Liberia, played a particularly important part in developing an African cash economy. They bought more consumer goods than their neighbors; they built new houses and sent their children to school. Local governments financed roads and bridge-building. New land for cocoa trees was purchased, and tens of millions of new trees were planted before 1914. To handle crop exports, new port facilities, railways, and roads had to be built.

Agricultural development was much slower to be pushed in the central and eastern colonies than in the west. The British South Africa Company in Rhodesia at first concentrated on mining, and little attention was given to the scientific aspects of agriculture. In 1908, however, the company embarked on an active policy to promote white farming, on the assumption that white colonization would provide the company with increased revenue from the sale of land and supply the mines with a steady and predictable supply of food, thus reducing the operating expenses of mining enterprises in which the company held an economic stake.

In that year E. A. Nobbs, a Cape expert, was engaged as director of agriculture; he was assisted by a few specialists, including a chemist, a botanist, an entomologist, a tobacco expert, and several veterinary surgeons. Between them, they studied local plant diseases and pests, soils, and products. The department distributed various kinds of improved seeds and plants; it advised on tobacco cultivation and succeeded in improving maize strains. Newly available information was widely spread among white farmers through the *Rhodesian Agricultural Journal* (1903), one of several professional publications initiated by agricultural departments throughout the empire.

The Rhodesian department tackled a variety of other tasks. Starting in 1904, measures were taken to ban the importation of diseased plants. As maize production in the territory began to expand, grading was introduced to prevent the export of inferior crops. The office became concerned with the quality of fertilizers; though the farmers were slow to make use of its findings, after 1913 or so they increasingly came around to the improved products. An engineer was appointed in 1910 to advise farmers on methods of irrigation; this led, in 1913, to the establishment of water courts to adjudicate water rights. In 1914 an ordinance made it compulsory for farmers to furnish certain statistical information to the Department of Agriculture, and a statistician was appointed to deal with the returns.

In settler colonies most agricultural resources were allocated to the Europeans. Nevertheless, the Africans progressed, too; they accepted the plow, the wagon, the use of manure, cash-cropping, improved strains of maize. The Southern Rhodesian government played its part in developing "tribal areas" (native reserves) by building boreholes, wells, and cattle dips, and by introducing plows, seeds, and new breeds of cattle. After the 1890's there was a significant increase in the African production of maize, beef, and other foodstuffs.

But resources were limited even in settler colonies, and successes were few. The British East Africa Protectorate did not establish an Agricultural Department until 1903. By 1907 it had experimental farms at Nairobi, Naivasha, Kibos, Malindi, and Mazeros to test the suitability of imported animals for cross-breeding with native cattle, sheep, and goats, as well as to study the suitability of certain crops for local growing conditions. The farms had nurseries for raising forest and ornamental trees, fibers, rubber, and other plants for sale to settlers. Areas for agricultural and pastoral resources were inspected by the department; it collected meteorological data and published bulletins and leaflets on agriculture. Because of the lack of staff and money, however, the results were limited. As late as 1907–8 only £11,618 was budgeted for agriculture and just £8,580 for veterinary affairs.

In 1904–5 the Veterinary Section and the Forestry Division of the Department of Agriculture were given separate status. There was only one veterinary officer in 1898, but in 1904 an assistant surgeon was appointed to control rinderpest, and two veterinary surgeons and one stock inspector were added the following year. Still, the department was too small and the area served too large for it to have an impact on pleuropneumonia, coast fever, piroplasmosis, intestinal parasites, and the many other diseases and pests that hindered the development of a livestock industry. Most of its time was spent in managing cattle herds collected during punitive expeditions against African tribes. Some work on livestock improvement was carried out—stock farms imported various breeds of cattle, sheep, and poultry to cross with African stock.

Some successes were recorded. John Ainsworth, as we have seen, was a major agricultural innovator in British East Africa before World War I, and his story is worth telling.[22] He was born in 1864 at Urmston near Manchester, but his health was bad, and his family moved to north Wales, where he was educated at home. Still, he yearned to see strange lands, and at twenty he went as a trader to the Congo, where he worked for a time with Roger (later Sir Roger) Casement. He stayed for five years, becoming a transport specialist. In 1889 Ainsworth signed on with the Imperial British East African Company; he served for over two years as transport superintendent in Mombasa, then went to Machakos. There he planted a vegetable garden, and his example encouraged other Europeans to do the same. His wheat and barley seeds made the Machakos area almost self-sufficient in these crops, but he did not have any influence on the local Kamba.

The years he spent in Nairobi, from 1899 to 1906, gave him a wider influence. Ainsworth believed Kenya's future lay in agriculture, and he set out to introduce new crops and techniques. He built a large experimental garden in Nairobi, established the East African Agricultural and Horticultural Society in 1901, and inaugurated *The East African Quarterly* (1904). In 1903 he purchased sisal plants from German East Africa and proved they could flourish in Kenya, so the Nairobi experimental farm and the Agricultural Department imported bulbils from the West Indies. At the yearly shows of the Agricultural and Horticultural Society he sought to encourage production of new crops by exhibiting what had been grown in his garden: cotton, sisal, grain seeds, coffee, castor oil. The Europeans were not enthusiastic about cotton, but they took readily to sisal, as had the German settlers of Tanganyika.

As the PC of Nyanza, Ainsworth worked just as diligently to encourage agricultural innovation among the Africans in his territory. The Kenya administration at this point (he took office in 1907) had done little or nothing to get Africans to grow cash crops. The prevailing view was that they should become laborers on European farms and government public works projects, and should not produce for the market.

Ainsworth opposed this policy, arguing that if the government could tax the Africans, it had a reciprocal obligation to help them, and that officials should promote agricultural development. To this end, Ainsworth mobilized his own staff to encourage cash-cropping and to improve food production; he gave away seeds, demonstrated how to grow new crops, and succeeded in introducing simsim, groundnuts, and improved varieties of maize and cotton. As a result of his work, the growth of agricultural exports in Nyanza province was spectacular. By 1908–9 their value was 287,460 rupees (about $93,000); in 1910–11 it was 987,623 rupees ($320,000). The improved maize seeds not only led to greater production with less work, but also revolutionized the people's way of life. Ainsworth's cotton-growing efforts were not successful during his lifetime, but lessons were learned from his experiments, and cotton later became an important cash crop in Nyanza.*

In addition to developing new export crops, colonial officials planted new trees and tried to conserve and develop forest resources. Before 1914 there was no program to train officers for the forestry services in British Africa. Oxford, Cambridge, and Edinburgh all had schools of forestry, but the Imperial Forestry Institute at Oxford was not opened until 1924, and the early colonial governments had to do the best they could with the few experts they could consult or recruit. The first step was usually to appoint guards to protect the forests. Some surveying delimited the forest reserves, and some experimenting with trees was undertaken. Deforestation took place rapidly until demarcation was well advanced. Nigeria had a conservator of forests from 1905 on, and in 1912 Sierra Leone set up a Forestry Department. Various colonies experimented with rubber trees, and by 1912 rubber plantations in the Gold Coast and Nigeria had replaced wild rubber.

Little work on tropical veterinary medicine was done in Great Britain before 1914, other than the government's publication of the *Tropical Veterinary Bulletin*. Only South Africa had a reasonable staff involved in veterinary research. A cure for piroplasmosis, which attacked domestic animals, was a great boon in this field. In 1894–95 Surgeon-Major David Bruce and his wife discovered that tsetse flies carried the disease *nagana* to cattle and horses, but a cure was slow to be found.

The total effect of these measures is difficult to evaluate. The main impulse to crop changes and other facets of production among the Africans did not come so much from the colonial administrators as from the private enterprise of the African cultivators themselves. It was the

---

*Cash-cropping helped to make the railway pay in the province and showed that the railroad did not have to depend solely on European agriculture.

TABLE 28
Value of Exports in Selected British African Colonies,
1902 and 1913
(Current prices in £)

Territory	1902	1913
Nigeria	1,337,000	7,352,000
Gold Coast	381,000	5,427,000
Zanzibar, Uganda, East Africa Protectorate	20,000	2,166,000
Sierra Leone	207,000	1,731,000
Gambia	228,000	867,000

SOURCE: David K. Fieldhouse, "The Economic Exploitation of Africa: Some British and French Comparisons," in Prosser Gifford and William Roger Louis, eds., *France and Britain in Africa* (New Haven, Conn., 1971), pp. 59–60.

African farmers who were responsible for the main agricultural triumphs during the period: the expansion of peanut and cocoa cultivation. The Africans, moreover, often had a better understanding of what was to their best advantage than the planners. In Northern Nigeria, for instance, the British tried to push cotton, but the local farmers discovered that they could make more money with less effort by growing groundnuts.

The principal driving force behind agricultural development was the expansion of transport facilities and the spread of village markets. Shippers and traders between them furnished Africans with new incentives; hence the exports of tropical crops grew by leaps and bounds in the decade preceding World War I. (See Table 28.) After the war, the great age of agricultural education and research began; but in extensive parts of Africa the British can claim to have created the original framework for state-supported assistance to agricultural enterprise, and by 1914 the experts' impact was apparent. Every British colony except Gambia had a Department of Agriculture, experimental farms, and a botanical garden. Research and information programs were in operation. There were some important successes in cash-cropping— cotton in Uganda, coffee in Kenya, cocoa in the Gold Coast, ginger in Sierra Leone, cloves in Zanzibar. New and improved strains of grain and fruits and improved breeds of cattle helped to increase African productivity. A beginning had been made on conservation and in experimentation.

The British thus laid the groundwork for later successes. Their immediate effect was limited with regard to food crops other than maize, peanuts, and cocoa. But given the lack of funds and their scanty knowledge concerning human and plant diseases, the restricted nature of the British impact is not surprising.[23]

Engineers and Surveyors

The British colonial administrative, military, and police apparatuses have all been well studied, but the less obvious colonial services—public works, forestry, veterinary medicine, education, agriculture, and especially engineering—have found few historians. The specialists' work was often arduous, undertaken in extreme discomfort and loneliness, with grave risks to health and life—as Kipling said, "in difficult surroundings without help or acknowledgement."

Great public works—mostly roads, bridges, ports, and buildings—were built throughout India and Africa on a scale that surpassed the engineering feats of the Roman Empire. Engineers in Africa had no achievement to rival the immense canal system that transformed the Punjab from a desert to a granary, or the 1,500-mile-long Grand Trunk Road;[24] but the railways, ports, roads, and public buildings that they constructed were significant achievements all the same.

The Colonial Office did not maintain an African equivalent to the Royal Indian Engineering College at Cooper's Hill, but army engineers provided skilled people. The Crown agents also helped supply the technicians of empire, the real builders of the administrations and the prosperity of the colonies. Engineers constructed the railways, roads, and ports that linked the various parts of a colony to the outside world. Engineers and some district officers put up bridges and dams, cleared the creeks and rivers, and constructed irrigation canals to allow men and goods to move more easily and safely, and to expand the growth and sale of crops and natural products. Most of their labor was done in the bush, the forest, the mountains, and the desert. Hence outsiders seldom knew of the problems these men had to overcome or appreciated their dangers or their privations. They spent months of isolation living on short and often monotonous rations while camped in remote, sometimes unhealthy, regions.

Victorian engineers were a diverse lot. There were several ways of rising to the top, with opportunities for men from the workshop as well as for men with an academic background. (Engineers were trained in a variety of ways: on the job, in Mechanics' Institutes, later in Polytechnics, in the so-called Central Technical College, South Kensington, and finally in various universities, with Cambridge taking the lead.)

Within the profession, power lay with the professional institutes. The oldest and most honored of these was the Institution of Civil Engineers (incorporated in 1828). The civil engineers enjoyed the highest prestige of all. Their training tended to emphasize practical skills. Their ethos prized individual initiative, panache, and the ability to complete a job speedily—qualities much in demand at a time when builders did not have to spend much time in placating timid committeemen and bureaucrats.

The engineering profession, like the medical profession, was dominated by striking individuals of great personality. They were culture heroes of the Victorian and Edwardian ages. The qualifications required of them were almost episcopal. In the magisterial language of the *Encyclopaedia Britannica*:

Qualifications include intellectual and moral honesty, courage, independence of thought, fairness, good sense, sound judgment, perseverance, resourcefulness, ingenuity, orderliness, application, accuracy and endurance. An engineer should have ability to observe, deduce, apply, to correlate cause and effect, to co-operate, to organize, to analyze situations and conditions, to state problems, to direct the efforts of others. He should know how to inform, convince, and win confidence by skillful and right use of facts. He should be alert, ready to learn, open-minded, but not credulous. He must be able to assemble facts, to investigate thoroughly, to discriminate clearly between assumption and proven knowledge. He should be a man of faith. . . . He should have extensive knowledge of the sciences and other branches of learning and know intensively those things which concern his specialties. He must be a student throughout his career and keep abreast of human progress. . . . The engineer is under obligation to consider the sociological, economic and spiritual effects of engineering operations and to aid his fellowmen to adjust wisely their modes of living, their industrial, commercial and governmental procedures, and their educational processes so as to enjoy the greatest possible benefit from the progress achieved through our accumulating knowledge of the universe.[25]

Graduates of British universities—especially Cambridge—and military officers trained in the Royal Engineers stood socially and professionally at the head of the pyramid. The Royal Military Academy at Woolwich (established in 1741) was the first military and, in its way, the first professional school in the kingdom. The intellectual qualifications required of its candidates were higher than those at Sandhurst, where rough horseplay was more common, and social snobbery more obtrusive. Woolwich men tended to be of middle class rather than gentry background. Woolwich also gave a chance to bright youngsters who were good at books and poor at games, men like Matthew Nathan, successively governor of the Gold Coast, Hong Kong, and Natal, the first professing Jew to reach this position in the British colonial empire. Woolwich men often had wider intellectual interests than their brother officers in other corps. Archaeological investigations abroad, for instance the pioneering research in Palestine, owed a great deal to Royal Engineers officers like Sir Charles Warren of Bechuanaland fame.

The corps was organized into something like its modern form after the Crimean War and, being a scientific formation, it subsequently developed many important branches of military science, including the Royal Flying Corps and the Royal Corps of Signals. Its officers were important to colonial development—from building barracks to unearthing archaeological treasures. They had a variety of skills: they knew how to construct fieldworks; they learned how to operate ports; they were familiar with the arts of adapting buildings for barracks, warehouses, and hospitals; they made tracks, railways, and roads; they became expert in providing water and light, and in disposing of sewage; they were experienced in building bridges, in conducting surveys, and in a host of other occupations. It was not for nothing that their regiment bore the motto *Ubique*.

Several engineers became governors and helped to develop the infrastructure of their colonies, men like Girouard, who built railways in the Sudan, Nigeria, and Kenya, and Guggisberg of the Gold Coast. Many colonial engineers were among the most highly trained men in their field. An example was W. McGregor Ross, a civil engineer with a B.A., an M.Sc., a B.E., and an M.Inst.C.E. He went to Uganda in 1900 as an assistant engineer and moved to Nairobi three years later as engineer in charge of the city's water supply. In 1905 he became director of public works for the colony, a position he held until 1923.

Public works departments did an outstanding job in providing houses and offices for officials, as well as roads and bridges, piers, harbors, ports, and embankments. The health and comfort of the officers were linked to their housing. Roads and bridges made administration easier and opened up the back country to trade. Even a simple bridge saved time and energy. Ross recounted that on a trip in 1906 it took his caravan two hours of dangerous work to cross a river; the previous year, when the bridge was intact, his men had passed in three minutes and lost no loads or people. Bridges were, of course, essential for getting bulky goods across rivers.

Though well-qualified from the technical standpoint, military engineers and Cambridge graduates alike regarded themselves as gentlemen rather than experts, and were so regarded by others. They fitted into the Establishment more easily than their German confrères; the Royal Navy, for instance, was much more effective in absorbing engineers into the officer corps than the German High Seas Fleet, where engineers remained a caste apart.

In the systematic expansion of higher technical education, however, the British lagged behind the Germans. The Technische Hochschulen, started in the 1880's, for long had no equivalent in Britain, and it was only in 1907 that the success of these schools induced the British to set up the Imperial College of Science and Technology in London. The middle layer of industrial leaders commonly came from such schools as the Regent Street Polytechnic, founded in the British capital in 1880. In addition, the British—more than the Germans—relied on a substantial group of practical men who had learned their skills on the job while supplementing their knowledge through evening classes. During the pioneering period of empire, the African colonies owed a special debt to these men, who were linked to the governing group of administrators but not wholly absorbed by it.

A. Beeby-Thompson, a government engineer who later became well known in the oil industry, will serve as an example. His father was headmaster of a county science school who specialized in geology and physics and who acquired a local reputation as a keen naturalist and editor of the Northamptonshire Natural History Society's journal, a position that brought him into contact with most of the country's leading scientists. He had an acute mind and taught his son all manner of subjects—from Darwin's theory of evolution to Spencer's views on the relationship between God and man. He took his son on numerous excursions about the countryside in search of fossils and botanical specimens, nurturing the boy's interests in nature and his powers of observation. Religion had a strong influence on young Beeby-Thompson's upbringing; he grew up to respect the doctrines of Christ, the superior position of the clergy, and the stern rectitude displayed by his father. *Robinson Crusoe* and *Swiss Family Robinson* were his favorite reading as a lad, followed later by the stories of Mayne Reed and Jules Verne and the accounts of explorers like Livingstone and Stanley. School was not a success; the classics bored him, but he acquired a sound reading knowledge of Latin, German, and French—subjects that proved useful in his later career.[26]

Since he was not inclined toward any particular profession, his father indentured him for five years with an engineering firm—a long apprenticeship that seemed little better than slavery. He worked from six in the morning to half-past five in the afternoon, leaving little time or strength for such pleasures as cards, taverns, playhouses—or matrimony—all of which were forbidden by the firm. The work inured him to hardship, for workshops were not heated in winter in those days, nor was any provision made for the health and comfort of the workers. On top of it, the young pupil was expected to attend evening science classes and rarely returned home before 10 P.M. Nevertheless, this "slavery" had its advantages. Beeby-Thompson's training was thorough; he acquired a good knowledge of office routine; he was taught how to handle machine tools and how to command men.

His apprenticeship completed, he secured a position with a firm of waterworks contractors and for the first time found employment under the most considerate and kindly masters he could have hoped for. Working with this firm gave him sound practical experience in well-boring, shaft-sinking techniques, pumping machinery, and the principles of hydrology. His opportunity came in 1896, when, at the age of twenty-three, he secured a position in the service of the Gold Coast government. His decision took a considerable degree of courage—a fact driven home to him when he tried to take out a life insurance policy before leaving. Only one company would even entertain a proposal, and it demanded a premium amounting to 50 percent of the coverage. But Beeby-Thompson was determined. He left for the Gold Coast without a policy, for he looked forward to proving himself on his first important job. His assignment was to search for subsoil water of potable quality within easy reach of Accra.

Despite his tough training, the first night ashore in Africa was an ordeal. The officers with whom he was to live regaled him for endless hours over drinks with the most harrowing stories of malaria, blackwater fever, and yellow fever, of hopes misplaced and comrades dead. An Irish physician drank himself into delirium tremens, raving interminably and confessing to a whole series of shameful crimes—including murder. Beeby-Thompson's misgivings about coast life were all too justified; he found himself in a society where disease was rife, where death was an ever-present companion, and where anyone who consumed less than a bottle of whiskey a day was a rank amateur. Eventually he met more temperate men, but almost all his acquaintances suffered in various degrees from debility, irritability, and anemia. The majority went down with fever, and most of them tippled to deaden their fears. The frequency of disease was hardly surprising. Stagnant mosquito-laden pools were everywhere. The drinking water was foul, and therefore required filtration and chemical treatment.

The work, however, was interesting. Nothing in the nature of a geological survey had ever been undertaken, leaving a virgin field to Beeby-Thompson. For an ambitious and energetic youth it was an exhilarating experience to be left to his own devices and to shoulder real responsibility. He got on well with the African workers whom he trained. He played polo. He found his study of life in West Africa so fascinating that on the expiration of his contract he accepted an offer from a consulting engineer for the Crown agents to act as assistant engineer for a firm engaged in surveying suitable sites for water reservoirs on the Gold Coast.

West Coast living conditions gradually improved. By the outbreak of World War I engineers could look forward to a reasonably healthy life and an income on a par or even superior to subalterns and of field officers in the army or the administration.* Their duties were extremely varied. They were employed in the engineering branch of the Post and Telegraph Department, on the railways, and in the Public Works Department. They built roads and bridges, public buildings, cisterns and waterworks. In more developed colonies like Southern Rhodesia, the bulk of the work was done through private contractors. But even in Rhodesia, the government engineers had many and varied tasks, including the supervision of government houses, the management of insurance matters, the upkeep of inventories of movable assets, the supply of water for government buildings, the inspection of explosives in magazines, the supply of government furniture, and the provision of fire appliances.

Southern Rhodesia, economically the most developed of the British colonial territories in southern Africa, also maintained a Mining Department to administer the affairs of a key industry. The Mines and Works Regulations of 1905 imposed a variety of duties on the office regarding health and sanitary inspection, and the government began to enforce measures to ensure structural safety in the mines. From 1910 onward, qualified inspectors joined the department. Though few in number, these men provided essential skills at relatively low cost, skills that never before had been exercised in the land of their adoption.

The Colonial Office began to organize some mineral surveys with a view to encouraging private entrepreneurs to exploit the mineral resources of various colonies. The task of mapping and surveying was

---

*A superintending sanitary engineer in the Gold Coast at the time made £600–700 (with allowances), compared with £480–580 for a DC, and £448 for a captain in the WAFF. An assistant engineer in the Public Works Department, at £350–400, made more than both an assistant DC (£300–400) and a WAFF lieutenant (£300–350). The director of the Public Works Department made £1,200, close to what the colonial secretary of the Gold Coast and the manager of the railway made.

rough. There was wild and unmapped country to cross. Prospectors had to watch out for insects, disease, and wild animals—one surveyor was knelt on by a water buffalo. There were other perils. An African policeman on patrol with surveyors near the Cross River went mad, killed seven people, bayoneted others, slaughtered all the camp animals, and burned all the supplies and equipment. The experiences of Major J. R. L. Macdonald, who surveyed 27,000 miles of possible route for the Uganda railway, were probably typical. He had soldiered and built railways in India, but he was not prepared for the difficulties he faced in East Africa. His donkey died; his men ran off. Once a stream burst its banks and swept away his camp. Bees attacked him in the forest, and then red ants. He came down with fever in the first month, and he and his men were all sick at various times. He had to climb to 10,000 feet and then descend to cross the Rift Valley. Hostile Africans gave him trouble, as did lions and elephants. Smallpox killed some of his followers; many carriers died of fatigue and accidents.[27]

Timber and gold concessions in the Gold Coast created problems of ownership and the marking of claims or leases. The Aborigines Protection Society battled the government to protect African landholdings. Governor Nathan, appointed in 1900, started the process of surveying and mapping the mining area of the Gold Coast. In 1902 he brought out Major Alan Watherston and later, the then-Lieutenant Gordon Guggisberg to do survey work. It was a hard job; high forest and damp tropical heat sapped the strength of the strongest. Guggisberg described it clearly: "In this cutting and measuring we encountered every variety of snake, poisonous scorpions and other biting insects, pestilential swamps, wide groves of thorny bush, and mosquito-haunted rivers. The work was very dreary, the eternal green and gloom of the forest, unrelieved by flowers, getting on the nerves after a few months."[28]

Malaria and blackwater fever were common and, devoid of medical aid, the members of the survey team could only dose themselves with quinine. They had to cut their way through the forest at the rate of a mile a day—hard, monotonous work. Surveyors operated during the dry season—October to May—then returned to London to work up their material until the next season. By 1907 there were 40 Europeans and 700 Africans at work mapping the colony. This was the largest survey group in tropical Africa, and all because of the presence of gold and timber resources in the Gold Coast. According to one Uganda surveyor, his department was the worst paid and housed but the hardest worked. Surveyors were almost continuously on safari. One man spent 498 days on tour in 1904–5. And after 14 years' service, his pay had only increased from £350 to £460.

Few colonies before 1914 could afford departments capable of making full geodetic, topographical, and cadastral surveys. Plots for cities, towns, and mining and plantation concessions were laid out, and border boundaries marked, even before geodetic surveys were completed. Accurate maps were not produced until the 1920's. South Africa first began official mapping and geological work in 1895, and retained a commanding lead on the continent in this, as in almost every other technical service. The Gold Coast had survey teams from 1902 and a separate Survey Department in 1908. Between 1908 and 1914 about 10,000 square miles of the Northern Territories were mapped, and nearly 150 concessions and 10 towns were surveyed; in 1911 a topographical survey of these territories was begun. Individual experts were employed elsewhere, and additional information was supplied by the Mineral Resources Department of the Imperial Institute. Not many colonies, however, possessed the resources needed to study hydrology and water supply, and meteorological data were often recorded by the DC. Similarly, there was little money to pay specialists to collect climatic information or to study soil and animal diseases. Despite these deficiencies, colonial pioneering did assure a not inconsiderable transfer of technical skills from the metropolis to the overseas dependencies, and by 1914 all the British possessions had at least the rudiments of specialist services.[29]

The Educators

Education in Great Britain was pioneered by ecclesiastical bodies; state-run schools developed later. The British followed the same system in their African colonies, where the bulk of educational pioneering was left to the missionary societies. These varied enormously in their financial background and educational capacities, with the result that schooling developed in an extraordinarily uneven fashion. Satisfactory literacy statistics are unavailable for British colonial Africa as a whole, but it seems clear that in most areas the mere ability to read and write stamped a man as a Westernized intellectual. In the most advanced regions—say, Lagos—the literacy rate may have been comparable to that of a backward Balkan kingdom; in Serbia, for example, the literacy rate in 1900 was estimated at about 16 percent.

The unequal impact of education had unforeseen social consequences. Until about 1910 the schools of British East Africa stressed education in local languages and not in English. Ugandans were especially handicapped in getting government jobs because they knew neither English nor Swahili. St. Andrew's College at Kuingani on Zanzibar was an exception in East Africa. It opened in 1869 as a primary school for freed slaves; it was made into a training college for teachers and clerics in 1884, and was the leading school in East Africa until the 1920's. Though the first students were freed slaves, after the 1890's families of high status sent their sons to St. Andrew's, where they received a literary education in English. Many graduates became teachers or clerics, but others joined the British civil service or went into commerce. In British Central Africa the Scottish missions in Nyasaland established an early lead, and Scottish-educated teachers, clerks, and evangelists traveled far afield to take up white-collar jobs in Barotseland and even in South Africa.

The quality of missionary education in Africa as a whole initially left much to be desired. The missionaries' first task was to convert rather than to teach; the study of the scriptures took precedence over the dissemination of secular skills. Literacy, moreover, was of no immediate use to tillers and herdsmen; many farming communities objected to sending their children to Western schools, since their services would be unavailable for domestic tasks such as guarding flocks and weeding. Those Africans who did go to school usually did not remain long enough to profit from their training; only a small percentage of those who stayed advanced beyond the elementary level. The students in village schools, especially, owed their instruction to African teachers only a little more knowledgeable than their pupils; hence standards remained low. In the Gold Coast, even in 1922 only 18 percent of the candidates passed the civil service examination for African clerks, and this despite the fact that some candidates managed to steal the questions.

Where standards began to improve, the courses naturally reflected the background and interests of the European teachers and clergymen, rather than the varied cultures of their students. When European planners later attempted to introduce more practical courses, educated Africans often became suspicious that, in devising such a curriculum, the schoolmasters were attempting to keep Africans in a subordinate intellectual and social position. They resisted vocational and industrial education because they thought they would be better paid and would have greater job opportunities if they received an academic education.[30] Government and missionaries alike were reluctant to give only literary training, but both had to bow to African pressures. The colonial administrations soon found they needed literate Africans more than they needed carpenters and mechanics. Moreover, the percentage of public funds devoted to education remained small (£25,374 in the Gold Coast in 1913 out of a total budget of £1,157,091) on the grounds that funds were limited, that missionaries ought to shoulder the main burden, and that the colonies did not need a large class of semi-educated Africans dependent on state employment.

Gradually the various colonial governments realized that they would have to supplement private church enterprise, and that African education was essential to the conduct of administration. Governments started to subsidize missionary education in the 1890's, and in order to get value for their money, they appointed inspectors to enforce minimum standards. In addition, a number of government schools were opened for the purpose of filling the gaps in the missionary system. By 1914 nearly all the African colonies under the sway of the Colonial Office had their own departments of education, which normally were headed by a director, assisted by one or more inspectors of education.

The system grew in a haphazard fashion and lacked central direction. But the general structure of education in the colonies came to follow a set pattern: (1) policy was fixed by a Board of Education consisting of the governor, members of the Executive Council, and nominated members; (2) boards of education also operated on the local level and advised the general board on the problems in their own areas; (3) policy was carried out by the Department of Education; and (4) missionary schools typically continued to exist side by side with government-established schools, and received some financial assistance.

Each colony, however, ran its schools more or less as local authorities saw fit. The relative homogeneity of the British educators' background made for a certain degree of uniformity, as did the British examination system for matriculation in the universities in England. There was also a certain degree of intercolonial consultation, initiated —characteristically—by the educators themselves rather than by the British government. In 1907 a number of educational administrators attending a professional conference in London approached the British government on the possibility of holding periodic imperial education conferences. London adopted this suggestion, and in 1911 the British Board of Education convened the first such meeting. Delegates included members from both the self-governing states and the colonies; but they could only recommend and not command.

State-run education was first developed on a substantial scale in Southern Rhodesia, where the settlers were influential. In 1898 they had managed to gain representation on the country's newly established

Legislative Council. They were aware of their economic power as tax-payers, and were determined to reconstitute the social services that they had known in their countries of origin, especially Great Britain and South Africa. In 1903 a Southern Rhodesian ordinance permitted the administrator to set up European schools from public funds in places where boards of managers could be found, and white children were the initial beneficiaries. But even though the territory was soon to become economically one of the most advanced in British Africa, the educational organization at first remained elementary.

Southern Rhodesia still depended on backwoods farmers and on mining, much of it carried on in small and scattered enterprises. The country was large and thinly settled; communications in the backwoods depended on horses, mules, oxen, and wagons. Many settlers lacked money to pay school fees, and the population in the mining townships was transient. Education had to be provided for children of different linguistic backgrounds—English, Afrikaans, and Yiddish. The country's administrative structure was rudimentary; in the beginning George Duthie, the first director of education, also had to act as government statistician, registrar of births and deaths, and director of the census.

In the 10 years between 1900 and 1910 the number of European schools more than quadrupled. Equally striking was the change from state-aided to state-run schools during the period. But attendance was voluntary, and in 1911 some 36 percent of the white children between the ages of seven and fourteen were still not going to school.[31] More-over, those who did attend often fared badly. "School C. Country School, 24 present," wrote a disillusioned inspector during a tour of farm schools attended mainly by poverty-stricken white children from the backveld; "21 were in Stds. 1–5 [the first five years of elementary school]. Fourteen professed never to have heard the name of Jesus, nor could they recall to mind, even when told, any incident of His birth, life or death."[32] By 1921 some 80 percent of the white children were enrolled in the elementary schools, but compulsory education for Europeans was not introduced until 1931.

As in the other British colonies, missionaries in Southern Rhodesia continued to educate the bulk of the African schoolchildren. The territory's first education ordinance, enacted in 1899, provided for small grants to mission schools on condition that industrial training would form part of their work. In 1906 the missionary societies held their first general conference. As a result of their recommendations, a new ordinance in 1907 divided schools into three classes for the purpose of making grants according to the work accomplished. The administration at first did not exercise any legal control over "non-grant-earning schools." But soon the authorities began to worry about the creation of "independent" African schools. In 1912 the chartered company decided to restrict the propaganda of dissenting bodies with strange religious doctrines, low academic standards, and social revolutionary sentiments by insisting that new schools could be set up only with the permission of the Education Department, whose staff would inspect the schools and, if necessary, close them.*

In the country's African areas the mission teacher became an important personage in the village. He was literate; he knew some English; he was expected to be familiar with the white man's ways. He was also relatively well remunerated; in 1898, even before government subsidies had been introduced in Southern Rhodesia, the Wesleyans paid their senior African teachers up to £5 a month, a salary that put its recipients well above all but the best-paid manual laborers. Normally, however, African teachers—like most African clerks—were allotted gardens in addition to their salaries, an arrangement that left the emergent African white-collar class in the dual position of being half professionals and half peasants.

The West Coast of Africa was the main center of academic instruction, and the Sierra Leone education system the most advanced. Fourah Bay College provided higher education for the upper classes, with a curriculum devoted to theology and the arts. A director of public instruction for the colony was appointed in 1869, but when he died in 1872 no replacement was named until 1909. The colony's schools were run by a Board of Education, made up of the colony's Executive Council and four nominated members, with one inspector assigned to serve the whole of British West Africa. In 1900 a teacher-training college was founded in Sierra Leone to supply qualified teachers to mission-run schools. A school for technical education had been opened earlier, in 1896, and artisans were given free courses in the building trades. Gradually schools thus developed to meet specific needs. Since the demand for educated and skilled workers was restricted in the colonies, there was little pressure to expand the school system.

For West Africa as a whole it appears that before 1914 even the limited number of schools and training programs turned out more skilled people than could be absorbed in the various British-held territories. Even a rapidly developing colony such as the Gold Coast had to export

---

*In 1912, 1,247 African students were at first-class (superior) elementary schools, 3,319 at second-class schools, 8,125 at third-class schools, and 1,830 at schools ineligible for grants. In Northern Rhodesia the government maintained the Barotse Native School with about 200 students.

some of its skilled labor. And Sierra Leone for many years saw its educated men move out to take jobs up and down the West African coast. Nevertheless, by 1914 the more-developed colonies had at least state-aided mission schools, a government teacher-training school, and a technical school.

But colonial authorities were still in need of educated "native" auxiliaries to help them run "native administration." Hence a government school for sons of chiefs or their nominees was opened in 1906 at Bo, in the hinterland of Sierra Leone, to train Africans to become "good and useful rulers of the country." The philosophy of the new school was that labor was as important as reading, writing, and arithmetic, or what one bishop called "The Gospel of the Carpenter's Shop." Students were to be given only the basic elements of an English education, with practical training in farming, carpentry, bridge-building, road-making, and surveying. And the *Sierra Leone Royal Gazette* reported on 29 September 1905: "Under existing conditions, pupils educated in Freetown almost invariably return home with a feeling of contempt for the native towns and even for their nearest relatives. To prevent this both the native teachers and the pupils will be expected to wear country clothes and their lives outside school hours will be spent in a small town, the government of which will be on ordinary native lines."

The schoolhouse at Bo was a large bungalow in the government compound with sports fields laid around the grounds. The boys lived beyond the compound in "towns" of round huts, each with a piece of ground to cultivate. European-style dress was forbidden. In 1909 there were 80 boys studying at Bo and working on their house plot or on the school farm. The boys stayed for eight years, and strong efforts were made to keep them in touch with their people and with village ways of life in order to ensure that they returned home to the hinterland and did not seek work in town.[33] The objective of Bo thus was not to train a cadre of government clerks for Freetown, but to turn out young men who would be useful to their villages. Nevertheless, by 1922 less than one-third of the graduates took jobs in "native administration." Most of them went on to earn their living in the modern sector of the economy; some became African civil servants, doctors, engineers, and lawyers.*

---

* In 1914 Sierra Leone had 13 government schools, a technical school, and 107 primary schools, as well as a number of Muslim schools. Their total enrollment was about 10,000. (F. H. Hilliard, *A Short History of Education in British West Africa*, London, 1957.)

At the Gold Coast Western missionary education dated from 1752, when the Reverend Thomas Thompson, one of the early missionaries of the Society for the Propagation of the Gospel, arrived from America. Thompson's first convert proved a disappointment to his mentor. Having "made an extraordinary progress in the Christian knowledge," and having acquitted himself splendidly before several learned gentlemen "upon many Points of Doctrine, beside the several Articles of the Creed," the neophyte then abandoned Christianity. Thompson, however, like many of his colleagues, never lost faith in the possibility of bringing Christianity and education to Africans on the grounds that they were a "more civilized People than the Nations in general."[34]

The nineteenth century brought many more missionaries to the Gold Coast, including emissaries from Methodist mission societies and the Basel Mission, most of them Germans. Complaints became common, from both official quarters and the business community, that the missions turned out nothing but white-collar employees, though it was precisely the government and the commercial interests that first called for clerks. The Basel Mission was an exception in combining a literary education with industrial training. It educated not only teachers and clerks, but also coopers, carpenters, blacksmiths, and wheelwrights.

In assisting education, the local governments primarily were guided by utilitarian considerations. Even a broad-minded governor like Sir Hugh Clifford had serious reservations about secondary education for Africans. Primary schools would train artisans and agriculturists, the kind of men the country badly needed; secondary education, however, produced "black Englishmen," who were apt to challenge the government. But neither artisans nor agriculturalists could be educated without teachers, and their availability in turn depended on training institutions capable of providing a form of higher education. By the outbreak of World War I the Gold Coast government was operating a Training Institution for Teachers, as well as a number of trade schools, among them the industrial school at Accra, which was set up in 1909.* In addition, the Posts and Telegraph Department gave some technical instruction, as did the Public Works Department, which trained its own foremen, building inspectors, and artisans. Africans served as telephone operators, engine drivers, stationmasters, and such, with far-reaching consequences for the country's future.

Whereas the Gold Coast had a unified educational system, Nigeria

---

*In 1914 the Gold Coast had 12 government schools and 124 "inspected" schools, with a combined enrollment of 20,246. In addition, there were 252 "unassisted" schools. (*The Statesman's Yearbook, 1915.*)

operated a dual system that reflected the divided nature of British policy. In the south the government encouraged missionary work and subsidized a number of mission schools, which were supervised through a staff of six inspectors (including Henry Carr, one of the Africans mentioned earlier, who rose to prominent positions in the Lagos administration). The great majority of mission schools, however, escaped official inspection altogether, especially those in the backwoods, which were staffed by poorly qualified village teachers. The mission schools were supplemented by several government schools, including King's College (set up in Lagos in 1909), an important institution that soon developed its own "old boys' network" of ex-pupils prominent in administration and business. English was the sole means of instruction in the more advanced classes—a natural choice for schools that aimed at satisfying a widespread demand for diplomas that would provide their possessors with white-collar jobs in government offices and commercial firms.

In Northern Nigeria, meanwhile, there was a well-established system of Islamic schools, the principal center being Kano. Missionary enterprise was restricted except in purely pagan areas, but was not totally excluded; a Christian mission was successfully established at Zaria, with the local emir's consent. But missionaries met with a great many difficulties, often officially inspired. A number of British officials disliked educated black Christians as much for their plebeian background as for their egalitarian notions. The government's educational policy was influenced by the practices followed in the Sudan. It also reflected the pro-Islamic bias of Lord Lugard, whose Letters of Appointment to the emirs never failed to mention that the government would not interfere with the Muslim religion, and Lugard put a generous construction on this promise.

In Northern Nigeria, moreover, many officials feared that missionaries might provoke Islamic resistance and thereby incite a Holy War. Above all, Lugard suspected that mission schools might become hotbeds of social subversion. To quote him, education

should train a generation able to achieve ideals of its own, without a slavish imitation of Europeans, capable and willing to assume its own definite sphere of public and civic work, and to shape its own future. The education afforded to that section of the population who intend to lead the lives which their forefathers led should enlarge their outlook, increase their efficiency and standard of comfort, and bring them into closer sympathy with the Government, instead of making them unsuited to, and ill-contented with their mode of life. It should produce a new generation of native chiefs of higher integrity, a truer sense of justice, and appreciation of responsibility for the welfare of the community. As regards that smaller section who desire to take part in public or municipal duties, or to enter the service of Government, or of commercial firms, education should make them efficient, loyal, reliable and contented—a race of self-respecting native gentlemen.[35]

As Lugard saw it, the mission schools were not doing their job. He felt that their graduates were apt to be unreliable, devoid of integrity, self-control, discipline, and respect for authority of any kind. At school they learned a deep-seated contempt for their elders and a constitutional unwillingness to work on the land. Cecil Rhodes put Lugard's point more bluntly; mission schools, he said, "produced nothing but 'Kafir parsons and editors.'" The remedy, however, was close at hand. Education should be remodeled on the principle of British boarding schools, where boys would be trained in character, play games, and learn how to exercise authority as school prefects. Religious teaching should be elevated in dignity by becoming a recognized examination subject so as to admit of government inspection. Lugard foresaw no trouble in reaching an agreed-on nondenominational system, noting that no less an authority than a British chief rabbi had avowed that the Anglican primate, the Catholic cardinal, and he himself could almost certainly arrive at some mutually acceptable system of religious instruction.

The Nigerian government therefore established some schools of its own, though their total impact at first remained small.* The government employees who ran or supervised them were a mixed lot. The education departments attracted a substantial number of men drawn from the same group of Public School and university graduates as the district officers, though a higher percentage appear to have been Scotsmen. Generalizations, however, are hard to make. The group included missionaries and teachers turned administrators; and also men with considerable administrative experience, like Herbert Irvine Wimberley, who had left his post as headmaster of Northampton Grammar School to become inspector of schools in Lagos in 1903. He retired in 1913 after three years as provincial inspector of schools in the Central Province.

---

*By 1914 the Northern Province had eight government schools, including one technical school, and 45 unassisted private schools. Total attendance figures were 485 and 1,079, respectively. In addition, some 200,000 students were said to attend Muslim schools, where they studied traditional learning. In the Southern Province there were 54 government schools with 5,757 students, 85 assisted schools, with 15,200 students, and some 700 private schools with 43,800 students. (*The Statesman's Yearbook, 1915*.)

Perhaps one of the most unusual educators was Hanns Vischer, a native of Basel who was educated in Switzerland and Germany. Later he attended Emmanuel College, Cambridge, and then served for a year in Northern Nigeria with the Church Missionary Society. In 1900 Vischer, then twenty-four years old, joined the Northern Nigerian administration and quickly advanced up the ladder to become resident. He also made a name for himself as a traveler by crossing the Sahara from Tripoli to Lake Chad and recounting his adventures in a book.[36] In 1909 he became director of education in Northern Nigeria, a post he retained until World War I, when he was seconded to the War Office. Affectionately called *"dan Hausa"* (brother of the Hausa), Vischer laid the foundation of education in Northern Nigeria during his five years as director of education. He did not want an educational system based on the English language, but one aimed at preserving the "racial feeling" of the students and at maintaining their contact with their parents and surroundings. Vischer's praise was reserved for men like Sir James Currie, director of education in the Sudan, who battled against missionary penetration and the disruptive effects of "pseudo-religious" ideas. Vischer was convinced that Africans should first of all acquire agricultural skills in tune with the daily life of the common people. Teachers should develop the "national and racial characteristics" of the youngsters under their charge; they should broaden the children's horizon without destroying their respect for their heritage. Vischer's principles had a profound effect on British educational policy in Africa. Yet they were full of contradictions. Ironically, Lugard, the proponent of indirect rule, fought with him, and came to favor a more liberal, Western-oriented system of education in English. Lugard lamented, in 1918, that out of a population of 9,000,000, Northern Nigeria could not supply a single clerk or artisan for government service from the local people.[37] After the end of hostilities Vischer represented the Colonial Office on a variety of important commissions concerned with education, such as the Phelps-Stokes Commission in East Africa. He also served for 16 years as secretary and member of the Colonial Office's Education Advisory Commission, and was a member of the International African Institute. In 1941, four years before his death, he was awarded a knighthood, a rare honor for anyone not born a British subject.

What did the work of these men amount to in the end? In purely numerical terms, not much. By 1914 educated Africans formed but a small proportion of the total population within their respective countries. In administrative and economic terms, however, their importance was already considerable. Except in British East Africa, British rule could not have functioned without African clerks, African teachers, African evangelists, African detectives, African police sergeants, African court interpreters, and African postmasters. Socially, their impact came to be immense. The British created a kind of social no-man's-land for literate blacks. To quote an elderly chief from Sierra Leone, writing in about 1961:

Forty years ago educated natives were between the Devil and the Deep [Sea] in the country. We were not liked by political officers nor trusted by our own people. Not liked by the officers, as they thought we were enlightening our people as to their rights and instead of co-operating with us for the welfare of our people and the smooth working of Government, they did not want us in the country, nor trusted by our own kin, they thinking that we have hands on all the woes and miseries brought on them, as being educated, we are hand in glove with them in all their doings.[38]

But it was these alienated men who allowed the new order to work, and who finally took over from their erstwhile mentors.

TEN

Conclusion

Four great notions dominated European thought in the nineteenth century—religion, race, class, and nationality. Of these sentiments, the strongest by far was nationality; even considerations of class and race were swept away in the mood of national enthusiasm that accompanied the outbreak of World War I. And British national feelings were among the strongest in all of Europe. The British, in their own estimation, had created the world's most successful society, prosperous by comparison with most of their neighbors, law-abiding and stable, secure from foreign invasion, safe from revolutionary subversion. Its people were wedded to the ideal of constitutional government and the rule of law, and united by a common code based on duty and self-restraint, a code shared by trade union leaders as much as by employers, by Christian believers as well as by atheists. Businessmen held the power of the purse. But theirs was not strictly a business mentality. British monied men valued money not merely as an end in itself, but as a means of social advancement into the landed gentry and the professions, social groups wedded in theory—and to a considerable extent in practice—to a common notion of good works, social responsibility, and patrician manners. Upper-class foreigners, to a great degree, accepted the British evaluation of themselves. Whereas the continental lower-middle classes tended to admire Germany, men of the world tended to be anglophile.

These values were reflected in British attitudes toward the Africans. Conquerors throughout history have been apt to despise the peoples whom they subdued, especially when the vanquished were poorly endowed with material goods. What requires explanation is not the sense of superiority that British soldiers and administrators felt toward their black subjects—mostly Early Iron Age warriors and cultivators wielding but the simplest tools. What requires explanation is rather the set of restraints that operated on the British, limiting that unbounded disdain that the Tutsi, Ngoni, or Masai had felt toward the peoples whom they despoiled.

The most powerful restraint was the notion of social class and of class responsibility. The British middle and upper-middle classes—the point bears repeating—were endowed for the most part with a strong sense of *bourgeoisie oblige*. Mistakenly or not, the bulk of British administrators were convinced that colonialism was an instrument of social reform. The heathen in the African bush should be uplifted, just like the poor in the British slums. Peace and good government, exercised according to the principles of "natural law and morality" (a favorite phrase in British proclamations), would extend the realm of human happiness—and so it did. The British workers, to the degree that they came into contact with Africans, were on the whole the most unabashed of overlords, and little troubled by trusteeship notions.[1]

The most militant "negrophilists" were groups like the Universities' Mission to Central Africa, which derived its main support from Oxford and Cambridge. Its membership was aristocratic in background and High Church in religious orientation. UMCA missionaries received no salary; they did not marry; they lived in a state of voluntary poverty, on a level with the African villagers they meant to convert. Many British administrators admired their sacrificing spirit, but most thought little of their work. To Sir Harry Johnston, for example, there was an almost caste-demeaning quality about these men who lived in African huts and subsisted on African food; they were the grown-up equivalents of "swots" (grinds) in Public Schools, gentlemen who took their religion to ungentlemanly lengths.

The ordinary British district officer preferred to think of himself as a kind of adult prefect, dedicated to an ethos of service for the betterment of his inferiors. Africans were like children—they must be raised slowly in the scale of civilization. Colonial officials should simply ensure that the natural evolution of Africans would take place without undue interference. This notion was usually coupled with a historical belief that late-nineteenth-century Africans were in a stage of development on a par with the ancient Saxons and Celts or, at best, with medieval Englishmen. Much damage would result if change were hurried beyond its natural pace. These trusteeship notions went widely with a firmly held belief that Africans should be protected against low-class Europeans, farmers, traders, mechanics, and entrepreneurs, men whose living depended on their ability to profit from selling their goods or their labor power, "economic men" whose ambitions frequently aroused the spurious disdain so often felt by the safely tenured for all those engaged in a competitive struggle for economic survival.

Class notions perhaps more than racial prejudice pure and simple determined the average British official's dislike for the "educated native." The "mission boy," supposedly boastful, obnoxious, and bent on success at any cost, was in some ways the African equivalent of the self-made man, proud of his sudden social advancement and impatient of restraint. The philosophy of the nineteenth century was replete with barroom aphorisms warning against the untrustworthiness of Sikhs who could speak French without the trace of an accent. In 1909 an official committee of inquiry into the liquor trade in Southern Nigeria found that habitual drinking went on among Christianized chiefs who had learned "the bad habits of the lower class of Europeans" in mission schools. Lugard went even further and posited that Europeanized Africans were "less fertile [and] more susceptible to lung trouble and other diseases"—a piece of nonsense that Lugard's medical officers could have easily dispelled.[2]

Official attitudes were far from static. The pioneers who conquered, say, the warlike Ngoni of what is now northeastern Zambia held ideas very different from those of their successors a generation later, men concerned with the more humdrum problems of managing an established colonial state. Nevertheless, certain stereotypes persisted. They were of a romantic kind. They assumed that the African was a cheerful, childlike warrior, the very opposite of the calculating Western businessman imbued with the notion of thrift and hard work, or as we would now call it, the Protestant ethic. These stereotypes may be summed up in Lugard's words in his classic exposition of indirect rule, published shortly after the end of World War I:

The typical African . . . is a happy, thriftless, excitable person, lacking in self-control, discipline, and foresight, naturally courageous and naturally courteous and polite, full of personal vanity, with little sense of veracity, fond of music, and "loving weapons as an oriental loves jewelry." His thoughts are concentrated on the events and feelings of the moment, and he suffers little from apprehension for the future. . . . The religious sense seldom rises above pantheistic animism. . . . The negro is not naturally cruel, though his own sensibility to pain and his disregard for life—whether his own or another's—cause him to appear callous to suffering. . . . He lacks the power of organisation, and is conspicuously deficient in the management and control alike of men or of business. He is an apt pupil, and a faithful and devoted friend.[3]

These ideas bore little relation to reality. They took no account, for instance, of the propensity for planning and saving demonstrated by

Hausa businessmen or Ashanti cocoa growers. (Later these stereotypes were oddly fused into the equally romantic generalizations produced by the enthusiasts of negritude in the post-colonial era.) Yet, given the context of colonial governance, this interpretation also had certain merits. It was surely better that British administrators should regard Africans as children to be educated than as raw manpower to be exploited. The "childhood" interpretation, moreover, allowed British officials to make a graceful exit during the era of "national liberation," when the children supposedly turned first into rebellious adolescents and finally into adults to be freed from their former tutelage. Trusteeship notions, however, were also interlinked with racial stereotypes. Their impact was probably less than has been assumed by post-colonial scholars, writing in an age in which racism is regarded in the same light as their ancestors regarded sin—as the most fundamental expression of human iniquity. The intellectual history of racism and its links to biological materialism and Social Darwinism have been much examined.

We shall confine ourselves to saying that nineteenth-century racism as a pseudo-scientific ideology derived from the European intelligentsia, with journalists, university lecturers, and metropolitan litterateurs as its foremost spokesmen. Racism went in hand with nationalism. The "higher" races arrogated to themselves a kind of aristocratic status in the world, but all members of the race supposedly shared in its virtues by reason of their common descent, rather than by individual merit or distinguished lineage. Racial interpretations colored national hostilities of all kinds, especially those between European races that could hardly be differentiated on physical grounds. Thomas Carlyle and James Froude believed that Irishmen lived in a stage of higher apedom. Serb nationalists of the period found the heredity of the Bulgarians equally suspect.[4]

Racial categories came to be widely applied in Africa, modified by considerations of class. The "Hamitic" races, aristocratic and aloof, were held superior to the Bantu-speaking peoples, who were likened to British workers, capable of hard labor under supervision, but not very bright. Bantu-speaking Africans in turn were supposedly on a higher level than Bushman and Pygmie hunters, among the most primitive groups in Africa, a kind of unemployable subproletariat, according to the standard notions of the time. The literature concerning these racial attitudes fills many library shelves. The impact of racist thinking as such, however, can easily be exaggerated. European behavior was affected more by situational needs than by racial theories. British foremen in the Rhodesian mines were more "reactionary" than clergymen, not because they were necessarily less enlightened, but because mining required a harsh discipline where the slightest breach might occasion disaster. British farmers took a harder line toward their African laborers than British officials, because the farmer's very livelihood depended on his ability to make the "boys" do their daily stint. British administrators took a less benign view of Africans than the more progressive kind of missionary, because the official's first duty was to rule, not to teach and preach. And however prejudiced a colonial might be, he always had his exceptions that proved the rule—the manservant or "boss boy" whom he enthusiastically extolled as a very pearl among Africans. Administrators in turn discovered unsuspected virtues in the African institutions that they tried to adapt to the purposes of British governance, so much so that some old-time administrators could even find all the virtues of their own government, complete with Crown, Lords, and Commons, in the Lozi royal government. Circumstances in fact helped to shape ideology. And circumstances in turn came to alter the misshapen orthodoxies concerning race.

The British Impact: A Summing Up

What, then, did the efforts of British administrators amount to in the end? The British came as colonizers; indeed, they prided themselves on that role. As a result, the impact of the British as soldiers and administrators cannot be disentangled from the wider record of colonialism. Therefore, at the risk of repeating material we have already discussed in other published works, we cannot avoid the wider task of drawing up a balance sheet of empire. This is not an easy task. Few words arouse as much hostility in the modern world as the word colonialism. Colonialism—the argument goes—accounts for much of the wealth accumulated by the rich nations of the world at the expense of the poor. Colonialism, moreover, must bear the blame not merely for the poverty, but also for the stagnation of the so-called underdeveloped world. According to Kwame Nkrumah, once one of Africa's most influential statesmen, the colonial powers left to the Africans nothing but their resentment, and it was only after the alien conquerors had gone that the Africans were sharply brought face to face with the destitution of their land. Nkrumah's views run essentially parallel with those of the modern Marxists, who have abandoned the view held by Marx himself that the conquering British bourgeoisie— for all their failings—had played a progressive role on the Indian subcontinent. Nkrumah's interpretation, of course, bitterly clashes with the philosophy of an old-style imperial administrator such as Johnston,

who took as his starting point the assumption that most truly construc-
tive endeavors in Africa had come from the foreign invaders, especially
the sword-bearers of late-Victorian imperialism. But neither Nkrumah
nor Johnston doubted that the European colonizer had taken a vital
part in the history of Africa, be he devil or demiurge.[5]

This view, however, has now come increasingly under challenge.
For the historian J. F. A. Ajayi, the colonial epoch was nothing more
than a brief interlude in the broad sweep of African history. For a
fleeting moment the conquerors held the reins of power, but the impact of their rule was uneven; their style of governance was shaped
to a considerable extent by African initiatives; hence the colonial epoch
was no more than an episode in the annals of Africa.[6] Ajayi's interpretation has considerable merit. When the Union Jack was pulled
down during the 1960's, imperial governance in most parts of the
continent had only been exercised for a brief span, usually no longer
than the lifetime of an octogenarian grandmother. The vast majority
of Africans continued to live on the land as they had always done; most
cultivators made their living by means of a few simple tools. Men
continued to rely on their kinsmen and neighbors to a much greater
extent than their contemporaries in Europe and America; they continued to honor their customs; they continued to speak their languages;
they thought of themselves as Bemba, Lozi, or Kikuyu, and certainly
not as black-skinned Britons.

What was true of Africa during the 1960's applied with even greater
force to Africa in 1914. Vast areas then remained little touched by
European rule; the penetration of Western enterprises into the continent was, for the most part, only beginning. Large parts of African
territory were just starting to pass from the Early Iron Age to the age
of steampower, from the age of the Homeric warrior to the age of the
twentieth-century bureaucrat. The British had made little more than a
beginning in spreading their language, their notions concerning government, and their religion in Africa. Africans quickly grasped the advantages of the white men's technology. Yet the moral impact of British conquest remained surprisingly small. Africans retained their own
languages and traditions. Even conquered people like the Shona-
speaking communities of southern Rhodesia remained convinced that
their ways, their ethics, their family system were superior to those
of the Europeans. Felicity in Shona life was still bound to the possession of many children. In a society where life was precarious and manpower always in short supply, the childless earned pity, and the man
with numerous offspring merited respect. Children were essential to

defend their parents, to help them at work, to look after them in old age, to honor their spirits when they died. The highest personal quality in Shona life remained *unhu*—the possession of a fine personality, measured, balanced, reasonable, judicious, in harmony with one's self, one's kinsmen, and one's community.

Yet there was change—change of a far-reaching kind, change on a scale never previously experienced in Africa in so short a space of time. The 30 years or so that preceded the outbreak of World War I saw a considerable increase in production in sub-Saharan Africa; trade expanded in a phenomenal fashion; new goods made their appearance, ranging from steam engines to wheelbarrows, sewing machines, plows, and bicycles. A host of new professions and new skills came into being. Sub-Saharan Africa's existing links to the world economy were broadened. The conquerors, moreover, set up a vast range of new institutions, political, administrative, ecclesiastical, and economic. Many different social groups—civil servants, engineers, merchants, missionaries, technicians, teachers—contributed in bringing about this transformation. It is almost impossible to single out one particular stratum, such as the "officials," in delineating the social revolution brought about by colonialism. There was a good deal of interaction between the various white groups: the activities of merchants influenced those of political officers; political officers in turn played an important part in economic affairs. Nevertheless, the officials stand out as an easily identifiable group, performing certain functions on their own. On these we propose to concentrate.

The Conquering State

The European monarchies of the seventeenth and eighteenth centuries laid the foundations of the modern state. They unified dispersed territories under a single, centralized administration; they created new boundaries; they exercised their power through a salaried army and a salaried civil service, with a royal court at the center. The colonizers in African performed a function not wholly dissimilar. The modern states of sub-Saharan Africa are all of imperial provenance except Ethiopia, an ancient Afro-feudal monarchy, and Liberia, a product of the Americans' humanitarian frontier. Precolonial Africa had been divided into a large number of polities, ranging from large kingdoms to small neighborhood groups without formal political cohesion. The British unified extensive regions into larger territorial units, all of them much bigger than anything that British rule had superseded. A territory like Northern Rhodesia came to include the lands of such erstwhile conquerors as the Lozi, the Bemba, and the Ngoni, as well as smaller groups like the Lamba and the Tonga, who previously had been victimized by their more powerful neighbors. The boundaries drawn across the map of Africa by the European conquerors have survived; they have been recognized by the colonizers' successors. These may be the most important heritage of European rule.

The new state depended on the conquerors' ideological dominance and technical superiority, and on the efficacy of their military and administrative machine. The new state also depended on a wide measure of coercion. Imperial governance, of course, involved armed conquest. It entailed the putting down of resistance, conspiracies, and rebellions. There was also economic coercion. The most straightforward form of exploitation involved the direct appropriation of movable wealth like cattle, a method that had been customary among indigenous warrior groups like the Ndebele, the Ngoni, and the Masai. White pioneers in Rhodesia also looted Ndebele herds after they had overthrown Lobengula's kingdom in 1893. But plunder for its own sake was comparatively rare. The conquering British found few currency hoards to loot in Africa, no merchant ships to seize, no industrial machinery to dismantle. The African precolonial economies rarely produced a surplus that would have made a warfare a paying proposition from the white man's standpoint.

Economic coercion was applied also through the appropriation of land in Southern Rhodesia, in parts of Nyasaland and Northeastern Rhodesia, and in Kenya. Pressure on the land, however, was confined to a few areas climatically suited to European settlement. In relation to the African land surface as a whole, white-occupied areas did not amount to much; in East Africa, for example, the amount of alienated land in 1914 was 338,033 acres. The impact of white settlement, moreover, was double-edged in that the European presence in itself came to stimulate African cash farming, especially in the Rhodesias.

European colonization entailed forced labor, both open and disguised. In the early phase of conquest, white caravan leaders often conscripted African porters and requisitioned African food supplies, both with disastrous effects to a backward village economy. Later on, DCs were enjoined—often much to their own distress—to produce labor for railway construction work and farms, a practice that was gradually being abandoned before World War I, when large numbers of workers were pressed into service, and then finally faded out in the decades following the war. In addition, the government itself conscripted workers for the construction of roads and other public works.

This form of economic compulsion only ceased when the railway and the truck largely eliminated the need for carriers, and when heavy earth-moving equipment did away with the need for large labor gangs.

Above all, the new state was peaceful and lawful. The new rulers were not torn by civil dissensions. There were no wars over inheritance and color, no civil wars, and no shifting fortunes under successive strong men. Individual DCs were moved around, to be sure, but as a group the new lords—unlike Ndebele or Zulu raiders—never departed. In place of tribal levies, they had at their command a salaried standing army. They relied on a permanent establishment of salaried civil servants. In lieu of tribute in kind, they imposed fixed taxes payable in cash. They stood for a wage economy in place of one based on kinship ties or slavery. They thought in terms of a hierarchical executive order, descending from the governor to the assistant DC. They governed through formal legislative instruments, Acts of Parliament, Orders in Council, and local ordinances, arranged in a sequential order, predicated on exact divisions of governmental functions and the rule of law, applicable to all and sundry of their subjects, Ndebele and Shona, Ngoni and Chewa—the erstwhile rulers and the erstwhile subjects—with supposedly predictable effects. According to Donald A. Low, imperial authority depended on:

(1) the gathering in of the threads of legitimacy where these existed; (2) the support for it of traditionally legitimate, if newly established, indigenous political authorities; (3) force, and a monopoly of coercive powers; (4) the establishment of a *Pax*, and the establishment of a new order offering a larger-scale existence; (5) (very often) upon the slow extension and remoteness of imperial authority, which prevented the colonial people from understanding what was happening until it was too late; (6) the vested interest that a number, sometimes a very large number, of local peoples had, for one reason or another, in the maintenance of the imperial regime; (7) the considerable strength and effectiveness of the imperial bureaucracy; and (8) the charismatic qualities which, at all events in the early years, imperial rulers possessed for many colonial peoples.[7]

The conquerors' belief that power was held in trust for the conquered—though widely disregarded in practice—was a revolutionary concept, one entirely incomprehensible to the old-time Ngoni, Masai, or Swahili warrior. So was the notion of a written constitution (enacted in British territories through published "Instructions to the Governor" and relevant Orders in Council). The assumption that the state should promote development was a Western importation, as was the belief that the state should provide social services—education, schools, agricultural instruction, meteorological observations, and such. The very notion of the state as a territorial entity independent of ethnic or kinship ties, operating through impersonal rules, was one of the most revolutionary concepts bequeathed by colonialism to post-colonial Africa republics. All of these base their territorial legitimacy on the colonial precedent. None of them have attempted to restore monarchies like Bornu or Barotseland. All of them have taken over, in some form or other, both the boundaries and the administrative institutions of their erstwhile Western overlords.

The creation of these new territorial entities was a matter of great moment. It helped to bring about one of the most radical social changes in Africa. The destruction or subordination of states like Ashanti or Buganda created markets of unprecedented size. Internal tolls disappeared. So did other restraints on trade, such as royal monopolies of ivory or the royal right of preemption that had given special advantages to kings over commoners in the marketplace. There was an end to sumptuary laws that prevented men of low degree from acquiring prestigious luxury goods. The British were equally determined to do away with all local forms of servitude that interfered with the working of a wage economy. Moreover, they clearly realized that neither white, brown, nor black merchants could prosper while potential customers were being murdered or abducted by warrior bands. Railway builders, miners, and plantation owners could not invest capital or recruit hired hands as long as able-bodied Africans were abducted to provide Zanzibari lords with plantation hands or Ngoni chiefs with military recruits. A wage-earning economy and a slave-raiding economy could no more exist side by side than a wage-earning economy and a warrior economy. The modern state—hierarchically organized, enjoying a monopoly of armed force, capable of legislating on a vast array of subjects, willing to enforce its rule throughout the area under its sovereignty, and capable of "remembering" its administrative decisions through the preservation of written files—had come to Africa.

The new state was permanent; to Africans it seemed to go on forever. The age of great tribal migration came to an end. *Völkerwanderungen* on the part of great armed hosts became a matter of history. The British had put an end to the age of precolonial slave-trading, raids, and conquests. In the Rhodesias, for instance, the British outtrekked the Boer *voortrekkers*. Afrikaners continued to make their way inland from the Transvaal; some of their great oxwagons even managed to cross the Zambezi. But the Afrikaners could no longer hope to establish political control over the region between the Limpopo and the Zambezi, most of which would almost certainly have fallen under their sway had it not been for Rhodes's intervention. British colonization likewise put an end to Islamic expansion in many parts of Africa—in the Sudan, in Nigeria, in southeast Africa. Swahili-speaking traders and freebooters, for instance, could no longer move into present-day Malawi and northeastern Zambia. The southernmost frontier of Islam was first brought to a halt and then rolled back.

The British occupation also prevented the growth of what might be called "bush feudalism" among some of the stateless peoples of Africa. Tough adventurers armed with rifles and followed by their own retainers could easily have set up independent lordships in, say, parts of Zambia. These local suzerainties established by alien invaders had depended on trade in ivory and slaves, on traffic with neighboring chiefs, and on the exaction of tribute. Their lords had spoken Portuguese, Swahili, or even English—like Changa Changa, a British frontiersman who carved out a short-lived principality in a remote area of eastern Zambia, where he levied his own taxes. But the "Arabs" and the Mambari (Portuguese-speaking Africans engaged in the exchange of slaves and elephant tusks) were driven out. Changa Changa experienced in his own person the transition from bush feudalism to capitalism; he ended his working days as a personnel manager for a Northern Rhodesian mine, and to this day his title denotes a gang boss.

The British, like the other colonial powers, tried to tighten their hold by controlling the distribution of firearms to Africans. This did not mean, of course, that the Africans were left without any guns at all. But the British controlled the ports, and they gradually began to control the frontiers as well. Merchants were no longer able to sell European surplus military equipment to African potentates. Firearms lost their former military significance for the African armies as new weapons became difficult to acquire. Guns had to be licensed, and the weapons remaining in private African hands were no match for modern magazine rifles. In many parts of Africa guns still maintained some value, but not so much for military as for social purposes. Sometimes they were treasured for ceremonial purposes or as a pledge for loans; more often—and more practically—they were useful for frightening off baboons and other pests. But they gradually ceased to play much of a part in intertribal or private conflicts, which came to be settled increasingly in the courts of the administration.

The Leveling State

The British usually came as conquerors, and the effect of conquest was often catastrophic. Military expeditions might burn a village in revenge for some real or imagined injury, seize cattle and crops, and abuse the women. But afflictions of this sort were familiar to African communities. Worse were the long-range effects of occupation. Once the new rulers established their authority, they conscripted labor for porterage or to construct roads, or at least enforced taxes. Migrant laborers in search of employment sometimes had to travel over long distances in discomfort or danger. Having obtained a job in a mine or on a railway construction project, they were exposed to new diseases, especially lung infections. But most devastating of all was the sense of disruption, brilliantly mirrored in Chinua Achebe's novel, *Things Fall Apart*.

The traditional religion, the old faith weakened, as missionaries were apparently able to resist with impunity the magic terrors of the haunted forest. The old distinctions between men of differing degree became less important as the white strangers admitted outcasts to their church on the same terms as men of honor. The old loyalties failed as men of renown were humiliated. The DC set up his court, where he judged cases in ignorance. He employed court messengers, strangers to the land, arrogant and high-handed. Prison guards oppressed the captives who had broken the white men's incomprehensible laws. Some of these prisoners had been put in jail for casting off newly born twins as harbingers of evil; others had harassed those of their fellows who had become Christians. But whatever their offense, they were beaten in jail and made to work for the whites. Among the prisoners were titled men who should never have had such disgraceful treatment. They grieved over their indignity and mourned over their neglected farms. But the most terrible suffering came from a pervasive sense of impotence.

"What is it that has happened to our people?" [asks Okonkwo, the hero of Achebe's novel, who later kills himself]. "Why have we lost the power to fight?"

"Have you not heard how the white man wiped out Abame?" asked Obierika.

"I have heard," said Okonkwo. "But I have also heard that Abame people were weak and foolish. Why did they not fight back? Had they no guns and hatchets? We would be cowards to compare ourselves with the men of Abame. Their fathers had never dared to stand before our ancestors. We must fight these men and drive them from the land."

"It is already too late," said Obierika sadly. "Our own men and our sons
have joined the ranks of the stranger. They have joined his religion and they
help to uphold his government. If we should try to drive out the white men
in Umuofia we should find it easy. There are only two of them. But what
of our own people who are following their way and have been given power?
They would go to Umuru and bring the soldiers, and we would be like
Abame."[8]

Some Africans indeed must have been seized by a sense that the very
universe was falling apart, that the Ancient of Days himself was failing.
As an aged Ila chief put it shortly after World War I: "To-day Leza
[God] has turned over and abandoned his old ways. To-day he is not
the same, he is altogether different, for he is not as he was in the
distant years before the white chiefs came. At that time he was truly
the Watergiver and all things were still sufficient on earth. . . . To-day
we say: Leza has grown old. . . . There is no flood to-day—no great
giver of floods."[9]

On the other hand, pacification also created many new opportunities. Some Africans found the new learning dispensed by the missionaries exhilarating, to judge from the extraordinary eagerness shown
for it by a growing minority. Literacy gave men access to the written
word, above all to the Bible, for many Africans the greatest—and
often the only—written literature to which they were exposed. The
art of reading and writing enabled its possessors to communicate with
friends and relatives over great distances. As time went on, literate
men were able to understand the workings of white government by
perusing the great mass of published reports issued by commissions
of inquiry into all manner of abuses, the legislative council debates,
and the published departmental reports, all of which became public
property under the British dispensation.

Once British rule was firmly implanted, there was, moreover, an
end to armed conflicts between one African community and another.
Slave-raiding gradually ceased; travel became easier. Typical of the
olden days in a war-torn land was the life story of Meli, a young girl
born in the frontier region that separated the Mambwe people from
the warlike Bemba in Northeastern Rhodesia. Meli's father, a headman, had earned the displeasure of a senior Bemba chief, prompting
the Bemba to dispatch a punitive expedition. In the raid Meli—then
aged about five—was captured, together with several Mambwe wom-
en, who were distributed to Bemba households. Meli's guardians
treated her reasonably well but soon sold her for four pieces of ivory.
She then received a Swahili name, had her nose pierced in the Swahili

TABLE 29
Population of the Principal British African Colonies Under
Colonial Office Governance, 1914

	Area	Estimated population	
Territory	(square miles)	1914	1963
East and Central Africa			
British East Africa Protectorate	224,960	4,000,000	8,636,000
Uganda	117,681	2,900,000	7,190,000
Nyasaland	39,801	1,000,000	2,900,000[a]
Southern Africa			
Northern Rhodesia	291,000	1,000,000	3,470,000
Southern Rhodesia	148,575	800,000	4,140,000
West Africa			
Nigeria	335,700	16,260,000	55,654,000
Gold Coast	24,200	900,000	6,726,000[b]
Sierra Leone	32,110	1,400,000	2,183,000
Gambia	4,003	152,000	315,000

SOURCE: *Statesman's Yearbook* for 1914 and 1963.
a 1961 figure.   b 1960 figure.

fashion, and learned Swahili ways. But she was a sickly child, a bad
investment, and was successively sold to other masters. Finally she
joined a trading caravan that was intercepted by white officials, who
liberated the slaves and repatriated those who knew their home village. Meli, now orphaned, went to live at a mission station, where she
was baptized and ultimately married to a young Mambwe carpenter
employed by the missionaries.[10] Under the new dispensation, men
and women ceased to be treated as salable objects, though domestic
slavery continued for some time.

Conquest benefited the conquered in other ways. The invaders introduced new notions of medicine and hygiene, and a new technology
that vastly improved health conditions. Colonial population statistics
are hard to come by for some areas and in general rather unreliable.
But from the turn of the century, or at least from the end of World
War I, the population of British Africa as a whole appears to have
experienced a steady increase. In all probability, its numbers came to
double every generation. (See Table 29.) In any event, survival ceased
to depend on prowess in war; the weaker communities had at last
found physical safety.

In some areas the colonial impact put an end to traditional "agro-
towns," such as the Lunda capital in Northern Rhodesia. But it created
many other towns in their stead. The new cities throughout Africa
owed their existence to European initiative; they were designed to

function as administrative centers or centers of capitalist production. They were sited according to considerations that would not have concerned an agricultural community of the traditional kind—considerations such as proximity to a railway line or to great mineral deposits.

In parts of Africa the white man's peace enabled villagers to spread out and use greater chunks of the land. Tillers could move farther afield without having to worry about the problem of defense. Discontented groups could break away from unpopular chiefs or from overly large parent villages without having to face the threat of armed punishment. British administrators in Rhodesia in fact wrote lengthy reports deploring the process because it rendered the tax collector's task harder, but they were unable to stop it.

The conquering state and the leveling state were also a tax collector's state. Tributes and labor services, tolls and presents of a more or less compulsory kind were of course nothing new to Africa. Rulers of great kingdoms such as the emirates or the Lozi and Bemba monarchies had elaborate devices for skimming their subjects' surpluses to the benefit of their own power and prestige. Control of the state machinery was a matter of both pride and profit; hence death struggles could arise between competing groups of aspirants for office. The new rulers, however, were different; they ended succession struggles. Sooner or later they called for taxes in cash rather than in kind. The switch-over appeared as arbitrary to the governed as it seemed rational to the governors. The feelings of the ordinary African toward the new policy were probably best expressed by a Nyika historian—who recorded the annals of his community in Rhodesia with some embellishments:

The Europeans reached this country in 1897 and after having been in this country for three years, they gathered all the chiefs in the country and said to them "Pay tax."

The chiefs said "What are we to give you as tax?" The Europeans said to them "Everything you own." The chiefs said "What do we own?" The Europeans said "Crops." So the chiefs and their subjects began paying tax with mealie meal.

The second year the Europeans said "We do not want mealie meal for taxation, we want fowls." And they were given. The third year the Europeans said "We want to substitute [goats and cattle for fowls] for taxation."

The chiefs and their subjects were very unwilling to give out their cattle for taxation and gave them goats only. The fourth year they asked for ten shillings instead of goats and it was so. All this was happening while the Englishmen were at Old Umtali in 1897 and the Africans were suffering much because of taxation.[11]

Taxation in other words began as tribute in kind, of a type not very different from the sort of impost that the African overlords had imposed on their subjects. But with a money tax an African could meet his obligations only by entering the money economy, either by working for the whites or by selling goods for coin; the need to earn cash became a steady and predictable feature of life, not an occasional problem that a man might face once or twice in the course of his career in order to get a pot, a knife, or a gun.

Imposts payable in cash depended on a system of wage labor and a market economy. Both were incompatible with personal servitude of any kind. Having conquered their colonies, the British had liquidated the slave trade where they found it. They also abolished hereditary dependency of the indigenous kind. In doing so, the colonizers acted from motives both of humanity and of self-interest. They considered themselves harbingers of liberty, and there is good evidence that they were thus regarded by a variety of servile groups. In Barotseland, for instance, the British found that they could not get the serfs to work for cash if their earnings were subject to confiscation by the ruling Lozi aristocracy; and if they were allowed to keep their wages, they could not at the same time perform traditional corvées and work in white employment. In 1906 the Lozi king, under considerable pressure from the British, allowed the serfs in his country to purchase their freedom. The abolition of serfdom provided workmen with a choice, however limited, of employers. As Lugard had argued with respect to Northern Nigeria, the system of free labor taught men to value freedom for the ability to earn wages and to buy what they liked.[12]

The tax collector was, in a sense, a great leveler, unconcerned with the social distinctions of the precolonial era, indifferent to the tax defaulter's clan affiliations or ethnic origins. British judges acted as equalizers in another fashion. They introduced a host of new offenses, applicable to all and sundry but unknown to precolonial societies, such as breaches of the trespassing laws or of the regulations for the protection of forests and the eradication of the tsetse fly. The British outlawed judicial methods once held to be efficacious—the poison ordeal and the water ordeal. They outlawed deeds once considered praiseworthy—human sacrifice to propitiate supernatural powers (practiced by some West African peoples) and the strangling of sick chiefs. In their punishments, the courts took no notice of whether an offender had been a Ndebele lord or a lowly retainer within the former tribal hierarchy. At the same time, the British refused to punish a great number of actions formerly considered crimes. Adulterous wives had nothing to fear from British courts. Neither had reputed witches. Indeed, the British penalized Africans who accused their neighbors of black magic, a legal innovation deeply resented by witch-finders but greatly welcomed by supposed witches. Not surprisingly, many Africans concluded that the invaders must be friendly to witches, and so caused their numbers to increase.

The British also put an end to certain kinds of bondage that existed among stateless people like the Ila, who dwelt in what is now central Zambia. In precolonial days these men and women were apt to lose their freedom by being kidnapped, convicted for crimes, sold in payment for debt, or sold to merchants from Angola; some even voluntarily put themselves into the hands of one of the great men. Their treatment as dependents varied a great deal. Some were practically treated as members of the family; others suffered a more unhappy fate. Some girls were treated little better than prostitutes. The most miserable of all—aging women, shivering with cold and dressed in ragged skins—were treated like beasts of burden.[13] Post-colonial romanticizers have since tried to reinterpret such features of precolonial society by identifying them as patriarchal relationships. But there seems little evidence that the ex-serfs themselves shared this assessment or agitated for the restoration of their former status.

British rule at once introduced new punishments and did away with the more lurid forms of criminal sanctions customary in many tribal societies. The British rejected both legal procedures and penal measures "repugnant," as legislation put it, "to natural justice or morality." They therefore no longer permitted the wholesale mutilation of convicted criminals, a practice customary, for instance, among the Bemba of Northeastern Rhodesia. Lozi prisoners could no longer be burned at the stake, or thrown to the crocodiles, or left to be eaten alive by fearsome black ants. The colonizers thereby greatly reduced the killing capacity of government. Executions became relatively rare under the Union Jack, and the new rulers thus laid down the very standards of humanity against which they were later destined to be judged.

The conquerors, and Africans brought up in the conquerors' schools, brought to the work of governance and conquest a new tool—the pocket watch, and with it, a new concept of time. For their purposes, Africans could reckon time quite accurately: they observed the heavenly bodies; they studied the growth cycle of staple crops. But most thought of time in much the same way as the ancient Hebrews had: "to everything there is a season and a time to every purpose under the heaven: a time to be born and a time to die; a time to plant, and a time to pluck up that which is planted." To Westerners, on the other hand, time was something that could be minutely subdivided. The sound of the church bells divided up time; and so did the bugle that called "Reveille" and "Last Post" in barracks. Time was a commodity for sale, time was money, and this was the first lesson for an African student enjoined to be punctual in a mission school, an African soldier ordered to be punctual on parade, an African clerk required to be punctual in the office, or a labor migrant working off his "ticket" (a labor certificate indicating the monthly period worked).

Imperial Superstructure

In establishing their African empire, the British set up a hierarchical order of a new kind. The British administration was more civilian in its ethos than the French administration in the Sudan or the Belgian administration in the Congo. Its members prided themselves on being gentlemen and amateurs in government, rather than on being military, legal, or administrative specialists. The British pioneers set up an administrative hybrid based partly on British metropolitan models and partly on models derived from colonial India and Ireland. They organized their empire in accordance with the hard facts of the situation rather than with imperial theories; they were forced to administer huge areas with insignificant budgets and military force, and with a minimum of administrators. In all essentials they did their work well. By 1914 the characteristic features of colonial administration in Africa, and to some extent, of post-colonial administration, had been established.

We have described previously the manner in which the British administered their new empire through salaried employees—titled, middle-ranking, lowly. The officials—with their elaborate rules of conduct, their games, their clubs, their rigid sense of honor and style of deportment—formed a distinct group within the white community, hospitable enough to military men and the Anglican clergy, but inclined to look askance at other whites. The mass of the missionaries likewise formed a definable layer of white society, distinct in their mode of living, heterogeneous in social and religious composition, aloof to some extent from the work of government but, for the most part, as loyal to the empire as the pukkah sahib. Officials and missionaries, as well as the senior employees of the railway and mercantile companies, differed sharply from the lowlier white strata. As salaried men they were economically more secure than the smaller white traders, farmers, and craftsmen, and therefore apt to assume a canting stance of moral superiority over those whose livelihood depended on the exigencies of the market.

The European "non-officials" were still relatively few and far between in 1914; in that year the East Africa Protectorate had only some 3,500 whites, the two Rhodesias just under 14,000. Elsewhere the Europeans were mainly birds of passage—merchants, planters, mine and railroad employees—who meant to return "home," usually to Great Britain, having managed to put by some of the money earned overseas. The top layer of the self-employed whites consisted of farmers who had carved out estates for themselves in the Kenyan or Rhodesian bush. In late-Victorian and Edwardian days, these men enjoyed an excellent press overseas. There are scores of prewar novels that tell of clean-limbed, clean-living young Englishmen who set out to seek their fortunes in Africa and built up a new country. The hardihood of the white man and the unblemished virtue of the white woman were an ever-attractive subject to the authors of books with titles like *The Settler's Eldest Daughter*. The settlers in short were idealized as the representatives of imperial power, of middle-class values, of sturdy enterprise and virtue. The reality, of course, was quite different. The great majority of early Rhodesian and Kenyan settlers were poor, as were the settlers on all the frontiers. They were men in search of work, as much subject to the strains and stresses occasioned by labor migrancy as the black migrants whose work they supervised. This was described in a few colonial novels of the time, such as the works of Stanley Portal Hyatt, who wrote about Rhodesia before World War I. A convinced imperialist, Hyatt tended to sound a note of disillusionment in his fiction, torn by the clash between the ideal to which he was committed and the reality that he observed.

The "better class" of Europeans—officials, settlers, and all—were in turn sharply differentiated from the lowliest whites. These included the "remittance men," black-sheep sons of wealthy families who obtained regular remittances from their families on condition they stayed abroad without besmirching the family's good name in England. There were also the DSBs, the "distressed British subjects"—drifters, ne'er-do-wells, deserters, the jobless, apparently hopeless cases whom the colonial governments often tried to deport lest the poor whites lessen white prestige. Hardly more acceptable in the social sense were whites engaged in caste-demeaning occupations like bush-trading, a livelihood most often taken up by the Portuguese, the Greeks, and Jewish immigrants from Eastern Europe. Foreigners, poor or even well-to-do, were rarely accepted socially by red-blooded Britons, even when they contented themselves with living in their own colonies. The settlers of Beira, in Mozambique, for instance, were described in a Rhodesian travel guide as "a perfect sample of polyglot rascality, male and female. They are unclean, physically and morally, lazy, dishonest, and altogether abominable. How they came there, why they came there, are unsolved riddles. . . . The eternal German is much in evidence of course; you will find him in any colony but his own—but Dagos predominate [and] even the bottles in the bar have a cosmopolitan look."[14]

However divided among themselves, the Europeans did form a recognizable caste. A poverty-stricken Greek could never expect to be received at Government House. But his Oxford-educated grandson might well have commanded a British battalion. This opportunity did not exist for British-educated Africans, who were divided from their rulers by color, if not necessarily by speech. The whites were united, moreover, by a system of kinship founded upon monogamy, by a common tradition of literacy in a Western language, and by a real or professed respect for the laws of Moses and Christ; silent skeptics among them were common, convinced atheists were few. Africans soon became perfectly able to distinguish between the various white classes and nationalities; they did, however, regard the bulk of the Europeans as what they were—members of a new Establishment.

African Vassal Kings and Their Subjects

During the last decade of the eighteenth century and the first decade of the nineteenth, French armies conquered Germany. The French profoundly changed the social and political configuration of Germany, but could not sustain their rule. In 1813 Austrian, Prussian, and Russian forces between them overthrew the French at Leipzig, and a new era began in German history. German historians then proceeded to slay Frenchmen in books and journals, just as German soldiers had slain them on the battlefield. The German people supposedly had arisen in a sacred union to drive out the invader; none but curs and traitors had liked the French or profited from their governance. The histories written in this vein now gather dust on library shelves; they do so deservedly, for they take no account of the complexities of French rule, or the various ways in which many Germans—princes, burghers, Jews, and peasants—had profited from French rule, and had become entwined in the network of Napoleonic domination. Worst of all, nationalist historians assumed a sense of nationhood that never existed among the mass of Hessians, Würtembergers, and Bavarians subject to Napoleon's sway.

Africa's post-colonial historiography is subject to similar flaws. History is apt to be written in terms of African resistance and its opposite, collaboration, seen as an iniquitous response to be roundly condemned. But British Africa, or even an individual territory like Kenya or Nigeria, had never been united before the British arrived. There was no sense of Kenyan nationhood. Even the very word African was a European importation, new to men who had previously considered themselves Nandi or Masai. In Victorian and Edwardian days, moreover, there was no clear-cut distinction between resistance fighters and collaborators of the kind that existed, say, in German-occupied France during World War II. In early colonial Africa, the resisters of yesterday might well have negotiated with the conquerors on the morrow. Just as some of the collaborators—men who originally looked on the British as convenient allies against local enemies—were perfectly capable of shifting their policy and opposing the new rulers.

That there was widespread popular resistance is undeniable.[15] In 1898, for instance, when the British imposed the hut tax in Sierra Leone the majority of the people took to arms. There were countless skirmishes; punitive expeditions burned villages and devastated crops. Families were disrupted. Prisoners were abused. The British sought out "cooperative" chiefs and helped them smash their local rivals. The disruption caused by these proceedings, the scramble to gain the good graces of the conqueror may in fact have stimulated local violence and incited desperate men to seek relief by magic means, including ritual murder.

Among the Lugbara of Uganda, on the other hand, change came in a more pacific fashion. A. E. Weatherhead, the pioneer administrator in the area, had to deal with a stateless people organized into small clans without a chief. There was continuous feuding between rival groups. There were no roads. There was no permanent government as understood by Europeans. Weatherhead put an end to serious fighting by making local alliances, by using demobilized Sudanese soldiers as agents, each responsible for certain areas, and by creating a new system of authority. A senior man from each subtribe was appointed as a representative; several subtribes were grouped into chiefdoms, with fixed territorial boundaries designed, as far as possible, to correspond to cultural or dialectical divisions. As late as the mid-twentieth century Lugbara memories of early colonization remained vivid.

Older people maintain that the country, its people and their culture, have been largely destroyed; whereas younger men are more aware of some of the advantages brought about by colonial rule. In the early 1950's most Lugbara thought that if the Europeans left, the Baganda and other southerners, or even worse, the Arabs of the Sudan, whom Lugbara remembered as slave-traders, would take over. They were thus ambivalent about the merits and demerits of colonialism.[16]

Ambivalence likewise marked the policy of the great kings in their dealing with the whites. Many African monarchs tried to adjust to British penetration by manipulating the newcomers to their advantage. Lewanika, king of the Lozi, placed his country under British protection in order to safeguard his own position in a country that had long been divided by civil war. The British were also expected to provide assistance in staving off the incursions of Ndebele raiders from the southeast, of the Portuguese from the west, and of Boer and British fortune hunters from the south. Lewanika's calculations, to some extent, miscarried. he had to give up much of his internal authority to a British resident. He had to relinquish much of his former sphere of influence to the Portuguese in the west and to British administrators in the east. He had to yield to British demands on such things as the abolition of serfdom and the imposition of taxation. Nevertheless, the Lozi ruling class retained a considerable measure of importance. Lozi courts continued to deal with minor cases. Lozi councils continued to function, albeit in a different form. The king retained a percentage of the revenue levied in his country by the British. The Lozi learned how to use some of the new administrative techniques that depended on the written word and a regular office routine. The Lozi thus continued to exercise a form of "sub-imperialism" over a variety of dependent communities, and Lozi chiefs—like the great chiefs in Buganda and Basutoland—retained substantial influence.

The Lozi, a preliterate people before the British arrived, adopted the Gospel, together with the art of writing, thanks to the work of Christian missionaries in the Zambezi valley. Northern Nigeria, on the other hand, formed part of the borderlands of Islam, and was ruled by lords conversant with Muslim law. During the nineteenth century the governance of Bornu fell into the hands of usurpers of Kanembu origin. In order to maintain their authority, they built up a standing military force. They changed the site of the capital city and redistributed the fiefs, as well as the leading state offices. Change, therefore, was not a new thing to the people of Bornu. Indeed, the British began

to make their power felt inland at the very time when Rabeh, a Sudanese warlord, was about to overrun the country. "In a sense," writes
a modern historian, "the colonial conquerors were also liberators, and
many older Bornu informants took just this attitude in describing the
coming of the British."[17]

The colonizers made use of the Bornu government. But in doing
so, they profoundly changed its character. In the olden days, Bornu
had been run by a ruler called the Shehu, who was assisted by a
variety of senior officials—judges, counselors, members of the palace
household, and titled courtiers. These men were themselves great
lords, each holding several territorial fiefs of varying size that could be
enlarged, diminished, or transferred to other feudatories at the
Shehu's pleasure. They were organized in such a manner that they
could incorporate shifting groups of nomads, settlers, and refugees.
Under the colonial dispensation this system was transformed into a
single hierarchy, descending from the Shehu at the top to the lowly
compound heads at the bottom. Each level of the hierarchy was identified with clearly delimited territorial boundaries. Under the new system, administration came to hinge on territorial units. Dispersed ethnic groups or clans could no longer be incorporated among the subjects
of Bornu, except by means of territorial divisions. The Shehu's court
gradually diminished in importance; a new salaried civil service became the pivot of the state, responsible for a great variety of duties
unknown to traditional rulers.

The reaction of educated men to the "native authorities" set up by
the British was double-edged. Men like James Africanus Horton insisted that, in advancing the material condition of the Gold Coast, the
British should not shy away from exercising "a little despotism," from
making an informed use of power to ensure progress. Ultimately, he
felt convinced, Ibo, Yoruba, Mandingo, and Temne were destined to
form a unified people. British rule should culminate in a unified West
Africa, with a common banking system, currency, educational system,
and administration—a new polity that would, in latter-day language,
attain dominion status.

As British government became more entrenched and as some chiefs
themselves acquired Western schooling or employed Western-educated counselors in their service, the attitude of educated men began
to change. In the Gold Coast, for instance, British enactments for
municipal reform violated traditional legislation and upset the customary patterns of landownership. As a result, a small group of educated Africans stepped forward to defend the authority of traditional

rulers, while at the same time advancing their own claims to increased participation in public affairs. One of the most outspoken of these men was John Mensah Sarbah, a Fante lawyer. Until his death in 1910, Mensah Sarbah used his training in British law to challenge the legitimacy, and indeed the utility, of British rule. Nevertheless, he recognized the realities of power. In later years, as a member of the Legislative Council, he maintained his earlier position, speaking for both traditional institutions and greater African participation in government.

The demand for unification became more insistent in the early twentieth century, when men like J. E. Casely Hayford, another brilliant African lawyer, took up the cry for a united British West Africa to be guided by educated Africans rather than chiefs.[18] These critics of colonial rule, taking as their point of departure the colonial structures set up by the British, advocated a far greater degree of union than anything ever contemplated by their rulers. They were nevertheless both the products and, ultimately, the heirs of empire.

Black Responses

Some Africans fought the white man when they first met him. Others took to arms only after they found colonial rule oppressive. Many cooperated with the whites, either to keep some control over their own destinies or to get the better of some rival group. Most African societies, however, responded to the white challenge in a selective fashion, taking only what they could assimilate into their way of life. Kamba men, for instance, would not work on white farms, but they accepted employment as askaris or laborers on railway construction projects. The Kikuyu and the Luo took even more quickly to the new opportunities presented by colonial rule. From about 1909 onward many of the Luo and Kikuyu welcomed Christianity; they began to acquire the new techniques taught by alien evangelists at a time when neither the Kamba nor the Masai were interested in the European's Gospel. But even the Luo and Kikuyu response was not of a piece. Kikuyu and Luo traditionalists developed new cults that rejected European influence, whereas the entire Kamba nation participated in a new Kathambi cult to resist the colonial authorities.[19]

Generalizations regarding the African response are therefore difficult to make. East Africa lacked that long period of commercial and missionary contact with the West experienced by the societies on the West African coast. When East Africa finally came under European control, the great majority of the indigenous communities in the interior were almost unaffected by Western civilizations. People like the Kamba, the Kikuyu, and the Masai of Kenya continued to live in small-scale societies, preliterate and acephalous, subsisting on rudimentary forms of farming and cattle keeping, dependent on simple technologies, and devoid of general purpose currencies. For their source of power they relied solely on human muscle—to bear burdens, to propel missile weapons, to paddle canoes, to hoe the soil. Nevertheless, the responses of these small-scale societies to white penetration varied a great deal. After a period of initial revulsion, the Kikuyu took easily to education and wage employment; the Kamba and the Masai, on the other hand, for long ignored schools. The Kikuyu chief became a mainstay of the new Kenya regime and, in the process, lost much of his former autonomy; the Kamba and Masai rulers would not cooperate so fully with the British and retained more of their accustomed independence and their traditional authority. From the British standpoint, the Kikuyu chiefs did well in their new jobs as peacekeepers and labor recruiters, whereas the Kamba and Masai heads failed to meet British expectations.[20]

The shape of the African response in West Africa was equally diverse. Some societies accepted colonial rule; others resisted. Some chose to cooperate with the new rulers to manipulate them to their purposes; others tried to opt out of the imperial system by force or by stealth. The same people, at different times, acted as "resisters" or as "manipulators"; hence generalizations are hard to make. By and large, the Africans who cooperated were convinced that the white men had come to stay. The "manipulators" therefore tried to use the British to strengthen their own position and the status of their village, town, or district. The "cooperators" tried to control and thereby to limit the impact of the new British dispensation. They enforced British regulations; they collected taxes; they provided labor for public works and for carrier duty; they suppressed practices that offended their new masters, like ritual sacrifice or the subjection of supposed witches to poison ordeals. But at the same time they tried to continue as many of the olden ways as they could.[21]

A third group might be called the "improvers"—those who considered colonialism a source of new opportunities, and who were determined to learn the new skills that seemed to give power to the white man. Some radical and nationalist historians recently have criticized these men as Quislings, charging them with deriving benefits for themselves at their people's expense and with derogating their own culture. The early clerks and teachers were indeed separate from their brethren by dint of acquiring a new education and converting to a new religion. They took Christian names, wore European dress, and tried to adopt Christian standards of social conduct; they gave up ancient ancestral cults; they more or less relinquished their accustomed trust in diviners and spirit mediums; they turned their backs on polygamy.

These converts, however, envisaged themselves not as traitors, but as harbingers of progress. The Europeans offered a new technology; the new regime also seemed to offer a degree of personal freedom unimagined under the old dispensation, when the claims of kinship and tradition took precedence over all others. Christianity assimilated its adherents into a wider world of believers. Christianity, moreover, was a traveling religion; the Bible was a portable fatherland that a traveler could take abroad more easily than the old gods, with their sacred shrines and burial grounds linked to particular localities. The early proselytes remained a small minority, recruited above all from great aristocrats anxious to learn the white man's new techniques—as in Barotseland and Lesotho—or from the ranks of slaves and outcasts who had nothing to lose and all to gain from the white man's new dispensation. The converts were among the first to enter into skilled wage employment as telegraphists, carpenters, clerks, teachers, printers' apprentices, and so forth. The great majority of the villagers remained loyal for the time being to the ancient divinities. Nevertheless, Christian education and Christian religious practices, as well as the new technology and the new economic system associated with the white man, posed a severe challenge to all. "Traditional society was based on a network of commonly accepted values, duties and expectations. Now the fabric was threatened." [22]

Before 1914 the European impact on the great majority of African societies was still limited. There were few administrators; their resources and their ability to promote change and economic development was restricted. A few miles away from the boma life seemed to go on much as before. The prudent DC left the offenses committed by Africans against Africans (except murder and slave-raiding) to be tried by the local people, according to their own custom. This was not entirely an easy matter, since the DC could not help employing "new Africans"—clerks and interpreters—whose very presence disturbed accustomed notions of power. The employment of minor African bureaucrats entailed a variety of abuses; the endeavors of the "new men" may, however, also have softened the colonial culture shock, with the new strata serving as a kind of social buffer.

The imposition of colonial rule, as we have seen, occasioned a great deal of violence and bloodshed. But in the end internecine warfare was stopped; the raids for women, cattle, and grain became distant memories; there were no more conflicts over tribal boundaries or over problems of a royal succession. Slave-trading disappeared; the use of coerced labor gradually gave way to the employment of free wage laborers, able to come and go in accordance with the dictates of the market. Freed from the menace of roving bands, African herdsmen, farmers, and traders could spread out farther afield and extend their range of economic choice.

Preserving law and order meant essentially stopping group conflicts and suppressing practices Europeans regarded as "inhuman." The imposing of Western moral values on African cultures, though ultimately good—liberating old women from witchcraft charges, slaves from being sacrificed, and twins from being slain—at first led to some injustices, for those who held to customary practices were punished even though by their own values they had done no wrong.

The social effect of these changes was contradictory in character. Old values were destroyed, for the missionaries' attack on animistic creeds and on polygamy struck at the very heart of traditional customs. Christian proselytes were sometimes segregated in villages of their own. Families broke up, as one or several members were converted. The new religion and the new ways, however, also provided a new source of moral inspiration and new economic opportunities. The mission-educated African became the indispensable auxiliary of European rule. He served the white man in the capacity of clerk, police sergeant, interpreter, government-appointed chief, and foreman. The interpreter played a particularly important role in consolidating imperial rule. Before 1914 perhaps only four British officials in Kenya knew an African tongue other than Swahili; and "Iboland's new rulers in no instance spoke the language of those they sought to rule."[23] Interpreters were the sole means of communication between the governed and their overlords. The same degree of power was available to the DC's clerk and the court clerk. They alone understood English; they alone grasped the new ways and the new laws; they had the ear of the white man. The power exercised by clerks and interpreters, as well as by policemen and court messengers, resulted in a great deal of abuse. There were never-ending complaints of bribery, corruption, and blackmail, stories that lost nothing when told in European clubs or committed to official reports. The "new men," however, also acted as intellectual pioneers; they represented the new order; they became the ultimate heirs of the imperial establishment.

The economic effects of colonial administration were equally double-edged. Colonizing caused some economic innovation. But African cultivators and traders for long had played the major share in developing the export crops, especially palm oil, peanuts, and cocoa. Unlike all previous conquerors, however, the Europeans introduced a new technology, new concepts of science, and new administrative techniques. Under the new dispensation, customary "restraints on trade" disappeared. The construction of roads, port facilities, and railways served military and administrative purposes; but new means of communication also expanded enormously, as did agricultural production. For the first time in the history of Africa, goods of great bulk and relatively low value—bags of maize, sacks of coal, and such—could be shifted over great distances at a reasonable cost. To cite but one example, once the rivers of Iboland were cleared of snags and trees, these watercourses became flourishing highways that vastly benefited Iboland: trade expanded; local particularism and dialects broke down; the burden on carriers and paddlers lessened. By 1906 Iboland's economic pattern was set; it became dependent on palm oil and peasant production for export, and large commercial concerns dominated its trade.[24]

The new rulers also spread new habits of consumption. Chiefs and wealthy men began to construct brick houses with corrugated iron or tiled roofs in place of round mud and wattle huts. These brick boxes lacked the picturesque quality of customary village architecture, but they were easier to keep clear of lice, bugs, and rats than the old houses; they also presented less of a fire hazard. Bicycles, sewing machines, kerosene lamps, iron bedsteads, china, enameled tableware, blankets, soaps, and European apparel gradually came into wider use. These innovations may be devoid of romantic appeal to intellectuals; nonetheless, they added immeasurably to the comforts of life and made for major, though little-noticed, improvements in public health. The Europeans brought new techniques of urban engineering—they improved sewage facilities and water supplies; they improved communications and opened the way for urban growth.

The new economy, however, also had its destructive aspects. Traditional crafts—for instance, the West African cloth industries—declined. Middlemen of the traditional kind suffered; for example, as did the Kamba traders in Kenya, whose special skills became obsolete under the new dispensation. Colonial rule, while expanding mobility by means of roads, railways, and river steamers, also imposed restraints on the movement of people. Internal migrations were controlled by administrative means. These regulations, coupled with the growth of population and the development of mining and other new forms of land use, often upset the habitual balance between land and population. In many of the more densely populated regions, settlements were fixed, and the soil wore out. Some peoples, such as the Ibo, suffered hardship because they could no longer move to fresh land. Many Ibo therefore left their villages and settled in towns throughout Nigeria; the Ibo diaspora, then, was a product of colonial rule.

The total effect of these changes on British Africa before 1914 is hard to gauge. There were enormous regional differences; change was uneven in both the qualitative and the quantitative sense. The bulk of the African people essentially remained subsistence farmers and herders. The market economy centered on certain "islands" where mining began or where cultivators produced cash crops for export. The indirect effects of economic development, however, were pervasive. An increasing number of villagers were drawn into the cash economy, at least briefly, for the purpose of paying taxes or acquiring some specially desirable piece of merchandise.

Economic change went in hand with a far-reaching political transformation. The new rulers all relied, to a greater or lesser extent, on the services of African intermediaries, including traditional chiefs able and willing to serve the new masters. At the same time, the colonial administration reduced the status and prestige of all the traditional African overlords. Any king, chief, or emir could be replaced if he failed to satisfy the white man's demands. As a result, Africans gradually came to look to the government rather than to the chief as the ultimate source of authority. They learned how to appeal to the DC from the decisions of traditional courts. They refused to carry out traditional obligations or traditional duties of hospitality and service to the chief and his retinue. African rulers lost the power to declare war, to organize slave raids and military expeditions, and to carry on independent diplomatic negotiations, major functions especially in martial communities like the Ngoni and the Bemba. Chiefs and their councilors surrendered many of their judicial roles, especially the right to kill or mutilate convicted criminals and dangerous political opponents.

Wherever white governance introduced new systems of land tenure, chiefs relinquished their ability to allot land to members of the community. Just as Christianity interfered with the ritual aspects of their authority, so the government changed the material basis of their rule. Chiefs became increasingly dependent on the favors of the colonial government. The traditional checks on their power, exercised by councils or custom, lost some of their former force. Chiefs no longer had to fear the threat of armed rebellion or civil war, but increasingly relied on subsidies or salaries paid to them by the government. As time went on rainmakers turned into road builders, warlords into hereditary bureaucrats. The chiefs were required to enforce new regulations and laws; they had to recruit labor for government projects, keep up roads, supply carriers, collect taxes, and sometimes enforce the cultivation of certain crops. Many local officeholders thus increasingly came to be looked on as mere agents of the white man's government.

Traditional obligations to the chief and the village community thus began to weaken. Accustomed patterns of giving and generosity were hard to maintain when food could be converted into cash and stored for individual use. In most parts of precolonial Africa, the individual African had not been able to accumulate much personal wealth; under the new dispensation money could buy goods, and money counted in raising a man to a higher social status. Money could also help to purchase an education. Education, in turn, brought power and influence. These new opportunities profoundly affected life in the village, and the village ceased to be an almost self-contained unit, absorbing all the interests of its people. Instead, cash-cropping and wage labor for limited periods gradually came to occupy a much more central position in the cultivator's life.

To sum up, British governance did not initiate all change in Africa. The so-called traditional societies had been subject to violent shocks and far-reaching dislocations brought about by famine and war, and by the introduction of new techniques in farming and trade. Colonial rule, however, vastly accelerated this transformation, spreading Western notions of trade, science, and government farther than ever before. There were new opportunities as well as new forms of social bondage. By 1914 the process had not yet gone very far. But change was under way, and Africa would never be the same again.

Reference Matter

Selected Data on the British Economy on the Eve of World War I

TABLE A.1

Great Britain's Foreign Capital Investments, 1911

(In £ 1,000)

Territory	Amount	Territory	Amount
BRITISH EMPIRE			
Canada, Newfoundland	372,541	India, Ceylon	365,399
Australia	301,521	Straits Settlement	22,037
New Zealand	78,529	Hong Kong	3,104
South Africa	351,368	North Borneo	5,131
West Africa	29,498	Other possessions	25,024
FOREIGN COUNTRIES			
United States	688,078	Italy	11,513
Cuba	22,700	Portugal	8,134
Philippines	8,202	France	7,071
Argentina	269,808	Germany	6,061
Mexico	87,334	Other European countries	36,319
Brazil	94,440	Japan	53,705
Chile	46,375	China	26,809
Uruguay	35,255	Misc. countries	61,907
Peru	31,986		
Other American countries	22,517	TOTALS	
Russia	38,388	Empire	1,554,152
Turkey	18,320	Foreign	1,637,684
Egypt	43,753	Total overseas	
Spain	18,808	investment	3,191,836

SOURCE: Sir George Paish, "Great Britain's Capital Investment in Individual Colonial and Foreign Countries," *Journal of the Royal Statistical Society*, 74, no. 2 (Jan. 1911): 186. This is an essential source for the study of British overseas investments during the period.

TABLE A.2
Value of British Trade, *1913*
(In £ 1,000)

Imports from foreign countries	577,544
Imports from British countries	191,191
TOTAL	768,735
Exports (British produce) to foreign countries	329,944
Exports (British produce) to British countries	195,310
TOTAL	525,254
Exports (imported merchandise) to foreign countries	95,957
Exports (imported merchandise) to British countries	13,610
TOTAL	109,567

SOURCE: *Encyclopaedia Britannica*, 14th ed. (1929), 10: 713.

TABLE A.3
Direction of British Trade, *1913*
(Percent)

Type of goods	Europe	Africa	Asia	North America	South America	Austral-asia
Imports	40.53%	6.10%	12.71%	23.86%	9.06%	7.74%
Exports	34.64	9.87	25.20	11.99	9.59	8.71
Re-exports	56.02	3.31	2.48	32.26	1.97	3.96

SOURCE: Same as Table A.2.

TABLE A.4
Index of Real Wages in the United Kingdom, 1850–1910

Year	Real wages of full-time workers	Adjusted for unemployment	Year	Real wages of full-time workers	Adjusted for unemployment
1850	100	96	1890	166	162
1860	103	101	1900	183	179
1870	118	113	1910	169	161
1880	134	127			

SOURCE: Same as Table A.2, p. 721.

NOTE: The figures given here are for illustrative purposes. The statistical information for the period 1850–80 leaves much to be desired. The statistics available for the subsequent years are more comprehensive but still leave room for wide differences in interpretation. By and large, experts agree that real wages rose about one-third between 1850 and 1880. The rate of salary gains slowed down after the 1890's, and progress more or less came to a stop during the two decades preceding World War I.

TABLE A.5
Comparative Percentage Increases in the Populations and Economies of the United Kingdom, Germany, and the United States Between 1893 and 1913

Category	United Kingdom	Germany	United States
Population	20%	32%	46%
Coal production	75	159	210
Pig iron	50	287	337
Crude steel	136	522	715
Exports, raw materials	238	243	196
Exports, manufactures	121	239	563
Railway traffic receipts, goods only	49	141	146

SOURCE: R. C. K. Ensor, *England 1870–1914* (Oxford, Eng., 1936), p. 503.

Top Colonial Office Officials, 1870–1914

Secretaries of State for the Colonies

1870 John Wodehouse Kimberley, 1st Earl of Kimberley
1874 Henry H. M. Herbert, 4th Earl of Carnarvon
1878 Sir Michael Hicks-Beach (later Earl St. Aldwyn)
1880 John Wodehouse Kimberley, 1st Earl of Kimberley
1882 Edward H. Stanley, 15th Earl of Derby
1885 Col. Sir F. A. Stanley (later Lord Stanley of Preston; later 16th Earl of Derby)
1886 Edward Stanhope
1887 Sir Henry Thurston Holland (later Viscount Knutsford)
1892 George F. S. R. Ripon, 1st Marquess of Ripon
1895 Joseph Chamberlain
1903 Alfred Lyttleton
1905 Victor Alexander Bruce, 9th Earl of Elgin and 13th Earl of Kincardine
1908 Robert O. A. Crewe-Milnes, 1st Earl of Crewe (later Marquess of Crewe)
1910 Sir Lewis Harcourt

Permanent Under Secretaries

1871 Sir Robert Herbert
1892 Sir Robert Meade
1897 Sir Edward Wingfield
1900 Sir Montague Ommanney
1907 Sir Francis Hopwood
1911 Sir John Anderson

Notes

Chapter One

1. Maurice Dobb, *Studies in the Development of Capitalism* (London, 1947), p. 315.

2. The rise of the population and the simultaneous decline of criminal convictions in the United Kingdom between 1850 and 1910 are shown in the following table. In 1973, according to the Department of Justice (*Criminal Victimization Surveys: 13 American Cities*; Washington, D.C., June 1975), the total number of aggravated assaults in San Francisco (pop. 1970: 715,674) was 17,800.

| Year | England and Wales | | Scotland | | Ireland | |
	Population	Convictions	Population	Convictions	Population	Convictions
1850	17,773,324	20,537	2,872,821	3,363	6,877,549	17,108
1860	19,902,713	12,068	3,054,738	2,414	5,820,960	2,979
1870	22,090,163	12,953	3,222,837	2,400	5,525,210	3,048
1880	25,714,288	11,214	3,705,994	2,046	5,202,648	2,383
1890	28,763,673	9,242	4,003,132	1,825	4,717,959	1,193
1900	32,249,187	8,157	4,436,958	1,835	4,468,501	1,087
1910	35,796,289	11,987	4,737,268	1,225	4,368,599	1,373

SOURCE: *Whitaker's Almanac* (London, 1912), p. 489.

3. *The Complete Writings of Oscar Wilde* (New York, 1909), 4: 42.

4. For a detailed summary concerning the various schools of thought regarding the Scramble, see G. N. Sanderson, "The European Partition of Africa: Coincidence or Conjuncture?," *Journal of Imperial and Commonwealth History* 3, no. 1 (Oct. 1974): 1–54. We have ourselves discussed the question in "Reflections on Imperialism and the Scramble for Africa," in L. H. Gann and Peter Duignan, eds., *The History and Politics of Colonialism, 1870–1914* (London, 1969), pp. 100–131 (vol. 1 of Peter Duignan and L. H. Gann, gen. eds., *Colonialism in Africa, 1870–1960*). Far more work has been done since. Recent works include William Roger Louis, ed., *Imperialism: The Robinson*

and Gallagher Controversy (New York, 1976); C. G. Eldridge, England's Mission: The Imperial Idea in the Age of Gladstone and Disraeli, 1868-1880 (London, 1973); and D. C. M. Platt, Finance, Trade and Politics in British Foreign Policy, 1815-1914 (Oxford, Eng., 1968), a valuable work. For an outstanding general interpretation of economic factors in West African history, see Anthony G. Hopkins, An Economic History of West Africa (London, 1973). Another valuable book is D. K. Fieldhouse, The Colonial Empires: A Comparative Survey from the Eighteenth Century (New York, 1971).

5. See J. A. Hobson, Imperialism: A Study (London, 1902); and Leonard Woolf, Empire and Commerce in Africa: A Study in Economic Imperialism (London, 1919). The literature on imperialism is enormous. Marxist works on imperialism alone fill many library shelves. But varied as they are, the Marxist and neo-Marxist interpretations are all embodied essentially in three pioneer works. V. I. Lenin, "Imperialism: The Highest Stage of Capitalism: A Popular Outline," in Imperialism and the Imperialist War (1914-1917), pp. 3-119 (vol. 5 of Selected Works, New York, 1935), represents present-day orthodoxy; Rosa Luxemburg, Die Akkumulation des Kapitals: Ein Beitrag zur ökonomischen Erklärung des Imperialismus (Leipzig, 1912, 2 vols. in 1), presages the critics of the New Left; and Karl Kautsky, Nationalstaat, imperialistischer Staat und Staatenbund (Nuremberg, 1915), reflects the liberal-reformist tradition of Marxism. The Marxist interpretations have been criticized by D. K. Fieldhouse, The Theory of Capitalist Imperialism (New York, 1967), and L. H. Gann and Peter Duignan, Burden of Empire (Stanford, Calif., 1971).

6. John E. Flint, "Britain and the Partition of West Africa," in John E. Flint and Glyndwr Williams, Perspectives of Empire (London, 1973), p. 95.

7. For a readable history, strong on local color, see Donald R. Morris, The Washing of the Spears: A History of the Rise of the Zulu Nation Under Shaka and Its Fall in the Zulu War of 1879 (New York, 1965).

8. Michael Glover, Rorke's Drift: A Victorian Epic (Hamden, Conn., 1975), p. 128.

9. The Times, the Morning Post, and the Standard (morning newspapers) were Conservative; so were the Globe, the Evening Standard, and the St. James Gazette (evening newspapers). The Pall Mall Gazette stood for a curious mixture of philosophical radicalism and jingoism. The Daily Chronicle and Daily Telegraph (morning newspapers) were Liberal-Unionist, combining liberalism with a strong belief in empire. The Liberal-Radical papers, which were apt to criticize colonial expansion, were the Daily News (a morning newspaper) and the Star (an evening newspaper).

10. Peter Marshall, "The Imperial Factor in the Liberal Decline, 1880-1885," in Flint and Williams, Perspectives of Empire, p. 142.

11. See Bernard Porter, Critics of Empire: British Radical Attitudes to Colonialism in Africa, 1895-1914 (London, 1968), pp. 50-55.

12. See James R. Boosé, Memory Serving: Being Reminiscences of Fifty Years of the Royal Colonial Institute (London, 1928), p. 62.

13. Trevor R. Reese, *The History of the Royal Commonwealth Society, 1868–1968* (London, 1968).

14. See James A. Edward, "Southern Rhodesia and the London Daily Press, 1890–1893," in National Archives of Rhodesia and Nyasaland, *Occasional Papers*, no. 1 (June 1963), pp. 58–70.

15. Porter, *Critics of Empire*.

16. For two excellent analyses of the role of Mary Kingsley, see John E. Flint, "Mary Kingsley—a Reassessment," *Journal of African History*, 4 (1963): 95–104; and Richard West, *Congo* (New York, 1972), part 1, chap. 3.

17. Quoted in West, *Congo*, p. 53.

18. Mary Henrietta Kingsley, *Travels in West Africa* (London, 1965), p. 217.

19. *Ibid.*, p. 494.

20. See Mary Henrietta Kingsley, *West African Studies* (London, 1964), pp. 392ff.

21. For Lloyd George's attack, see Great Britain, *Parliamentary Debates*, House of Commons, 4th ser. (Dec. 1900), 8: 397–421. For Chamberlain's masterly defense, *ibid.*, pp. 432–47.

22. Elie Halévy, *Imperialism and the Rise of Labour* (London, 1951), 5: 15–16.

23. See especially John E. Flint, *Sir George Goldie and the Making of Nigeria* (London, 1960); Hopkins, *Economic History*; Allan McPhee, *The Economic Revolution in British West Africa* (London, 1971); Frederick Pedler, *The Lion and the Unicorn in Africa: A History of the United Africa Company (1787–1931)* (London, 1974); and K. O. Dike, *Trade and Politics in the Niger Delta, 1830–1885* (Oxford, Eng., 1956).

24. John S. Galbraith, *Mackinnon and East Africa, 1878–1895* (Cambridge, Eng., 1972), p. 139. Galbraith summarized the composition of the board as follows: "Among the subscribers were men who had been involved with East Africa for many years, including Kirk, Sir Lewis Pelly, and Holmwood. The humanitarians were prominently represented by Thomas Fowell Buxton, William Burdett-Coutts, husband of the celebrated Baroness, and Alexander L. Bruce, the son-in-law of Livingstone who had devoted much of his fortune from breweries to missions in East Africa and to the African Lakes Company. Among the prominent businessmen were Mackinnon's long-time associate James F. Hutton, now also a director of the Royal Niger Company; Lord Brassey, who had been Civil Lord of the Admiralty in Gladstone's post-Midlothian administration, and had formerly been a director of the British North Borneo Company; Mackinnon's old friend and business associate, James M. Hall; Henry J. Younger, a partner with Bruce in an Edinburgh brewery; Robert Ryrie, a prominent London merchant; and George S. Mackenzie, a partner in Gray, Dawes, and Company, and a director of the British India Steam Navigation Company. Also included were General Sir Donald Stewart, who had recently retired as Commander-in-Chief of the Indian Army; General Sir Arnold B. Kemball, who after a long career in the Indian Army and in

various diplomatic capacities in South Asia, had retired to become a business associate of the Duke of Sutherland; and Sir Francis de Winton, recently Administrator General of the Congo Free State."

25. The list of books and articles written about him fills a whole volume; see Central African Rhodes Centenary Exhibition, *The Story of Cecil Rhodes* (Bulawayo, Rhodesia, 1953). The best are Basil Williams, *Cecil Rhodes* (London, 1938); and John E. Flint, *Cecil Rhodes* (Boston, 1974). For the best work on the chartered company, see John S. Galbraith, *Crown and Charter: The Early Years of the British South Africa Company* (Berkeley, Calif., 1974).

26. *Who Was Who . . . 1897–1916* (London, n.d.), p. 595.

27. For details on charter negotiations, see Peter Duignan, "Native Policy in Southern Rhodesia, 1890–1923," unpublished Ph.D. dissertation, Stanford University, 1961, pp. 62–68.

28. Williams, *Rhodes*, p. 132.

29. Great Britain, Parliamentary Command Papers, *Further Correspondence Respecting the Affairs of Bechuanaland*, C. 5918 (1890), no. 88.

Chapter Two

1. L. S. Amery, cited by Sir Anton Bertram, *The Colonial Service* (Cambridge, Eng., 1930), pp. 2–3.

2. Trevor Ternan, *Some Experiences of an Old Bromsgrovian: Soldiering in Afghanistan, Egypt, and Uganda* (Birmingham, Eng., 1930), p. 324.

3. Cited by Sir Charles Joseph Jeffries, *The Colonial Office* (London, 1956), p. 15.

4. Brian L. Blakeley, *The Colonial Office, 1868–1892* (Durham, N.C., 1972), p. 19.

5. Henry L. Hall, *The Colonial Office* (London, 1937), p. 118.

6. G. W. Johnson was a Scholar of Trinity College, Cambridge, and an 8th Wrangler (a candidate who had been placed in the First Class in the Mathematical Tripos). Herbert J. Read, a Brasenose man, had a First in mathematics at Oxford. C. Strachey had come up through the Foreign Office. H. C. M. Lambert, an Old Etonian, obtained a First in classics at New College, Oxford. A. E. Collins, educated at the City of London School and at Trinity College, Cambridge, was a Scholar of the college and took a First in the Classics Tripos. W. D. Ellis went to Winchester and then to New College, where he received a First in *literae humaniores*, a junior Greek Testament prize, and the Chancellor's Prize for a Latin essay. G. A. E. Grindle was a Scholar of Corpus Christi College, Oxford, where he took a First in classics and won the Chancellor's English essay.

7. Jeffries, p. 18.

8. See, for instance, J. H. Warren, *The Local Government Service* (London, 1952), *passim*.

9. Cited by Blakeley, p. 118.

10. See Frederick John Dealtry, Baron Lugard, *The Dual Mandate in British Tropical Africa*, 5th ed. (London, 1965), chap. 8.

11. Hall, p. 37.

12. *Ibid.*, p. 86.

13. See especially Robert V. Kubicek, *The Administration of Imperialism: Joseph Chamberlain at the Colonial Office* (Durham, N.C., 1969).

14. See R. Kesner, "The Builders of the Empire: The Role of the Crown Agents in Imperial Development, 1880–1914," *Journal of Imperial and Commonwealth History* (in press). Sir Montague Ommanney later became a director of the North Borneo Company and a vice-president of the Royal Colonial Institute.

15. Sir Ralph Furse, *Aucuparius: Recollections of a Recruiting Officer* (London, 1962), p. 44.

16. Inspector-General Wilkinson, cited in *ibid.*, p. 26.

17. See I. F. Nicolson, *The Administration of Nigeria, 1900–1960: Men, Methods and Myths* (Oxford, Eng., 1969).

18. Kubicek, p. x.

19. Cited by Hall, *Colonial Office*, p. 62.

20. M. P. K. Sorrenson, *Origins of European Settlement in Kenya* (Nairobi, 1968), p. 85.

21. Philip E. Chartrand, "Churchill and Rhodesia in 1921: A Study of British Colonial Decision-Making," unpublished Ph.D. dissertation, Syracuse University, 1974.

22. See A. W. Abbott, *A Short History of the Crown Agents and Their Office* (for private circulation; London, 1959), pp. 1–4.

23. Cited by Vincent Ponko, Jr., "Economic Management in a Free-Trade Empire: The Work of the Crown Agents of the Colonies in the Nineteenth and Twentieth Centuries," *Journal of Economic History*, 26, no. 3 (Sept. 1966): 363–77; Ponko, "History and Methodology of Public Administration: The Case of the Crown Agents for the Colonies," *Public Administration Review*, 27, no. 1 (March 1967): 42–47. See also Great Britain, Parliamentary Command Papers, *Committee of Enquiry into the Organisation of the Crown Agents . . .*, C. 4474 (1909).

24. Vincent Ponko, Jr., "The Colonial Office and British Business Before World War I: A Case Study," *Business History Review*, 43, no. 1 (April 1969): 39–58.

Chapter Three

1. Friedrich Immanuel, *Was Man von englischen Heere wissen muss* (Berlin 1912), p. 4.

2. *Rudyard Kipling's Verse: Definitive Edition* (Garden City, N.Y., 1940), p. 45. Reprinted by permission of the Executors of the Estate of Mrs. George Bambridge and Doubleday & Company, Inc.

3. Correlli Barnett, *Britain and Her Army, 1509–1970: A Military, Political, and Social Survey* (London, 1970), p. 335.

4. Cited in Sir James Handyside Marshall-Cornwall, *Haig as Military Commander* (New York, 1973), p. 60.

5. C. E. Callwell, *Small Wars: Their Principles and Practice*, 3d ed. (London, 1909), pp. 90–91.

6. H. J. Hanham, "Religion and Nationality in the Mid-Victorian Army," in M. R. D. Foot, ed., *War and Society* (London, 1973), pp. 159–83, especially p. 163.

7. We thank Professor D. G. M. Muffett for this information on the Cameronian Scottish Rifles.

8. John C. M. Baynes, *Morale: A Study of Men and Courage; The Second Scottish Rifles at the Battle of Neuve-Chapelle* (London, 1967).

9. See Sir Charles W. Gwynn, *Imperial Policing* (London, 1939), pp. 10–33, on the principles of imperial policing; and Sir Charles Reith, *A New Study of Police History* (Edinburgh, 1956), on the development of the British police force.

10. Cited by Joseph H. Lehmann, *The First Boer War* (London, 1972), p. 71.

11. *Ibid.*, pp. 123, 125.

12. The cited verse is from Newbolt's poem "Vitai Lampada."

13. W. H. Goodenough and J. C. Dalton, comps., *The Army Book for the British Empire* (London, 1893), p. 416.

14. Gwyn Harries-Jenkins, *The Army in Victorian Society* (London, 1977), p. 44.

15. Byron Farwell, *Queen Victoria's Little Wars* (New York, 1972), p. 273.

16. For the standard histories of these three units, see Peter Gibbs, *The History of the British South Africa Police*, 2 vols. (Salisbury, Rhodesia, 1972–74); A. Haywood and F. A. S. Clarke, *The History of the Royal West African Frontier Force* (Aldershot, Eng., 1964); and Hubert Moyse-Bartlett, *The King's African Rifles: A Study in the Military History of East and Central Africa, 1890–1945* (Aldershot, Eng., 1956), the last-named being the best of its kind.

17. Winston S. Churchill, "The Makaland Field Force," reprinted in *Frontiers and Wars* (New York, 1962), pp. 115–16.

18. Trevor Ternan, *Some Experiences of an Old Bromsgrovian: Soldiering in Afghanistan, Egypt, and Uganda* (Birmingham, Eng., 1930), p. 2.

19. See Adrian Preston, ed., *The South African Journal of Sir Garnet Wolseley* (Cape Town, 1973), for a literate account of a military organizer and reformer at work in pacifying Zululand after the British defeat at Isandhlwana.

20. E. S. Turner, *Gallant Gentleman: A Portrait of the British Officer 1600–1956* (London, 1956), p. 265.

21. Sir Robert Harry Inglis Palgrave, *Dictionary of Political Economy*, 3 vols. (London, 1926), 3: 798–800.

22. Goodenough and Dalton, p. 422.

23. Karl Marx, "The Future Results of the British Rule in India" (22 July 1853), reprinted in *On Colonialism: Articles from the 'New York Tribune' and Other Writings by Karl Marx and Friedrich Engels* (New York, 1972), p. 82.

Chapter Four

1. Adrian Preston, ed., *The South African Journal of Sir Garnet Wolseley* (Cape Town, 1973), p. 225.

2. For two excellent and succinct modern accounts of these events and the subsequent war, see John Keegan, "The Ashanti Campaign, 1873–1874," in Brian Bond, ed., *Victorian Military Campaigns* (New York, 1967), pp. 161–98; and J. K. Fynn, "Ghana-Asante (Ashanti)," in Michael Crowder, ed., *West African Resistance: The Military Response to Colonial Occupation* (New York, 1971), pp. 19–52.

3. See Jeffrey Andrew Fadiman, "Traditional Warfare Among the Meru of Mount Kenya," unpublished Ph.D. dissertation, University of Wisconsin, 1973.

4. Our discussion of the WAFF is based largely on A. Haywood and F. A. S. Clarke, *The History of the Royal West African Frontier Force* (Aldershot, Eng., 1964); and S. C. Ukpabi, "Recruiting for British Colonial Forces in West Africa," in *Odu: A Journal of West African Studies*, n.s., 10 (July 1974).

5. Sir Bryan Sharwood Smith, *Recollections of British Administration in the Cameroons and Northern Nigeria, 1921–1957: But Always as Friends* (Durham, N.C., 1969), pp. 139–40.

6. Cited by Ukpabi, p. 91.

7. Cited by W. D. Downes, *With the Nigerians in German East Africa* (London, 1919), pp. 260–61.

8. See Hubert Moyse-Bartlett, *The King's African Rifles: A Study in the Military History of East and Central Africa, 1890–1945* (Aldershot, Eng., 1956), pp. 19–20.

9. Richard Meinertzhagen, *Kenya Diary, 1902–1906* (Edinburgh, 1957); John Lord, *Duty, Honour, Empire: The Life and Times of Colonel Richard Meinhertzhagen* (New York, 1970), pp. 184, 185, 197–99.

10. Meinertzhagen, pp. 41ff; Lord, pp. 197–200.

11. See Frank Johnson, *Great Days: The Autobiography of an Empire Pioneer* (London, 1940); A. S. Hickman, *Men Who Made Rhodesia: A Register of Those Who Served in the British South Africa Company's Police* (Salisbury, Rhodesia, 1960); and British South Africa Company, *Regulations for the Instruction of the Pioneer Corps and Expedition* (Cape Town, 1890).

12. See L. H. Gann, "The Development of Southern Rhodesia's Military System, 1890–1953," National Archives of Rhodesia, *Occasional papers*, no. 1 (1965), pp. 60–79.

13. R. F. H. Summers, "The Military Doctrine of the Matabele," in *NADA* (Salisbury, Rhodesia), 32 (1955): 7–15.

14. The section on the BSAP is based largely on L. H. Gann, *A History of Southern Rhodesia: Early Days to 1934* (London, 1965); Gann, "Development of Southern Rhodesia's Military System"; Hickman, *Men Who Made Rhodesia*; and Peter Gibbs, *The History of the British South Africa Police*, 2 vols. (Salisbury, Rhodesia, 1972–74).

15. There is an immense body of literature on the subject, too large to be even tentatively listed in a note. The most exhaustive study of military operations is L. Amery, ed., *'The Times' History of the War in South Africa, 1899–1902*, 7 vols. (London, 1900–1909). For a German view, see Germany, General Staff, *The War in South Africa from October 1899 to September 1900*, authorized English translation by W. Waters and H. DuCane, 2 vols. (London, 1904–6). A large-scale Afrikaans study is H. J. Breytenbach, *Die geskiedenis von die tweede vryheidsoorlog in Suid-Afrika, 1899–1902* (Pretoria, 1969—).

16. Weston Alexander Jarvis to Lady Jarvis, 9 May 1900, JA/4/1/2, National Archives of Rhodesia.

17. Charles R. N. Robinson, *Celebrities of the Army* (London, 1900), p. 10.

18. Cited by Byron Farwell, *Queen Victoria's Little Wars* (New York, 1972), p. 344.

19. From the poem "Delilah Aberystwyth."

20. Leonard Cooper, *British Regular Cavalry, 1644–1914* (London, 1965), pp. 198–201.

21. See Crowder, *West African Resistance*, p. 2. The discussion that follows is taken from Crowder's excellent introduction and the essays in the volume.

22. John Ainsworth, "Reminiscences," mss. Afr. S. 380, Rhodes House Library, Oxford University.

23. See Richard Waller, "The Masai and the British, 1895–1905: The Origins of an Alliance," *Journal of African History*, 17, no. 4 (1976): 529–54.

24. Hogard's "Ten Rules of Anti-Revolutionary Tactics" have been reprinted in George Armstrong Kelly, *Lost Soldiers: The French Army and Empire in Crisis, 1947–1962* (Cambridge, Mass., 1965), pp. 120–21.

25. Winston S. Churchill, "The Makaland Field Force," reprinted in *Frontiers and Wars* (New York, 1962), p. 110.

26. See Meinertzhagen, *Kenya Diary*.

27. Cited by A. J. Hanna, *The Beginnings of Nyasaland and Northeastern Rhodesia, 1859–1895* (Oxford, Eng., 1956), p. 188.

28. I. F. Nicolson, *The Administration of Nigeria, 1900–1960: Men, Methods and Myths* (Oxford, Eng., 1969), p. 88.

29. *Ibid.*, p. 108.

30. Colin Harding, *Far Bugles* (London, 1933), p. 101.

31. See Robert 'Cummings, "A Note on the History of Caravan Porters in East Africa," *Kenya Historial Review*, 1, no. 2 (1973): 110–38. In West Africa a district commissioner on tour was entitled to eight hammock-men, and a WAFF company of 62 on the march would use 607 carriers and 23 headmen.

32. See Meinertzhagen, p. 265.

33. A 1904 campaign against the Irryeni and the Embo killed 1,046. See *ibid.*, p. 152.

34. "Instructions . . . for the Guidance of Officers," by H. F. Ruxton, resident at Muri, 3 March 1910; H. M. Brice-Smith, "Nigeria: Notes on the Munsih [Tiv]," both in mss. Afr. S. 662, Rhodes House Library, Oxford University.

35. Quoted in Donald Anthony Low, *Lion Rampant: Essays in the Study of British Imperialism* (London, 1973), p. 23.

36. H. Belloc, *Sonnets and Verse* (London, 1923), p. 157.

37. James Clyde Mitchell, *The Kalela Dance: Aspects of Social Relationships Among Urban Africans in Northern Rhodesia*, Rhodes-Livingstone Paper no. 27 (Manchester, Eng., 1956).

Chapter Five

1. A. H. M. Kirk-Greene's works include *The Emirates of Northern Nigeria: A Preliminary Survey of Their Historical Traditions* (London, 1966), with Sidney John Hogben; *Adamawa, Past and Present: An Historical Approach to the Development of a Northern Cameroons Province* (London, 1958); and *The Principles of Native Administration in Nigeria: Selected Documents, 1900–1947* (London, 1965). At the time of this writing he was preparing a biographical dictionary of British governors in Africa and a history of the British colonial service; we are indebted to him for allowing us to draw on his manuscript for this chapter.

2. Sir Hesketh Bell, *Glimpses of a Governor's Life: From Diaries, Letters, and Memoranda* (London, 1946), p. 117.

3. Elizabeth Rosetta, Lady Glover, *Life of Sir John Hawley Glover* (London, 1897), quoted by Roy Lewis and Yvonne Foy, *Painting Africa White: The Human Side of British Colonialism* (London, 1971), p. 139.

4. Cited by Sir Anton Bertram, *The Colonial Service* (Cambridge, Eng., 1930), pp. 56–57.

5. Theo Williams to his mother, 5 Dec. 1912, mss. Afr. S. 779, Rhodes House Library, Oxford University.

6. R. S. T. Cashmore, "Your Obedient Servant," mss. Afr. S. 1034, Rhodes House Library, Oxford University.

7. Bertram, p. 50.

8. Henry L. Hall, *The Colonial Office* (London, 1937), p. 93.

9. Colin A. Hughes and I. F. Nicolson, "A Provenance of Proconsuls: British Colonial Governors, 1900–1960," *Journal of the Imperial and Commonwealth History* (London), 4, no. 1 (Oct. 1975): 77–106. Their paper is so good that we can do no better than to summarize their findings, and combine these with our own. They have excluded quasi-gubernatorial posts (residents and administrators), governorships of island fortress posts that were usually filled by senior officers of the armed services, and wartime appointments and military governorships.

10. "Matilda," *The Oxford Dictionary of Quotations* (London, 1959), p. 41.

11. Sir William Milton to his wife, 25 Sept. 1896, MI 1/1/2, National Archives of Rhodesia.

12. Peter Stansky and William Abrahams, *The Unknown Orwell* (New York, 1972).

13. Herbert Branston Gray, *Public Schools and the Empire* (London, 1913), pp. 172–73.

14. Edward Clarence Mack, *Public Schools and British Opinion Since 1860: The Relationship Between Contemporary Ideas and Evolution of an English Institution* (New York, 1941), pp. 123–24.

15. See Norman Dixon, *On the Psychology of Military Incompetence* (London, 1976); Correlli Barnett, *The Swordbearers: Studies in Supreme Command in the First World War* (London, 1963), pp. 113–99; and Barnett, *The Collapse of British Power* (New York, 1972), *passim*.

16. Nigeria, Federal Ministry of Education, *Investment in Education: The Report of the Commission on Post-School Certificates and Higher Education in Nigeria* (Lagos, 1960), p. 5.

17. Chauncy Hugh Stigand, *Administration in Tropical Africa* (London, 1914), p. 9.

18. Johnston to Foreign Office, 31 May 1897 (FO 2/128, Public Record Office, London), cited by L. H. Gann, *A History of Northern Rhodesia: Early Days to 1953* (London, 1964), pp. 94–95.

Chapter Six

1. Cited by Robert Heussler, *Yesterday's Rulers: The Making of the British Colonial Service* (Syracuse, N.Y., 1963), p. 9.

2. See Anthony Sillery, *John Mackenzie of Bechuanaland, 1835–1899: A Study in Humanitarian Imperialism* (Cape Town, 1971).

3. T. H. R. Cashmore, "Studies in District Administration in the East African Protectorate, 1895–1918," unpublished doctoral dissertation, Cambridge University, 1965.

4. "Chant-Pagan," *Rudyard Kipling's Verse: Definitive Edition* (Garden City, N.Y., 1940), p. 459. Reprinted by permission of the Executors of the Estate of Mrs. George Bambridge and Doubleday & Co., Inc.

5. See C. A. Baker, *Johnston's Administration: A History of the British Central Africa Administration, 1891–1897* (Zomba, Malawi, 1970).

6. L. H. Gann, *The British of a Plural Society: The Development of Northern Rhodesia Under the British South Africa Company, 1894–1914* (Manchester, Eng., 1958), pp. 104–7.

7. Heussler, p. 14.

8. See Melvin Richter, *The Politics of Conscience: T. H. Green and His Age* (London, 1964). See also J. M. Winter, "Balliol's Lost Generation," in *Balliol College Annual Record*, 1975, pp. 22–26; and *Balliol College Register, 1916–1967* (Oxford, Eng., 1969).

9. Sir Geoffrey Archer, *Personal and Historical Memoirs of an East African Administrator* (London, 1963), p. 25.

10. Oliver Ransford, *Livingstone's Lake: The Drama of Nyasa* (London, 1966), quoted by Roy Lewis and Yvonne Foy, *Painting Africa White: The Human Side of British Colonialism* (New York, 1971), p. 151.

11. Sir Alan Cuthbert Burns, *Colonial Civil Servant* (London, 1949), p. 9.

12. G. N. Lord Curzon, "The True Imperialism," *The Nineteenth Century and After*, Jan. 1908, pp. 151–65.

13. Winston Churchill, *The River War: An Account of the Reconquest of the Sudan*, 3d ed. (London, 1951), pp. 8–9. Originally published in 1899.

14. R. S. T. Cashmore, "Your Obedient Servant," mss. Afr. S. 1034, Rhodes House Library, Oxford University, p. 30.

15. Heussler, *Yesterday's Rulers*, pp. 24–25.

16. Passages from "We and They," copyright 1926 by Rudyard Kipling, and "The Mother-Lodge" (which follow) and from "Exiles Line" (cited here) are from *Rudyard Kipling's Verse: Definitive Edition* (Garden City, N.Y., 1940). Reprinted by permission of the Executors of the Estate of Mrs. George Bambridge and Doubleday & Company, Inc.

17. Sir Bryan Sharwood Smith, *Recollections of British Administration in the Cameroons and Northern Nigeria, 1921–1957: But Always as Friends* (Durham, N.C., 1969), pp. xiv–xv.

18. Theo Williams to his father, 28 May 1913 and 12 June 1913, mss. Afr. S. 799, vol. 1, Rhodes House Library, Oxford University.

19. I. F. Nicolson, *The Administration of Nigeria, 1900–1960: Men, Methods and Myths* (Oxford, Eng., 1969).

20. See the excellent article by Adele Ebereciukwu Afigbo, "The Consolidation of British Imperial Administration in Nigeria: 1900–1918," *Civilisations* *XXI*, 4 (1971): 436–59.

21. *Ibid.*, p. 443.

22. See Adele Ebereciukwu Afigbo, *The Warrant Chiefs: Indirect Rule in Southeastern Nigeria, 1891–1929* (Ibadan, Nigeria, 1972).

23. Sir Charles Eliot, *The East African Protectorate* (London, 1905), p. 186.

24. "The Lost Legion," in Rudyard Kipling, *Collected Verse* (New York, 1910), p. 108.

25. Robert O. Collins, "The Sudan Political Service: A Portrait of the 'Imperialists,'" *African Affairs*, July 1971, pp. 293–303.

26. We are indebted to Professor David Brokensha for information on the DC in fiction and as ethnographer.

27. W. R. Crocker, *Nigeria: A Critique of British Administration* (London, 1936), pp. 135–37.

28. See the excellent article by Bethwell A. Ogot, "British Administration in the Central Nyanza District of Kenya, 1900–1960," *Journal of African History*, 4, no. 2 (1963): 249–73.

29. See Robert M. Maxon, "John Ainsworth and Agricultural Innovation in Kenya," *Kenya Historical Review*, 1, no. 2 (1973): 151–61.

30. Ogot, p. 255.

31. Henry L. Hall, *The Colonial Office* (London, 1937), p. 120.

32. See R. A. Dick, "Ulendo . . .," mss. Afr. S. 952, Rhodes House Library, Oxford University.

33. See C. L. Temple, "Annual Report for Kano" (1909) and "Quarterly Report for Kano Province" (12 Dec. 1912) in H. M. Brice-Smith reports, mss. Afr. S. 230, Rhodes House Library, Oxford University.

34. For a superb account of the life of a resident, see C. L. Temple, *Native*

Races and Their Rulers: Sketches and Studies of Official Life and Administrative Problems in Nigeria (Cape Town, 1918).

35. Temple, "Annual Report," 1909.

36. Quoted in Cashmore, "Your Obedient Servant," p. 87.

37. *Ibid.*, p. 85.

38. Diary of Alfred Harry Sanders, Royal Commonwealth Society, London.

39. Joyce Cary, *Mister Johnson: A Novel* (New York, 1951), p. 6.

40. Cashmore, "Your Obedient Servant," p. 48.

41. Quoted in *ibid.*, p. 60.

42. Colonial Secretary to Controller of Customs, Gold Coast, 12 Dec. 1893, in correspondence with Colonial Secretary's Office, Accra, regarding Customs and Medical Department, 1893–1900, mss. Afr. S. 215, Rhodes House Library, Oxford University.

43. Quoted in Cashmore, "Your Obedient Servant," p. 55.

44. *Ibid.*

45. *Ibid.*, p. 59.

46. Quoted in Baker, *Johnston's Administration*, p. 71.

47. Quoted in Cashmore, "Your Obedient Servant," p. 80.

48. *Ibid.*, p. 79.

49. Preface to Sir Alfred Claud Hollis, *The Masai: The Language and Folklore* (Oxford, Eng., 1905).

50. R. T. Coryndon, cited by Gann, *Birth of a Plural Society*, p. 92.

51. Lord Hailey, *An African Survey: A Study of Problems Arising in Africa South of the Sahara* (London, 1938), p. 298.

52. For Shona notions of morality, see, for instance, Michael Gelfand, *African Crucible: An Ethico-Religious Study with Special Reference to the Shona-Speaking People* (Cape Town, 1960). For the concept of the "reasonable man" in Lozi jurisprudence, see Max Gluckman, *The Judicial Process Among the Barotse of Northern Rhodesia* (Manchester, Eng., 1955), the most brilliant work on African jurisprudence in existence.

53. See Ronald Hyam, *Britain's Imperial Century, 1815–1914: A Study of Empire and Expansion* (London, 1976), pp. 135–47.

54. Quoted by Cashmore, "Your Obedient Servant," p. 67.

55. *Ibid.*, pp. 68–69. Note also this confidential circular, issued by the office of the colonial secretary of the Gold Coast, 25 March 1907:

1. I am directed by the Governor to inform you that His Excellency's attention has been drawn, with much regret, to the alleged prevalence in this Colony and its Dependencies of very undesirable relations being maintained by European Government Officers with Native women.

As such relations, apart from their demoralizing tendency, seriously detract from the value of an officer's services, not merely by creating jealousy and ill-feeling among the Natives, but also by destroying their confidence in his integrity and impartiality, His Excellency relies upon Commissioners and Heads of Departments to take every means in their power to put an end to this abuse; and, if their Subordinates disregard the warning, to report the matter officially.

2. I am also to inform you that should any case of this description be definitely brought to the Governor's notice and the Officer concerned fail to exculpate himself, His Excellency will report such case to the Secretary of State forthwith.

3. I am therefore to request that you will be so good as to communicate confidentially the contents of this Circular to your European Subordinates.

56. British South Africa Company Minutes 23.3.1909, Annexes 12 and 16, 1909, National Archives of Rhodesia.

57. Richard Meinertzhagen, *Kenya Diary, 1902–1906* (Edinburgh, 1957), p. 192.

58. Laura Boyle, *Diary of a Colonial Officer's Wife* (Oxford, Eng., 1968), p. 96. The diary dates from World War I.

59. Cited by Oscar Wilde in "Literary and Other Notes," in *The Complete Writings of Oscar Wilde* (London, 1909), 4: 224–25.

60. Mrs. C. H. Hart-Davis, "Personal Reminiscences, 1908–1935," mss. Brit. Emp. S. 346, Rhodes House Library, Oxford University.

61. For details on Olive MacLeod, see Joan Alexander, *Whom the Gods Love: Boyd Alexander's Expedition from Niger to the Nile, 1904–7, and His Last Journey, 1908–10* (London, 1977), chap. 21.

62. Boyle, p. 16.

63. *Ibid.*

64. *Ibid.*, p. 1.

65. *Ibid.*, p. 96.

66. In later years, according to one account, her "self-centered-ness and self-aggrandisement" ruined their marriage (R. E. Wraith, *Guggisberg*, London, 1967, p. 39).

67. Decima Moore Guggisberg and F. G. Guggisberg, *We Two in West Africa* (London, 1909).

68. See mss. Afr. S. 1058, Rhodes House Library, Oxford University.

69. See Lewis and Foy, *Painting Africa White, passim.*

Chapter Seven

1. Davidson Nicol, ed., *Black Nationalism in Africa, 1867: Extracts from the Political, Educational, Scientific and Medical Writings of Africanus Horton* (New York, 1969), p. 33. See also Christopher Fyfe, *Africanus Horton, 1835–1883: West African Scientist and Patriot* (New York, 1972).

2. Quoted in David Kimble, *A Political History of Ghana: The Rise of Gold Coast Nationalism, 1850–1928* (Oxford, Eng., 1963), pp. 89, 93.

3. *Ibid.*, p. 94.

4. Kwame Arhin, ed., *Papers of George Ekem Ferguson: A Fanti Official of the Gold Coast, 1890–1897* (Leiden, 1974). Ferguson was murdered on one of his boundary-making tours.

5. Kimble, p. 98.

6. See Gold Coast Colony, *Blue Book, 1914* (Accra, 1915).

7. For details of J. C. Smith's life, see "Library Notes," *The Royal Commonwealth Society*, n.s., 181 (May 1972).

8. Sir William Geary, cited by I. F. Nicolson, *The Administration of Nigeria, 1900–1960: Men, Methods and Myths* (Oxford, Eng., 1969), p. 51.

9. See Sir Ronald Ross, *Memoirs* (London, 1923), pp. 445ff, for a sketch of Lagos.

10. G. O. Olusanya, *The Evolution of the Nigerian Civil Service, 1861–1960: The Problems of Nigerianization* (Lagos, 1975), pp. 1–24.

11. According to the figures collected by R. S. T. Cashmore ("Your Obedient Servant," mss. Afr. S. 1034, Rhodes House Library, Oxford University, p. 33), the government employees in British East Africa around 1914 included 2,057 Indians and Parsees; 735 Goans; 83 Arabs, Baluchis, and Africans; 18 persons from the Seychelles and Mauritius; and 6 Malays.

12. See Nizar A. Motani, "The Growth of an African Civil Service in Uganda, 1912–1940," doctoral dissertation, University of London, 1972.

13. Report of the Secretary, Northeastern Rhodesia, British South Africa Company Minutes, 23 March 1904, annex 17, 12 March 1904, National Archives of Rhodesia.

14. H. A. Fosbrooke, trans. and ed., "The Life of Justin. An African Autobiography," *Tanganyika Notes and Records*, 2 parts, 41 (Dec. 1955): 30–56 and 42 (March 1956): 19–30.

15. Margery Freda Perham, ed., *Ten Africans* (London, 1936); see chapter on Kayamba.

16. See Margaret Read, "The Ngoni and Western Education," in Victor Turner, ed., *Profiles of Change: African Society and Colonial Rule* (London, 1971), pp. 346–92 (vol. 3 of Peter Duignan and L. H. Gann, gen. eds., *Colonialism in Africa, 1870–1960*); and Lucy Mair, "New Elites in East and West Africa," *ibid.*, pp. 167–92.

17. Robert I. Rotberg, *The Rise of Nationalism in Central Africa: The Making of Malawi and Zambia, 1873–1964* (Cambridge, Mass., 1965), p. 117.

18. Nxobbe to Lobengula, 3 March 1893, WI 6/1/1, National Archives of Rhodesia.

Chapter Eight

1. See Robert Cummings, "A Note on the History of Caravan Porters in East Africa," *Kenya Historical Review*, 1, no. 2 (1973): 110–38.

2. Our discussion of the department is based on the Migeod papers, Royal Commonwealth Society, London.

3. He put his complaints into a parody of the twenty-third Psalm:

The "Ford" is my car,
I shall not want—another—
It maketh me to lie down in wet places,
It soileth my soul,

It leadeth me into deep waters,
It prepareth a breakdown for me in the presence of mine enemies.
Yea, though I run down the valley, I am towed up the hills.
I fear much evil while it is with me.
Its rods and engines discomfort me.
It anointeth my face with oil.
Its tank runneth over.
Surely to goodness the damned thing won't follow me all the days of my life,
or I shall dwell in the house of the insane forever.

To him a Ford was "A little spark, a little coil, / A little gas, and a little oil, / A piece of tin, and a two-inch board; / Glue them together and you've got a 'Ford.'"

4. The pioneers of the truck were usually private merchants. On the Gold Coast, for example, many merchants used trucks during the first decade of the twentieth century. A truck in that period carried from one to two-and-a-half tons, as against a hand-truck load of 1,500 pounds to one ton and a headload of about 60 pounds. The first trucks traveled at a speed of just over five miles an hour.

5. See D. T. S. Sinclair, "History of the Nigerian Marine," mss. Afri. S. 809, Rhodes House Library, Oxford University.

6. Cited in Mervyn F. Hill, *Permanent Way: The Story of the Kenya and Uganda Railway* (Nairobi, 1950), p. 54.

7. The poem, frequently quoted, was first printed in *Truth*, and is cited by L. H. Gann and Peter Duignan, eds., *Burden of Empire: Colonialism in Africa South of the Sahara* (New York, 1967), p. 223.

8. Richard Hill, *Sudan Transport: A History of Railway, Marine and River Services in the Republic of Sudan* (London, 1965), pp. 152–56.

9. Approximately 2,493 Indians died in Africa, and about 1,400 soon after they were repatriated. Some 25,000 were ill or died during the building of the railway (Mervyn Hill, *Permanent Way*).

10. *Ibid.*, p. 203.

11. Great Britain, Parliamentary Command Papers, *Private Enterprise in British Tropical Africa*, C. 2016 (1924), pp. 9, 19.

12. R. Szereszewski, *Structural Changes in the Economy of Ghana, 1891–1911* (London, 1965), pp. 63–64.

13. *The Communist Manifesto of Karl Marx and Friedrich Engels* (London, 1930), pp. 21–23.

Chapter Nine

1. Allan McPhee, *The Economic Revolution in British West Africa* (London, 1971), p. 275.

2. For an excellent survey that we have used heavily, see William Forman, "Science for Empire: Britain's Development of the Empire Through Scientific Research, 1895–1940," unpublished Ph.D. dissertation, University of Wisconsin, 1941.

3. *Ibid.*, pp. 15–16.

4. See Gerald C. D. Dudgeon, *The Agricultural and Forest Products of British West Africa* (London, 1911).

5. See Christy Papers, Royal Comonwealth Society, for details on patients with blackwater fever.

6. Michael Gelfand, *Livingstone, the Doctor, His Life and Travels: A Study in Medical History* (Oxford, Eng., 1957).

7. Cited in Andrew Balfour and Henry Harold Scott, *Health Problems of the Empire* (London, 1924), pp. 77–78.

8. Great Britain, Parliamentary Command Papers, *Vital Statistics of Native Officials in West Africa*, C. 920 (1919).

9. Report by Professor W. J. Simpson dated 1909, cited in Balfour and Scott, p. 81.

10. See I. F. Nicolson, *The Administration of Nigeria, 1900–1960: Men, Methods and Myths* (Oxford, Eng., 1969), pp. 78–79.

11. Figures for one colony are given by Michael Gelfand, *Northern Rhodesia in the Days of the Charter: A Medical and Social Study, 1898–1924* (Oxford, Eng., 1961), p. 167.

12. See Great Britain, Public Record Office, "Professor Simpson's Report on Mombasa, 1913," CO 533/127.

13. See Dr. P. A. Clearkin, "Ramblings and Recollections of a Colonial Doctor, 1913–1958," mss. Brit. Emp. R. 4/1, Rhodes House Library, Oxford University.

14. *Ibid.*, p. 21.

15. H. C. Squires, *The Sudan Medical Service: An Experiment in Social Medicine* (London, 1958).

16. Ralph Schram, *A History of the Nigerian Health Services* (Ibadan, 1971), pp. 43–44, lists 17 prominent early Nigerian medical practitioners. Of these, 11 had Edinburgh degrees; the rest came from London, Liverpool, and other universities.

17. For the nurse's account, see Lady Clifford, ed., *Our Days on the Gold Coast, in Ashanti, in the Northern Territories, and the British Sphere of Occupation in Togoland* (London, 1919).

18. For an account of the work done by pioneer administrations in British Central Africa, see Michael Gelfand's trilogy: *Lakeside Pioneers: Socio-Medical Study of Nyasaland, 1875–1920* (Oxford, Eng., 1964); *Northern Rhodesia* (cited in note 11 above); and *Tropical Victory: An Account of the Influence of Medicine on the History of Southern Rhodesia, 1890–1923* (Cape Town, 1953). For other areas, see Ann Beck, *A History of the British Medical Administration of East Africa, 1900–1950* (Cambridge, Mass., 1970); Squires, *Sudan Medical Service*; and Schram, *Nigerian Health Services*.

19. In that year 282 Africans died in the Southern Rhodesian mines. Pneumonia accounted for 113. The others died of scurvy (42), malaria (24), dysentery (24), malaria and scurvy together (16), peripheral neuritis (4), beriberi (3), peritonitis (2), dropsy (1), measles (1), senility (1), other causes (51).

20. Cited in Geoffry Bussell Masefield, *A History of the Colonial Agricultural Service* (Oxford, Eng., 1972), p. 27.

21. See Nicolson, *Administration of Nigeria*.

22. See Robert M. Maxon, "John Ainsworth and Agricultural Innovation in Kenya," *Kenya Historical Review*, 1, no. 2 (1973): 151–62; and F. H. Goldsmith, *John Ainsworth, Pioneer Kenya Administrator, 1864–1946* (London, 1955).

23. See Montague Yudelman, "Imperialism and the Transfer of Agricultural Techniques," in Peter Duignan and L. H. Gann, eds., *The Economics of Colonialism* (London, 1975), pp. 329–59 (vol. 4 of Peter Duignan and L. H. Gann, gen. eds., *Colonialism in Africa, 1870–1960*).

24. See Maud Diver, *The Unsung: A Record of British Services in India* (London, 1945), for the engineers' role in developing India.

25. "Engineer, Professional," *Encyclopaedia Britannica*, 14th ed. (1928), 8: 443.

26. See A. Beeby-Thompson, *Oil Pioneer: Selected Experiences and Incidents Associated with Sixty Years of World-wide Petroleum Exploration and Oilfield Development* (London, 1961).

27. See J. R. L. Macdonald, *Soldiering and Surveying in British East Africa* (London, 1897).

28. Quoted in R. E. Wraith, *Guggisberg* (London, 1967), p. 31.

29. On the development of scientific and technical bodies during the colonial period, see Edgar Barton Worthington, *Science in Africa: A Review of Scientific Research Relating to Tropical and Southern Africa* (London, 1938); and both editions of Lord Hailey, *An African Survey: A Study of Problems Arising in Africa South of the Sahara* (London, 1938, 1957).

30. According to F. Ekechi, *Missionary Enterprise and Rivalry in Igboland, 1857–1914* (London, 1972), p. 187, the Ibos "demanded the best of Western education not merely for its utilitarian purposes but also to use . . . as a weapon against colonial exploitation. Hence they aspired to a *good* education and not merely a vocational education that would consign them to menial tasks and keep them under colonial tutelage forever."

31. At that point 1,327 white children in this age group were attending government or government-aided schools, many of them as boarders, and about 100 more were attending private school. Just over 800 were receiving no education at all. (L. H. Gann, *A History of Northern Rhodesia: Early Days to 1953*, London, 1964; Gann, *A History of Southern Rhodesia: Early Days to 1934*, London, 1965.)

32. Cited by Gann, *History of Southern Rhodesia*, p. 207.

33. See T. J. Alldridge, *A Transformed Colony: Sierra Leone As It Was, and As It is: Its Progress, Peoples, Native Customs and Undeveloped Wealth* (London, 1910), chap. 16.

34. Cited by W. E. F. Ward, *A History of Ghana* (London, 1963), p. 202.

35. Frederick John Dealtry, Baron Lugard, *The Dual Mandate in British Tropical Africa*, 5th ed., (London, 1965), pp. 425–26.

36. Hanns Vischer, *Across the Sahara from Tripoli to Bornu* (London, 1910).

37. See A. H. M. Kirk-Greene's introduction to Sonia F. Graham, *Government and Mission Education in Northern Nigeria, 1900–1919, with Special Reference to the Work of Hanns Vischer* (Ibadan, 1966), pp. iv–ix.

38. "Memoirs of the 1898 Rising: Paramount Chief J. K. Mana-Kpaka," in *Eminent Sierra Leoneans in the Nineteenth Century* (Government Printer, Freetown, c. 1961), p. 73.

Chapter Ten

1. The *Livingstone Mail*, published by a chemist in Livingstone, Northern Rhodesia, appealed principally to local white farmers, prospectors, and railwaymen. The paper criticized existing labor practices. It argued that the native labor problem, as the whites saw it, "is to obtain a sufficiency of unskilled labour at less than its value. At less than its value because obviously, if it were fully remunerated, there would be no margin of profit." Still concerned by the situation 10 years later, the *Mail* noted: "The relationship between white and black is purely economic. Except to gratify idle and morbid curiosity, no interest is taken in the Native. No one knows or cares what he thinks, hopes, or aspires to." (See issues of 14 Oct. 1911, and 30 April 1920.)

2. Cited by Charles H. Lyons, *To Wash an Aethiop White: British Ideas About Black African Educability, 1530–1960* (New York, 1975), p. 115.

3. Frederick John Dealtry, Baron Lugard, *The Dual Mandate in British Tropical Africa*, 5th ed. (London, 1965), pp. 69–70.

4. to quote T. R. Georgevic, *Macedonia* (London, 1920), pp. 18–19: "The physique of the modern Bulgars is very striking. . . . Certain Mongol features appear at first glance. . . . The moral qualities of the Turanian Bulgar can also be traced in the Bulgars of to-day. . . . The insatiable lust of possession which characterized the Bulgars when they first came to the [Balkan] Peninsula is equally strong in the Slavicized Bulgars. The only difference is that whereas the Turanian Bulgars were an intrepid warrior horde, the Slav Bulgars are insatiable grabbers only when there is a prospect of profit without risk. The old Turanian cruelty [is] toned down even to servility."

5. See Kwame Nkrumah, *Africa Must Unite* (London, 1964); and Sir Harry Hamilton Johnston, *A History of the Colonization of Africa by Alien Races* (Cambridge, Eng. [1889], 1930).

6. See J. F. A. Ajayi, "Colonialism: An Episode in African History," in L. H. Gann and Peter Duignan, eds., *The History and Politics of Colonialism, 1870–1914* (London, 1969), pp. 497–509 (vol. 1 of Peter Duignan and L. H. Gann, gen., eds., *Colonialism in Africa, 1870–1960*).

7. Donald Anthony Low, *Lion Rampant: Essays in the Study of British Imperialism* (London, 1973), p. 28.

8. Chinua Achebe, *Things Fall Apart* (London, 1966), p. 159.

9. Edwin Williams Smith and Andrew Dale, *The Ila-Speaking Peoples of Northern Rhodesia* (London, 1920), pp. 198–99.

10. Marcia Wright, "Women in Peril: A Commentary on the Life Stories of Captives in Nineteenth-Century East Africa," *African Social Research*, Dec. 1975, pp. 800–819.

11. J. Machiwanyika, "History and Customs of the Manyika People," MA 14/1/2, Rhodesian National Archives.

12. Lugard, pp. 364–65.

13. Smith and Dale, pp, 408–12.

14. Stanley Portal Hyatt, *Off the Main Track* (London, 1911), pp. 209–10.

15. The literature is now extensive and includes such excellent studies as Terence O. Ranger, *Revolt in Southern Rhodesia, 1896–1897: A Study in African Resistance* (Evanston, Ill., 1967), an important pioneer work; I. N. Kimambo and A. J. Temu, *A History of Tanzania* (Nairobi, 1969); and Robert I. Rotberg and Ali Mazrui, eds., *Protest and Power in Black Africa* (New York, 1970).

16. John Middleton, "Some Effects of Colonial Rule Among the Lugbara," in Victor Turner, ed., *Profiles of Change: African Society and Colonial Rule* (London, 1971), p. 7 (vol. 3 of Peter Duignan and L. H. Gann, gen. eds., *Colonialism in Africa, 1870–1960*).

17. Ronald Cohen, "From Empire to Colony: Bornu in the Nineteenth and Twentieth Centuries," in *ibid.*, p. 122.

18. See, for instance, Kenneth D. Nworah, "The Integrative Strand in British West Africa, 1868–1914," *Genève-Afrique*, 13, no. 1 (1974): 22; and David Kimble, *A Political History of Ghana: The Rise of Gold Coast Nationalism, 1850–1928* (Oxford, Eng., 1963).

19. See John Forbes Munro, *Colonial rule and the Kamba: Social Change in the Kenya Highlands, 1889–1939* (London, 1975).

20. See Robert L. Tignor, *The Colonial Transformation of Kenya: The Kamba, Kikuyu and Masai from 1900 to 1939* (Princeton, N.J., 1976).

21. See Elizabeth Isichei, *The Ibo People and the Europeans: The Genesis of a Relationship—to 1906* (New York, 1973), pp. 173–74.

22. *Ibid.*, p. 181.

23. *Ibid.*, p. 160.

24. *Ibid.*, pp. 172–73. Road-building had been so successful that by 1905 Governor Egerton could travel from Lagos to Calabar by bicycle, a distance of over 300 miles.

Index

Abercorn, Duke of, 43
Aberdeen, Lord, 25
Aberdeen University, 50
Aborigines Protection Society, 24–25, 34, 41, 326
Abrahams, William, 176
Accra (Gold Coast), 247–50, 297f, 305–6
Achebe, Chinua, 220, 349–50
Achimota College (Gold Coast), 168
Acholi people, 119
Administrators, colonial: positions and functions, 164–68, 221; recruitment for, 183–86, 197–201; motives for joining, 201–8; use of direct and indirect rule, 208–13; compared with French and Germans, 213, 219 table; social and living conditions, 219–20, 226–33, 240–43; contacts with indigenous chiefs, 224; and women, 239–52, 386–87. See also Colonial Office; and individual positions by name
Adultery, in African law, 235, 353–54
Afghanistan, 21
Africa, Scramble for, 8–20
African Affairs, 27
African Association, 27
African Lakes Company, 32–33, 43, 117
African Steamship Company, 38
Afrikaners, 29, 87, 129–37, 347–48
Agriculture, colonial research and development of, 61–62, 222, 296, 310–20; botanical research, 57, 61, 293, 312–13, 314; state experimental work in, 294–95; export crops developed, 310–11, 319 table; African innovations, 311–12; government cooperation with private development, 313–14; forestry service,

318; veterinary research, 318; cash-cropping related to railroad development, 318n. See also individual crops by name
Ainsworth, John, 141, 185, 222, 227, 317–18
Ajayi, J. F. A., 343
Akamba people, 220
Aldington, A., 227
Allenby, Gen. Edmund H., 177
Anderson, J. J., 185
Anthropology, as hobby of colonial administrators, 220
Anti-Slavery and Aborigines Protection Society, see Aborigines Protection Society
Archer, Geoffrey, 160, 200–201
Argentina, British investments in, 1f
Aristocracy, 5, 37, 91, 174
Army, British, 5, 21, 71–101; organization and training of, 71, 73, 77–79, 80–82; officer corps, 72–73, 89–98; in India, 73–74; impact of colonial experience on, 75–77, 96–97; regimental traditions, 81, 82–83; civilian-mindedness of, 83–84; in Africa, 84–89; noncommissioned officers, 98–101; black forces in, 106–22. See also Military organization and campaigns; Weapons technology; and individual units by name
Army Medical School, 295
Ashanti campaign, 102–6, 115n, 134
Ashanti people, 11, 103–5, 141
Association for Moral and Social Hygiene, 53
Association of Northern Rhodesian Farmers Resident, 37